MARY QUEEN OF SCOTS

In this new biography of one of the most intriguing figures of early modern European history, Retha Warnicke, widely regarded as the leading historian on Tudor queenship, offers a fresh interpretation of the life of Mary Stewart (Stuart), popularly known as Mary, Queen of Scots.

Mary became Queen of Scotland at six days old, was crowned Queen of France at seventeen on the death of her husband Francis II, and was the cousin and rival of Elizabeth I, who ultimately had her executed for treason. A devout Catholic, who lived during an era of intense religious discord, Mary's turbulent life was characterized by treachery, violence and tragedy.

Setting Mary's life within the context of the cultural and intellectual climate of the time and bringing to life the realities of being a female monarch in the sixteenth century, Warnicke also examines Mary's three marriages, her constant ill health and her role in numerous plots and conspiracies. Placing Mary within the context of early modern gender relations, Warnicke reveals the challenges that faced her and the forces that worked to destroy her.

This highly readable and fascinating study will pour fresh light on the much-debated life of a central figure of the sixteenth century, providing a new interpretation of Mary's impact on politics, gender and nationhood in the Tudor era.

Retha M. Warnicke is Professor of History at Arizona State University. She has published widely on Tudor and Stuart history, women's history and cultural history and is the author of *The Marrying of Anne of Cleves: Royal Protocol in Tudor England* (2000) and *The Rise and Fall of Anne Boleyn: Family Politics at the Court of Henry VIII* (1991).

ROUTLEDGE HISTORICAL BIOGRAPHIES

SERIES EDITOR: ROBERT PEARCE

Routledge Historical Biographies provide engaging, readable and academically credible biographies written from an explicitly historical perspective. These concise and accessible accounts will bring important historical figures to life for students and general readers alike.

In the same series:

MARY QUEEN OF SCOTS

Retha M. Warnicke

Routledge
Taylor & Francis Group

LONDON AND NEW YORK

First published 2006
by Routledge
2 Park Square, Milton Park, Abingdon, OX14 4RN

Simultaneously published in the USA and Canada
by Routledge
270 Madison Avenue, New York, NY 10016

Routledge is an imprint of the Taylor & Francis Group

© 2006 Retha M. Warnicke

Typeset in Garamond by M Rules
Printed and bound in Great Britain by
TJ International Ltd, Padstow, Cornwall

British Library Cataloguing in Publication Data
A catalogue record for this book is available from the British Library

Library of Congress Cataloging in Publication Data
Warnicke, Retha M.
  Mary, Queen of Scots / Retha M. Warnicke.
    p. cm. — (Routledge historical biographies)
  Includes bibliographical references and index.
1. Mary, Queen of Scots, 1542-1587. 2. Scotland—History—Mary Stuart, 1542-
1567. 3. Great Britain—History—Elizabeth, 1558-1603. 4. Queens—Scotland—
Biography. I. Title. II. Series.
  DA787.A1W37 2006
  941.105'092—dc22
                                                              2005024109

ISBN10: 0-415-29182-8 ISBN13: 9-78-0-415-29182-8 (hbk)
ISBN10: 0-415-29183-6 ISBN13: 9-78-0-415-29183-5 (pbk)

Contents

PLATES

ACKNOWLEDGMENTS

After deciding to write this biography of Mary Stewart, I read widely in the field of Scottish history before turning to studies of her and then to the primary sources. I discovered that I knew more Scottish history than I had originally thought, but not nearly enough to complete this book. In the last few decades, many historians have provided significant revisionist approaches to the Scottish Renaissance and Reformation by exploring new research topics, especially on gender issues but also on other social and cultural topics. Scotland's political, religious and cultural importance on the British Isles has also received attention even from historians who have traditionally focused on England.

In completing my research I had the assistance of Dr Deborah Simonton and Dr Karen Miller in the United Kingdom, Katia Scio in France, and my Ph.D. student, Tara Wood. My thanks are due also to Dr Philip Soergel, University of Maryland at College Park, Dr Mack Holt, George Mason University, and Dr Robert Mueller, Utah State University, Utah Basin Campus, for their helpful suggestions. I am grateful for the financial assistance of Arizona State University's Center for Religion and Conflict and History Department, which made possible my trips to various libraries and archives. The Center for Medieval and Renaissance Studies here has also long supported my scholarly endeavors.

The Hayden Library Inter-library Loan Department at Arizona State University has diligently obtained numerous books from around the world for me. The cooperation of the staffs of several other libraries and archives was important to the completion of this book: the British Library, the Institute of Historical Research, the Public Record Office, the National Library of Scotland, the Folger Shakespeare Library, the Huntington Library, and the Bibliothèque Nationale.

I have presented some of my findings on Mary, Queen of Scots, at sessions of the Renaissance Society of Southern California Conference and at the Pacific Coast Conference on British Studies. At a conference on Tudor history sponsored by the Huntington Library, I also gave a paper on the marriage of women rulers, which contained a few excerpts from this book and which appeared in *Studies in Medieval and Renaissance History*, co-edited by Philip Soergel and Andrew Barnes.

I am grateful for the willingness of Robert Pearce, the editor of this biographical series, to read and reread the manuscript, offering many insightful criticisms. The staff at Routledge, Liz Gooster, the acting commissioning editor, and Philippa Grand, her editorial assistant, led me through the publication process expertly, choosing anonymous readers who helped clarify some misstatements and inaccuracies. My family, as always, has been extremely supportive: my husband, Ronald, my daughter Margaretha, my son Robert, and his wife Cynthia, who gave birth to my granddaughter Winter in January 2005. Members of Ronald's law firm, especially John Dionne, provided copying services and other assistance, and Margaretha read the book's original introduction, offering a few key suggestions that I gladly incorporated.

I discovered in reading about this first Scottish queen regnant that modern writers have often been more critical of some of her decisions, especially the one to seek aid in England, than was Sir Francis Knollys, her first, reluctant English guardian. He was of the opinion in 1568 that she fled to his realm because she had no safe refuge in Scotland and no secure means of going to France. Historical analysis has seldom been so generous.

During her seven years in Scotland from 1561 to 1568, she faced four armed rebellions, two unrelated abduction scares, had an intruder secrete himself in her bedchamber twice, witnessed a murderous assault on her French secretary, lost her husband to foul play, underwent abduction, rape, and a forced marriage that led her to threaten suicide, faced a public attack on her honor in which she was called a whore, was imprisoned at Lochleven, and was compelled to abdicate. In the midst of these adversities, she managed to give birth to her son, who succeeded her. She also suffered from a chronic illness that left her crippled by the time she was 40 years old.

It seems appropriate that while I was writing this book about the first queen regnant on the British Isles that my first grandchild was born female. I hope that when it is time for Winter to seek employment that she will find no path left untrod by earlier females and that the opportunities and pitfalls of becoming the first woman in a field will no longer exist. It is true that unlike this first Scottish queen regnant, most modern first women do not have to encounter life-threatening assaults or abduction threats, but they have faced professional challenges that have and can be very troubling. I, therefore, dedicate this book to these pioneering women, from the early modern queens regnant to modern faculty members, astronauts, prime ministers, and others in less prominent employments. Understanding Mary Stewart's life reminds us of how difficult the first woman's journey for professional acceptance and respect has been and can still be.

CHRONOLOGY

Year	Personal	Political	General
1538	James V and Mary of Guise married		
1542	Mary's birth		Battle of Solway Moss
1543		Treaties of Greenwich James Hamilton, second earl of Arran, future duke of Châtelherault became her governor Mary's coronation	Rough Wooing commenced
1544	Birth of Francis, the French Dauphin		
1545	Birth of Henry Stewart, Lord Darnley		
1547			Battle of Pinkie
1548	Mary sailed to France		
1550	Mary of Guise visited France		
1551		Robert Stewart's plot to poison Mary	
1553–54	Establishment of Mary's household		
1554	Mary wrote Latin epistles	Mary's regal majority recognized Mary of Guise became regent	
1555	Mary gave Latin Oration		

Year	Personal	Political	General
1558	Mary and Francis wed	Mary signed secret documents concerning Scotland	
			Mary Tudor died Elizabeth's accession
1559		Mary quartered the arms of England with those of Scotland and France Francis's coronation	Henry II died
1560	Mary of Guise died Francis II died	Treaty of Edinburgh Reformation Parliament	Conjuration of Amboise
1561		Mary returned to Scotland Mary's Edinburgh Entry Meetings with John Knox	
1562		Privy Council decision to distribute finances of benefices	First French Religious War
		Attempts of Mary to meet Elizabeth failed	
		Imprisonment of James Hamilton third earl of Arran and James Hepburn, fourth earl of Bothwell, for abduction conspiracy Defeat of George Gordon, fourth earl of Huntly	
1563	Pierre de Châtelard incident	Commissaries established First parliament convened Mary's final meetings with Knox	Francis, duke of Guise, assassinated
1564	Negotiations to wed Don Carlos and Robert Dudley, earl of Leicester		
1565	Mary and Darnley wed	Mary gave Darnley title of king	Chaseabout Raid

Year	Personal	Political	General
1565–68			Bannatyne Manuscript collected
1566	Mary gave birth to James	David Riccio murdered	Marriage of Bothwell to Jean Gordon
		First complete edition of Statutes of the Realm published	
		Mary at Jedburgh and the Hermitage	
	Mary seriously ill Craigmillar meeting discussing a divorce and raising funds for James's christening		
1567	Mary escorts the sick king to Kirk o'Field		
	The king's murder		
	Bothwell's abduction of the queen	Bothwell ennobled as duke of Orkney	
	Mary wed Orkney	Carberry Hill surrender	
		Mary abdicated at Lochleven	James Stewart, earl of Moray, became regent for James VI
1568		Mary escaped from Lochleven	Battle of Langside
		Mary fled to England	
		York inquiry into Mary's involvement in the king's death	Third French Religious War
1569	Mary planned to wed Thomas Howard, fourth duke of Norfolk	George Talbot, fourth earl of Shrewsbury, became her custodian	
			Northern Rising
1570		Removed to Sheffield	Moray assassinated
			Excommunication of Elizabeth
			Matthew Stewart, fourth earl of Lennox, became regent
1571		Ridolfi Plot	Lennox assassinated
			John Erskine, first earl of Mar, became regent

Year	Personal	Political	General
1572			Death of Mar James Douglas, fourth earl of Morton, became regent
		Elizabeth offered to return Mary to Scotland for trial and execution	
			St Bartholomew Massacre Execution of Norfolk
1573		Scottish Civil War over	
1574		Elizabeth again offered to return Mary to Scotland for trial and execution	
1577	Mary considered marrying Don John of Austria	Don John planned to invade England	
1578	Orkney's death		
1581		Mary proposed associating with son in governance of Scotland	Execution of Morton
1583		Throckmorton's plot: Henry, duke of Guise, planned to invade England	
1584		Sir Ralph Sadler became Mary's custodian Bond of Association to protect Elizabeth drafted	
1585		Sir Amyas Paulet became Mary's custodian	Treaty of Joinville
		Mary moved to Chartley Failure of the Treaty of Association	Dr William Parry's Plot
1586		Mary bequeathed Scotland to Philip II Babington Plot	Treaty of Berwick

Year	Personal	Political	General
1587	Mary buried at Peterborough Cathedral	Mary's treason trial at Fotheringhay Castle	
1603			James I's accession
1612	Mary re-interred at Westminster Abbey		

ABBREVIATED GENEALOGICAL CHARTS

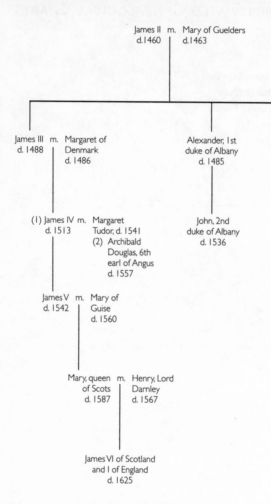

James II m. Mary of Guelders
d.1460   d.1463

James III m. Margaret of
d. 1488   Denmark
               d. 1486

Alexander, 1st
duke of Albany
d. 1485

(1) James IV m. Margaret
    d. 1513   Tudor, d. 1541
              (2) Archibald
                  Douglas, 6th
                  earl of Angus
                  d. 1557

John, 2nd
duke of Albany
d. 1536

James V m. Mary of
d. 1542   Guise
             d. 1560

Mary, queen m. Henry, Lord
of Scots   Darnley
d. 1587   d. 1567

James VI of Scotland
and I of England
d. 1625

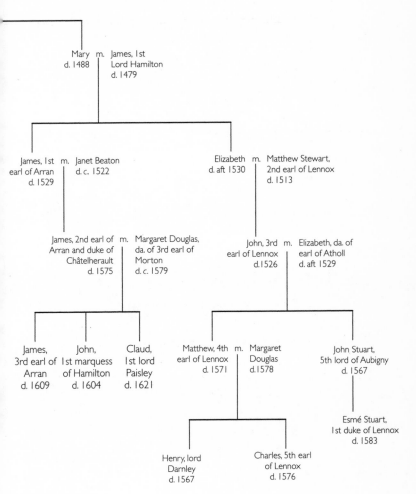

1 Scottish Succession

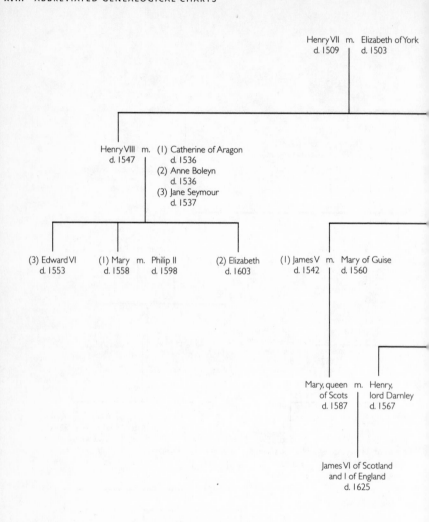

Henry VII m. Elizabeth of York
d. 1509   d. 1503

Henry VIII m. (1) Catherine of Aragon
d. 1547   d. 1536
                  (2) Anne Boleyn
                     d. 1536
                  (3) Jane Seymour
                     d. 1537

| (3) Edward VI | (1) Mary m. Philip II | (2) Elizabeth | (1) James V m. Mary of Guise |
| d. 1553 | d. 1558   d. 1598 | d. 1603 | d. 1542   d. 1560 |

Mary, queen m. Henry,
of Scots   lord Darnley
d. 1587   d. 1567

James VI of Scotland
and I of England
d. 1625

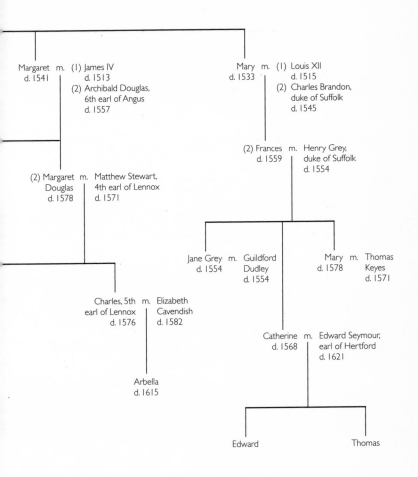

Margaret m. (1) James IV
d. 1541   d. 1513
             (2) Archibald Douglas,
                 6th earl of Angus
                 d. 1557

Mary m. (1) Louis XII
d. 1533   d. 1515
           (2) Charles Brandon,
               duke of Suffolk
               d. 1545

(2) Margaret m. Matthew Stewart,
    Douglas   4th earl of Lennox
    d. 1578   d. 1571

(2) Frances m. Henry Grey,
    d. 1559   duke of Suffolk
               d. 1554

Jane Grey m. Guildford
d. 1554   Dudley
            d. 1554

Mary m. Thomas
d. 1578   Keyes
          d. 1571

Charles, 5th m. Elizabeth
earl of Lennox Cavendish
d. 1576   d. 1582

Catherine m. Edward Seymour,
d. 1568   earl of Hertford
            d. 1621

Arbella
d. 1615

Edward

Thomas

2 English Succession

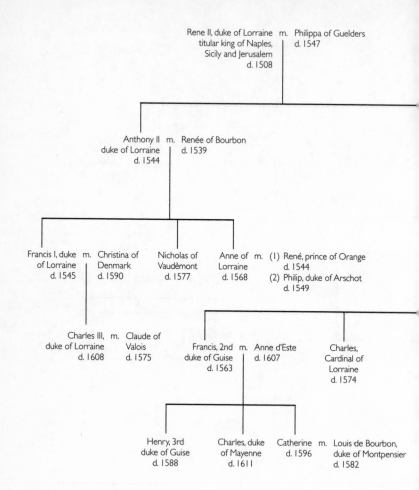

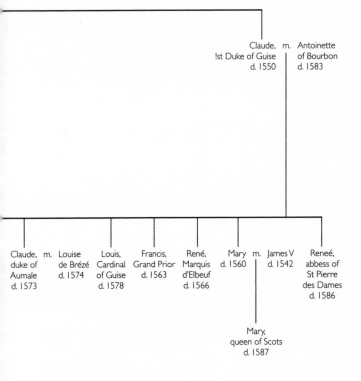

Claude, m. Antoinette
1st Duke of Guise   of Bourbon
d. 1550   d. 1583

Claude, m. Louise   Louis,   Francis,   René,   Mary m. James V   Reneé,
duke of   de Brézé   Cardinal   Grand Prior   Marquis   d. 1560   d. 1542   abbess of
Aumale   d. 1574   of Guise   d. 1563   d'Elbeuf   St Pierre
d. 1573   d. 1578   d. 1566   des Dames
d. 1586

Mary,
queen of Scots
d. 1587

3 Lorraine-Guise Family

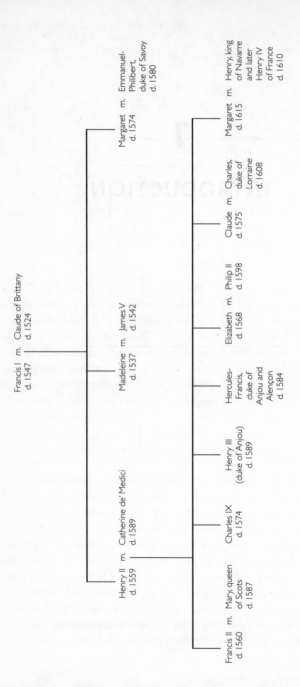

Francis I m. Claude of Brittany
d. 1547   d. 1524

Henry II m. Catherine de' Medici
d. 1559   d. 1589

Madeleine m. James V
d. 1537   d. 1542

Margaret m. Emmanuel-
d. 1574   Philibert,
     duke of Savoy
     d. 1580

Francis II m. Mary, queen
d. 1560   of Scots
     d. 1587

Charles IX
d. 1574

Henry III
(duke of Anjou)
d. 1589

Hercules-
Francis,
duke of
Anjou and
Alençon
d. 1584

Elizabeth m. Philip II
d. 1568   d. 1598

Claude m. Charles,
d. 1575   duke of
     Lorraine
     d. 1608

Margaret m. Henry, king
d. 1615   of Navarre
     and later
     Henry IV
     of France
     d. 1610

4 Valois Dynasty

1

INTRODUCTION

On 8 February 1587 with two English soldiers supporting her under her arms, the crippled Mary Stewart, queen of Scots, encountered Andrew Melville, the master of her household, at the entrance to the execution hall at Fotheringhay Castle.[1] During their brief conversation, she asked Melville to testify to the world that she died a true woman to her religion and a true woman of Scotland and France. Although her English succession rights were important to her, she clearly identified herself in those last critical moments as a Catholic of Scotland and France. Mary's final thoughts focused on her lineage and faith, not her alleged romantic marriages in Scotland that culminated in her long English imprisonment and ultimately her violent, tragic death.

By contrast, beginning even in Mary's lifetime, her defenders and detractors have mostly been more concerned with the formation and dissolution of those marriages than with her self-identification and understanding of her royal responsibilities and religious commitments. In 1570 John Leslie, bishop of Ross, her ambassador to England, was the first to deny in print that the imprisoned queen had aided and abetted the murder of her second husband, Henry Stewart, Lord Darnley, in order to marry James Hepburn, fourth earl of Bothwell, his assassin and her abductor. About two years later, a treatise, written by George Buchanan, a Protestant humanist and Mary's former tutor, was published to counter Leslie's defense. Depicting her as an evil, lecherous woman, it claimed she colluded both in Darnley's death and in Bothwell's capture of her.

During the more than four centuries since the polemical works of Leslie and Buchanan appeared, many historians have supported one of their two contrasting characterizations, although some scholars have also favored a third position that somewhat amends Leslie's stance. Doubting she was totally innocent concerning Darnley's death, they speculate that she must at least have suspected that a conspiracy against him was afoot but usually agree that Bothwell forcibly seized her.

MARY'S HISTORY

Mary's life that ended in England had begun in Scotland 44 years earlier on 8 December 1542. The basic outlines of her history are well known. She was the child of Mary of Guise and James V, who died six days after her birth, leaving his crown to her. That she was not only the Scottish queen regnant but also as the granddaughter of Margaret Tudor a claimant to the English throne, caused many parents, including her great-uncle Henry VIII, to seek her as a bride for their sons. In 1548 her mother and her governor, James Hamilton, second earl of Arran, arranged for her transportation to France as the betrothed of Francis, the dauphin. In 1558 she wed Francis, who succeeded as king about one year later. After his death in 1560, she returned home to a realm controlled by Protestants but insisted on continuing Catholic worship at court. She remarried twice: in 1565 to Darnley, the father of her son, and in 1567 to Bothwell, her abductor. Her outraged rebels then imprisoned her at Lochleven, forced her to abdicate, and crowned her son as James VI. In 1568 she escaped, raised an army that was defeated, and fled to England. After holding an inquiry into whether Mary should be restored to her throne, Elizabeth decided to retain her in England, leaving Scotland to the rule of James and his Protestant regents. In 1587 having discovered that Mary consented to Anthony Babington's plot, which included a scheme for her assassination, Elizabeth signed the warrant for her cousin's execution, prompting Catholic desires for Mary to be recognized as a martyr to their faith. In 1603 her son succeeded Elizabeth as James I of England.

RECENT STUDIES OF MARY

The most well-known biography of Mary, which was published in 1969 and reprinted in 1993 and 2001, was composed by Antonia Fraser, a popular writer.[2] A volume of over 600 pages, it romanticizes her life, claiming she married Darnley for love but wed Bothwell only because he abducted and ravished her. It includes moving passages about the queen's four attendants also called Mary, who were undoubtedly Mary of Guise's namesake goddaughters, as their parents were her allies and dependants. Fraser ended the book with references to the corpse of Mary's son James, which was interred in the tomb of Henry VII in the Tudor king's chapel at Westminster Abbey, and to Mary's coffin, which rests under her tomb in that same chapel, surrounded by her many tiny descendants who died in their infancy. In contrast, the remains of the childless queens regnant, Mary and Elizabeth Tudor, lie together by themselves under the latter's tomb, ironically also in Henry's chapel. By thus highlighting Stewart fertility and Tudor barrenness, Fraser emphasized the Stewart subsumption of the Tudor dynasty.

Missing from Fraser's conclusion are two salient facts: first, Mary selected as James's godmother Elizabeth, who became by contemporary standards in some sense his second mother and who eased his succession when she politically isolated English pretenders to her throne. Second, in May 1586 less than a year before her execution, Mary promised Philip II of Spain through an intermediary, Bernardino de Mendoza, his ambassador in France, to bequeath her English inheritance claims to him if James failed to convert to Catholicism. Her son's accession in England was definitely more complex than mere biological destiny.

Fraser's biography has other problems. It presents a too benign view of Mary's long, difficult captivity, repeats inaccurate facts, and relies on outdated information and interpretations. Since it was first published in 1969, numerous histories of early modern Britain have appeared, an impressive number specifically on Scotland: its Renaissance and Reformation, court life, politics and constitution, and gender and family history. Among them is Michael Lynch's excellent volume of 1988, which was a special issue of the *Innes Review*. Written by a mixture of experts on Scottish, French, and English history, these essays explore selected topics, like "The Release of Lord Darnley and the Failure of the Amity" by Simon Adams.[3] In the Introduction, Lynch claimed correctly that a major problem for biographers of a woman, who was queen of two kingdoms and a pretender to another, is that they have mostly received academic training within a particular national historiography.

Jenny Wormald's negative study of Mary, which appeared the same year as Lynch's edition, is an analysis of the queen's personal rule rather than a true biography.[4] When Wormald, an expert on Scottish history, reissued it in 2001, she included Lynch's volume and other recent publications in her bibliography but did not revise her text to incorporate their findings. Focusing on what she considered was the best scenario for Scotland, Wormald claimed that Mary's reluctance to return home after Francis's sudden death led her to linger frivolously in France for several months. Surely, however, arrangements for moving to her overseas realm that Protestant rebels controlled would have taken longer than a few weeks to complete. After beginning her personal rule in Scotland, Mary rarely attended the privy council meetings identified in its register. Among other facts, Wormald cited this absenteeism to rate Mary the most unsuccessful monarch since Robert III who died in 1406. As the register lacks reference to many council sessions that are identified in other contemporary records, it is hardly appropriate evidence for forming this negative judgment. It is also interesting that, according to the register, the attendance of the noble councilors was extremely erratic.[5] Furthermore Wormald denied that some of Mary's regal difficulties were gender based despite the published research confirming the marginalized status of early modern women that appeared before her book was reissued. Agreeing with Fraser that Mary wed Darnley for love, Wormald conceded Bothwell's abduction and apparent rape of her.

James MacKay published his study in 1999 specifically to refute Wormald's analysis.[6] An experienced biographer of male subjects who lived in later centuries than Mary's, he presented a somewhat different nationalistic perspective than Wormald's, identifying parallels in Anglo-Scottish relations between the 1560s and the modern devolution debate and referendum. Throughout the text his prejudices flow unchecked, describing, for example, John Knox as the Ayatollah. Like Fraser and Wormald, MacKay claimed Mary fell in love with Darnley and acquitted her of complicity in Bothwell's abduction.

Susan Watkins's beautiful book about the queen, which appeared in 2001, contains photographs by Mark Fiennes.[7] The strength of her publication is that it not only relates Mary's life through the medium of photography but also offers vivid descriptions of artifacts and clothing. As Watkins previously utilized this method to present the lives of Jane Austen and Marie Antoinette, she lacks experience in writing sixteenth-century history and sometimes shied away from documentary analysis, merely commenting, for example, that Mary may or may not have consented to Bothwell's abduction.

Like Fraser's study, the biography of Mary published in 2004 by John Guy, a prominent Tudor political historian, provides a romantic conceptualization of her. Validating claims that Mary wed Darnley for love, Guy argued that after Bothwell's forcible abduction of her, she consented to sexual relations with him because she never would have married her rapist, thus transferring modern sensibilities on to early modern people. In his memoirs, however, Sir James Melville, a witness to Mary's abduction, claimed that Bothwell raped her, and although the aged Melville knew well her subsequent history, including the imprisonment in Scotland and the flight to England that led to her life-long captivity, he still maintained that she "could not but marry him, seeing he had ravished her and lain with her against her will."[8]

Guy also maintained – unrealistically – that if Mary had not fallen in love with her captor within two or three days after he seized her, she could have escaped from Dunbar Castle or, at least, kept her chamber door locked. It must be noted that it took her almost one year to win release from Lochleven prison.

A major reason Guy turned to this biography was to establish that William Cecil, Elizabeth's principal secretary, schemed to engineer Mary's downfall. In 1566 Cecil instructed his ally, Francis Russell, second earl of Bedford, to persuade Mary to pardon her exiled rebels, especially James Douglas, fourth earl of Morton, because Cecil anticipated that upon reaching home Morton would join Bothwell and other Protestants in murdering Darnley. Guy cited extensive evidence to prove his conspiracy theory but failed to explain why Catholics, such as Darnley's kinsman, John Stewart, fourth earl of Atholl, and even members of the French government, also pressed for Morton's return.

Like most recent scholars, Guy pronounced as forged the Casket Letters, which include eight French love letters allegedly written by

Mary to Bothwell. To prove that her adulterous love for Bothwell caused her to collude in Darnley's murder, her illegitimate half brother, James, earl of Moray, who served as her son's regent, introduced these documents into the English inquiry commissioned to determine whether she should be returned to Scotland. As the originals have disappeared, Guy turned to extant sixteenth-century transcripts and discovered that Cecil altered the English translations of the French versions to make it appear as though she had referred to Darnley's murder. It is difficult to judge the impact of Cecil's mistranslations, however, as some commissioners could read French. Furthermore, one of their charges was comparing the handwriting in the French Casket Letters to that in French documents unquestionably composed by Mary. Ultimately, the Englishmen seemed far less interested in validating the letters' contents than in understanding why Moray was so willing to besmirch his half sister's honor and reputation.

Besides these manuscripts, Guy utilized other archival evidence for his biography of over 500 pages. Despite its length, the book fails to refer to some significant issues, for example, Wormald's arguments about Mary's ineffectiveness as a ruler, and gives relatively limited attention to her extended captivity. Finally, it relies on unconfirmed diplomatic gossip and contains several surprising factual errors.[9]

That Alison Weir, a popular writer who was intrigued by the mystery surrounding Darnley's murder, also published a romantic study of Mary in 2004 indicates the continuing public demand for works on her life.[10] This highly readable book relies on a manuscript attributed to Claude Nau, who became Mary's secretary for French affairs in 1575 while she was an English prisoner. Weir treated this manuscript as though it were the queen's memoirs, although Mary's authenticated writings contradict some of its statements.

APPROACHES TO MARY'S LIFE

These earlier studies generally reflect their authors' interest in British political history as well as photography. By contrast, this biography represents not only an understanding of political history but also my experience in researching a wide range of cultural rituals, mores, and behavior. Since the 1980s, I have examined queenship conventions, gender relations, family networks, the honor code, death customs, religious conflict, aristocratic education, court politics, and royal protocol. In interpreting Mary's controversial decisions at critical moments in her life, I have also utilized works by anthropologists, such as Victor Turner, which remind us of the limited range of choices, specific to their culture, which individuals have when responding to personal crises.

In some sense all Marian scholars have benefited from and have even built upon their predecessors' studies of her. Besides becoming familiar with this extensive historiography, I have turned to recent research on early modern cultural, legal, and social topics, especially concerning Scotland, which highlight information that makes possible new approaches to her life. Her royal status, her kinship networks and French upbringing, her dynastic vision, her marital difficulties and gender relations, her religious views, the conspiracies against Elizabeth, and the preparations for her execution – these all gain richer and fresher nuances when examined for the first time within early modern frameworks.

EARLY MODERN FRAMEWORKS: ROYAL KINSHIP AND DYNASTIC VISION

It is significant to the development of Mary's character and personality that as she was growing up, she could not remember a time when she was not the queen of her realm. As she moved from infancy to childhood, she must have slowly become aware that in social groups and at every public and private moment she occupied the premier place. She headed a social hierarchy in which the royal family held a superior status to that of dukes, who, in turn, took precedence over earls. Below them were situated lesser members of the titled classes. In Scotland the royalty, noblemen, and lesser aristocracy even wore different kinds of helmets to confirm visually their social standing. Their placement in public processions or ceremonies also reinforced their status in the pervasive early modern pyramid.

After reaching France, Mary learned from Henry II, her future father-in-law, important lessons about Scotland's diplomatic status in Christendom. He granted her first place at court among his daughters, but although she was a queen regnant, he situated her behind Catherine de' Medici, his queen consort, and his sons. That Mary was destined to marry his heir Francis, the dauphin, was the reason Henry advanced her to this high ranking. Following the medieval papacy's protocol, European leaders had customarily privileged the princes of the blood of France above all others, except the pope, the emperor, and his heir the king of the Romans. At diplomatic conferences and festive occasions French envoys were placed immediately after papal and imperial legates. When Emperor Charles V no longer governed Spain, however, its monarchs challenged their demotion to the second-place position. Shortly after the accession of the emperor's son, Philip II, to the Spanish throne in 1556, he began unsuccessfully to dispute the French primacy. Meanwhile, Henry VIII claimed third place for England but occasionally, as, for example, at the imperial court, his envoys had to acquiesce in the loss of their status to Portugal, whose infanta, Isabella, was Emperor Charles's wife. Scotland came further down the list, after Sicily but before Cyprus and Denmark. Monarchs, as well as their aristocratic subjects, jealously guarded their social and diplomatic standings, sometimes responding violently when threatened with displacement.

In France Mary also became aware of the prominence of her Guise uncles, her mother's brothers, who dominated the royal council and government after her husband Francis's accession. They taught her the political and social advantages of their powerful kin networks. Her mother had, after all, chosen to match Mary with the dauphin rather than an English prince in order not only to ally Scotland with the more prestigious realm but also to enhance the influence and authority of her French relatives in their native land.

During Mary's residence in France while receiving a humanist education similar to Francis's, she was instructed in the strategies conducive to political survival at royal courts. Her mother's brother, Charles, cardinal of Lorraine, taught her how to manipulate protocol to mask her opinions, to shun gossips that might spread rumors about her, to prevent enemies from entering her household, and to employ ciphers and codes in her sensitive correspondence. Her life in France may have been happy but it was never carefree.

Earlier in 1543 Henry VIII had demanded her as a bride for his son Edward, partly because Mary was also a claimant to the English throne.

Scottish officials agreed to the Treaties of Greenwich, arranging for her removal to England as Edward's betrothed when she was ten years old, but rejected those treaties a few months later. In retaliation English raids, which have been termed the Rough Wooing since Sir Walter Scott coined the phrase in the nineteenth century, devastated parts of her realm, attempting to capture her and remove her to England. In his will which set out the English succession, Henry ignored the Stewarts, apparently intending that Mary would become England's queen only if she wed Edward, his heir.

These childhood experiences and Henry II's endorsement of her English rights in 1559 after the accession of Henry VIII's Protestant daughter Elizabeth, whom Catholics viewed as illegitimate, may have strengthened Mary's dynastic resolve. It would, however, have been uncharacteristic for an early modern ruler to surrender a hereditary asset like hers without a struggle. Henry II and his father, Francis I, for example, fought ruinous wars with Emperor Charles, trying to capture Milan to which they held only a remote claim.

GENDER ISSUES AND MARITAL DIFFICULTIES

Believing that it was more appropriate for men than women to wield monarchical power, many British people deplored the rule of queens regnant. When Parliament entailed the Scottish crown in 1373 to Robert II's sons, it noted the "evils and misfortunes" that had in many places "arisen from the succession of female heirs."[11] In 1542 the crown had reverted to Mary only because her father's heir apparent and cousin, John Stewart, second duke of Albany, had died childless in 1536. Among the multitudinous early modern voices preferring kings to queens regnant were besides John Knox, a leading reformer, David Lindsay the herald, David Calderwood, historian of the Kirk, and her own son James VI. In a sermon at the court of Edward VI, the English preacher, Hugh Latimer also publicly expressed concerns about the possible accession of the king's sisters.[12]

Before Mary's reign the only attempt to crown a Scottish queen regnant occurred in the late thirteenth century when Margaret, the Maid of Norway, granddaughter to the deceased Alexander III, died on her voyage to the realm to serve as its queen. Her demise resulted in civil wars, English intervention in Scottish politics, and ultimately the accession of Robert Bruce, who possessed the junior lineal claim to Alexander's throne.

If Mary failed to marry and give birth to a legitimate heir, two families with royal pretensions: the senior Hamilton branch, possessing the earldom of Arran and the dukedom of Châtelherault, and the junior Stewart branch, holding the earldom of Lennox, would surely have competed for her crown, perhaps provoking a civil war. Indeed, the heads of both families had schemed to wed their heir to Mary, and when the Stewarts succeeded in their marital ambitions in 1565, the Hamiltons joined the earl of Moray to challenge her authority in the unsuccessful Chaseabout Raid. Ironically, it was Mary's weddings in Scotland that ultimately led to her captivity. Darnley her second husband was an English subject with strong claims to the Scottish throne, as the heir of Matthew Stewart, fourth earl of Lennox. Like Mary, Darnley also possessed English inheritance rights as a grandson of Margaret Tudor. While Mary was the granddaughter of Margaret and her first husband, James IV, Darnley was a grandson of Margaret and her second husband, Archibald Douglas, sixth earl of Angus.

About eight months after their wedding, Darnley orchestrated a conspiracy to murder David Riccio, Mary's secretary for French affairs, who, some believed, was exercising undue influence at court. Darnley seems to have been frustrated personally because he had mistakenly anticipated that his royal wedding would endow him with actual regal authority. It is relevant to his participation in this crime that a man's honor held both public and private facets, public by displaying personal bravery especially on the battlefield, private by maintaining his household authority and his wife's sexual loyalty.

Unfortunately for Mary, who was six months' pregnant, rumors had spread that she was Riccio's lover. Whatever were her husband's motivations in conspiring against Riccio – whether or not he believed he was defending his honor – it is possible that his goal was to injure both her and her unborn child in order to claim the kingship in fact as well as in name.

After Darnley's murder in 1567 and her marriage to Bothwell three months later, Mary's rebels crowned her son with the intention of raising him as a Protestant. Why she married Darnley and then Bothwell are questions that will never be answered to everyone's satisfaction. There is compelling evidence, however, that she wed Darnley for his lineage, that she was unaware of the conspiracy to murder him, and that she neither colluded in Bothwell's abduction nor had consensual sexual relations with him while his prisoner at Dunbar. The importance of Darnley's English claims, the forcible marriage of early modern heiresses, and the Scottish tradition in which men signed bands or bonds agreeing to support a variety of enterprises, such as the murder of Riccio and Darnley, will be explored more fully in later chapters.

Regardless of the specific details of Mary's three marriages, they served generally to fulfill contemporary expectations about the husbands of female rulers. If the women chose foreigners, the men might interfere in their realm's diplomacy and seize its assets or possessions on behalf of their native lands. If they selected one of their subjects, his political ambitions could generate internal strife. No bridegroom in Mary's likely candidate pool could assuage the fears of the entire Scottish aristocracy, and, indeed, all three of her alliances generated rebellions against her authority.

After she married Bothwell, her enemies probably created the Casket Letters to prove that her love for him caused her to collude in the murder of her second husband, an act that many condemned as the most despicable crime a woman could commit. It is relevant to the English inquiry in which the Letters were introduced in 1568 that English law categorized husband-killing as petty treason and that English trial judges routinely accepted as evidence testimonies that explained what witnesses and plaintiffs believed had happened, even when referencing fictional and supernatural acts. Despite this inclusive evidentiary standard, which slowly died out after 1700, it is noteworthy that the Letters failed to gain enough credibility for Elizabeth to have Mary condemned as her husband's murderer. The later publication of them did, however, cause many contemporaries to claim that Moray, as her son's regent, had irreparably harmed Mary's reputation, and, of course, she remained in captivity without full exoneration.

Any analysis of the Casket Letters and other defamations of her character must consider early modern views about female sexuality. Possessing wombs that were said to wander about their bodies causing them to become hysterical, women were thought to be dominated by their biological drive to conceive babies. The easiest means of dishonoring a woman in this society in which female virginity was highly valued, was to spread rumors that she had committed fornication or adultery.

Concerned about the alleged inability of women to suppress their biological urges and weaknesses, husbands and male guardians sought to supervise the activities of their female dependents closely. Because contemporaries expected all women to be subject to the headship or authority of men, the power of husbands over their wives and family members was rarely disputed. In her study of political culture in Elizabethan England, Anne McLaren discovered that even queens regnant were strongly admonished to accept the advice of their male councilors. In realms, such as England and Scotland, which experienced both the Protestant reformation and the accession of queens regnant, McLaren found that male reformers viewed "social order and male primacy" as interdependent. They presumed not only that they should be the ones counseling women rulers but also that their advice should be heeded. In 1572, for example, Thomas Digges, a member of parliament, threatened to withdraw his allegiance from Elizabeth if she did not agree to Mary's execution.[13]

A study comparable to McLaren's does not exist for Scotland, but Roger Mason has examined the long-held Scottish tradition of challenging monarchs who relied on evil councilors.[14] Functioning within this cultural and political context, William Maitland of Lethington and the future earl of Moray began to discuss whether Mary upon returning to Scotland in 1561 would accept their advice rather than that of her Guise uncles. They believed that if she would "trust only in her native subjects" that she would convert to Protestantism.[15] That Mary should seek appropriate counsel was also a concern of the English government. In February 1561 Sir Nicholas Throckmorton, the English ambassador in France, wrote home with assurances that Mary would be ruled by good counsel and wise men.

That it was assumed she was incapable of individual judgment, of weighing advice, and coming to an independent conclusion is proved by the developing events after her decision to marry Darnley was revealed. Rumors spread, repeated by Thomas Randolph, the English ambassador to Scotland, that in selecting him she had followed the advice of the Italian David Riccio and Darnley's uncle, the earl of

Atholl, among others. These rumors helped fuel the animosity that led later to Darnley's conspiracy against Riccio.

To clerics, especially, it also seemed critical for the queens regnant to accept male advice, reigning, as the women did, over tiers of religious institutions mostly staffed by men. Presenting themselves as God's messengers, preachers often gave advice to their queens publicly. In a sermon in 1587, which was later printed, for example, Edward Harris criticized the activities at Elizabeth's court and portrayed her as a helpless victim who needed to depend on God for her successes.[16] The warnings of John Knox to the Scottish queen are well known and will be briefly described below.

MARY'S CATHOLIC STATUS AND CONSPIRACIES AGAINST ELIZABETH

Another of Mary's political disadvantages when she returned to Scotland in 1561 was her commitment to Catholicism. While a majority of her subjects still clung to her faith,[17] Protestants, including her half brother, the future Moray, had previously gained control of the government and had outlawed the mass. One of his early allies was the outspoken Knox, who has been likened to an Old Testament Prophet by both friends and foes. In 1558 he attacked women rulers in *The First Blast of the Trumpet Against the Monstrous Regiment of Women*, criticizing the persecution of Protestants by Mary Tudor and to a lesser extent by Mary of Guise, her daughter's regent in Scotland. Claiming it was monstrous for a realm to have a woman as its head, Knox validated rebellion against the rule of ungodly governors. Too much attention can focus on Knox, however, for Protestantism was a strong international movement seeking far-reaching changes. In France, the Catholic Guise family participated in murderous civil wars against Huguenots, including the future Henry IV.

Citing Mary's tolerant attitude toward the reformed religion and her Protestant marriage to Bothwell, some skeptics have doubted that she merits recognition as a Catholic martyr. While early in her English captivity, Mary also agreed to wed an English Protestant, Thomas Howard, fourth duke of Norfolk, she viewed the marriage as a means of gaining liberation, her restitution to Scotland, and recognition of her

English rights. Later, however, she promoted a series of Catholic plots against Elizabeth and the return of Britain to the Roman confession. After her execution, many contemporary Catholics revered her as a martyr. Indeed, Christians do not need to behave in a pious manner during their entire lifetime to gain recognition for holiness after death.

FEARING ASSASSINATION AND PREPARING FOR DEATH

Although Mary approved Anthony Babington's scheme to rescue her in 1586, she probably did not support as a first step toward her freedom his plan to murder Elizabeth, the charge for which she was beheaded. Mary had long worried that when Elizabeth died, whether by natural causes or violence, her jailors would assassinate their captive. These fears became more acute after 1584 when thousands of Englishmen endorsed the Bond of Association, promising to kill the perpetrators and anyone for whom an assassination attempt against Elizabeth was made. Mary fully understood that the Bond, enacted as a statute in 1585, was directed at her. Fearing for her own life if Elizabeth were killed, Mary also endorsed the Bond. Like Elizabeth who later exhibited great reluctance to sign her cousin's death warrant, Mary belonged to an early modern royal network that deplored regicide. Monarchical honor dictated, for example, that rulers ransom their royal prisoners, even enemies captured on the battlefield, rather than have them executed.

In the weeks preceding her death in the spirit of the *ars moriendi*, the continuing medieval tradition instructing Christians in how to die well, Mary prepared through a series of devotional exercises to accept the fate God planned for her, that is to face calmly the violent end of her pilgrimage on earth. Her faith sustained her in those final moments when she publicly forgave both her captors for imprisoning her and her executioner for the task he would shortly carry out. Even hostile commentators testified to her good Christian death.

As this introduction indicates, when her royal positions, her inheritance rights, and her family relationships are analyzed in the context of early modern culture, they gain richer and fresher nuances. Clearly, her upbringing and socialization instilled in her the duty to marry and provide her dynasty with legitimate heirs. Most individuals, even those who remained single, accepted the contemporary impulse to strengthen their familial networks and to transmit enhanced political, social, and financial assets to the next generation. In that respect, Mary fulfilled her society's expectations, but her marriages created alternatives to her rule in the persons of her husbands and son. Her status as a female monarch lent her a certain vulnerability when confronting assertive reformed clerics and aggressive, power-hungry noblemen.

PRIMARY SOURCES

Fortunately, Marian scholars have access to extensive primary documentation, most of which is in print but much of which is flawed and requires cautious treatment. Scottish chronicles are, for example, riddled with inaccuracies, since the annalists, writing usually long after the events occurred, sometimes failed to authenticate rumors or other scurrilous reports they repeated. Many assertions in Buchanan's and Leslie's polemical works, as well as in some memoirs composed in their authors' old age, also require careful analysis. Public documents, especially diplomatic dispatches, contain much problematic data, as rulers often deliberately leaked false information to ambassadors, who spread through the rumor mill that information, as well as unconfirmed gossip forwarded to them by their paid spies.[18] In addition, further questions will be raised about the governmental records that have been employed to condemn Mary's personal rule.

The most important of the primary sources is her voluminous correspondence; many, but not all, of her letters are available in Alexandre Labanoff's nineteenth-century edition.[19] Some of her personal writings contain statements that are obviously contradictory because she sometimes pursued conflicting goals. For example, in 1565 she simultaneously negotiated to marry Don Carlos of Spain, Robert Dudley, earl of Leicester, and Darnley. She was not the open, trusting, uncomplicated woman described by some of her sympathetic biographers. She remembered well and routinely employed the strategies, such as putting her communications in cipher and keeping her personal matters secret, that she learned from her Guise uncles to overcome the notorious backbiting and snooping at royal courts.

SUCCEEDING CHAPTERS

The chapters following this introduction are arranged chronologically, although occasionally within chapters chronology is dispensed with to complete discussions of specific topics. All begin with movements or with journeys that indicate a new phase in her life, starting with her father's search for a French wife in 1536 and his daughter Mary's birth in 1542 and ending with her death in 1587, her burial at Peterborough Cathedral, and re-interment at Westminster Abbey in 1612.

2

SCOTTISH BEGINNINGS TO 1548

On 1 September 1536 James V, king of Scots, sailed for France with a fleet of six ships and some 500 men and reached Dieppe eight or nine days later. He undertook the voyage to wed a French lady, as first arranged in 1517 by his governor, John Stewart, second duke of Albany, with Francis I in the Treaty of Rouen. Having initially appointed one of his daughters for James to wed, Francis retracted this promise in 1534 and offered him a substitute bride, Mary of Bourbon, daughter of Charles, duke of Vendôme. Departing from his court which removed to Rouen, James rode on horseback with John Tennant and six servants to Vendôme's home at St Quentin, Picardy, to make her acquaintance. Traveling with so small an escort required that he go incognito not only for security reasons but also for greater speed since he could thereby avoid the usual pomp of royal progresses.

The fifth consecutive Scottish monarch with this name, James was a descendant of Robert Bruce, who succeeded in founding an independent dynasty despite civil war and English aggression. Beginning in 1296 Edward I had invaded Scotland almost yearly in attempts to enforce his suzerainty on the realm. Bruce and his successors countered English threats and attacks by adhering to a military agreement with France first negotiated in 1295 that ultimately gained recognition as the auld alliance. The Treaty of Rouen proposing a French bride for James continued that Franco-Scottish tradition.

The chronicles detailing personal information, such as James's visit to St Quentin, are replete with errors, partly because their authors often composed them long after the events they recorded. It is possible, nevertheless, that Robert Lindsay of Pitscottie was correct in asserting that Mary of Bourbon had some deformity, perhaps a misshapen back.[1] A disability such as this appalled her contemporaries, who believed God caused the birth of monstrous children to punish their parents for their sins, especially sexual ones.

Whether her appearance repelled James or whether he planned to take the opportunity his incognito visit to the Vendôme home offered to pressure Francis into substituting one of his two daughters for Mary cannot now be determined. After rejoining his court, James traveled toward Francis at Lyons and proposed to wed Madeleine, the elder princess.

In 1536 James was seeking a bride because of a recent adverse papal decision. At the age of 24, he was the father of some nine illegitimate children, including six sons who held monastic posts *in commendam*, a status that provided them with church revenues without requiring them to enter religious orders. James considered wedding his favorite mistress, Margaret Erskine, daughter of John, fifth Lord Erskine, and legitimizing their son Lord James, who was born in 1531. The obstacle to these plans was that she was the wife of Robert Douglas of Lochleven and was probably married to him when she gave birth to James's son. After Paul III refused to nullify her marriage, James did not challenge papal authority but chose to seek the wife arranged in 1517, partly because he relied on Church revenues to supplement his limited income.

James's dependence on papal funds was caused by the crown's poverty; unable to afford a royal army, for example, he had to rely on noblemen's lieges during troubled times. His realm, which was much poorer economically and financially than England, was also regionally and politically diverse. The approximately 850,000 Scots, whose occupation was mainly farming and cattle-grazing, lived in distinctly different areas, covering some 30,500 square miles, much of which was rugged and mountainous. From one-third to one-half of the population inhabited the Lowlands, which contained the realm's capital Edinburgh with a population of some 12,000. The remainder lived in the Highlands and the Borders. The Highlanders, who spoke Gaelic rather than Lowland Scots, held stronger allegiance to their clan leaders than to the monarch, and many Border inhabitants, both Scots and English, were notorious criminals.

Writers have characterized the marriage in January 1537 of the reputedly handsome Scottish king to 16-year-old Madeleine as a love match, partly because she seems to have helped him overcome the reluctance of her father, who was concerned about her fragile health. Aware that as the elder princess, she might have to marry a stranger she had never seen, she preferred to wed the king she had met. Monarchs' daughters, like her, often harbored ambitions to marry kings or their heirs. In 1560 Juana, the younger sister of Philip II and the widow of Emanuel John of Portugal, refused a match with Francesco Maria de' Medici because his father Cosmo was only the duke of Florence.

In May 1537 when travel on the North Sea was less risky than in the winter, James and Madeleine sailed for Scotland accompanied by, among others, Pierre de Ronsard, the greatest of the Pléiade group of French poets. They arrived safely at Leith, Edinburgh's harbor, on the 19th, but her father's fears about her health were soon realized, as she died on 7 July some six weeks later. On that same day, her widowed husband wrote a letter to Francis, reporting her demise and stating that he was sending its bearer, David Beaton, abbot of Arbroath, the future cardinal archbishop of St Andrews, with a proposal, which was, as it turned out, a request for another French bride.

MARRIAGE TO MARY OF GUISE

Rather than attempting to persuade James to wed the still available Mary of Bourbon, Francis offered him Mary of Guise, the widow of Louis II, duke of Longueville, who died about a month before Madeleine. Pregnant with Longueville's second child Louis, who was born in August but who died four months later, Mary was displeased about the possibility of marrying a foreigner. If she wed James, she would have to move to his realm and leave behind her two-year-old son Francis, the new duke. James had probably met Mary at his wedding to Madeleine, which she and her late husband Longueville attended. The advantages of Mary's candidacy were that James was acquainted with her and obviously approved of her appearance, that she had a dowry of 150,000 livres, and that she had proved her fertility.

Ironically, after Jane Seymour died in childbirth in October 1537, Henry VIII chose to compete with his nephew for this alliance and sent Sir Peter Mewtes, a gentleman of his privy chamber, to visit Mary twice at Châteaudun Castle, the Longueville home on the Loire River. Having learned that she was a tall person, Henry informed Louis de Perreau, sieur de Castillon, the French ambassador, that as he was a big man, he required a big wife.

Henry's diplomacy failed to prevent the marriage on 9 May 1538 of Mary and James at Châteaudun with Robert, fifth Lord Maxwell, serving as the groom's proxy and with Erskine and Beaton in attendance. Maxwell placed a diamond ring on her finger valued at 300 crowns;[2] the one for Madeleine was worth four times as much, but these varying amounts reflected the difference between a gift suitable for a king's daughter and one for his cousin.

The descendants of Charlemagne as well as John II of France through the female line, the Guises were originally from Lorraine, a semi-autonomous duchy of the Holy Roman Empire that was incorporated into France in 1766. Before his death in 1508, René II of Anjou, titular king of Naples, Sicily and Jerusalem, and duke of Lorraine, divided his territories between his two older sons, the first Anthony, succeeding to the duchy of Lorraine, and the second Claude, inheriting many of his father's French estates and later gaining the dukedom of Guise. Claude's wife, Antoinette of Bourbon, gave birth to ten surviving children, the oldest of whom was Mary, born on 20 November 1515 at Bar-le-Duc, their château built above the Ornain River, and the youngest of whom was René, future marquis of Elboeuf, born in 1536. After Claude's mother Queen Philippa of Guelders retired to a nunnery in 1519, he moved his family into the ancestral home at Joinville, which was situated on a hill above the Marne River.

On 10 June 1538 Mary and her household left Le Havre in three royal galleys and landed at Crail in Fife on Trinity Sunday. They traveled to Balcomie Castle, some two miles distant where James met her the next day and escorted her to St Andrews, which lies about ten miles away on a promontory jutting into the North Sea. Sir David Lindsay of the Mount, the king's herald and future Lyon King of Arms, produced her entry pageants. In the high middle ages, citizens began celebrating their rulers' first entries into their towns in festivities that extolled and justified royal policies and applauded their realm's peace and prosperity. James encouraged this practice, recognizing that the creative achievements and wealth displayed on these occasions helped to reinforce his realm's position among the states of Western Europe.

Before the new Abbey Gate at St Andrews, a lady disguised as an angel stepped from an artificial cloud and delivered the keys of Scotland to Mary. Subsequently, Lindsay gave an oration exhorting her to serve God, obey her husband, and live in a pure state according to God's will. Afterward, James accompanied her to the archbishop's guest house for the night, and they were married for a second time in the cathedral the next morning.

On 16 November Lindsay supervised the festivities for Mary's entry into Edinburgh. She followed the traditional path, entering the city at the West Port, processing up the hill to the castle, then moving down High Street, and exiting at the Netherbow Port, the entrance to the Canongate, on the way to Holyrood Palace. At set locations, the citizens presented pageants featuring biblical scenes, moral allegories, and mythological topics, the splendor and creativity of which signaled the existence of a flourishing Renaissance culture in Scotland.

Evidence of it could also be found in royal architecture. James had continued his father's remodeling efforts at Holyrood, Linlithgow, Falkland, Dunfermline, and the two nearly impregnable castles of Stirling and Edinburgh, although the latter was mostly used as a prison before its apartments were refurbished in 1566. Constructed on a smaller scale than Mary of Guise had known in France, where the Loire châteaux, for example, are truly grand structures, the new facades and decorations of the Scottish palaces represented some of the earliest and finest examples of Renaissance building on the British Isles. Foreign developments inspired James's architectural vision, but his innovations were refined into an unmistakable and impressive native style.

In the first phase between 1534 and 1536, he may have followed Henry VIII's lead, as the northwest Tower at Holyrood, a quadrangular structure on the west side of the Augustinian Abbey, and the gatehouse and fountain at Linlithgow recall English designs. Overlooking a loch about 19 miles west of Edinburgh, Linlithgow, the queen's jointure house, reportedly greatly pleased her. It had castellated chivalric imagery, a noble courtyard, and an elaborate fountain with three tiers of basins decorated with medallion heads that spouted out water to basins below. Its long galleries on the east and south also possessed an Italianate air.

On returning from France James brought with him wines, jewels, tapestries, and works of art and introduced architecture reflecting his admiration for French Renaissance models of Italianate style. At Falkland in Fife, his favorite palace, and at Stirling, James employed masons sent to him by the duke and duchess of Guise. With its delicate classical buttresses fronted by columns on the facades, Falkland reflects the architecture of Villiers-Cotterets, a French château. However, the royal house at Stirling, with its life-sized sculpted statues and decorated ceilings with wooden roundels, is Scotland's finest example of Renaissance architecture and compares favorably with Châteaudun and Joinville. A final palace at the royal Benedictine Abbey of Dunfermline was created by enlarging the king's guest house there. Funds extracted from the Church made possible this extensive building program.

In the autumn of 1539, one year after Mary's Edinburgh entry, James accompanied her on a pilgrimage to St Adrian's Shrine on the Isle of May in the Firth of Forth. Believing that childbirth required a special divine intervention, barren women customarily visited this shrine to seek assistance in conceiving. Many women also assumed that touching something infertile or barren would affect their childbearing abilities. Catherine de' Medici, for example, refused to ride on a mule for fear she would somehow take on its infertility. When in 1539 shortly after the St Adrian pilgrimage, Mary discovered she was pregnant, James ordered her coronation to take place, and Cardinal Beaton crowned her on 22 February 1540 at Holyrood Abbey.

Their first child, his father's namesake, was born on 22 May. The next year, on 24 April, another son, christened Robert, was born. To their parents' dismay both infants died within a week of Robert's birth. In a six-year period, Mary was delivered of four children, only one of whom, Longueville, was still alive, but in 1551 he also died prematurely. Historians have estimated that some 34 per cent of all early modern English children died before the age of ten. When compared to the modern English percentage of 2.4 for this age group, this toll was exceedingly high but even higher for Mary's male offspring, 75 per cent of whom failed to reach their tenth year.

BIRTH OF MARY, QUEEN OF SCOTS

On 8 December 1542, the day of the Immaculate Conception of the Virgin Mary, the queen gave birth to a namesake daughter. Although other dates, especially the 7th, have been credited, the 8th was the day on which Mary celebrated her birthday. It is likely that she was born at midnight or shortly thereafter, since contemporaries were often inconsistent in dating an event that occurred in the early morning hours. In recounting Darnley's death, for example, Mary related that on the evening of 9 February about two hours after midnight, his house was blown up.[3] Even the official trial record placed his murder on the 9th, although it actually occurred about 2:00 a.m. on the 10th.

Born at Linlithgow, Mary was christened at nearby St Michael's during a time of great trouble for her realm. On 24 November a Scottish raiding party lost the Battle of Solway Moss to the English, and although only a few were killed, some 1,000 became English prisoners. Afterwards, James, who was not present at the defeat, visited his consort at Linlithgow en route to Falkland where by 6 December he lay seriously ill with a fever. Lindsay of Pitscottie's claim that when James learned about Mary's birth, he predicted, "Adieu, farewell, it came with a lass, it will pass with a lass," was undoubtedly an invention, perhaps created by the chronicler.[4] During the days before his death on 14 December, James was mostly delirious and incoherent from "a serious illness of the mind," possibly suffering from cholera or the plague.[5] James's alleged comment alluded to the Stewarts' descent through Bruce's daughter, Marjorie, the wife of Walter Fitzalan, sixth Grand Steward of Scotland, but Mary's accession did not eliminate her family's name from the dynasty. She married Darnley, who was a Stewart and the father of her son, who took his family name.

The biological difference between a male and a female was and is the basic social distinction overriding all others, and in the early modern period, that organizing principle was translated into specific gender roles and expectations. Medicinal and philosophical treatises taught that women were not only naturally passionate, hysterical, and irrational but also inferior to men anatomically and intellectually. Religious tracts generally proclaimed God had subjected women to men as punishment for Eve's sins. These theories were applied at all social levels. David Calderwood, the historian of the Scottish Church, stated, for example, that in 1542, "all men lamented that the realm was left without a male to succeed."[6] As the 1373 parliamentary entail of the crown had expired on Albany's death in 1536, Mary's accession went unchallenged, although most who accepted her rule, like Lindsay the herald, remained hostile to the notion of a female ruler:

> Ladyis no way I can commend,
> Presumptuouslie quhilk dois pretend,
> Till use the Office of ane King,
> Or Realmes tak in governing.[7]

In contrast to her undisputed accession, James Hamilton, second earl of Arran, born in 1516, had difficulty enforcing his claim to be her governor, the office to which as the heir presumptive he had the best hereditary right. Since the direct male line was extinct, Arran had gained recognition as heir presumptive because his father, the first earl of Arran, was the heir of Mary, daughter of James II (d. 1460) by her husband, James, Lord Hamilton. Arran's difficulty was Beaton's testimony that the king had committed his infant to the cardinal's care. An extant notarial instrument dated on the day of his demise named Beaton, Huntly, Archibald Campbell, fourth earl of Argyll, and James, earl of Moray (the king's illegitimate half brother), to Mary's governing council. Denying the legality of this council, Arran alleged its authority derived from the king's will that Beaton had manufactured for his own advancement. Although, unlike Beaton, Arran had not witnessed James's death, his accusation gained credibility because churchmen did fabricate documents favorable to themselves, justifying their behavior with the excuse that they were furthering God's cause. Many great abbeys, for example, possessed invented charters validating their property rights. Indeed, forgery was an increasingly popular medieval practice that did not level off until the fifteenth century. Unless the crime involved forging the king's coins or seal or an over-lord's seal, it was treated as a misdemeanor even when it included introducing false documents into court.

A competition ensued between Beaton and Arran for custody of the young queen and for control of her marriage, which English intrigue made more complicated. Before releasing the Solway Moss prisoners, Henry's officials forced them to pledge to promote a match between his heir Edward and their queen. For additional leverage, Henry also sent to Scotland two allies, the earl of Angus, the divorced husband of his sister Margaret Tudor, and Sir George Douglas, the earl's brother. Angus had originally fled to England to escape the hostility of his royal stepson James V.

To gain recognition for his double role as governor and heir presumptive, Arran favored the English alliance and succeeded in imprisoning the cardinal at the Douglas castle of Dalkeith. In March 1543 Arran convened a parliament, which confirmed his authority as Mary's governor and approved reform measures, such as criticizing the papacy, promoting Protestant preachers, and translating the scriptures into English or Scots. Later that month when support for the English policy was declining, Beaton was transferred to St Andrews and in April gained his freedom.

On 1 July 1543 the governments of Scotland and England agreed to the Treaties of Greenwich, the first ending the war and the second stipulating that at the end of Mary's tenth year, she would marry Edward by proxy and move to England. A clause also confirmed Scotland's right to retain its laws and liberties. In the negotiations leading to this amity, the English ambassador, Sir Ralph Sadler, obtained Mary of Guise's reluctant, momentary agreement to her daughter's marriage to Edward. On 22 March Sadler was permitted to view the infant naked to reassure his monarch about her health and appearance, most importantly about her lack of deformity, and observed that she was "as goodly a child as I have seen of her age, as like to live, with the grace of God."[8]

Opposition to the alliance mounted because of the agreement to send the queen to England while she was still a child. On 24 July having gathered an army larger than Arran's, Beaton and his allies challenged the earl's control of her. Among Beaton's supporters were Argyll, Huntly, and Lennox, who had recently reached Scotland as the ambassador of Francis I. Eleven years earlier possibly for safety reasons, Lennox had moved to France where he became a French subject. Usually, when two Scottish forces encountered each other, the side with fewer numbers withdrew, as occurred at this confrontation. On the 27th Beaton supervised the transfer to Sterling of Mary, who was teething, and her grateful mother, who had earlier expressed the opinion to Sadler that it was inappropriate for Arran, the heir presumptive whom she considered untrustworthy, to have sole custody of her child. At their young queen's removal to Stirling, Arran and Beaton each appointed two guardians for her: Arran chose Alexander, fifth Lord Livingston of Callendar, and John, fifth Lord Lindsay of the Byres, while Beaton selected Lord Erskine, and William Graham, second earl of Montrose.

After meeting with the queen dowager at Stirling, Sadler reported on 10 August her opinion that "her daughter did grow apace; and soon, she said, she would be a woman, if she took after her mother." He also commented, "She is a right fair and goodly child, as any that I have seen, for her age." A week later, responding to an inquiry about whether she was ill with a childhood disease, Sadler related that she had contracted smallpox but had been fully recovered from it for at least ten days.[9] Often reports were vague and contradictory about childhood diseases. As Mary later suffered smallpox in France, the ailment to which Sadler referred was probably chickenpox.

On Sunday, 9 September, Beaton crowned her at Stirling; in the procession to the chapel, Arran marched with the crown, Argyll with the sword of state, and Lennox with the scepter. This was the first occasion on which these regalia, obtained by James IV and James V, were carried together to symbolize royal power. The usual festivities, tournaments, and masques celebrated the event. Although Sadler criticized the day's meagerness, remarking that she was crowned with such ceremony as they employ in Scotland, which was not very costly, comparisons of later versions of the ceremony to their English and French counterparts indicate a great similarity.

It is, furthermore, unclear just what evidence Sadler was using for his assessment since he was unable to attend the ritual. His enforced seclusion at Edinburgh, 38 miles from Stirling, could have prompted his disgruntled remark, as ambassadors usually held places of honor on these occasions. Three days before the coronation, he reported that someone had shot at and almost hit one of his men. He also complained that Edinburgh's citizens were so hostile: "I dare not go, nor almost send out of my doors, and much less might I ride or travel abroad in the country . . . without suspicion and danger."[10] In somewhat different circumstances, the imperial ambassador, Francis van der Delft, who marched in Edward VI's procession from the Tower of London to Westminster Abbey on the eve of his coronation but was not invited to the ritual itself, reported that it was "no very memorable show of triumph or magnificence."[11]

Since Scotland was Mary's dowry, Henry VIII was not the only father seeking to match his heir with her. Before confirming the English treaties, Arran proposed her for his namesake son, who was about five years her senior; another contender was Argyll, a descendant of James II, who settled for his namesake heir's union with Jean, one of James V's illegitimate daughters. It was the 26-year-old Lennox, who was momentarily successful, signing a secret pact in October with the queen mother to wed her infant daughter.[12]

After Lennox returned to Scotland as a French subject, Beaton and Mary of Guise agreed to recognize him as the young queen's heir presumptive. Like Arran, Lennox was a descendant of James II's daughter Mary but through her daughter Elizabeth, not her son. Lennox and his allies argued, however, that because Arran was born to his father's wife, Janet Beaton, during the lifetime of his former divorced spouse, Janet Home, he was illegitimate and therefore ineligible for the succession. If this allegation were to win acceptance, Lennox would be declared the true heir presumptive, but most Scots continued to favor Arran's claim.

In November Sadler reported the unconfirmed rumor that Beaton had tried unsuccessfully to reconcile Arran and Lennox with two proposals: Arran was to divorce his wife and marry the queen mother and Lennox was to wed her daughter. No evidence suggests that Beaton approved Arran's union with Mary of Guise although Lennox did agree to wed her child. Not wishing to wait well more than a decade before marrying, however, Lennox began competing with Patrick Hepburn, third earl of Bothwell, for Mary of Guise, who had earlier expressed her feelings about remarriage to Sadler: "Since she had been a king's wife her heart was too high to look any lower."[13]

Mary of Guise would not normally, of course, reveal her marital inclinations to the English ambassador, but her invocation of early modern hierarchical social standards was tactful and went unquestioned. That she spent the remainder of her life protecting her daughter's patrimony indicates her major concern was that child's well-being. She undoubtedly believed it would not facilitate her daughter's rule as queen to advance a Scottish nobleman as her stepfather. Although Lennox ultimately departed for England, Bothwell procured a divorce from his wife, Agnes Sinclair, known thereafter as the Lady of

Morham, to make it possible for him to wed Mary of Guise should she decide to accept him as her husband.

Meanwhile, having lost control of the young queen and observing a growing hostility to her English marriage, Arran had retreated in September from his reformist stance, sometimes referred to as his Protestant fit, and was reconciled to the Church and Cardinal Beaton. Fear that his anti-clericalism might lead the Church to revoke his father's divorce from Janet Home and declare Arran illegitimate may have prompted this policy change. Three months later in parliament, he rejected the Treaties of Greenwich. Reacting angrily to this negative decision, Henry sent armed forces into Scotland under the command of Edward Seymour, future duke of Somerset, as part of a strategy known as the Rough Wooing, which spanned two hostile periods, first from late 1543 to mid-1546 and then from late 1547 to the spring of 1550. During the first phase, raiding parties destroyed many buildings and fortifications and burned several towns but failed to capture the young queen. In May 1544, according to a letter co-authored by the future Somerset, Charles Brandon, future duke of Suffolk, and Sadler, when English forces approached within six miles of Stirling, Mary's guardians removed her temporarily to Dunkeld, 44 miles away on the edge of the Highlands.

After Arran began favoring the French alliance, Lennox left for England to champion the young queen's marriage to Edward; thus the Scottish claimants switched their diplomatic stances. In 1544 Lennox transferred his allegiance from France to England and agreed to capture Mary for Henry, who planned to serve as her protector. The king then permitted Lennox to wed Margaret Douglas, the daughter of his sister, Margaret Tudor, and her second husband, the earl of Angus. On 7 December 1545 the countess gave birth to Darnley, who possessed claims to the English and Scottish thrones through his mother and father, respectively. Some writers have questioned whether this was his birth year, but after his death, Mary recalled that he was nineteen on their wedding day in July 1565.

Between 1543 and 1548 Mary resided mostly at Stirling in the care of her nurse, Janet Sinclair, and her guardians, whose number was reduced in 1545 to two lords: Erskine and Livingston. Her spiritual advisers were her almoner, John Erskine, prior of Inchmahome, and

Alexander Scott, canon of the chapel royal of Stirling and parson of Balmaclellan.

After Arran rejected his reformist stance, Henry encouraged his collaborators in Scotland to support anti-papal behavior, hoping to promote a religious understanding between the two realms that would result in the reinstatement of the Treaties of Greenwich. One Scotsman pressing for reform was John Knox, a tutor of Alexander, son of John Cockburn of Ormiston. Knox condemned Cardinal Beaton's crusade against heresy and his decision in March 1546 to burn the charismatic reformer, George Wishart, a Cambridge alumnus and probably an English agent.

In retaliation for his execution, some Fife men, disguised as stone-masons, invaded the castle at St Andrews in May 1546 and assassinated Beaton. Others, including Knox, who were associated with Wishart, joined the murderers, known as the Castilians. With some limited English aid, they controlled the castle until July 1547 when a French fleet forced their surrender. Their conquerors sent some Castilians of high social rank to French prisons but employed others as galley slaves, including Knox and James Balfour.

Some months following the castle's surrender, the second phase of the Rough Wooing commenced. After Edward's accession in January 1547, his uncle, Somerset, the Lord Protector, decided to use force to complete his nephew's marriage to Mary. In September after he defeated the Scots at the battle of Pinkie Cleugh near Musselburgh, Mary of Guise transferred her daughter to the priory of Inchmahome, which lies on an island in the Lake of Menteith. Their short residence led to the growth of many legends, among them that the little queen planted a garden there, but she was much too young for this achievement and was back at Stirling by early October. After William, Lord Grey of Wilton, and Lennox led armies into Scotland in February 1548, Grey to the east and Lennox to the west, the queen mother had her child removed on the 29th to Dumbarton, the most important strategic castle in western Scotland. The English captured several fortifications, built two new forts, and created an area regarded as their pale that centered on Haddington, which lay 18 miles from Edinburgh.

Having requested assistance from Henry II, the successor of Francis I in 1547, Arran and Mary of Guise agreed on 7 July that the queen should wed Francis the dauphin, who was born 19 January 1544. Arran had earlier pledged that in return for a French duchy and a marriage for his namesake son with Frances, the elder daughter of Louis of Bourbon, duke of Montpensier, he would seek parliamentary consent for Mary's union with the dauphin, her removal to France, and French control of certain Scottish fortifications. Clearly interested in this alliance because Mary was also a claimant to the English throne, Henry II promised Arran full authority in Scotland during her minority and support for his accession in the event of her death without children.

These were substantial concessions, as Henry subsequently granted Arran the dukedom of Châtelherault with an annual income of 12,000 livres. Although his son, referred to hereafter as the earl of Arran, moved to France, he failed to win Montpensier's daughter. In March during these negotiations, Mary contracted a case of measles, which because of its rumored severity may have been rubella. Her illness raised concerns about the Scottish succession, since measles had a high mortality rate among children in the early modern period, but by the 23rd the crisis was over.

Meeting in tents erected near the Abbey of Haddington in July, parliament approved Mary's French marriage and residence and the employment of Henry II's forces to expel the English invaders, thereby transforming Scotland into a French protectorate. Although French fleets had provided occasional assistance to the queen mother, the Treaty of Haddington, which agreed to a permanent French military presence in the realm, moved Henry II far beyond a short-term level of commitment. On 19 June even before parliament confirmed the treaty, a French armada reached the Firth of Forth and several days later a joint Franco-Scottish army began besieging Haddington.

Nicholas Durand, sieur de Villegaignon, and Artus de Maillé, sieur de Brézé, took four galleys from the fleet northward around the realm to Dumbarton to transport the queen to France. On 29 July Mary and her train, including four maids named Mary, representing the Fleming, Livingston, Beaton, and Seton families, boarded the galleys. Some accounts have greatly exaggerated the importance of the queen's having four attendants named Mary, but they surely gained selection because of their royal connections and their nearness in age to her and not because of their names. Seton and Beaton were daughters of two of Mary of Guise's French attendants; Fleming's mother, Janet, the widow of Malcolm, third Lord Fleming, and an illegitimate daughter of James IV, was Mary's governess; Livingston's father was one of her guardians. Although Mary was a generic name for Scottish maids of honor, these four girls were all christened Mary and were surely goddaughters of the queen mother. Godparents, especially royal ones, regularly named their godchildren after themselves. In England during Jane Seymour's brief queenship, four noblewomen gave birth to girls christened Jane, almost certainly because the queen was one of their two godmothers. Had Jane's young Edward been female, four Janes might well have attended him.

Besides the Maries, the queen's escort of some 200 individuals included three of her illegitimate half brothers, Lords James, Robert, and John, the commendators of St Andrew's, Holyrood, and Coldingham, respectively. On board also were Erskine and Livingston, her two guardians, nurse Sinclair, governess Fleming, her spiritual advisers, and other attendants. For several days the fleet remained in the harbor, waiting for the adverse winds to change.

3

FRENCH UPBRINGING,
1548–61

When they boarded the galleys, de Brézé promised to keep Mary of Guise informed about how her daughter fared during the voyage. On 3 August 1548 he assured her that the winds tossing them about in the harbor had not made her child sick, and three days later reported that the fleet had sailed but storms had forced its return to port. Despite this and other misadventures, such as a broken rudder, they left Dumbarton on 7 August and disembarked at St Pol de Léon near the port of Roscoff in Brittany on 15 August.[1] He reported on the 18th that Mary had been less ill than everyone else and that Henry had sent his *valet de chambre*, Antoine Cabassoles du Réal, to welcome her to France.[2]

Following a two-day rest at Morlaix's Dominican convent, Mary's party reached Nantes, where she made her entry on the 22nd. Surely following the prompting of her guardians or governess, she explained to her greeters at Nantes that she believed they were honoring her as Henry II's daughter. When informed about the five-year-old queen's statement, the gratified king repeated it several times, affirming he held her as his true daughter.

From Nantes Mary and her escort traveled by barge up the Loire River, rested at Ancenis, were welcomed at Angers on 21 September, and continued on to Tours, where the joyous duchess of Guise greeted her granddaughter. On 1 October she predicted to her son, Charles, archbishop of Rheims, future cardinal of Lorraine, that Mary would become a beauty, for she was pretty, intelligent, and graceful. A brunette, she had white skin, a fine and clear complexion, small deep-set eyes, and a long face.[3] After lingering at Maille, they passed by Amboise and Blois and disembarked at Orléans to complete the journey overland.

On 14 October they reached the nursery, which was located at the château of St Carriéres in St Denis during the refurbishing of the palace at St Germain-en-Laye, its usual headquarters some 12 miles from Paris. Away on a progress, Henry sent instructions to its director, Jean de Humières, sieur de Mouchy, and his wife, Frances de Contay, to prepare for Mary's arrival. As his heir's betrothed, Henry raised her in rank above his daughters and granted her the privileges held by his consort, Catherine de' Medici, to grant pardons and release prisoners.[4]

After meeting Mary, probably on 9 November at St Germain, Henry judged her the prettiest and most graceful princess he had ever seen, an opinion reflecting the views of the whole court, according to de Brézé. Catherine echoed her husband's praise and later remarked that the little queen needed only to smile to turn all French heads.[5] Lord Erskine also confided to Mary of Guise that the royal family greatly honored her child.

De Humières taught the four-year-old Francis how to welcome Mary, and he apparently rose to the occasion admirably. His greeting impressed Henry's long-time mistress, Diane de Poitiers, duchess of Valentinois and widow of Louis de Brézé, count of Maulévrier. She counseled the tutor that if he wanted to please Henry he should continue coaching Francis to perform those small courtesies. De Humières followed her advice so well that Anne de Montmorency, constable of France, could report to Mary of Guise in March 1549 that Francis paid her six-year-old daughter little attentions, proving they were born for each other.

Mary was immediately introduced to the court's protocol. The children assembled daily in the nursery's great hall to pay homage to the dauphin and his betrothed as their social superiors. Imitating their elders' dinnertime etiquette, Mary and Francis dined at the same table while their young attendants sat elsewhere according to their rank. In 1553 her French governess, Frances d'Estamville, madame de Parois, assured her mother that Mary behaved very well toward Francis.

Whenever possible, parents arranged for betrothed children to be brought up together so that they could become acquainted and emotionally attached to each other. Representing the perfect examples of this practice, Francis and Mary impressed observers, as they approached adolescence, with their caring relationship. In January 1555 when she was 12 and Francis was 11, Giovanni Capello, the Venetian ambassador, characterized their intimacy as love after witnessing them caressing each other and whispering together in a corner of the room.[6]

Capello almost certainly was referring to an emotional rather than a physical attachment. Modern studies indicate that the onset of puberty was later in the sixteenth century than in the twenty-first century. Although the church permitted twelve-year-old girls and fourteen-year-old boys to marry, when children did wed at this young age, parents and guardians usually delayed their sexual intimacy until the bride, at least, was about sixteen.

As soon as the Treaty of Haddington was ratified, the children's supervisors began teaching them the significance of their future marriage, which would unify their realms as well as join them together personally. Early modern Europeans customarily placed a romantic gloss on these matches to obscure their economic and political underpinnings. In 1548, for example, Francis, the future second duke of Guise, wrote to his sister, Mary, that for their family's honor their father Claude traveled south toward Italy to greet Anne d'Este, the elder daughter of Hercule II, duke of Ferrara, and praised her to him so that he fell in love with his future bride at a distance. Michel de Montaigne later remarked: "Men do not marry for themselves, whatever they may say. They marry as much or more for their posterity and house. The custom and profit of marriage concerns our race much more than ourselves."[7]

At a time when family honor was a high priority, Mary's and Francis's commitment to these dynastic arrangements could bind them together in a relationship as compelling, perhaps more compelling, than that of a romantic liaison. In 1554 under the guidance of Claude Millet, her classics tutor since 1550, Mary addressed a Latin letter to Francis as part of a classroom assignment in which she explained that her love prompted her to advise him to honor his instructor, as Alexander the Great honored Aristotle.[8]

The nursery was most often situated at St Germain, although when it needed cleaning the children were moved to other châteaux. Deeply interested in their well-being, Henry kept them at St Germain because he favored staying at this palace when he had business in Paris. Its main building contained 55 lodgings with his apartments on the second floor since no one but a member of the royal family could be housed above him. As social rank also dictated the children's room assignments, Mary shared the best bedchamber with Princess Elizabeth, who was born in 1545. At this time, only one other royal child, Claude, who was born in 1547, resided in the nursery, but Catherine gave birth in early 1549 to a prince named Louis for whom Mary of Guise was selected as godmother. By 1556 Catherine was delivered of six more children, four of whom survived to adulthood: the future monarchs Charles IX and Henry III, Hercules-Francis, duke of Anjou and Alençon, and Margaret, queen of Navarre.

Shortly after Mary's arrival, the court began to participate in gala festivities. In December her uncle, Francis, wed Anne d'Este, whose mother, Renée, duchess of Ferrara, was the younger daughter of Louis XII. Some observers claimed that the Guises achieved this important connection because of their kinship with the dauphin's betrothed. Henry wrote Mary of Guise that in plain view of all the ambassadors at the wedding's festivities, he gave Mary and Francis little caresses and insisted that they dance together, delighting everyone, he thought, except Dr Nicholas Wotton, the English ambassador. The next year in June, Catherine was crowned on the 10th; Francis and she made their Paris entries on the 11th and 18th respectively, and Henry on the 16th.

Soon after reaching St Germain, many of Mary's attendants lost their positions to French appointees. Henry, like other monarchs, routinely culled the trains of foreign-born brides to reduce expenditures and to limit the number of potential spies at court. These changes also facilitated the absorption of Mary's household into the French nursery. While the Maries were sent to the Dominican convent at Poissy to be educated, nurse Sinclair was permitted to remain with Mary but lost her authority in the nursery.

A scandal that led to governess Fleming's expulsion from France was probably an episode in Montmorency's political struggle with Valentinois and the Guises, who were related to her through her daughter Louise de Brézé's marriage to the duke's namesake son Claude of Guise, future duke of Aumale. During Valentinois's absence, Henry impregnated Fleming, who boasted at court about her condition, outraging both the queen and the duchess. Blaming Montmorency for encouraging the liaison, Valentinois joined Catherine in persuading Henry to send Fleming home after she gave birth to his namesake son in April 1551.

For her successor Lorraine chose madame de Parois, a former attendant of Anne d'Este, duchess of Guise, his sister-in-law. As Mary approached adolescence, she was involved in several disputes with Parois, who complained, for example, that her mistress slighted her when distributing her wardrobe to her attendants. In 1557 on the recommendation of Lorraine, Catherine, and Valentinois, Mary took the opportunity of Parois's chronic illness to replace her with Maréchalle de la Marche, countess of Brêne. In Brêne's absence, Antoinette de la Marck, mademoiselle de Bouillon, a granddaughter of Valentinois, agreed to bear Mary's train and a niece of Brêne, an old widow, was appointed to sleep in her chamber. Gratified by these arrangements, Mary informed her mother that year of the duchess's many kindnesses. Lorraine had earlier assured his sister that her daughter could not be better behaved if she had a dozen governesses.

Partly because of Henry's relationship with Valentinois, some writers, mainly Protestants ones, have characterized his court as licentious and have assumed that Mary's French upbringing adversely affected her character. Despite some lapses, Henry was devoted to the duchess, who was solicitous about his children's needs and made efforts to be agreeable to his queen. Some contemporaries even claimed that Henry's court was outwardly more respectable than his father's and praised Valentinois for this refinement. Catherine's attitude contributed to this atmosphere; although privately resentful, she emphasized publicly her love for her husband and bore Valentinois's presence with equanimity. Actually, Henry's court was as respectable, if not more so, than some Scottish ones. His three illegitimate offspring, for example, were far fewer than the nine James V sired with his serial mistresses. Sir James Melville, who visited Mary in France, even credited her upbringing there for her virtuous behavior and natural judgment.[9]

MARY OF GUISE'S FRENCH VISIT

After the Treaty of Boulogne ended the Anglo-French war in 1550, Mary of Guise began planning a trip home. Both personal issues and official business prompted her visit; she longed to see her family again, especially her children, and needed to inspect her dower estates. She also hoped to persuade Henry to aid war-torn Scotland and to discuss plans with him for its governance when her seven-year-old daughter reached her majority. While preparing for the journey, she was saddened to learn of her father Claude's April death.

Attended by numerous Scottish subjects, including the earl of Huntly and Gilbert Kennedy, third earl of Cassilis, she reached France in September 1550 and joined the royal family and her children on the 25th at Rouen, Normandy, where the king's entry was scheduled for 1 October. Her delighted daughter, who had been looking forward to greeting her, had just recovered from a ten-day bout of the flux, a form of dysentery. Perhaps it was her second illness in France, since rumors claimed she contracted measles in March 1549.

Besides Fleming's disgrace, several other significant events occurred during Mary of Guise's sojourn, which began on a sad note. Her godson Louis died of smallpox in October 1550. At Blois the next February, Henry seems to have decided to appoint her as her daughter's regent when she reached her majority. The queen dowager apparently expressed a desire to return to France permanently, but after the Scottish noblemen in her train informed Henry that they preferred her to any other French regent he might select, she agreed to remain in Scotland to protect her child's interests.

In April 1551 she was horrified to learn of Robert Stewart's plot to kill Mary. An ally of Cardinal Beaton's murderers, he had, after serving as a galley rower, become an archer in the French Scottish Guard. While on leave in England, he was imprisoned for trying to generate support for a plan to poison Mary with the aid of friends in the nursery kitchen. After successfully demanding his extradition, Henry authorized his execution at Angers in June.

That same month on a happier note, William Parr, marquess of Northampton, headed an embassy that reached Châteaubriand with a proposal for Mary to wed King Edward, but anticipating failure, his instructions provided that if she were unavailable, Elizabeth of Valois could be substituted for her. An agreement was reached concerning the French princess, but Edward's death in 1553 ended that possibility. Northampton visited Catherine's chamber and witnessed the two Scottish queens dancing together.

After enjoying her children's company for almost a year, the queen dowager left them at Fontainebleau to condole with her widowed mother at Joinville. Then in early September 1551 she began her return trip to Scotland, traveling to Amiens with her son who became ill and died suddenly on the 22nd, about a month before his 16th birthday. On 18 October, having lost her fourth son as well as her father and her godson, the mourning queen departed for Scotland by way of England, leaving her daughter, whom she had seen for the last time, to continue her education in France.

FRENCH EDUCATION

From October 1548 when Mary reached the royal nursery, besides learning court etiquette, she began to acquire language and dance skills. In December after she had studied French only two months with her tutor, Mahault des Essarts, demoiselle de Curel, diplomats were spreading rumors that Mary was gifted and able to speak the language very well. They were, of course, greatly exaggerating her talents, but she may have acquired a child's French vocabulary more quickly than had been anticipated. Probably to prepare her and his children for the festivities at Francis of Guise's wedding, Henry appointed Paul de Rege as their dance instructor. Among other steps, Mary learned the galliard, which reportedly she performed as well as anyone.

Acting as her mother-substitute, Catherine monitored both Mary's academic and domestic training, initially correcting her Latin exercises and also teaching her how to embroider. In Latin letters of 1554, which, like the one to the dauphin, formed part of a classroom assignment, Mary referred to Catherine several times: they attended vespers together and the French queen advised her to follow her tutors' directions because it was only by learning to obey that she could learn to command. During that same year, under Catherine's direction, Mary, acting as Sybil, the oracle at Delphi, joined with other Sybils, among them Mary Fleming and Mary Livingston, in reciting quatrain verses, composed by Mellin de St Gellais, Henry's favorite poet, to welcome the king back to St Germain.[10]

Besides these pastimes, Mary played chess, wrote poetry, composed emblems, painted, and enjoyed sports, such as tennis, horseback riding on two favorite horses, Bravane and Madame la Réale, and hunting with dogs and falcons. In 1554 she noted in another Latin letter that Henry permitted her to hunt deer in the park with his illegitimate daughter, Diane, duchess of Castro.

In addition, Mary had lessons in geography, history, music, and languages. She sang with a pleasant voice and played the lute, virginals, and other instruments. Besides gaining fluency in French and Italian and studying Latin, she acquired a rudimentary knowledge of Spanish and possibly a smattering of Greek and Hebrew. Books in these languages appear on a 1573 inventory of her library.

When Mary was eleven, her tutor required her to render some French letters into Latin, a few of which were cited above. In a neat Italic script, she wrote 64 translations in a small red leather volume now at the Bibliothèque Nationale in Paris. She left blank the pages next to the Latin epistles, which she entered in the book on various days from July 1554 to January 1555. Later a scribe copied on the blank pages the French versions, which it has been assumed her tutor composed because of their references to Plutarch, Aesop's Fables, the Scriptures, and Erasmus's colloquies. Since they were mostly addressed to her acquaintances, especially Elizabeth, and contained personal data, it is more likely that Mary created them. After returning home, she drafted her speeches in French before rendering them into Scots, a procedure she learned in the schoolroom. That the epistles referred to classical literature is not surprising since Jacques Amyot, the translator of Plutarch, a copy of which Mary owned, and Pierre Danès, Greek professor at the Collège de France, resided at court.

Her letters represent the conventional Renaissance education of children, who were instructed in the classical pagan and Christian writings on the Erasmian model. Humanists believed that by relating ancient experiences to the issues of their day, they could educate rulers to cure social ills. Mary's epistles confirm she was taught that princes should be better read than their subjects to demonstrate that learning was the root of virtue. They should not, she warned, read for entertainment but for knowledge and self-improvement. In a letter to

Lorraine, she related a story that condemned flatterers. Its author pointed out that royal children often learned nothing well except horsemanship because their high rank led their tutors to overrate their achievements. In contrast, the horses, unaware of their riders' status, tossed off those with inadequate skills. Teachers favored the letter-writing genre to keep their pupil's hands busy, since idleness was considered the *mere de tous vices* (mother of all vices). Among her epistles is one to John Calvin in which she argued for the existence of purgatory, but a copy of it was probably not forwarded to him, and perhaps none of her addressees actually read her compositions.

As they were schoolroom exercises, her translations do not display a profound knowledge of Latin, but they do indicate a solid grounding in the language. In 1562 in Scotland although she understood the Latin oration of Nicholas de Gouda, a Jesuit, she indicated a preference for responding in French or Scots. She must have been a better classicist than the other royal children, as apparently only she had the opportunity to deliver a Latin oration before Henry and Catherine at the Louvre in early 1555. For her speech responding to detractors who denied women should be taught Latin, she drew upon her letters, 15 of which extolled learned women. The Ramist rhetorician, Antoine Fouquelin, claimed in the *Rhètorique Française*, which he dedicated to Mary in 1557, that her oration elicited praise for its eloquence. On returning home in 1561 she must have carried a copy of it with her. In her 1573 inventory was listed "Ane Oratioun to the King of Franche of the Quenis Awin Hand Write."[11]

Although several individuals supervised Mary's upbringing, the person ultimately most responsible for it was the cardinal of Lorraine. According to governess Parois in 1554, he loved and honored Mary like a daughter. Later, Parois revealed to her mother his assiduous care for his niece's well-being. One important lesson he imparted was the value of family solidarity in achieving public and private goals. Lorraine and his brother, the duke of Guise, possessed somewhat different personalities. The cardinal, a skilled diplomat, was quite comfortable at court, while the duke, the realm's premier general, was at ease on the battlefield. Despite these differences, they successfully cooperated together to advance Guise interests and seemed never to have disagreed about how to accomplish their objectives, but if they did, they kept their quarrels private. Besides maintaining their family's honor and prestige, they also sought to enlarge and preserve their fortune and estates for transmission to the next generation. One of their greatest achievements was their young relatives' excellent marriages. In 1552 at the birth of Guise's daughter Catherine, future duchess of Montpensier, Lorraine observed that although he would have preferred a boy, he had already been considering several splendid matches for her.[12]

Romanticists have characterized Mary's French upbringing as carefree and happy, but while she may have been happy, her childhood was not carefree. She was taught several survival tactics for residing at royal courts, which were criticized for housing gossips and spies who sought data about others to advance their self-interests. Lorraine especially warned her of the dangers. In February 1553 he explained to her mother in a note written in his hand that because of the rumormongers, he often reminded his ten-year-old niece to speak with a guarded tongue. The ubiquitous prying forced the aristocracy to adopt various strategies to keep their personal lives secret in order to prevent the spread of information that might reflect adversely upon their reputations and honor. In short, courts were highly artificial communities in which individuals learned to suppress their personal feelings and to follow prescribed etiquette rather than to act spontaneously or naturally.

Mary's letter to her mother in 1552, dated a year earlier than Lorraine's, proves that she was learning about Scottish governance and the need for maintaining secrecy about her business affairs. She confessed that despite her mother's warning to keep the documents forwarded to her private, she had asked the duke of Guise to read them. Otherwise she would not have understood them. The reason she failed to send the letter in cipher, she also explained, was because her secretary assured her it was an unnecessary precaution. As an adult, she routinely used ciphers or symbols that stood for the letters of the alphabet to communicate sensitive material. The ciphers were placed on a wheel which could be shifted to rearrange the 26 letters that they represented. She also created codes to represent the names of individuals. Finally, in this letter to her mother, she revealed that she was denying strangers access to her household officers, remembering perhaps the foiled poisoning plot of 1551.

Lorraine regularly kept his sister informed about her progress. In February 1553 at Amboise, he was gratified to see his beautiful, virtuous, and accomplished ten-year-old niece attract the attention of Henry, who occasionally spent up to an hour chatting with her. She entertained him, Lorraine boasted, with discussions on sensible topics, as though she were 25 years old. Others extolled her maturity, including Anne, duchess of Guise, who explained that Mary could no longer be treated as a child because her conversation was not that of a child.

As Mary matured, she became increasingly aware of the material requirements of her rank. In 1554 after learning that she was to witness the marriage of her cousin, Nicholas of Lorraine, count of Vaudémont, to Jean, daughter of Philip of Savoy, duke of Nemours, Mary asked for a new gown of cloth-of-gold and cloth-of-silver like those Elizabeth and Claude recently wore to a wedding. This plea demonstrated her realization that she should dress in accordance with her royal position. It was inappropriate for females of lesser status, even princesses, to possess richer or more stylish clothes than she. At the time of her request, she did not lack gowns, for in 1551, alone, she acquired 16 new ones.

HEALTH ISSUES

Lorraine also monitored her physical well-being. In April 1554 Mary visited his palace at Meudon near Paris when his nephew, Charles, Guise's second son, the future duke of Mayenne, was christened with Valentinois acting as godmother and the duke of Ferrara and the cardinal, who named the child after himself, serving as godfathers. Afterwards, Lorraine assured his sister that Mary was healthy and expressed surprise that she had heard her daughter was sickly. Because her daughter possessed a strong constitution, he continued, the doctors had predicted a long life for her. Conceding that she sometimes suffered a little faintness or indigestion after overeating, Lorraine planned to supervise her diet more carefully. This eating disorder, first mentioned when she was 11 years old, was probably an early symptom of later, more serious health problems, but it did not inhibit her physical development since she became a large woman like her mother and grew to be about six-feet tall.

Perhaps the worried queen mother was reacting to a September 1553 letter from Claude, seigneur d'Urfé, the successor of de Humières, revealing Mary's recent recovery from an illness. Another message from Parois in 1553, lacking a more specific date, could have cited the same sickness, which lasted one day only, although it may have described a separate attack. Except for these reports and two complaints about toothaches, all other references to her during the years 1551 through 1555 rated her healthy. In 1554, for example, Lorraine revealed that Catherine was at Rheims with Mary, who was well and who was visiting Renée of Guise, their sister, at the convent of St Pierre-les-Dames.

From 1556 when Mary was thirteen, reports of her sickness became more frequent and serious. On 8 August at Fontainebleau during a hot summer, she contracted a painful fever for which her physicians ordered the usual blood-letting, a treatment that surely did more to weaken her condition than to improve it. Lorraine, who was with the king at Anet, a château belonging to Valentinois, assured his sister that Catherine had remained constantly with Mary during her attack. Since women of all ranks were expected to oversee the medical needs of their close relatives, Lorraine, who hurried to Mary's bedside, was gratified but not surprised at Catherine's solicitude. She happened to be at the nursery because she was recovering from her difficult delivery on 24 June of twin girls: one was still-born and the other died on 17 August. Lorraine also reported that after Mary's first feverish bout ended, she had three more attacks and that the doctors predicted at least seven in all. To escape the heat he removed her to Meudon for the curative effects of its air. Recalling her earlier eating disorder, he also noted that she had indigestion in August after consuming too much melon. The fevers endured intermittently into the autumn, but by October she was convalescing at the Hôtel of Guise in Paris and receiving visits from Henry and Catherine. In November for two or three weeks, she suffered from an ague, probably a form of malaria.

Eight months later in July 1557 when she was fourteen, Lorraine reported to Guise that Mary had recovered from a recent attack of smallpox. In Scotland in 1562 after learning that Elizabeth had contracted the disease, Mary related to her that the late Jean Fernel, the king's court physician, had protected her face from the usual scarring with some lotion but had not revealed its recipe to her.

During the next few years, Mary's illnesses elicited further comments. From March through June 1559 diplomats observed that she looked ill, pale, and green. In May she appeared short breathed and swooned two or three times and in June was allowed to drink some wine from the church altar after almost fainting. Later that month she swooned again. Her ill health returned in August and September when she became sick after eating, swooned, and was revived with spirits. In November she appeared pale and ill again. The next month, after improving enough to go horseback riding near Blois, she suffered minor injuries when a tree limb knocked her off her horse. Then in January 1560 she developed a fever and had attacks that were called fits, perhaps a recurrence of the swooning.

SEPARATE HOUSEHOLD AND REGAL MAJORITY

By 1556 when these illnesses commenced, Mary resided in a separate household. Lorraine began recommending this arrangement in February 1553 when he learned that Henry was preparing a separate establishment for Francis but that Catherine intended to retain her daughters with her until they married. Since Henry also planned for Francis and Mary to leave the nursery after Lent and reside at court, Catherine's decision meant that Mary must share her quarters. Opposing this plan, Lorraine advised his sister to fund her daughter's independent establishment. Having compiled a list of candidates, he wished not only to appoint attendants loyal to him but also to use the existence of her own apartments to pressure his sister into seeking recognition of Mary's regal majority. In setting up the household, he warned her mother to include nothing mean or superfluous, as Mary had such high spirits she visibly disapproved all unworthy treatment.

In late December 1553 at the end of her daughter's 11th year, Mary of Guise funded her separate household. On New Year's Day Mary celebrated the occasion by entertaining Lorraine at supper in her quarters. Possessing her own rooms, including a presence chamber, also meant that she could hold audiences, as in February 1555, when she received some Scotsmen whom she welcomed as her countrymen. Her accounts for the year 1556–57, signed by her and Lorraine, indicate 58,000 livres were allotted for her maintenance, 25,000 from

Scotland's revenue and the remainder from her mother's assets. On the list of her more than 100 servants can be found the names of the four Maries.[13]

During a long discussion in August 1553 with Henry Cleuten, seigneur d'Oysel, Henry II's lieutenant general of Scotland and the queen dowager's close advisor, Lorraine argued that his niece should assume her regal authority at the end of her 11th rather than 12th year, as was usual in her realm. He believed that her governor Châtelherault could not be trusted and bore her great ill-will. In December 1553 the *Parlement* of Paris decreed Mary was of perfect age. The following April the Scottish estates confirmed her majority and, responding to her request, appointed her mother as regent amidst protests that this action treated Châtelherault unfairly. Mary later explained that the nine months she spent in her mother's womb were counted to make her 12 years old that spring. As a further sign of her adulthood, on Easter Day 1554 at Meudon in the presence of her grandmother and Lorraine, she received her first communion, utilizing personal ceremonial vessels, perhaps a precaution against poisoning.

MARRIAGE ARRANGEMENTS

When Henry arranged his heir's marriage with Mary in 1548, her uncles' enemies, led by Montmorency, opposed the match and continued to agitate against it. In October 1557 during France's war with Spain and England, Montmorency lost some of his political clout when the Spanish defeated his army at St Quentin and captured him and his nephew, Gaspard de Châtillon, seigneur de Coligny, admiral of France. Fearing a Paris invasion, Henry named Guise lieutenant general and recalled him from the Italian front. That winter Guise besieged Calais, an English possession for 220 years, and won acclaim as a great hero by conquering it in early January.

Meanwhile, Henry asked the Scottish parliament to send representatives to the French court to negotiate a marriage contract between Francis and her. In March 1558 nine Scottish commissioners reached Fontainebleau and obtained authorization to proceed with the arrangements from Mary and her grandmother, the dowager duchess of Guise acting on behalf of her daughter, the Scottish queen regent. One of the commissioners was Mary's half brother, Lord James, who had returned home after accompanying her to France and had recently converted to Protestantism. Probably at the commissioners' behest, Mary promised on 15 April to maintain Scottish laws and liberties. On the 19th Francis joined her as she reiterated this pledge and granted the additional concession that if she died without issue the Scottish heir presumptive would succeed. On that same day the commissioners signed the contract, providing for Mary's and Francis's eldest son to become king of France and Scotland, but if they had only daughters, for their eldest daughter to become queen of Scotland but not of France, where the female succession was forbidden. The contract also offered Francis the crown matrimonial and title of king of Scotland. If he died, she would receive a dower of 60,000 livres and the choice of living in France or Scotland but would have to obtain the consent of the French and Scottish governments before remarrying. On 30 April, six days after their wedding, Francis and Mary repeated their promises of the 19th, and Francis made a similar declaration in June.

On 4 April, 11 days before Mary and Francis began making these official pledges, she endorsed three secret documents stipulating that if she died childless, Scotland would descend to Henry II and his heirs and pledging to him one million crowns from Scotland's revenues to pay for its defense against the English and for her education. Finally, Mary voided all the future demands of the estates that were prejudicial to these concessions.

As Henry had been acting as Scotland's ruler not its protector since 1548 and had insisted on the appointment of a French regent in 1554, surely no major European leader would have been surprised to learn of the existence of these documents. Indeed, in November 1548 Jean de St Mauris, the imperial ambassador in France, referred to Henry as the king of Scotland. His wish to draw upon that realm's funds was surely a response to the ongoing expense of his occupation forces there, since by 1550 the costs had already amounted to some two million livres.

Even so Mary behaved with duplicity in approving secret documents that negated the later official ones. Some scholars have contended that at the age of 15 she was too young to understand the meaning of her behavior, but others have more correctly maintained that she was following the advice of Henry and the relatives she trusted. Like most other monarchs, she viewed her realm as a private estate, which she could dispose of as she deemed necessary. Later in a 1577 draft will and in a 1586 secret communication with Mendoza, the Spanish ambassador in France, she specified that if her son James VI refused to convert to Catholicism, she would cede her English succession rights to Philip of Spain.

When arranging marriages with queens regnant, early modern rulers sought to create prenuptial documents justifying their retention of their bride's realms if they died childless. In 1554 Philip signed a secret document, absolving himself from observing some restrictions in his marriage contract with Mary Tudor, which he later publicly approved. The clauses to which he objected denied him a claim to her throne if she died without issue and rejected English support for Spain's war against France. Even in initial courtship discussions, the succession issue could be raised. In 1559, Emperor Ferdinand I asked Elizabeth I of England to promise in the proposed marriage treaty with his son, Archduke Charles of Styria, that he would inherit England if she died childless.

Furthermore, Mary Stewart and her relatives viewed as untrustworthy the duke of Châtelherault, whom her secret documents, if implemented, would have deprived of his right to succeed her. In 1548 Henry attempted to win his loyalty by offering to match his son, Arran, with Montpensier's daughter. Although Arran removed to France anticipating this union, Montpensier declined to approve this marriage for his child, as did the parents of three other potential brides the king proposed. Two of those ladies wed Mary's relatives: Louise de Rieux, daughter of the count of Montford, to her uncle, Elboeuf, and Jean of Nemours, to her cousin, Vaudémont.

After Valentinois's granddaughter, Bouillon, joined Mary's household in 1557, she obtained the king's consent for Arran to wed her. The duchess decided, however, to seal hers and Montmorency's political reconciliation with a family alliance, matching Bouillon with his son, Henry, seigneur de Damville. In failing to find Arran a noble wife, Henry deeply offended the Hamiltons, already alienated by the duke's loss of the regency. Besides assuming that they had the right to dispose of their realms, monarchs also occasionally acted as though they need not consult their inhabitants' opinions about a change of rulers. Scottish kings had earlier displayed this behavior.

When James III married Margaret of Denmark in 1469, her father Christian I pledged his Shetland and Orkney estates for her dowry. Following Christian's defaulting on her dowry, James annexed the territories without seeking their residents' permission. The expressed wishes of local officials could also be ignored. In 1538 disregarding Anthony, duke of Lorraine's claim to succeed the childless Charles of Egmond as duke of Guelders, William of Cleves accepted its estates' invitation to govern the duchy. After expelling Cleves from that principality, Emperor Charles seized it for himself, ultimately transferring it to his son Philip.

It is noteworthy that Mary's secret documents left Scottish laws and traditions intact. Structurally, in fact, many early modern realms were composite monarchies, ruling dependent territories that held positions similar to that of the French protectorate Mary had validated for Scotland. Many principalities, such as those the Habsburgs governed, continued to enjoy separate identities and local traditions. This pattern, which went out of fashion in the 1620s, made the transfer of lands from one ruler to another somewhat more palatable to their inhabitants.

The French kings' ambitious Italian and Scottish campaigns indicate they hoped to create composite monarchies similar to those of the Habsburg rulers in Spain and the Empire. Despite charges that France had absorbed contiguous duchies, like Brittany, their inhabitants continued to speak regional dialects, possess their institutions, and enjoy their traditions. It was even more likely that under French rule a distant land like Scotland would continue to enjoy its local customs and laws. Even so, many Scots chaffed at the prospect of becoming permanently another Brittany under French rule.

To defend their independence, Catholic Scots, at least, could evoke the Declaration of Arbroath, their letter of 1320 to Pope John XXII, requesting assistance in maintaining their freedom from England. Some two hundred years later, however, their divisive politics hindered their goal of independence. The competition between the Châtelherault-Hamiltons and the Lennox-Stewarts meant that the family that scored a success with England, as Lennox had in 1544, would prompt the other one to turn to France. The earl of Cassilis's boast that he was neither French nor English was understandable but somewhat unrealistic given the existence of these regal disputes.

MARRIAGE FESTIVITIES

On 19 April 1558 the day their marriage contract was signed, Mary and Francis were formally betrothed at the Louvre. Henry escorted her, and Anthony Bourbon, king of Navarre, accompanied Francis into the great hall where Lorraine conducted the official betrothal ceremony in which Francis and Mary, while holding hands, pledged their troth. They afterwards attended a banquet and then a ball, which Mary and Henry opened with the first dance. On the 23rd, the eve of the wedding, the royal family moved into the bishop's palace near the Cathedral of Nôtre Dame, the place appointed for the ceremony. It was to be the first marriage of a dauphin in the city for over 200 years.

On the pavement before Nôtre Dame was erected an observation platform to hold prominent officials, including the Scottish commissioners. In addition, a 12-feet-high gallery in the shape of an arch and decorated with green boughs connected the door of the bishop's palace to the cathedral door before which stood a pavilion, adorned with fleurs-de-lis. At 11:00, to trumpet fanfare, Eustache du Bellay, bishop of Paris, accompanied by his cross-bearer and choir-boys carrying lighted tapers, opened the cathedral door. From the palace emerged Guise, the grand master for the occasion, and the Swiss Guard in charge of security. Mounting the platform Guise instructed the aristocracy not to crowd too closely and thereby obstruct the view of the other onlookers.

The Swiss Guard musicians in their regimental red and gold then moved through the gallery toward the bishop. Behind them marched more musicians, 100 gentlemen of the royal household, the princes of the blood, 18 bishops and abbots, seven cardinals, including the papal legate, Antonio of Trivulzio, who granted a dispensation to the bride and groom because they were related in the fourth degree, their French grandfathers having been second cousins. Next came the dauphin, accompanied by Navarre and by Princes Charles and Henry. After more trumpet fanfare at the palace door appeared Mary, escorted by the king and her cousin Charles III, duke of Lorraine. She was clothed in a robe of white satin with a mantle of blue velvet that complimented her hazel eyes, her fair complexion, and her reddish-brown hair, which seems to have lightened as she grew older. It hung loose down her back, the usual bridal hairstyle. On her head sat a golden crown, adorned with rubies, diamonds, sapphires, emeralds, and pearls of great value; around her neck hung diamonds and rich gemstones. Two maids of honor carried her long, blue velvet train, embroidered with white silk and pearls. Behind them walked Catherine, accompanied by Louis Bourbon, prince of Condé, a prominent Huguenot and brother of Navarre, her daughters, Elizabeth and Claude, the king's sister Margaret, and the duchesses of Valentinois and Guise, among other dignitaries.

At the pavilion Charles Bourbon, the cardinal archbishop of Rouen, performed the ceremony, and following the couple's exchange of vows, Henry removed a ring from his hand, which Bourbon blessed and presented to Francis for placement on Mary's finger. After the bishop's oration, they entered the cathedral in the order they marched through the gallery. As they processed, the heralds cried largesse three times and tossed numerous gold and silver coins into the crowd. The rush of people scrambling for them caused great confusion: some fainted; some lost pieces of clothing; others were so frightened they begged the heralds to cease the distribution.

While the wedded pair sat on a throne beneath a canopy of cloth-of-gold, the bishop celebrated the nuptial mass at the high altar. Afterwards, the heralds again tossed coins, this time inside the cathedral. Finally, the bishop blessed the bride and groom as they stood under a silver cloth suspended over their heads. Departing in the same order as before, the wedding party attended a banquet and enjoyed various festivities at the bishop's palace. Later that afternoon, they journeyed to the Palais of Justice, the official residence of the *Parlement* of Paris, for a banquet, dancing, and masques. The evening's highlight was a pageant of ships, the duke of Lorraine's gift to the bridal couple. An artificial wind supposedly blew six miniature ships, adorned in cloth-of-gold and crimson velvet and equipped with silver sails and masts, across an undulating blue cloth covering the floor. On each ship sat a masked nobleman dressed in cloth-of-gold, who invited a lady to sit beside him. The duke of Lorraine selected Claude, his future bride; Henry chose Mary; the dauphin took Catherine; Jacques of Savoy, duke of Nemours, claimed Margaret; Navarre summoned his wife; Condé opted for the duchess of Guise and away they sailed.[14]

In the early hours of the morning at the Hôtel of Guise, the royal family bedded down the bride and groom, as custom dictated. Scholars have assumed that the chronically ill and physically immature 14-year-old dauphin was incapable of consummating the marriage and had probably not done so at his death in December 1560 when he was still 16. Even so, as Mary and her relatives deemed divine intervention necessary for conception, they could petition God to bless this union and make it fruitful. During their short marriage, two interesting but contradictory rumors, both of which lack confirmation, circulated concerning their marital relationship: some diplomats claimed she would never be able to bear children while others surmised that she had a miscarriage. The day after the bedding-down ceremony, the wedding party dined at the Palais of Justice before moving to the Louvre for several days of festivities.

Poets composed verses in at least three languages to honor the marriage: French, Neo-Latin, and Scots. Two prominent ones were by Sir Richard Maitland of Lethington and George Buchanan. Lethington's verse welcomed Francis as Scotland's ruler:

> O michtie Prince, and Spous to our Mistreiss!
> Ressaive this realme in loive and heartliness;
>   Set Furth our lawis, mantein our libertie;
> Do equall justice bayth to mair and less;
> Reward vertew; and punishch wickedness;
>   Mak us to leive in gude tranquillitie.[15]

Buchanan, an eminent Latinist who held a private teaching position in France, composed a Neo-Latin *Epithalamium* in which he called Mary the "most accomplished lady of her kind," confirmed she was "Maturely grave ev'n in her tender years" and promised Francis:

> If matchless Beauty your nice fancy move,
> Behold an Object worthy of your Love![16]

Afterwards, Mary and Francis traveled to Villiers-Cotterets, some 50 miles northeast of Paris, for several days of rest. In May they returned to the court at Compiègne, and in September Francis joined his father at Amiens to oversee military operations, although a truce with the Spanish and English was signed shortly thereafter.

DEATH OF MARY TUDOR, 1558

During the next two years, four royal deaths impacted on Franco-Scottish relations. First, on 17 November 1558 Mary Tudor died, leaving her throne to Elizabeth, whom Catholics deemed illegitimate and, therefore, ineligible to succeed. Henry II and the Guises claimed that as Mary Stewart was the granddaughter of Margaret Tudor, she had the best hereditary claim to the English throne and was the rightful monarch. In January 1559 at the marriage celebrations of Henry II's daughter, Claude, to the duke of Lorraine, the king had Mary proclaimed queen of Scotland, England, and Ireland.

That June Henry publicized Mary's rights at festivities honoring the two marriages arranged by the Treaty of Cateau-Cambrésis, which ended France's war with Spain and England. Having accepted Elizabeth as queen in the treaty, Henry decided to counter that diplomatic concession by again displaying his daughter-in-law's rights to the English crown publicly. On the 21st at the Louvre, his daughter, Elizabeth, was betrothed to the widowed Philip II, a bridegroom of more than twice her age. Alvarez de Toledo, duke of Alva, acted as his proxy for the betrothal and for the wedding the next day at Nôtre Dame in which Mary and Claude carried the bride's train. On the 27th Henry's sister Margaret was betrothed to Emmanuel-Philibert X, duke of Savoy. At the subsequent three-day tournament, the king dauphin and the queen dauphiness sat under a canopy on which the English arms were incorporated with those of Scotland and France. When the English ambassador, Sir Nicholas Throckmorton, protested this employment of his realm's arms, French officials responded that his queen bore the French arms, although the Salic law barred her from the succession. Despite losing Calais, the last vestige of their French empire, English monarchs continued to claim the French kingship until the Treaty of Amiens in 1802.

ACCESSION OF FRANCIS II, JULY 1559

The wedding festivities on 30 June ended with a joust between Henry and Gabriel de Lorges, count of Montgomery and captain of the Scottish Guard. Montgomery's lance accidentally splintered into the king's throat and eye, critically wounding him. Royal aides carried Henry to the nearby Hôtel de Tournelles, where upon recovering consciousness, he ordered the completion of his sister's marriage. Instead of the planned Nôtre Dame ceremony, Margaret married Savoy privately at the nearby chapel of St Paul on 9 July. Henry died the next day and was buried on 13 August at St Denis, the cardinal of Lorraine having conducted the funeral service.

After hearing of the king's death, Lennox sent his 13-year-old son, Darnley, who traveled incognito with his tutor, John Elder, to condole with Mary and to request her assistance in recovering the family's Scottish estates that were confiscated in 1544 when the earl became an English subject. Darnley probably stayed with his paternal uncle, John Stuart, fifth seigneur d'Aubigny, the successor of Montgomery as captain of the Scottish Guard. At Chambord Darnley caught up with Mary, who rejected his father's petition but invited him to Francis's coronation and gave him a gift of money.[17]

In September Mary journeyed with her 15-year-old husband to Rheims, making their separate entries on the 15th and attending vespers at the cathedral on the 17th. The next day, the cardinal of Lorraine presided at Francis's coronation, which Mary witnessed as an independent sovereign, sitting in the gallery with Elizabeth, the Spanish queen.

After Francis's accession, the Guises assumed control of his government, and Montmorency and Valentinois departed from court, but only after the duchess had surrendered the crown jewels to Mary. Although Navarre headed the Bourbon family that would succeed if the Valois dynasty failed in the male line, he was not offered a governmental position. In fact, when he reached court after Henry's burial, Navarre withdrew from the political competition by agreeing to escort Elizabeth to Spain. Mary, Francis, and Catherine accompanied Navarre and Elizabeth to Châtelherault, near Poitou, and bade farewell to them in late November. Here and elsewhere Mary displayed the arms of England with those of France and Scotland. The royal party then returned to Blois, their headquarters for the winter season.

By this time the political and religious measures of Francis's government had generated controversy. His councilors not only diligently enforced his father's repressive policies against the Huguenots but also insisted on drastic financial entrenchment to counter the crisis created by his military expenditures that left the crown 41 million livres in debt. Although these were Henry's policies, protestors associated them narrowly with the Guises, especially the cardinal of Lorraine, widely denounced as a tiger and a viper.

The animosity culminated in a conspiracy called the Conjuration of Amboise, led by a Huguenot adventurer, Jean du Barry, seigneur de la Renaudie, who planned to assault the royal family at Blois, murder Lorraine, and release Francis from his control. Mary's uncles, however, viewed it as a plot to abduct Francis, force Protestantism upon him, and murder his family. In February 1560 when rumors of the conspiracy reached Guise, he transferred the court to Amboise, the most defensible royal château, and organized search parties that arrested armed raiders as early as 11 March. Some, including la Renaudie who died on the 19th, were killed in the skirmishes; some drowned in the Loire while others were hanged from the château's balconies. As some rebels had connections to the Bourbons, Lorraine and Guise blamed Navarre's brother Condé for the conspiracy.

DEATH OF MARY OF GUISE AND THE SCOTTISH REFORMATION

Because Mary was still recovering from this frightening and bloody experience, Lorraine delayed informing her until 28 June of her mother's death on the 11th of that month. The news overwhelmed her with sadness, manifested by her bitter tears and her retirement to her bedchamber to mourn in seclusion. Her family and friends feared that her profound grief would cause her to become seriously ill.

While the French government was facing religious and political challenges, so was the queen regent of Scotland. In late 1557 five Scotsmen, known as the Lords of the Congregation, had first signed a band promoting reform:

> We do promise . . . that we shall . . . maintain, set forward,
> and establish the MOST BLESSED WORD OF GOD, and
> His Congregation: And shall labor . . . to have faithful
> ministers purely and truly to minister Christ's
> evangel and sacraments to his people.[18]

In the next two years by downplaying doctrinal matters and demanding the expulsion of French troops, the Congregation attracted increasing numbers of supporters.

In France in May 1559, two years after the endorsement of the first band, Arran, himself a Protestant convert, learned that Montpensier's daughter, the bride promised him in 1548, planned to wed Valentinois's grandson, Henry Robert de la Mark, duke of Bouillon, at the Louvre on 11 June. To prevent the alienated Arran from returning home and complicating the queen regent's political problems, Henry II had ordered his arrest. Eluding governmental officials, Arran fled France with the aid of English agents and in August reached England, met with Elizabeth, and then returned home. The next month supported by English allies in Scotland who accused Mary and her relatives of having mistreated him, Arran persuaded his father Châtelherault to join the Congregation. Once again, the duke changed his religious stance, this time in response to concerns that Mary's French marriage had negated his succession rights. As the heir presumptive, his public support enhanced the Congregation's political viability, and in October the Lords, with Châtelherault and Arran holding leadership roles, issued a proclamation, deposing the queen regent and claiming the governance of Scotland.

Rejecting their authority and attempting to cause the English to suspect Châtelherault's loyalty, Mary of Guise had a letter from the duke to Francis II forged in which he promised to serve as the French king's faithful and loyal servant. She instructed Michel de Seurre, the French ambassador in England, to present it to Cecil. When the duke of Norfolk learned about it, he sent a message on 15 March about its contents to the putative author, Châtelherault. Challenging Seurre to a duel, the outraged duke offered personally to fight with anyone equal to him in status or to appoint one of inferior quality to fight a like individual. Later that month English agents intercepted the queen regent's message to Lorraine and Guise, condemning the ambassador for not more effectively utilizing the forgery. She noted that the letter in question was written on one of two blank papers she had obtained with the duke's seal.

Concerned that the French army might invade England from its Scottish headquarters, Elizabeth ratified the Treaty of Berwick, negotiated with the Congregation in February 1560, which provided for joint military action for mutual defense in the British Isles, including Ireland. Although the English army had small success against the French at Leith, the expected French navy failed to arrive, first because storms destroyed an armada commanded by Elboeuf, whom the king appointed as lieutenant general and successor of his ailing sister, the queen regent, and second, because domestic discord, including the Conjuration of Amboise in March 1560, prevented him from sailing with another fleet that was outfitted for departure that spring. Elboeuf's disappointed niece had already assured Throckmorton that she would be a better neighbor to his queen than the Scottish rebels.

After the queen regent's death, Châtelherault and Lord James, along with William Maitland of Lethington, her secretary, as representatives of the Provisional Government, became the effective rulers of Scotland. In July, the month after her demise, French and English commissioners negotiated the Treaty of Edinburgh, requiring Mary to cease bearing English arms, providing for the withdrawal from Scotland of all foreign troops, authorizing the calling of a Scottish parliament, and establishing procedures for appointing a government that would basically leave the Congregation in control of the realm. When in November the treaty was finally presented to Mary and Francis for their approval, they refused to ratify it, mainly from concerns that its language might be interpreted to deny her English succession rights. In the meantime, all troops had departed Scotland, except for 120 Frenchmen.[19]

In August without Francis's and Mary's authorization, the Provisional Government had summoned a parliament, known as the Reformation Parliament because of its religious enactments. It abolished the mass and papal authority and established a reformed Confession of Faith, although it left untouched the Catholic clergy's jurisdiction within their benefices. The estates then proposed to Elizabeth that she wed Arran to consolidate the Anglo-Scottish alliance and to set up the possibility of a British monarchy if Mary died without heirs.

LAST MONTHS OF FRANCIS'S REIGN

While these setbacks were occurring in Scotland, religious and political discord continued in France. Even before the Conjuration in early 1560, Francis's government had adopted a more moderate stance, promising in the Édict of Amboise, for example, to pardon all religious prisoners who were not pastors or conspirators. Despite these conciliatory measures, the Huguenots continued their demonstrations.

Having acquired a bodyguard, Francis accepted his advisers' recommendation to convene a Council of Notables on 21 August in his mother's chamber at Fontainebleau, to discuss the problems he had inherited. In attendance were Catherine, Mary, Guise, the cardinal of Lorraine, the princes of the blood, and other royal officials. The absence of Navarre and Condé fueled further suspicions about the latter's involvement in the Conjuration. On the 23rd, Montmorency's Protestant nephew, Coligny, argued unsuccessfully for the establishment of two equal churches, Catholic and Huguenot. Before adjourning on the 26th, the council recommended summoning the Estates General and convening an assembly of the Gallican Church. More convinced than ever of Condé's guilt, the cardinal of Lorraine had him arrested on 30 October at Orléans where Francis and Mary made their entries on the 18th, amidst heightened security measures because of Huguenot disturbances in neighboring towns.

At Orléans Francis became ill, and although on Sunday, 17 November, Catherine kept him in bed, his condition worsened. For three weeks he suffered crippling headaches and drainage from an infected middle ear; when the drainage ceased, it caused excruciating pains in his jaws and teeth and a swelling behind his ear. During his illness his wife and mother remained at his bedside, witnessing his death on 5 December after Lorraine administered the last rites. He left a grieving widow, his crown to his ten-year-old brother, and a reprieve for Condé, whom Catherine ultimately freed.

Custom required that the widow of a French king dress in white mourning clothes, *en deuil blanc*, and spend 40 days in a darkened room, hung with black cloths and lighted only by a few candles. On 6 December before entering seclusion attended by her grandmother, Mary surrendered the crown jewels to Catherine. The grief she reportedly displayed was surely genuine. Throughout their marriage, Francis and she related to each other as they had from childhood. That interaction resulted in the development of sincere emotional ties, and no observer ever questioned their mutual esteem.[20] Michele Surian, the Venetian ambassador to France, who was not a Guise client, reported in early December that all pitied the young, beautiful, and graceful widow, who was full of tears because she lost a beloved husband, was deprived of France, and possessed small hope of recovering Scotland, her patrimony and dowry. A month later after condoling with her, he informed his government that although overwhelmed with grief, she expressed thanks in a few sorrowful words.[21]

In the mourning room social precedence prevailed. For the first 15 days, only the king, his brothers, Navarre, her Guise uncles, and Montmorency could enter. Four or five days later the bishops and the elder knights of the Order of St Michael could pay their respects. The younger knights, except for the married one, were denied admission, as their presence was considered inappropriate because of her youth. Afterwards, ambassadors were permitted to condole with her. Speculation was already rife about her next husband, and in late December Lorraine proposed to Thomas Perrenot, seigneur de Chantonnay, the Spanish ambassador, that she wed Philip's heir, Don Carlos. Although other names were mentioned, the queen dowager ultimately concluded that her honor was best served by marrying another prince.

4

RETURNING HOME, 1561–63

On 15 January 1561 having changed from white into black mourning clothes, 18-year-old Mary emerged from seclusion to attend a memorial service for Francis at the Grey Friars' Church. Shortly thereafter she moved with her grandmother to a private residence and ordered the erection of an elegant marble pillar in the Cathedral of St Croix at Orléans where, according to custom, his heart was buried apart from his body, which was interred at St Denis. The bodies of prominent individuals, especially monarchs, were often buried in two places, providing pilgrimage renown and, therefore, honor to the interment sites.

Later in Scotland Mary continued dressing in black in honor of Francis's memory until after her marriage to Darnley in 1565. On the day before the first anniversary of his death, she had a dirge said for him at Holyrood chapel and in a solemn procession the next day she presented a huge wax candle draped in black velvet. Sometimes mourners scheduled for their deceased loved ones ceremonies one month after their demise, which were called the month's mind, but more often they held the services on the first anniversary of their death.

While adjusting emotionally to widowhood at Orléans, Mary began making plans for returning home. On 18 January she wrote to Elizabeth for a passport for four commissioners to travel through England to Scotland with a letter for the parliamentary estates, informing them of her decision. Her letter to the estates was conciliatory; she sent them promises of immunity and requested they dispatch a representative of the Provisional Government to finalize the arrangements for her personal rule. In the event storms interrupted her voyage home, she also hoped to obtain Elizabeth's permission to journey through her realm or at least to seek shelter in an English harbor. Unless absolutely necessary, travelers did not venture on to the North Sea before summertime and even then the weather could be challenging.

Throckmorton visited Mary in seclusion on 31 December, but for his queen's official condolences to her, he awaited the arrival in France of the earl of Bedford, Elizabeth's special envoy. Between 16 and 19 February, Bedford met with Mary three times at Fontainebleau, where she had accompanied the court on the 3rd, to tender Elizabeth's condolences, to blame her French marriage for her realm's disturbances, and to request she ratify the Treaty of Edinburgh. Looking sorrowful, according to Throckmorton who accompanied Bedford, she replied that she could make no decisions concerning the treaty without her estates' advice. This was an appropriate response, since the prevailing wisdom was that British queens regnant should seek and follow their male councilors' recommendations.

Soon after Francis's demise, rumors began to circulate about her remarriage;[1] among the proposed candidates were Charles IX, Eric XIV of Sweden, Frederick II of Denmark, William of Nassau, prince of Orange, Don Carlos, Archduke Charles of Austria, Alfonso II, duke of Ferrara, Albert III, duke of Bavaria, Don John of Austria, her uncle, Francis, Grand Prior of the Knights of St John of Jerusalem in France, and the earl of Arran. Philip's decision to send Don Juan Manrique to condole with her in late January fueled reports that a Spanish marriage was imminent. To all inquiries she responded that previous agreements required her to obtain the estates' consent before remarrying. Throckmorton believed she valued her honor so highly that she would select only someone who would enhance her rank and reputation.

CHANGING POWER AT COURT

Meanwhile after becoming Charles's regent in December 1560, Catherine persuaded Navarre, who had a hereditary claim to that high office, to serve as lieutenant general. Consequently, Mary's uncles lost political authority, a change in their fortunes that surely explains her estrangement from Catherine. As recently as late 1559 Mary reported sympathetically to her mother that if Francis did not obey Catherine as well as he did, she would die and that would be disastrous for France. During his short reign the two French queens dined at the same table and attended sermons together daily. Three months after his demise, however, Catherine had begun to suspect that Mary was operating as a spy for Lorraine, who had left court, and his brother, Guise. In a letter to Sébastien de l'Aubespine, bishop of Limoges, the French ambassador in Spain, she explained that Mary was as obsequious as ever but that she was undeceived about the true feelings of her daughter-in-law, who undoubtedly favored her Guise relatives.[2]

From December 1560 Catherine's activities, focusing as they did on the future of her three small children whom she believed God had placed in her care, seem to have caused Mary concerns that she was neglecting the appropriate mourning for her deceased son. Apparently pleased that the French dynasty's future was no longer tied to that of the Guise family, Catherine sought to perpetuate that separation, opposing Mary's union with her son, Charles, and also with Don Carlos. Catherine especially hoped to prevent Guise influence spreading in Spain because her eldest daughter was its queen and because she had been attempting to marry her youngest daughter Margaret to the Spanish prince.

Rumors of the French queens' estrangement must have circulated at court. In June 1563 almost two years after Mary's departure for Scotland, Prospero Publicola Santacroce, cardinal bishop of Chessamos and the papal nuncio to France, claimed that Catherine developed a grudge against her daughter-in-law after overhearing her demeaning her, a de' Medici, as a shopkeeper's daughter. Since Santacroce had replaced Sebastian Gualtier, bishop of Viterbo, as papal nuncio in 1561, it is odd that he should have so belatedly reported this gossip. Diplomats often repeated unconfirmed even stale rumors, as this surely was. Given Mary's upbringing, it seems unlikely that she would have criticized her late husband's mother within her hearing, and Catherine's letter to Limoges confirms that she was not breaching court protocol. Catherine's appointment of Coligny to the *conseil des affaires* and her conciliatory religious policies led Guise to conspire against her authority. In April after forming a triumvirate with Jean d'Albon, Marshal St

André, and Montmorency, his former enemy, Guise sought Spanish aid to bolster the Gallic Church. While Philip felt obliged to support his mother-in-law's regency, he felt sympathy for her opponents. He also disliked her policies, which many believed were encouraging the spread of Protestantism.

PREPARING TO RETURN TO SCOTLAND

On about 18 March Mary left for Rheims to celebrate Easter, breaking her trip at Paris on the 20th to inventory her possessions in preparation for returning home to Scotland. Surian explained that she departed Fontainebleau because she anticipated the Scottish envoy's arrival to discuss her realm's affairs. Diplomatic protocol was precise. According to him, it was inappropriate for these deliberations to occur at the French court since Francis's death officially ended his realm's concern with Scottish business.[3] Earlier, during his reign, English ambassadors conferred with him in his presence chamber about his kingdom's affairs and with Mary in her presence chamber about her realm's business.

After reaching Rheims on the 26th, Mary celebrated Easter at St Pierre with her Aunt Renée and then left on 10 April for Nancy via Joinville, intending to return later to Rheims for Charles's coronation. On the 14th while in transit with Lorraine, Guise, Aumale and other relatives, she encountered John Leslie, future bishop of Ross, at the village of Vitry-le-François in Champagne. Representing Catholic Scotsmen, most notably the earl of Huntly, the lord chancellor, Leslie suggested that she disembark at Aberdeen, meet up with the earl, who would gather a large army and overthrow the Protestants. Since Huntly had joined the Lords of the Congregation in April 1560, Mary distrusted him and refused this request. Unwilling to place herself under his control and to plunge Scotland into civil war, she was probably following her uncles' advice to form at least a temporary alliance with the Protestant lords to facilitate her return.

The next day her half brother, Lord James, representing Scotland's Provisional Government, caught up with her at St Dizier, 138 miles from Paris. In their discussions over a five-day period, she promised to uphold the Protestant settlement on the condition that she be allowed to worship privately as a Catholic and pledged to seek the estates' consent before marrying a foreign prince but still declined to ratify the Treaty of Edinburgh. Her refusal to permit him to accompany her to Nancy caused him to surmise that she was going there to pursue secret marriage negotiations. His concern that she was withholding important information from him is understandable since he, himself, was duplicitous. He did not inform her of his discussions with Cecil and Elizabeth *en route* to France.

Furthermore, he later revealed his conversations with Mary to Throckmorton in Paris and to Cecil and Elizabeth on his return home through England. Regardless of whether Mary harbored personal reasons for preventing his journey to Lorraine, it was inappropriate for him and his attendants to arrive at the duke's court, representing the Provisional Government of Scotland, without an official commission or an invitation. As noted earlier, Surian maintained that, if she had met with the Scottish envoys at the French court, she would have violated diplomatic protocol. She, herself, explained on 22 April that Lord James had no commission except to do his duty to her as his monarch.

The conversations with her half brother and with Leslie on Huntly's behalf alerted Mary to the existence of deep political divisions in Scotland, only partly rooted in religion, that ultimately erupted into revolts against her authority. By compounding her differences with Lord James and other Protestants, she signaled to Huntly her unwillingness to challenge overtly the governmental and religious *status quo*.[4]

At Joinville she met her grandmother, renewed her friendship with a cousin, Anne of Lorraine, dowager duchess of Arschot, and greeted Archibald Crawfurd, parson of Eaglesham, her mother's almoner. He had recently brought her corpse to Fécamp, Normandy, where it lay in state at the cathedral before its interment at St Pierre. The grateful queen appointed him her almoner until she could grant him a benefice.

The purpose of Mary's visit to Nancy was to witness the baptism of Vaudémont's child, her godson and Lady Arschot's nephew, but it is possible that Lord James was correct and that discussions about her possible marriage did occur. Until 1564 Lady Arschot remained hopeful that Philip would name his son Don Carlos the regent of the Spanish-controlled Netherlands and that Mary would become the regent's wife. The House of Lorraine possessed a claim to Guelders through the marriage of King René, Lady Arschot's grandfather and

Mary's great-grandfather, to Philippa, the sister and heiress of Charles, the last Egmond duke of Guelders, who died childless. Lady Arschot's father, Duke Anthony, lost his bid to enforce his mother Philippa's claim to Guelders when Emperor Charles seized it in 1543 from William of Cleves, who had attempted to exercise an even more ancient claim to the duchy than Lorraine's when he became its ruler in 1538. If Mary did wed Don Carlos after he became the Netherlands' regent, her maternal relatives could view her marriage as a means of recovering their lost rights.

Lady Arschot's presence also fed rumors that Mary might wed William of Orange, whom she had met at the Paris wedding of Elizabeth to Philip's proxy. William was the cousin and heir of Lady Arschot's first husband, René of Nassau, prince of Orange. Shortly after reaching Nancy on the 22 April where guests were entertained with hunting and plays, Mary was stricken by tertian fever and decided to return with her grandmother to Joinville, convalescing there until late May and missing, therefore, Charles's coronation on the 15th.

On the 28th after spending two days at Rheims, Mary departed for St Germain, where the king, the queen regent, Prince Henry, Navarre, Condé, and others greeted her on 10 June. Shortly thereafter, she left court for the Louvre and then for Lorraine's castle at Dampierre. On the 18th, having returned to the Louvre, she assured Throckmorton of her determination to go home that summer, despite not having fully recovered her health. While awaiting Elizabeth's response to her request for a passport to land in England in case of an emergency at sea, Mary suffered another, shorter bout of tertian fever. Then on 20 and 21 July, after Throckmorton explained that Elizabeth had denied her a passport because she refused to ratify the Treaty of Edinburgh, Mary replied that she would consult with her estates about the treaty and reminded him that she had not worn England's arms since her husband's death, implying that she had been following his and his councilors' advice. Indeed, in late December 1560 Throckmorton commented on her former subjection to Francis and thought, considering her youth, she was showing wisdom, modesty, and great judgment. Even without the passport she planned to return home because her arrangements were well advanced and her baggage had been dispatched to Le Havre. The seas that could be treacherous to navigate even in the summer months could not deter her.

DEPARTING FRANCE

On 25 July after the royal family hosted a four-day series of parties for her at St Germain, she began the 148-mile trip to Calais with six Guise uncles and the duchess of Guise. As their route took them through Normandy and Picardy, she hoped to honor her mother's body at Fécamp, but the illness of Lorraine and Guise that delayed them at Méru on the 28th ended this plan. They were at Beauvais on 3 August, rested at Abbeville on the 7th and 8th, then left for the Abbey of Forest Monstrier, and reached Boulogne on the 10th and Calais on the 11th. About noon on the 14th, her fleet set sail. Realizing that refusing to grant Mary a passport was a breach of etiquette and opposed, as Surian said, "to the dictates of humanity,"[5] Elizabeth belatedly forwarded one that arrived after her cousin's departure.

Although not with her on this voyage, Buchanan, her future tutor and court poet, later alleged that Lorraine advised his niece to leave with him her furniture and wardrobe, presumably including her jewels, from concerns that they might be lost at sea. She reportedly responded: "When she ventured upon danger, she did not see why she should take greater care of her valuables, than of her person."[6] This was surely Buchanan's little joke about the cardinal's alleged greed, since when he wrote it, he was one of Mary's bitterest enemies. Jewels did actually figure in her farewell, as she gave a string of pearls to Lorraine and a necklace of assorted gems to the duchess. Much more important than mere decorative trinkets, jewels constituted portable wealth that during perilous times could be buried in the ground without fear of decay. As coins were scarce and bullion was rare and inferior, a government's prime asset was its gems that could be substituted for money. Both Châtelherault and her mother had exchanged many pieces for equipment and supplies to defend against English aggression. In 1556 the duke forwarded to Mary in France the items he still possessed, including 31 rings, many jeweled ornaments, 12 pieces of cloth-of-gold or silver tapestry, and a bejeweled dagger presented to her father by Francis I. Her inventory in 1561 included 159 items, many of which were deposited in the Jewel House at Edinburgh Castle.

Among her attendants on the two galleys, one painted red and the other white, and two other ships were three Guise uncles, Aumale, Elbeouf, and Francis, the Grand Prior, and five other noteworthy

Frenchmen, Damville and his servant, Pierre de Boscosel de Châtelard, Pierre de Bourdeille, seigneur de Brantôme, Michel de Castelnau, seigneur de Mauvissière, who had been raised in Guise's household, and, René Benoist, her confessor. A few Scots also accompanied her, including Leslie and the four Maries. As the fleet departed, according to Brantôme's later account, they witnessed the sinking of a vessel with its entire crew, a tragedy interpreted as a bad omen for the voyage.

Brantôme also recalled Mary's despair and repeated her sad words of farewell at their departure: "*Adieu, France! Beloved France, Adieu!*" When it was supper time after five hours at sea, the grief-stricken queen, he noted, could eat only a salad and chose to spend the night on deck. Before retiring, she asked the agreeable pilot to awaken her in the morning if the coast were still visible. He kept his promise, and she again said good-bye to the realm where she had lived for 13 years. Expressing sadness as she was leaving was an appropriate way for her to show respect for the land of her upbringing, but Brantôme surely exaggerated the signs of her grief. On a seafaring ship the deck is the best place to stay to avoid seasickness, and others, including Châtelard, slept there. The ship's movement could also have been as responsible for her diminished appetite as her melancholy. The main meal, furthermore, was served before the voyage began.[7]

Brantôme's recollections have led writers to emphasize her reluctance to leave France, but despite Elizabeth's decision to withhold the passport, Mary insisted on sailing home, risking the stormy weather that might force her to land illegally in England rather than using her cousin's unfriendliness as an excuse to linger. And why should she act any differently? Although Scotland was not Christendom's most prestigious realm, the papal list of precedence in 1504 ranked it above Navarre, Cyprus, Bohemia, Poland, and Denmark. Many in this hierarchical society avidly sought to maintain and achieve regal status. In a letter of 1549 complaining about the lack of French support for Scotland, for example, her mother claimed that nothing ought to be spared to save a kingdom. Princess Madeleine had fulfilled her royal ambitions by marrying James V in 1537, and Charles the Bold, the last great duke of Burgundy, had died at Nancy in 1477 while attempting to wrest Lorraine from Mary's ancestor, René II. Because in the Middle Ages, Lorraine had gained recognition as the kingdom of Lotharingia,

Burgundy had hoped possession of it would make possible his advancement to kingship.

In 1561 Scotland was Mary's dowry: without it she might be unable to arrange another prestigious marriage. When quizzed about her union with his son, Archduke Charles, Emperor Ferdinand I responded that after her realm received her, he would consider the proposal. In fact, neither he nor most other potential fathers-in-law or husbands were prepared to fund a Scottish conquest for her. Later as Elizabeth's prisoner, she repeatedly requested English, French, and Spanish assistance for recovering Scotland and then became irate when her son refused to associate with her in its governance.

In France she realized that the royal family valued her betrothal to Francis partly because Scotland was her dowry. She did not reject her heritage, which lent her a certain distinction or charm. The courtiers affectionately called her *La Petite Sauvage*, and she sent for Scottish ponies and terriers to amuse them. Brantôme remembered her dressing in highland plaids and speaking melodiously her native tongue, which he deemed barbaric. She even conversed in Scots with Throckmorton, doubtlessly a political strategy because he could communicate in French. Since in less than two years, Guise would be assassinated in the first of eight religious wars, Mary was leaving behind in 1561 neither a peaceful realm nor a sympathetic court.

Although Surian blamed the French for mistreating her, "a widow unarmed and almost banished from her own home,"[8] she said good-bye to many friends two of whom were her favorite poets: Jerôme de l'Huillier, seigneur de Maisonfleur, and Ronsard. Another poet she greatly admired was the deceased Joachim du Bellay, whose elegy by William Aubert she owned. The most well known of them was and is, of course, Ronsard, who composed a farewell elegy in the Petrarchan style, claiming that the court would miss her as a pasture would miss its flowers, the sky its stars, or the sea its waves. The next year, he again lamented her absence and recalled her loveliness:

> Even so your beauty, brilliant as the sun,
>> In one brief day for France has risen and set;
> Bright as the lightning, 'twas as quickly gone,
>> And left us only longing and regret.[9]

This and other references to her beauty have caused skeptical historians, after closely examining portraits of her, to accuse her
contemporaries of flattering her looks. Since artistic conventions and
practices have altered over time, studying images of her to determine
her beauty is at best an unproductive exercise. Modern likenesses usually exude warmth, vitality, and sometimes friendliness, while early
modern portraits are often stylized representations, intending to display the rank and wealth of their subjects as embodied in their clothing
and jewelry. Ultimately, since beauty is in the eye of the beholder and
is culture bound, it seems sufficient to note that not only poets but also
relatives, diplomats, and other observers lauded her attractiveness
beyond the level that the royalty might usually have expected. Indeed,
in December 1559 even d'Oysel reported to Mary of Guise that her
daughter was gentle and beautiful and that the king, her husband,
greatly esteemed her. It is possible that those who praised her were
influenced by her height of six feet, which provided her with a special
presence at a time when males were on average only about five feet,
four inches tall.

Meanwhile, Mary's fleet moved northward, all but one of her ships
outdistancing an English squadron. Its crew captured the vessel with
her stable of horses and escorted it to England but subsequently
released it with apologies, although the warden of Tynemouth
impounded the horses for a month. A thick, normal summer fog, a
Forth ha', descended as they sailed into Leith about 9:00 a.m. on 19
August, discharging cannons to announce their arrival.

REACHING SCOTLAND

Because the voyage went so smoothly and quickly, Mary reached
Scotland before Holyrood Palace was prepared to receive her. Andrew
Lamb invited her to his Leith home where Châtelherault, Arran, and
Lords James and Robert welcomed her. Later she and her attendants
rode to Holyrood on borrowed ponies, which Brantôme ridiculed as
inferior beasts. Since she expected to utilize her own horses, which
remained at Tynemouth, she had not anticipated transportation difficulties and was probably grateful for any animals that could be
rounded up on such short notice. In June 1562, moreover, Mary later

viewed Scottish horses as suitable gifts for her French friends. Brantôme also disparaged the serenade sung and played on violins and rebecs by several hundred Edinburgh youths, but she seems to have appreciated their thoughtfulness in welcoming her and thanked them for their efforts. As he wrote after her death, it is not surprising that he was critical of the Scots, who usurped her throne. Some of his assertions were obviously inaccurate, for example, that her fleet left France in the autumn and that she died on 7 February. In his memoirs, Mauvissière also indicated he retained mostly vague memories of her reception, noting incorrectly, for example, that no one greeted her until she removed to Holyrood.[10]

From her arrival, which caused astonishment since she lacked a personal bodyguard, she exercised her right to hear mass in her chapel. On Sunday, the 24th, Lord James kept his promise and barred her door from those trying to disrupt her services while Lords Robert and John prevented attacks on her priests. The next day at Edinburgh's Mercat Cross, the central meeting place for announcing laws and punishing criminals, she issued a proclamation, forbidding religious changes, promising to obtain her estates' advice at a convenient time, and ordering her subjects to keep the peace and refrain from molesting her French attendants. Her order may have raised some reformers' hopes that when parliament did meet, it would re-enact the Reformation Acts of 1560, which she had not ratified. Others may have worried that her proclamation represented only a temporary reprieve for Protestantism, leaving it with an uncertain future. Mary's private court services and this public religious stance prompted Knox to storm against Catholic idolatry on the next Sunday. Like many other preachers he believed that it was his duty to act as God's prophet in the Old Testament sense and denounce the sinfulness of all people, especially of female monarchs.

Mary scheduled an audience with him for 4 September and then turned to official Edinburgh business. On 2 September the day after its provost and magistrate hosted a banquet for her, she made her official entry into her capital, which, as it unfolded, seemed more an occasion for religious baiting than for welcoming her. Although Catholics outnumbered Protestants in Edinburgh, the council supervising the entry was selected in 1560, shortly after the dissolution of the Reformation Parliament. Its actions later prompted her to order the replacement of its members but on 2 September the day belonged to them.

Some of the evidence is obscure but the following account generally reflects the occurrences.[11] Entering at the West Port, she rode to the castle to dine; afterwards, she was met on capital hill by 50 young men, dressed as Moors, symbolizing the forces of disorder that needed taming. Then probably at the Butter Tron, the weighing station, citizens arrived with a pall of purple velvet to hold over her head and with a cart carrying musicians that followed her through the town. The cart also contained a golden propine or coffer with a gift for her perhaps of wine. Next, a cloud descended from which emerged a boy dressed as an angel, who not only delivered the keys to the town to her but also gave her a vernacular Bible and a Psalm book, two well-known Protestant symbols. At the Tolbooth, which functioned as a prison as well as the meeting place of the council and the courts of justice, she observed a double pageant: fortune standing on the upper story above three ladies on the lower story, appearing as Love, Justice, and Policy. Mary continued on to the Mercat Cross, viewed four virgins representing the traditional virtues and drank wine from the fountain. Next she approached the Salt Tron with the day's *coup de grâce*. In his dispatch Randolph, the English resident ambassador, reported that Huntly had intervened to prevent the citizens from burning an effigy of a priest celebrating mass. Regardless of the report's accuracy, they did set afire effigies of Korah, Dathan and Abiram, the Old Testament rebels against Moses whom God destroyed, a sacrifice that seemed to warn that similar punishments awaited the enemies of Protestantism. At the Netherbow actors also burned a dragon, which represented the apocalyptic Antichrist and, therefore, the pope in the reformers' view. Finally, with the cart still following her, she reached Holyrood only to hear a speaker admonish her to relinquish the mass.

Two days later Mary was surely in less than a cheerful mood when she received Knox, whose opposition to women rulers was well known. In early 1558 while on the continent, he published his treatise against women rulers, claiming that a woman's rule violated natural, civil, and divine law and equating a realm governed by a woman to that of a monstrous body with its head where its feet should be. In discussions with Mary and in correspondence with Elizabeth, he explained that his treatise applied specifically to Mary Tudor, whom he labeled an English Jezebel for approving the execution of almost 300 Protestants. Even so he never altered his theoretical position concerning female rulers.

According to Knox's later account of the audience, which only Lord James witnessed, Mary accused him of inciting a rebellion against her mother and of writing a book against her own authority. He responded it was his duty to disclose the tyranny of the pope, the Antichrist, and while he detested female rule, as long as her subjects found hers convenient, he was willing to accept her governance, noting that Paul had been willing to live under Nero's rule. Knox also remarked that if monarchs exceeded their lawful limits, they might be resisted, even by force. The audience was ended when she was called to dinner.

Reactions to her exchanges with Knox varied. Maitland of Lethington informed Cecil that she behaved reasonably and remarked he wished Knox would treat her more gently; although she was not a Protestant, she still displayed a wisdom in dealing with him far exceeding that expected from one of her young years. Randolph heard that she wept, but Knox did not refer to any emotional response in his later account, although he did recall her weeping during their fourth interview in 1563. It is possible that the ambassador, who wrote shortly after this first audience, was correct since he did later observe her tearful reaction to other bad news. About her alleged weeping during Knox's harangue, Randolph explained, "there be of that sex that will do that, as well for anger as for grief."[12]

In reporting on his conversation with Mary in May 1562, Randolph offered another interpretation for her outbursts. After merely raising the possibility that the conference she hoped to arrange with Elizabeth might be postponed, he was astonished to observe tears rolling down Mary's cheeks. He realized that her reaction must have led observers to believe that the news he conveyed seemed rather worse that it actually was. She thus used her tears to manipulate the views not only of listeners but also of witnesses out of ear shot. In fact, Buchanan claimed that she was "well qualified to conceal her emotions."[13]

Early modern Europeans often used excessive gestures and facial expressions to indicate the depths of their feelings. In 1562 Bishop Alvaro de la Quadra, the Spanish ambassador to England, informed Philip that when Elizabeth learned about a conversation at the home of Henry Fitzalan, 12th earl of Arundel, concerning the succession rights of Catherine Grey, sister to Jane Grey, and a descendant of Mary Tudor, Henry VIII's younger sister, the queen wept with rage. Five years later during Throckmorton's meeting with the earl and countess of Lennox in London to discuss how Elizabeth intended to react to their son's recent murder, Lady Lennox wept bitterly and her husband sighed deeply.

GOVERNANCE ISSUES

Meanwhile at Holyrood on 6 September 1561, Mary appointed 16 men to her privy council, four Catholics, including Huntly, who retained the lord chancellorship, and virtually all the important Congregation leaders. Privy council guidelines required six noblemen to reside at court, but Lord James and her secretary, Lethington, played the major governmental roles. In addition, Robert Richardson, treasurer, James Makgill, clerk register, and John Bellenden, justice clerk, also served on the council.

Interested in becoming reacquainted with her realm, Mary departed in early September with Elboeuf, Huntly, Archibald, fifth earl of Argyll, and Lord James, among others, for Linlithgow, her birthplace, and then for Stirling, her childhood residence. On the evening of the 14th at Stirling, an accident threatened her life when a lit candle burned the drapery around her four-poster bed, releasing smoke that almost suffocated her. Another assault on the priests singing high mass in her chapel on that day reportedly left some of them with minor injuries. In Edinburgh Randolph heard that Argyll and Lord James were the attackers, but since her half brother was seeking an earldom from her, it was more likely a scuffle initiated by their households. Randolph later claimed that at Holyrood Lord James heard sermons in his lodgings, which lay near the royal chapel where her priests celebrated mass, and that these two groups of clerics sometimes exchanged blows. These confrontations continued, as a servant of Lord Robert's beat up her priests celebrating the choral mass on All Hallows' Day.

At Stirling just before Mary set out for Perth on the 15th, Arthur Lallart presented a petition from Lennox, requesting the recovery of his Scottish estates. She responded that she was unable to offer a remedy but would do what she could for his family at the appropriate time. Then continuing northward to Perth, she reportedly swooned during the entry festivities, which, according to Randolph, featured anti-Catholic pageants. He also explained that she often suffered sudden attacks such as this after experiencing great unkindness. She recovered her senses enough to depart the next day for Dundee. After visiting St Andrew's, where on the 24th Huntly apparently disputed with Lord James about permitting the public celebration of mass, she was back at Holyrood on the 29th.

Three days later the Edinburgh council ordered the expulsion of monks, friars, priests, nuns, adulterers, fornicators, and all filthy people. Mary subsequently met with the council at the Tolbooth and insisted on the removal of the provost and four bailies. Thomas McCalzean, a moderate reformer, was then selected to replace Archibald Douglas of Kilspindie, the provost chosen in 1560 and 1561. During the remainder of her personal rule, she usually did not attempt to advance Catholics to the council but supported moderate Protestants, thus dividing them politically from their more extreme colleagues.

In governmental policy she also maintained a conciliatory attitude toward the reformers and in December summoned a convention, her first great advisory council, to address the Kirk's financial problems. Conventions, like parliaments, contained the three estates sitting in one chamber: nobles, senior clergy, and commissioners from the burghs. Differences between the institutions did exist, however, as par-liaments required a 40-day notice before meeting and possessed judicial as well as advisory and legislative authority. By contrast, con-ventions could be summoned on shorter notice and could advise the crown, enact temporary laws, and authorize taxation but not dispense justice.

The convention's deliberations concerning the need to provide funds from Catholic benefices for Protestant ministers formed the backdrop to the privy council's decision in February 1562 to approve a settle-ment for offering salaries to reformers and for supplementing crown revenue. The holders of Catholic benefices retained two-thirds of their income for their lifetimes, and the crown confiscated the other one-third to cover governmental costs and to support Protestant ministers. This arrangement accepted the existence of two religious entities, one reformed and one Catholic, although priests still could not celebrate mass except at court. In time the amount distributed to reformers decreased. In 1562 the crown obtained for its use £12,700 but in 1565 £32,033. Even with this revenue stream, because of an eroded customs income and the lack of a sound tax base, the deficit continued to mount reaching £33,000 by 1565. The only tax Mary levied was for her son's christening in 1566. Her annual jointure of 60,000 livres, although she received only about two-thirds of this amount, funded her household.

Her determination to avoid religious controversy kept her from acknowledging officially the visit of the papal envoy, Nicholas de Gouda, who reached Scotland in June 1562 to request her participation in what was to be the last session of the Council of Trent. After a lengthy delay, she agreed to meet him secretly in late July but declined to send envoys to Trent. About a month later, the disappointed de Gouda departed disguised as a sailor, having been able to confer with only one of her Catholic ecclesiastics, Robert Crichton, bishop of Dunkeld. In May the next year Lorraine read a letter from Mary to the Council of Trent, explaining that she was resolved to live and die a loyal Catholic and promising to abide by all their decrees. Both Pius IV, who later sent her two copies of Trent's printed canons, and the delegates expressed satisfaction with her explanations.

Even some who did not complain publicly about her mass longed for her to abandon it. In August 1562 Randolph reported that she was recently ill at chapel and hoped if it happened again, her sickness would cause her to stay away from Catholic services. Unlike Randolph, Knox continued to harass her publicly. On 15 December 1561, two days after he preached against royal frivolities, such as dancing and banqueting, she summoned him in the presence of Lord James, the earl of Morton, and Lethington to her Holyrood bedchamber, which was utilized for daily activities beyond merely sleeping. To her claim that he attempted to engender contempt for her, he responded that he had spoken generally about princes and not specifically about her and that if she wanted to know his exact words, she should attend his services. He went on to characterize her uncles as God's enemies and predicted they would not spare the blood of many innocents to maintain their noble life and worldly glory. When he questioned what others might think about his being absent from his book so long, she turned away, reminding him that he could not always be at his book.

The festivities that offended him may have been more boisterous than those to which Edinburgh residents had become accustomed during the rule of her mother and the provisional governors. In October 1561 the month after Aumale returned home with the galleys, a second Guise uncle, Francis, the Grand Prior, along with Damville, Châtelard, Brantôme, and Mauvissière, obtained Elizabeth's permission to travel through England to France. Before they left, Mary arranged a farewell banquet and masque in which the Grand Prior and Damville took parts. For this occasion, Buchanan may have written the *Apollo et Musae Exceles*.

During the next two months Mary enjoyed more entertainments. On 18 November Randolph noted that her ladies were merry and dancing, lusty, and attractive. Then at Leith Sands on two Sundays in late November and early December, the ambassador witnessed competitions called running at the ring, which pitted two teams of six men against each other. On 30 November one team led by Lords Robert and John, which was disguised as women, defeated the other team led by Elboeuf, which was dressed in elaborate masks and costumes. Although masking was a usual noble amusement, reformers inveighed against cross-dressing, citing Deuteronomy 22:5 as their authority, and Knox probably deplored the victory of men masquerading as women. His complaints may have had some effect. In December 1562, after he had preached for more than a year against Mary's festivities Randolph blamed him for the decrease in the usual court dancing.

Although Mary enjoyed disguised entertainment, she was also aware that some popular practices could lead to public unrest. In April 1562 on the authority of a 1555 act against masquerading as Robin Hood and Little John, she forbade her subjects at Edinburgh and St Andrews to dress up as these legendary figures because of the uproarious celebrations that had occurred in May 1561 before her arrival.

Randolph had relatively easy access to her court because Mary wished Elizabeth to understand by her ambassador's treatment just how deeply her Scottish cousin valued her friendship. Shortly after returning home, Mary began corresponding with Elizabeth about negotiating an Anglo-Scottish accord that recognized her English succession rights. On the other hand, Elizabeth still hoped Mary would ratify the Treaty of Edinburgh. On 5 January 1562, Mary explained to Elizabeth she would not ratify the treaty because it was prejudicial to her lineage, but she also promised either to fulfill its reasonable requirements or to enter into a new amity that would secure her claims to the English throne next after those of Elizabeth and her issue.

Mary hoped Elizabeth would approve her official succession rights and override Henry VIII's will, which ignored the descendants of Margaret his elder sister and privileged the Grey descendants of Mary his younger sister. Publicly authenticating her Scottish cousin's claims was an act Elizabeth would not concede. She feared a rebellion favoring Mary Stewart like the one Sir Thomas Wyatt the younger waged on her behalf in 1554 against her sister Mary Tudor; as a Protestant Elizabeth also worried that validating her cousin Mary's claims would encourage Catholic conspiracies against herself. Furthermore, she suspected that many of her advisors supported the pretensions of the Protestant Greys. In 1561 Elizabeth ordered Catherine Grey imprisoned for marrying without royal consent Edward Seymour, earl of Hertford, a union that produced two sons who were declared illegitimate. Elizabeth seems to have been ambivalent about the Greys, who in 1553 took advantage of their status in Henry's will to attempt to usurp his daughters' premier places in the succession.

Since her contemporaries believed that failing to enforce their royal claims would compromise their honor, it was virtually impossible for Mary to relinquish her English succession rights at this time. Both Francis I and Henry II, had, of course, fought ruinous wars, attempting to conquer Milan, which a distant ancestor once ruled. Mary's English claim was not only much more recent than their Italian ones but many Catholics also considered it more valid than Elizabeth's. One major difference between these queens regnant was that Elizabeth recognized no worldly superiors to herself, as all her advisers were her appointees and were, in some sense, her creatures. Mary, by contrast, possessed religious superiors with great expectations of her. Pius IV, for example, advised her to marry a Catholic prince and to model herself after Mary Tudor. That in Scotland Mary condoned the Protestant settlement seems to have caused her to be more concerned about protecting her reputation as a loyal Catholic than she might otherwise have been.

On 7 December attempting to build a lasting Anglo-Scottish amity, Lethington wrote to Cecil, exploring the possibility of scheduling a personal interview between their monarchs. A stream of correspondence ensued with Mary sending Elizabeth a heart-shaped diamond ring, emphasizing to her cousin the importance she placed on arranging this meeting. At special occasions like these, exchanging jewelry, particularly rings valued for their talismanic and symbolic functions, conveyed the sentiments held by both the presenters and recipients and served to recognize and validate their mutual standing and relationship in the social hierarchy.

In early May 1562 at Falkland Palace, a serious riding accident in which Mary's arm and the right side of her face were injured delayed deliberations until the 19th, but her councilors finally agreed on a rendezvous between 20 August and 20 September somewhere in northern England. Elizabeth postponed it when the first French religious war flared up again that summer after a short truce. Guise had set off the initial conflict in March 1562, when his forces killed some 70 Protestants and wounded 100 others at an illegal prayer-meeting at Vassy, which was part of Mary's jointure lands under his administration.

Although the warfare's renewal led Elizabeth at first to delay the conference, she postponed it again in July after deciding to aid Condé at Rouen and Dieppe in exchange for English control of Le Havre, which she planned to trade for Calais. According to Randolph, Mary shed many tears to emphasize her deep disappointment when she learned of Elizabeth's decision. The English intervention in France, which began in October, was a failure; Guise defeated Condé in December and French troops expelled the English from Le Havre in the summer of 1563. Some months earlier in February, a Huguenot assassinated Guise, causing Mary, of course, great sorrow, but his death did not end the conflict, which lingered into 1564.

ABDUCTION SCARES

Meanwhile in Scotland attempts were afoot to besmirch Mary's honor. Previous analyses of these confrontations have failed to consider adequately contemporary attitudes concerning abductions. In most realms noble competition for custody of monarchs who were minors occurred because control of them also meant control of their governments. Kidnappers seized both Mary's father and her son, and Henry VIII attempted to remove her forcibly to England, when she was a child. In political terms noblemen viewed women rulers as naturally subordinate to them and susceptible, like children, to their authority. In Scotland and elsewhere, moreover, men occasionally abducted heiresses and ravished them with the intention of pressuring them into marriage. Hence, they utilized the sexual act as a political tool to dishonor the victims, who had little recourse except to wed their abductors. Official documents used interchangeably the words, ravishment and abduction, because the two acts were so closely associated together. The heiresses' abductors were required to pay a compounded amount to their new wives' parents or guardians for their property losses.[14] Occasionally an heir, who was a minor, might also be abducted, but this convention mainly affected heiresses.[15] It was not until 1612 that the problems of abduction and rape prompted the Scottish privy council to promulgate an act against the ravishment of women.

If committed independently of abduction, rape was a crime but a greatly under-reported one. The rapes that reached court dockets mostly involved children although sexual assaults against adult females who were of higher social status than their attackers or who were mauled might also be adjudicated. In the latter cases the punishment meted out was more for the women's injuries than for the rapes. This cavalier attitude stemmed from the notion that women were more passionate and lecherous than men. As a final insult, if the victim became pregnant, she could not claim it was the result of a rape. Her contemporaries believed that conception occurred only when both partners enjoyed the sexual act, the weakness of her flesh causing her to become responsive despite her initial refusal.[16]

In November 1561 Mary's first abduction scare in Scotland arose from an alleged comment of Arran, whose father wanted him to wed her. Arran reportedly asked why it would not be as easy to take her from the abbey, as others had once thought it would be to seize her mother. On the 16th at 9:00 p.m. when Lord James was away from court, rumors that Arran had crossed the Firth of Forth with an armed band greatly frightened Mary. Lords Robert and John kept watch that evening to calm her, and later she decided to form a personal bodyguard of 19 archers for protection.

A dispute between Arran and Bothwell in December may have been related to this incident, as the two had been enemies since Arran's return home two years earlier. Bothwell, born in 1535, remained a loyal supporter of Mary of Guise despite his conversion to Protestantism. In October 1559, he ambushed Cockburn of Ormiston, wounded him in the face, and seized the English gold he was delivering from Berwick-on-Tweed to the Congregation. In retaliation, Arran and Lord James, accompanied by 300 armed men and some artillery, attempted to capture Bothwell at Crichton Castle, a few miles from Haddington. As he had already fled, they sacked his castle and seized his papers. Subsequently, Bothwell challenged Arran to single combat to settle the points of honor between them; early modern men wore their swords as weapons for fighting not merely as clothing accessories. Denouncing him as a liar, Arran refused the offer.

Two years later in December 1561 the month following Mary's panicked reaction to Arran's alleged abduction scheme, Bothwell, Elboeuf, and Lord John, wearing masks, entered an Edinburgh merchant's house, seeking Arran's mistress, Alison Craik, the stepdaughter of Cuthbert Ramsay and Agnes Stewart, James IV's sometime mistress and Bothwell's grandmother.[17] After gaining admission the first night, they forced their way in the next evening. This intrusion is often dismissed as a drunken frolic, but the cooperation of Mary's uncle and her favorite half brother with Bothwell lends a more serious complexion to it; they surely did not concoct this conspiracy over some chance glasses of wine. Bothwell had a close relationship with Lord John, who intended to marry his sister, Janet Hepburn, and the earl must also have become acquainted with Elboeuf in France. Dispatched on a mission to that realm by Mary of Guise shortly before her death in 1560, Bothwell reached Paris in September. It is likely that he met with Elboeuf, who had planned to succeed his ailing sister as the Scottish governor. In November after Francis appointed Bothwell to his privy chamber and supplied him with financial support and Mary named him as one of her commissioners for summoning the estates, he returned to Scotland. The next year in 1561, Elboeuf escorted his niece home, and while his two brothers departed for France, he remained as her special councilor to advise her about handling governmental emergencies and difficulties.

That December at Edinburgh, it seems likely that these three men, one Arran's determined enemy and the two others Mary's beloved relatives, conspired to harass Arran's mistress to retaliate for his having caused the queen's recent abduction fright. The controversy almost escalated into a pitched battle the third evening when the Hamiltons gathered to challenge Bothwell and his allies, but Lord James, Argyll, and Huntly arrived with a royal proclamation and successfully disbursed the posturing warriors. On this final evening of the dispute perhaps responding to his niece's request, Elboeuf remained at Holyrood. It was partly his share in this controversy that prompted Randolph, a Hamilton sympathizer, to rate the marquis's judgment as inferior to that of his brothers, although the ambassador had already been complaining about his expensive dining habits. In February 1562 Randolph was delighted to learn that Elboeuf would return home earlier than expected because of his wife's serious illness.

Meanwhile in January 1562 during the interval between the Arran–Bothwell conflict in December and another that was to occur in March, Mary attended Lord John's and Janet Hepburn's wedding at Bothwell's Crichton Castle. Responding positively to Mary's reconciliation efforts, Lord James first joined Cockburn of Ormiston in exchanging with Bothwell promises to keep the peace before the privy council and then agreed to witness this marriage at the castle he had helped Arran to sack less than three years earlier.

A few days later at Lithlingow, Arran submitted to Mary and promised to attend with his father the wedding on 8 February of Lord James and Agnes Keith, sister of William, fourth Earl Marischal, at St Giles' Church in Edinburgh. Along with Châtelherault, Arran, Huntly, and Randolph, Mary was present at the marriage banquet, the lavishness of which elicited complaints from Knox who conducted the wedding. The day before the ceremony, Mary granted Lord James the Mar earldom, but after John, sixth Lord Erskine, the son of her deceased guardian, protested that the title was his family's perquisite, she substituted the richer Moray earldom. In some sense it was an appropriate ennoblement because its last holder was their father's illegitimate brother who died childless. She momentarily kept the grant a secret to postpone the anticipated negative reaction of Huntly, the administrator of the Moray and Mar estates since 1549. The Gordon family had actually been attempting to acquire these properties for two centuries.

Another confrontation the next month with Cockburn of Ormiston prompted Bothwell to attempt to end his estrangement from Arran. While horseback riding with his wife and his son Alexander, Ormiston learned that Bothwell and eight companions were lying in wait for them. Retreating with his wife, he left Alexander to check on the intruders' intentions. When Alexander discharged his gun at the earl, he seized the young man and attempted unsuccessfully to carry him off to Crichton.

Probably because this confrontation displeased both Mary and the privy councilors, Bothwell requested Knox, whose father and forbears were Hepburn dependents, to mediate an understanding between him and Arran. The two earls' subsequent reconciliation fell apart after they dined together on 26 March at Hamilton House in the parish of St Mary-in-the-Field, known as Kirk o'Field. The next day Arran informed an unsympathetic Knox that Bothwell planned to capture Mary, take her to Dumbarton Castle, which was held by Châtelherault, and murder Lord James and her other advisers. He also sent a message to Mary that his father the duke supported the abduction scheme. Because he was descending into madness, Arran was somewhat incoherent, making it difficult for observers to separate facts from fantasy.

After meeting with the two earls, the privy council ordered the incarceration ultimately at Edinburgh Castle of both Arran and Bothwell, the latter protesting his innocence. In late August Bothwell escaped from the castle and was shipwrecked in England, a flight that led many to credit Arran's testimony. When in early 1564[18] Mary finally agreed to forward permission to Elizabeth for Bothwell's departure to France, Randolph condemned his character as worthless and complained about Arran's continued imprisonment. Although never completely regaining his senses, Arran was freed in 1566 but remained under house confinement until his death in 1609. Meanwhile, indicating that she gave some credence to his accusations, Mary took the opportunity this dispute offered to remove Dumbarton from his father's control. Châtelherault's possession of that stronghold had long been of some concern to her. The memoirs written later either by Sir John Maxwell of Terrigles, who became fifth Lord Herries in late 1566, or more probably by one of his descendants, claims that Bothwell did concoct this plot. It is interesting that Buchanan, a Lennox ally, believed that both Bothwell and the Hamiltons planned to abduct her but that Randolph, a Hamilton ally, blamed only Bothwell for the scheme.

HUNTLY'S REBELLION

An examination of Châtelard's writings is helpful to an understanding of yet another assault on the queen's honor in late 1562. After accompanying her to Scotland, Châtelard, a maternal grand-nephew of Pierre du Terrail, chevalier de Bayard, and a poet of the Ronsard school, expressed grief at her attentions to three men: Damville, Arran, and Sir John Gordon of Findlater, the third son of Huntly. Rumors spread even before Damville accompanied Mary to Scotland that a friend had offered to poison his wife so that he might wed the queen. In short, Châtelard's writings indicate that these suitors had something more serious on their minds than mere dalliance. The poet ultimately concluded that Gordon of Findlater had captured Mary's heart and described him in glowing terms:

> the paragon of excellence in man ... the youthful Gordon ... what majesty was in his port; ... Upon his knees he came to greet his queen; ... such grace was in his motion, that had Apollo's self been there, the god had been a Gordon.[19]

In August 1562 after the meeting with Elizabeth was postponed, Mary traveled northward, reached Old Aberdeen by the 27th, and visited the university. In her train were Lord James, still addressed as the earl of Mar, James Ogilvy of Cardell, master of her household, and Randolph, among others. As she entered Gordon territory, Elizabeth Keith, countess of Huntly, attempted to intercede for her son, Findlater, a fugitive from justice. Two months earlier, he was imprisoned in the Edinburgh Tolbooth for mutilating the right arm of James, fifth Lord Ogilvy of Airlie, but had since escaped and fled to Aberdeen.

The assault on Lord Ogilvy was an episode in an ongoing inheritance dispute between Findlater and Ogilvy of Cardell, master of the queen's household. Lord Ogilvy was drawn into it as the guardian of Walter, the grandson and heir of Cardell. After Cardell's deceased father had married as his second wife Elizabeth Gordon, he disinherited Cardell and bequeathed the Ogilvy estates to his wife's cousin, Findlater. Reportedly, Findlater kept Elizabeth Gordon, who became his mistress, imprisoned so that he could control her jointure lands.

Following a conversation with Findlater's mother Lady Huntly, Mary ordered him to appear before Aberdeen's court of justiciary. After it demanded that he repair within seven days to Stirling for confinement, he departed but failed to appear at the castle. Besides this incident, the Gordons nurtured other grievances. As Huntly disliked both English and French interference in Scotland, he opposed Mary's efforts to meet with Elizabeth and boycotted the privy council meeting that approved the conference. Moreover, as noted above, Huntly administered both the Mar and Moray estates and could be expected to react with hostility when he learned that Mary had granted the Moray earldom to Lord James, his old enemy.

As she departed Aberdeen, Mary anticipated trouble and declined to visit Huntly's home, Strathbogie Castle. She continued on to Darnaway Castle, the earl of Moray's hereditary seat, and at a privy council meeting on 10 September, decided to respond to Gordon of Findlater's defiance with force and to recognize her half brother as Moray. The councilors also ordered Findlater and his pretended spouse to release the Ogilvy estates to the crown. When Mary reached the royal castle at Inverness, which the Gordons had largely built and controlled for 50 years, its keeper, Alexander Gordon, refused to admit her on Huntly's orders as sheriff of Inverness. Since she had to spend that night in private lodgings rather than the more secure castle, the earl apparently was planning to make it easier to capture her and forcibly marry her to his son Findlater. Obtaining local support, she ordered Gordon to open the gates and had him hanged when he complied, thus enforcing the statute that declared this illegal behavior a treasonable act. After she left the castle, Findlater harried her forces. Finally on 28 October, eleven days after she ordered Huntly declared a traitor with three blasts of the horn at Aberdeen's Mercat Cross, Mary's army of about 2,000 led by Moray defeated the attacking Gordon force of some 700 or so at Corrichie, near Aberdeen. As she approached this showdown, Randolph reported that he had not seen her merrier and never thought she would be able to stomach these violent events. Indeed, her physical endurance must also have impressed him. He described as a miserable experience their more than two-month journey on horseback that covered difficult terrain amidst cold and foul weather.

After the battle Huntly died probably of a stroke; his heir George was imprisoned, but Gordon of Findlater was executed in November at Aberdeen. The axe man was so inept that Mary, probably witnessing her first beheading, fainted while observing the bloody deed. In France Châtelard surmised that her presence was required to prove she lacked passion for Findlater, but others remarked that she needed to witness it to confirm that the execution was not merely Moray's avenging himself on the Gordon family. Randolph believed Findlater meant to kill Mary, but Knox more realistically claimed Huntly intended to seize her and murder Moray. The Herries memoirs also state Huntly wanted to match her with his son, Findlater.

A controversial aspect of these events was that Huntly headed the most prominent Catholic family in Scotland, and scholars have charged that Mary destroyed him because of his opposition to her plans for meeting with Elizabeth. That she invited Randolph to join her progress does seem to lend credence to this claim. It remains true, however, that Huntly and his sons defied her, seized the master of her household's inheritance, refused her admission into Inverness Castle, threatened to abduct her, and rallied their allies, including John Gordon, 11th earl of Sutherland, to attack her forces. Since she delayed ordering Huntly declared a traitor until mid-October, she undoubtedly hoped to obtain his submission and avoid violence. Disregarding traditional practice, the Gordons chose not to retreat and end the conflict after encountering a larger armed force. The family's ruin created a power vacuum in the northeast that was not filled until 1565 when Mary responded to the challenge of the Chaseabout raiders by releasing Huntly's heir, who resumed control of his inheritance as the fifth earl and remained thereafter her loyal supporter. Later, as an English prisoner, she recalled that Huntly blamed Moray not her for his father's and brother's deaths.

THE CHÂTELARD INCIDENTS

That November while Mary was still on this progress, Châtelard reached Scotland, ending a one-year absence. Although he declared at his departure that he was leaving Scotland forever, he changed his mind and returned via London where he reportedly confided to a friend he was going to see his lady love. Having found Mary at Montrose on the 12th, he delivered to her from Damville a long letter, which according to Randolph, greatly pleased her. Indeed, she longed to receive news from France, and James Melville remembered that she enjoyed conversing with individuals returning from abroad. In late December Randolph reported that only one packet and two letters from France had arrived since Châtelard's return and that no prince received fewer messages from there than she. Lethington also complained about not hearing much news in their corner of the world. It is no wonder then that she rewarded Châtelard for bringing Damville's letter to her with a ride on a gelding presented to her by her half brother Lord Robert. Randolph did not report, as did others, who were not witnesses to their exchanges, that she gave her horse to the poet. Continuing toward Holyrood, she reached the palace by the 21st and succumbed to the influenza, called the New Acquaintance. There she was to face still another challenge to her honor.

In the next few weeks Randolph revealed no more information about Châtelard, although he noted that an illness kept Mary in bed for several days in January 1563. He later discovered that on 12 February before she left Holyrood on another progress, two chamberlains found Châtelard under her bed armed with his sword and dagger. After learning about this intrusion the next morning, Mary banished him from court. Undeterred he followed her to Dunfermline and apparently became persuaded that her anger had abated. On the 14th *en route* to St Andrews, she stopped at Rossend Castle, Burntisland, where, having hidden in a corner of her bedchamber, according to Randolph who was not present, Châtelard set upon her with such force and impudence that she and her two attendants cried for help. When Moray came to her rescue, she allegedly demanded that he stab Châtelard but her half brother arrested him instead, and on the 22nd the poet was executed at St Andrews. Meanwhile, Mary Fleming began sleeping in her mistress's bedchamber.

When Châtelard returned to France in 1561, he fought in the religious wars on behalf of the Huguenots, but his Protestantism did not prevent him from obsessing about his feelings for Mary. Knox and others charged her with somehow leading the poet on, accusations that highlighted the ambivalence about women at court, who were expected to please men but somehow to demonstrate a modesty that kept them at bay. It is noteworthy that although Randolph, unlike Knox, observed some of Mary's interactions with Châtelard, he did not accuse her of over-familiarity with the poet until after learning about the bedchamber confrontations.

In his writings Châtelard revealed that he played the lute for her, that she gave him a book by Petrarch, and that he read to her some of Ronsard's and Petrarch's poetry, the latter bringing tears to her eyes.

He never referred to any beguilement on her part but confessed only to suffering an unrequited passion for her. His obsession seems to have led him to follow or tail her; today we would say that he stalked her. Such individuals do not require encouragement; they inhabit a deluded world, focusing on their inner feelings and harassing their victims even after courts issue restraining orders. If he had ulterior motives for following her, the belief of Mary's Catholic friends that he meant to assassinate her seems implausible. He did admit, however, to attempting to sully her reputation in hopes of preventing her from remarrying. Perhaps he even thought that the bedchamber intrusions might make her feel compelled to wed him. Randolph regretted these attempts to dishonor Mary on whom he predicted a scar would ever remain.

Indeed, females often believe lewd attacks pollute them. Earlier in August 1562 when Mary was walking in Holyrood's garden with Sir Henry Sidney, who was sent by Elizabeth to explain why she was postponing their conference, a Captain Hepburn delivered a document to her. She handed it to Lord James, who opened it to discover four ribald verses and crude sketches of women's and men's genitalia. To provide a context for her offended reaction, candid treatments of sexual matters in medical books even horrified some members of the medical profession. The outraged Mary ordered the captain's arrest because she feared his lewd gift would in some sense cast doubts upon her honor, prompting individuals to wonder if she deserved to be so insulted.

Confirming Mary's concern for her honor, Lethington reported to Cecil in December 1564 that her reputation was dearer to her than her life. In May 1565 when outraged by her plans to wed Darnley, Randolph even claimed he previously had deemed her to be prudent, wise, and honorable in all matters and James Melville recalled in his memoirs that she detested all lewd and vicious people. In the future, she would have to deal with even more damaging attacks on her honor and reputation that would result in her flight to England and life imprisonment.

5

RULING SCOTLAND, 1563–66

In early 1563 Randolph reported that from the beginning of her sorrows, Mary had ridden restlessly from place to place hawking and hunting. During the previous six months, she had faced troubling times: Huntly's defeat at Corrichie, Châtelard's execution for secretly entering her bedchamber twice, and the duke of Guise's death on 24 February during the first of the French religious wars. After accompanying her to Falkland on 19 March, Randolph departed for St Andrews. Six days later Mary journeyed to Petlethie, Moray's residence some four miles from St Andrews. As Randolph dined with her there on the 29th, a packet arrived from France notifying her of the death on 6 March of her uncle, Francis, the Grand Prior, which her concerned attendants had been concealing from her. She shed tears during the reading of his testament, displaying grief that was undoubtedly sincere although his high rank also deserved this emotional reaction. When Catherine de' Medici learned of Guise's death, for example, she wept and fainted.

Because of her French upbringing, it is appropriate in judging Mary's personal rule to examine a schedule Catherine recommended to Charles IX that was based on his father's routine. After the morning *lever*, he met for an hour or two with the *conseil des affaires*, a small advisory body, to hear despatches requiring his attention. At 10:00 a.m. he attended mass and by 11:00 a.m. had dined. Then, twice weekly he held audiences for an hour or two; at that same time the *conseil privé*, his larger council, convened, but he needed to attend it only occasionally. In the afternoons when unengaged in these affairs, he enjoyed free time, although at 3:00 p.m. on two or three days, he entertained his nobility with sports and other exercises. Every evening he supped with his family and twice weekly gave a ball.[1]

This document not only informs about Mary's understanding of how French kings obtained counsel but also offers evidence that is useful in highlighting the diversity of early modern royal routines. Unlike France, England had only one small advisory council, called the privy council, the meetings of which its queens regnant, Mary and Elizabeth Tudor, rarely attended. When Philip II was resident in England, he met with his wife's privy council, pointing out that this was a masculine task. Scotland also had only one small advisory council, the privy council, sometimes called the secret council.

During Mary's personal rule, she did not substitute French governmental practices for Scottish ones. To be sure, her household continued to be largely Catholic and French, although containing some Italian members, but her realm was already familiar with French culture; her father's court, especially after his marriages, has been described as Franco-Scots. Her mother Mary of Guise had also served as her regent from 1554 to 1560.

Like their French counterparts, Scottish rulers were more visible and accessible to their subjects than English rulers. Beginning in Henry VII's reign, Tudor monarchs routinely withdrew at mealtime to their privy chamber, its staff carefully monitoring those approaching the royal presence. Neither the French nor the Scottish court developed a department equivalent to the English privy chamber. Like the Valois kings, Mary dined daily in open court. She also conducted much of her business in her bedchamber, conferring with her council and even ambassadors while resting in bed. In contrast to her mainly French household, she filled governmental offices, including the privy council, mostly with Protestant Scotsmen.

No agenda comparable to the above French royal schedule exists for Scotland, but two extant documents are revealing about its monarchs' activities.[2] The first is a poem in the *Bannatyne Manuscript*, an invaluable collection of late medieval Scottish poetry, which confirms that rulers should entertain their nobility with sports and games. In January 1560 Makgill, clerk register, and Bellenden, justice clerk, composed the second manuscript, the *Discours Particulier D'Écosse*, which Mary of Guise sent to French officials, who were considering a charge of treason against Châtelherault after he joined the Congregation. Besides treason law, the document details crown revenue and the legal system.

Whether or not Mary was aware of these documents, she gained a practical understanding of royal procedures from observing her father-in-law's and husband's habits. Indeed, when her mother notified her in France that Huntly was petitioning for the reversion of an office, Mary responded that Henry always waited until possessors died before designating their successors. Even so she did not require a routine for council meetings echoing French custom.

In 1561 her privy councilors agreed to meet daily from 8:00–10:00 a.m. and from 1:00–3:00 p.m. in the council chamber unless she summoned them to her. They decided that six of their noble members should reside at court, but it was difficult for so many to be present especially during the summertime; on 10 August 1562, for example, only one was in attendance. To remedy this problem, eight councilors amended the procedures on the 15th, naming three slates of four noblemen to alternate staying at court for two-month periods. Their meeting times were rescheduled to 8:00–11:00 a.m. and 2:00–5:00 p.m. on Mondays, Tuesdays, Thursdays, and Saturdays. Unfortunately, the privy council register is incomplete; in 1563, for example, it contains one meeting for April and none for May. Nevertheless, it seems likely that noble participation remained erratic in Scotland as it did in other realms, partly because the men understood they could gain more from personal attendance on the monarch than sitting for long periods at the council table.[3]

Although the guidelines did not address Mary's presence in the council chamber, historians have concluded that she was an unsuccessful ruler partly because she appeared at only a few of the meetings listed in the register. A comparison of her record to her son James VI's, who is usually judged a competent Scottish ruler, casts serious doubts on the register's use as negative evidence for her governance. From 1585 for several years when he was about her age, his attendance at the sessions printed in the register was not much greater than hers. Only in the 1590s did he meet with his council regularly.

The condemnatory studies of Mary's rule have overlooked Randolph's references to her habit of seeking her councilors' advice.

Although her motivations and the rationale behind her comments frequently eluded him, he usually knew her whereabouts and sometimes the nature of her business. He observed that she often attended part of the council meetings and sewed while listening to the discussions. She may have learned this practice from observing Catherine, who embroidered every afternoon while heeding conversations around her. A non-threatening female activity, it afforded her opportunities to hear as well as to conceal her reaction to others' opinions.

The register's inadequacies become more obvious when searching in it for the specific meetings Randolph identified. In late 1561 he named five occasions when Mary sat with her council that are missing from the register. On 22 October he reported that he was with her and the councilors in the council chamber, but the register lacks an entry for that date. Subsequently, he referred to other unrecorded gatherings.

When absent, she could have been disposing of more pressing business. On 17 February 1566 she informed Sir Robert Melville, her English ambassador and the brother of James, that she had just pardoned John Johnston, an Edinburgh lawyer, for delivering funds the previous summer from Randolph to Lady Moray for the use of her husband, who was organizing a rebellion to protest Mary's wedding to Darnley. Since Randolph was conferring with the council during her audience with Johnston, Mary continued, she was able immediately to remind him of Elizabeth's promise not to aid her rebels and to banish him from her realm.[4] Randolph's meeting with the council is missing from the register.

Sir Thomas Craig, a Protestant and the crown advocate in Mary's reign as well as the justice depute for the justice general in criminal cases, praised both his queen's and Elizabeth's interactions with their councilors. In a treatise defending James's accession as king of England, which was written before 1603 but not published until the eighteenth century, Craig reminisced about Mary:

> I have often heard the most serene Princess Mary queen of Scotland, discourse so appositely and rationally in all affairs which were brought before the privy council, that she was admired by all; and when most of the councillors were silent; being astonished, or straight declared themselves of her opinion, she rebuked them sharply, and exhorted them to speak freely, as becomes unprejudiced councillors, against her opinion,

that the best reasons only might overrule their determinations: And truly her reasonings were so strong and clear, that she could turn the hearers to what side she pleased . . . ;

He further complimented her understanding of equity and justice:

She had not studied Law, and yet by the natural light of her judgment, when she reasoned of matters of equity and justice, she oft times had the advantage of the ablest Lawyers, her other discourses and actions were suitable to her great judgment, No word ever dropped from her mouth that was not exactly weighed and pondered. As for her liberality and other virtues, they were well known.[5]

Best known for claiming a common origin for Scottish and English feudal law in *Jus Feudale*, Craig was the only Scottish legal expert to gain a European audience. Recent academic historians, such as Jenny Wormald, who denounced Mary's personal rule, and John Guy, who admired her governance skills but failed to discuss her council attendance, have ignored the importance of Craig's comments.[6]

Another of Mary's royal responsibilities was the convening of legislative and advisory bodies: altogether she held five parliaments or conventions in six years.[7] On 26 May 1563 wearing her crown and royal robes, she processed into the parliament house to open her first parliament, the most important of her personal rule. With an attendance of 78, it was also slightly larger than the usual 50–60 membership. Before her marched Châtelherault with the crown, Argyll with the scepter, and Moray with the sword. In honoring these noblemen, she confirmed publicly her practice of relying on the advice of Protestants. After delivering an oration, she attended daily the debates of the lords of articles, the parliamentary steering committee preparing the legislation for the full body's approval. She also witnessed the condemnations of Huntly, his corpse displayed in a coffin, the exiled Sutherland, and 11 others. By touching bills with her scepter, she assented to several laws, among them, declaring it a capital crime to practice witchcraft, sorcery, or necromancy and to commit adultery, and ordering the confiscation of the property of individuals bringing false coins into the realm.

Despite having refused to ratify the Reformation acts of 1560,

Mary's support for the Protestant settlement and her failure to advance Catholicism beyond retaining mass privately at court, had gained her the trust of moderate reformers. These strategies had enabled her to avoid an unwanted confrontation at this, her first parliament, with the extremists who had expected her to confirm the Reformation acts. Even her half brother Moray would have needed to call upon the moderates she had conciliated had he attempted to impose the Kirk's agenda at this parliament. By avoiding religious enactments in 1563, Mary kept her ability to promote compromise and maintain the viability of her personal worship at court.

It is possible that she summoned Knox to Lochleven, where she held court in April, with this future parliament in mind. The interview was the only one of the four with him that did not respond to an attack of his on her or her faith. It was also the only one occurring on two consecutive days. Her stated reason for seeing him shortly after the 11th, Easter Sunday, was to request he persuade his people not to penalize Catholics for following their religious beliefs. She was especially concerned about numerous priests imprisoned for celebrating Easter mass. As anyone could easily have predicted, Knox demanded the punishment of all lawbreakers.

The next morning in a more conciliatory mood, she promised to punish all who celebrated or attended mass except at court. At that time, she also discussed with him the marital problems of the earl of Argyll and his countess, her illegitimate half sister. Perhaps, she created the opportunity for this interview, just a few weeks before the opening of parliament, to pledge her support for the Reformation acts to one of her loudest critics, who would reveal her comments to his Protestant friends. Certainly, Knox claimed that she subsequently incarcerated John Hamilton, archbishop of St Andrews, the illegitimate brother of Châtelherault, and 47 other priests for saying mass outside her court because of the scheduled parliamentary meeting.

Knox, himself, chose to take advantage of the legislative session to preach against her and her faith, possibly on 30 May, the last Sunday before parliament was dissolved. In his sermon before most of the lords, he warned that if she married an infidel, a favorite name of his for a Catholic, she would endanger Scottish Protestantism. When summoning him to Holyrood, Mary must have felt particular annoyance since she had just promised him in April to support the Reformation acts and since he seemed to be attempting to generate parliamentary opposition to Catholicism. To her tearful questioning of what business he had referring to her marriage, he retorted that he was one of her subjects. In similar circumstances Elizabeth insisted on enforcing the sedition statute passed in her sister Mary's reign against John Stubbs, who lost his right hand for publishing a treatise opposing her marriage to a French prince. The difference in the two queen's reactions indicates not only that England's monarchy was more powerful than Scotland's but also that Knox held a more influential leadership position among Scottish Protestants than Stubbs among English Puritans.

A later dispute in 1563 concerning Holyrood's Catholic services led to another confrontation between Mary and Knox. In August Patrick Cranstoun and Andrew Armstrong were arrested for entering the palace on the 15th in her absence to identify Edinburgh citizens attending mass. The incarceration of the two men prompted Knox on 8 October to summon his brothers in the faith to Edinburgh on the 24th, when their trial was scheduled, to advance the glory of God, the safety of their imprisoned colleagues, their own security, and even the preservation of the Kirk. In December the privy councilors summoned him to a meeting in the presence of the queen for which his reminiscences are the only transcript, as the register lacks references to it. They asked whether he had convoked his brothers to raise a riot or for religious purposes. If the latter goal were intended, as he claimed, he had not committed treason. To Mary's complaint that he accused her of cruelty, he replied he had only charged with cruelty the wicked Papists who caused her to have the men incarcerated without reason. After he departed, the councilors voted against accusing him of treason, greatly displeasing Lethington and others, whom Knox denounced as court flatterers. The queen then passed to her private chambers, but Lethington presently decided to request her return for another tally, which only reaffirmed the earlier decision. That two votes were taken, which overrode the opinion of Lethington and apparently the queen, indicates that the Scottish councilors had considerably more influence than their English counterparts. As noted earlier, Elizabeth rarely attended council meetings, usually relying on the more flexible practice of discussions with one advisor or two or three of them at a time to frame public policy.

Because Knox did not witness the dispute, whether Mary and

Lethington were as offended as he claimed cannot be confirmed. Craig's statements about her influence with the councilors were probably too favorable, but Knox's negative account was surely exaggerated. It is more likely that she and the councilors reached the consensus that official action against him would prove to be a divisive step, both religiously and politically. In practical terms it would have been extremely difficult, if not impossible, on the basis of this evidence to empanel an assize or jury that would actually convict a leading reformed preacher like Knox of treason. If a trial were held, even before the verdict was reached, the government would probably have had to deal with Protestant riots.

In March 1564, three months later, Randolph repeated rumors that the queen was aggrieved to learn that Knox, who was about 50, intended to marry 17-year-old Margaret Stewart, the daughter of Andrew, second Lord Ochiltree, because his bride was of Mary's blood and name. It would be reasonable to assume that when Mary learned about it, regardless of her reaction to Knox's proposed wedding, she also recalled her earlier audience with him concerning his public denunciation of her possible marriage to a Catholic.

Despite these troubles, Mary continued to address legislative and legal matters. In 1566, recognizing that Scotland's laws needed to be made available in an accurate version, she assigned this task to a commission, whose members included Balfour, Leslie, and Edward Henryson. Their deliberations resulted in Henryson's publication of the first complete edition of the acts of parliament, a milestone in the history and use of statutory law. It became known as the *Black Acts* because of the blackness of the type in which it was printed. A copy of the volume at the British Library, which was especially bound for Mary in dark brown calf, is one of only seven books that have survived from her library.[8]

Randolph's dispatches reveal that Mary also took great interest in the courts of law adjudicating civil matters. In March 1563 by her council's advice, she entered the Edinburgh Tolbooth to expedite the court of session's disposition of poor people's bills. She instructed the lords thereafter to hear cases three days a week, both mornings and afternoons, and enlarged their stipends accordingly. Her contemporaries expected royal women to have special concern for poor people's problems, and Randolph later noted approvingly other occasions when she attended the session to hear their petitions. In 1563, furthermore, to replace the old ecclesiastical courts, she signed a charter erecting the commissary court of Edinburgh, which possessed original jurisdiction in questions of testaments, succession, and marital relations, and appellate authority over provincial commissariats. Her decision with the council's advice to collect one-third of the revenues of benefices has previously been cited. She also utilized her resources for charitable and patronage purposes: in 1563 funding five bursaries for poor students at the University of Glasgow and granting the property of Edinburgh's Dominican friary to the burgh for the foundation of a poor hospital, in 1564 giving the temporalities of the Abbey of Crossraguel in Ayrshire to Buchanan and an annual pension for life to James White for the study of good letters, and in 1566 granting monastic revenue to the city of Glasgow to support its ministers.

An important Scottish criterion for rating the success of their monarchs was their willingness to be seen going on progresses and dispensing justice throughout the realm. Travel was extremely difficult and slow-going, the rough terrain and inadequate road system requiring individuals to ride on horseback. In her short personal rule Mary stayed with 82 hosts in all sections of Scotland, except the Northern Isles, the Hebrides, and the northwest Highlands. Riding sidesaddle on her horse, the mode she learned in France, she covered some 1,200 miles between August 1562 and September 1563, penetrating into the north, the south, and the west. In 54 days between July and September 1564, she traveled 460 miles, reaching Inverness for a second time, honoring her hosts by instructing her court to wear Highland dress; in early 1565 she journeyed into Fife as far as Balmerino Abbey and in the summer made her way to Dunkeld and Perth. In 1566 she held a justice ayre at Jedburgh. Most of the lords she visited on these journeys later supported her during the civil wars that were fought after her flight to England.

MARRIAGE PROPOSALS

Meanwhile in 1563 when Knox was warning Mary against marrying a Catholic, Lorraine was attempting to match her with Archduke

Charles, who, he believed, would assist her in governing Scotland. In early 1563 Lorraine left the Council at Trent to confer with Emperor Ferdinand at Innsbruck, but her uncle had small chance of success. James Melville returned home in early 1564 claiming that Maximilian, the emperor's heir, opposed his brother's union with her. Mary did not favor Charles because he lived in a remote country without adequate resources to advance her affairs. Although aware of her lack of interest, Lorraine was still assuring Pius IV in late 1564 that she would only be able to re-establish Catholicism if she married Charles.

While Lorraine's priority was finding a Catholic husband to assist her in governing Scotland, Mary's goal was to connect her realm and ultimately England to the Netherlands by marrying Don Carlos, whom she hoped his father would name as the regent at Brussels. The resulting composite monarchy had the potential of becoming even grander when he succeeded his father as Spain's monarch. In June 1563 Philip agreed to commence secret marriage negotiations with her primarily to distract her from a French alliance. For about a year her envoys, including Pierre Raulet, her secretary for French affairs, discussed the match with Philip's ambassadors in the Netherlands, England, and France, since he did not maintain a Scottish embassy.

In August 1564 Philip decided to end the discussions, using as his excuse Lorraine's attempts to marry her to his cousin, the archduke, whom he was loath to offend. Worried that her uncle's diplomacy might thwart her ambitions, she had shown Randolph a letter in March from Lorraine in which he denied seeking her alliance with Charles. Either his letter was forged, the more likely possibility, or he was being disingenuous. Other evidence indicates he pressed for this marriage. Mary also publicly complained about her uncle's unkindness, knowing that her comments would circulate in the diplomatic rumor mill. Her tactics did not and, indeed, could not serve to change Philip's decision about Don Carlos marrying her. The king did not intend to match anyone with his ill son, who behaved erratically even before he hit his head in a fall. In late 1567 Philip locked him in a chamber where he died a few months later.

Philip had worried needlessly about Mary's selecting a French husband. Catherine opposed Mary's alliance with both her son Charles and Don Carlos and dispatched Mauvissière in mid 1564 to offer another son, the duke of Anjou. Mary declined the proposal, explaining that

France was dear to her because she had been its queen, but she would not return to a position inferior to the one she previously held and risk the loss of Scotland. She also confirmed to Mauvissière her interest in Don Carlos especially if he should move to the Netherlands.

In 1563 concerned that Mary might wed Don Carlos or the arch-duke, Elizabeth intervened in the negotiations. She instructed Randolph to warn Mary against selecting either candidate and to offer her any English nobleman, but if she must marry abroad, she should choose someone below princely rank. After Mary repeated this message to Argyll, he asked if the queen of England had become a man, mean-ing that no English person, except Elizabeth, was worthy of his queen. When they speculated about which candidate was meant, Randolph noted that none guessed Robert Dudley, Elizabeth's master of the horse, some suggested his brother, Ambrose, earl of Warwick, but most named Darnley. Randolph also predicted that she would not debase herself by marrying anyone of a lesser rank than hers.

In March 1564 following further instructions, he revealed to Mary that Elizabeth was recommending Dudley to her. When she asked why it stood with her honor to accept him, Randolph responded that the match might bring England to her. Many Scots opposed her selecting someone of Dudley's inferior lineage, but it is true that when Jane Grey attempted to become queen in 1553, she was married to his brother, Guildford.

To make Dudley more acceptable to Mary, Elizabeth ennobled him as the earl of Leicester. James Melville witnessed the ceremony in September 1564 and recalled in his memoirs without criticism that she lightly touched the earl's neck, an intimate gesture that was not part of the usual protocol. Interpreting this behavior as a spontaneous display of her feelings, some writers have argued that Elizabeth was insincere in offering Dudley to Mary. If they are correct, the public behavior the ambassador observed not only revealed Elizabeth's deceit but also con-stituted an insult to Scotland and its queen. Considering the nature of court etiquette, this gesture was more likely a deliberate act to convey visually to Melville that Elizabeth's esteem for Dudley, if Mary accepted his suit, would ensure amicable relations between their realms. Almost always a breach of protocol was not the result of spon-taneous behavior.

The governments arranged for Bedford and Randolph to confer

about the marriage with Moray and Lethington at Berwick in November. There the Scotsmen's hopes were dashed. Mary would only wed Leicester if Elizabeth promised legislation naming her the heir apparent, a commitment her cousin consistently refused to make. The petition of Elizabeth's second parliament, requesting her to name a successor, may have fueled Mary's resolve for statutory validation. One member, John Hales, the clerk of the Hanaper, wrote a controversial treatise, *A Declaration of the Succession of the Crown Imperial of England*, a copy of which Lethington obtained. In it, Hales validated the claims of Catherine Grey, whose succession rights were recognized in Henry VIII's will, and argued that Elizabeth should legitimize her two sons. He also denounced the pretensions of the foreign-born Mary, whose family rights Henry ignored, and claimed even if that king's will were invalidated, Edward III's statute of 1351, barring alien inheritance applied to the crown. When learning about the tract in 1564, Elizabeth ordered Hales imprisoned, although his ideas reflected the views of many parliamentary members as well as many privy councilors.

After parliament failed again in 1566 to persuade Elizabeth to marry or name a successor, Edmund Plowden, a lawyer of the Middle Temple, responded to Hales's tract *in A Treatise . . . Proving the Queen of Scots by her Birth is Not Disabled by the Law of England to Receive the Crown of England*. In it, Plowden denied that Edward III's statute, establishing exceptions to the common law ruling that aliens could not inherit in England, affected the royal succession. The statute exempted from the prohibition concerning alien inheritance both the children of English kings wherever and whenever they were born and the children of parents in allegiance to English monarchs who were born abroad. He argued that this inheritance rule and the statute were applicable to bodies natural but not to the crown, the body politic, and its succession.

In December 1564 as this debate was raging in England, the disappointed Moray and Lethington explained to Cecil that Mary would swear obedience for life to Leicester, becoming in a sense his slave or "thrall" while Elizabeth needed only to confirm her cousin's succession claims, a concession that would not adversely affect her during her lifetime. Mary may have guessed that Leicester was a reluctant suitor because he still hoped to wed his monarch, but she continued to pursue the marriage with him, hoping to obtain official confirmation of her English succession rights.[9]

ROYAL COURT

While this diplomacy was underway, Mary went on progresses and supervised court activities. In February 1564 her four Maries swore to remain single until she remarried. Although Livingston broke her vow when she wed John Sempill of Beltries in March 1565, the approving queen funded her dowry and wedding costs. Two other Maries took husbands only after her own remarriage, Beaton wedding Alexander Ogilvy of Boyne in 1566 and Fleming marrying Lethington in 1567. Except for Fleming's wedding that followed Calvinist tradition and was not celebrated with dancing, Buchanan composed masques to honor these occasions. Mary Seton, who joined her mistress in England in 1568, remained single.

Mary Stewart was the first Scottish monarch to use regularly the imperial title of majesty rather than grace, adopting, as were other contemporary monarchs, the style and protocol of the Holy Roman Emperor. She also observed traditional royal etiquette, which was especially visible in dining procedures. Here and at other courts, eating habits defined and authenticated social status. At the formal midday dinners, food from her table was passed downward to other tables following the hierarchical guidelines regulating seating. For example, at the table next to Mary's sat nine ladies, including the four Maries, and at a more distant table sat 19 valets of the chamber, among them the French and English musicians and Riccio, who entered her court in 1561. Occasionally, Mary invited Randolph to her table not to privilege him personally but to honor his queen.[10]

The kind of food served varied, depending on the diners' status. The queen and those seated nearest her in the chamber would have enjoyed the food usually provided in elite Scottish households. They would have consumed wine, ale, meats, and bread, but humble servants dining in other rooms partook only of bread and ale. The meats included beef, veal, mutton, poultry, seafood, and wild game that Mary took delight in hunting.[11]

The queen enjoyed outdoor and indoor entertainments. All her palaces possessed gardens in which she took walks and practiced archery, usually shooting at the butts (mounds on which targets were erected). In April 1562 Randolph observed her and Patrick, the future sixth Lord Lindsay of the Byres, competing against Moray and his wife in this archery contest. As the roads were primitive, she mostly traveled on horseback. When Elizabeth granted her a license in 1561 to obtain six or eight geldings, Lethington responded that she needed at least 15 or 16.

Randolph characterized her indoor pastimes as pleasant and comely. Despite Knox's complaints, the ambassador recorded only occasional festivities. He noted banqueting, masking, and running at the ring in early May 1563, probably in celebration of May Day. Annually on 6 January, Twelfth Day, her courtiers played a game in which the person who found a bean concealed in a cake reigned as the night's sovereign. In 1564 the queen permitted the winner, Mary Fleming, to dress in her robes and jewels. For that night and for two succeeding nights, Buchanan composed Latin verses for the banquet servers to sing. In February 1564 before Shrovetide, she hosted a feast that Randolph judged as sumptuous as those usually honoring royal marriages. The following October after Lennox returned ending a 20-year absence, Mary, while masked, lost to him in a dice game a crystal jewel set in gold.

Six months later at Stirling on Easter Monday, 1565, Mary and her ladies twice dressed up as bourgeois wives and walked out to take pledges from individuals for a coin to attend her banquets, which were held at the house where Randolph usually stayed. To the guests' amazement, she hosted the meals as their queen. In July 1565 about two weeks before their wedding, she strolled with Darnley twice into Edinburgh in disguise. Early modern monarchs often favored incognito visits with local people, avoiding the pomp and ceremony required for royal appearances. The disguises also provided them opportunities to be judged for their virtue rather than their lineage or status.

During quiet moments Mary studied languages and history. With Buchanan after dinner, she read Livy; one lesson included the Oppian Law, a criticism of women's finery and a denunciation of their wielding political power. During the negotiations with Philip in 1564, she was observed studying Spanish. She also indicated a willingness to learn about other religions. When a copy of Theodore de Beza's oration to the Gallic religious assembly at Poissy was forwarded to her in 1561, she and Elboeuf read it, and Buchanan dedicated an edition of his Latin paraphrases of the Psalms to her in 1564. She also owned a copy of the reformer, Peter Martyr's treatise on the sacrament, which, of course, denied Catholic doctrine.

Several Scotsmen besides Buchanan composed poetry at her court, which was culturally as important and up to date as her father's more famous one. As a New Year's gift in 1562, Alexander Scott, her court's most outstanding vernacular poet and a canon of the chapel royal at Stirling, wrote a poem welcoming her home. Alexander Seton penned elegant Latin verses, and the important heterogeneous *Bannatyne Manuscript* was collected by 1568. In addition, Alexander Montgomerie, an imitator of Ronsard's style, and John Stewart of Baldynneis, a translator of Ariosto, were at her court but which, if any, of their compositions can be traced to her reign has not been established. Foreign scholars also visited her: Charles Utenhove, a Greek writer who probably reached Scotland in 1563, composed a sonnet for her, and Pietro Bizarri, an Italian Protestant who arrived in 1564, dedicated his *De Bello ac Pace* to her. He later testified that "she was beloved and esteemed in the highest degree by the whole kingdom and that the island enjoyed her most prudent and courageous government."[12]

HEALTH PROBLEMS

Meanwhile she continued to endure bouts of ill health. An indisposition in June 1563 briefly kept her bedridden, but her first serious attack in Scotland occurred that December. Her attendants believed her excessive dancing on her birthday caused her sickness, but Randolph, noting that during the past two months she had often wept without cause, thought she caught cold from lingering too long at divine service or from her despair at failing to arrange her marriage. Although still unwell on 11 December she invited Randolph to her chamber to accept a ring from Elizabeth that she kissed several times signaling her desire for the friendship that this gift customarily validated. She possessed two jewels, she explained, that she would keep until her death, this one and a ring from Francis. By the 21st she was complaining of a pain near her spleen, which the physicians treated as a symptom of melancholy, since they believed an excessive display of emotion adversely affected the spleen. For several days, she underwent purgations to cleanse her body through bowel movements, and her attendants feared for her life, but she soon began to recover and was completely healed by February 1564.

END OF THE EARLIER COURTSHIPS AND DARNLEY'S ARRIVAL

By the end of 1564 both Mary's Spanish and English marriage negotiations had stalled, but she did not relinquish hope that one of them might still have a successful outcome. While communications with England continued, Mary tried deceptive politics with Spain. She required her French resident ambassador, James Beaton, archbishop of Glasgow, to schedule audiences with Catherine in January 1565 to delude others, particularly Philip, into believing that a French marriage was afoot.[13] In the meantime, she began to consider marrying a bridegroom of Scottish and English descent.

That in February 1565 Darnley joined his father in Scotland to recover their family estates proved to be timely for their royal ambitions. Although Lennox, an English subject, had repeatedly petitioned Mary to restore his property, his requests only won serious attention in June 1563 when Elizabeth recommended that Mary give positive consideration to returning his lands that were forfeited in 1544. Since then, Lennox's foe, Châtelherault, remained in possession of his estates despite conspiring against Mary of Guise's authority. Sympathetic to the Hamiltons, Randolph challenged Lennox's reinstatement not from fear that Mary might wed his son but from concerns about internal dissension. When Elizabeth retracted her permission for Lennox's departure, Lethington and Moray protested that Protestantism's survival did not depend upon his absence and that Mary considered a breach of promise as dishonorable. Elizabeth relented, and Lennox arrived at Edinburgh in September 1564, having left his family behind as hostages. Mary attempted to reconcile him and Châtelherault, but the offended duke only belatedly attended the December parliament that ratified her restoration of the earl's title and estates. As she explained, since Lennox was of her blood and name, she could not be so unkind as to refuse his petition.

When he requested permission for Darnley to join him so that they could be enfeoffed in their property together, a common legal procedure, Elizabeth assented, still retaining his mother as hostage. Later after Mary and he were wed, some contemporaries, including Elizabeth, charged that Mary solicited Darnley's visit because she believed his lineage made him an eligible husband for her.[14] After reaching Edinburgh in February 1565 and learning that Mary was at the castle of Sir John Wemyss, her lieutenant in Fife, Darnley, who was three years her junior, crossed over to the northern side of the Firth of Forth and met with her on the 17th. According to James Melville, who surely could not remember her precise words, she exclaimed that he was "the lustiest and best proportioned long man that she had ever seen; for he was of a high stature, long and small, even and erect, and from his youth well instructed in all honest and homely exercises."[15]

Biographers who believe she was enamored with Darnley assume that the word, lustiest, referred to his sexual allure. *A Dictionary of the Older Scottish Tongue*, however, contains numerous definitions for lust, including among others: cheerful, light-hearted persons, filled with or giving pleasure, delightful to look at, lovely faces, good-looking people, handsome, gallant, dashing, well-built, sturdy men, vigorous, healthy people, even fair, gallant ships, and finally, carnal, sensual pleasures.

Melville's usage of this word seems similar to Randolph's, who referred to Mary as lustier, probably meaning more vigorous or healthier, than she was before leaving to brave the winter storms. Earlier, in response to Elizabeth's remark that he preferred Darnley to Leicester as Mary's spouse, Melville characterized the young man as inappropriate for a woman of spirit because he was more like a woman than a man, lusty, beardless, and with the face of a lady. In the sixteenth century, facial hair was thought to confer masculinity: the beard made the man. Later, Robert Melville even called the infant James lusty. On 18 February, meanwhile, Darnley departed to visit his father who was at Dunkeld with their kinsman, the earl of Atholl, but returned to Wemyss on the 24th and traveled with Mary to Holyrood. Two days later in a conciliatory gesture, he attended Knox's service with Moray before going to Holyrood and dancing a galliard with her.

During the next few weeks while Darnley attended court daily, Mary still hoped that Elizabeth would agree to obtain official recognition of her English succession rights, making it possible for her to marry Leicester. On 16 March Mary received extremely disappointing news. Elizabeth sent a letter, informing her cousin that she would not allow her successor to be named until she decided not to marry or notified her determination not to marry. After a tearful audience with her about Elizabeth's decision, Randolph reported that Mary's grief sprang from the "dishonor and shame" she felt from having been so deceived.[16]

From Darnley's arrival, Randolph carefully monitored Mary's behavior toward him. On 15 March he assured Cecil he saw no great "goodwill borne to him" and on the 31st informed Henry Sidney that he had seen no evidence that Mary's heart was affected.[17] On the latter day Randolph traveled with the court to Stirling where he continued to observe Mary's interactions with Darnley; the ambassador and his partner, Mary Beaton, defeated the two of them in a game of billiards called biles. Shortly thereafter, Darnley contracted a serious case of measles but was past danger by 6 April.

By then Randolph had detected a change in Mary's treatment of Darnley. The ambassador was astounded to learn that she was greatly honoring the ailing patient by sending him food from her own table. Later, because Darnley continued to suffer pains in his stomach and head, she delayed departing for Perth.

After 16 March, the day that the greatly disappointed Mary had received Elizabeth's written refusal to name her successor, the Scottish queen had been considering measures that might change her cousin's mind. She probably demonstrated a public interest in Darnley in early April because she was finalizing plans to send Lethington to London for discussions with English officials about marrying Leicester. Her behavior toward Darnley, which she knew Randolph would reveal to his government, can be interpreted as a warning that she had a groom in reserve if arrangements to wed Leicester could not be worked out to her satisfaction.

Reaching London in mid-April, Lethington discussed the Don Carlos match with Diego Guzman de Silva, dean of Toledo, the Spanish ambassador, and Mary's succession claims with English officials. Lethington's instructions required him to discover if Mary's diplomatic ploy in January to make Philip believe she was arranging a French alliance had caused him to rethink his previous rejection of her marriage to Don Carlos. Lethington dispatched de Silva's and Elizabeth's responses, which reached Stirling on 3 May, that Philip would not reopen the negotiations[18] and that Elizabeth would not name Mary as her successor.

While Lethington was checking on the viability of her English and Spanish courtships in London, Cecil was digesting Randolph's dispatch, written at Berwick on the 15th, that Mary was favoring Darnley over all other suitors. When questioned about this report, Lethington confirmed Randolph's assertions but denied the rumors that Darnley's relatives had been spreading in England that she risked her life to "attend upon him" with "much diligence" during his infectious bout.[19] Overlooking this denial, all her recent biographers, including Antonia Fraser, Jenny Wormald, and John Guy have credited the rumors that she fell in love with Darnley while nursing him. As a queen regnant in this hierarchical, honor-driven culture, Mary would have seriously damaged her reputation by attending to the medical needs of a young, unmarried man. It should also be noted that it is usually the grateful patient not the nurse who falls in love.

A concerned Elizabeth decided to send Throckmorton to warn Mary not to wed Darnley. In the ambassador's initial instructions, drafted by Cecil on 24 April, can be found the confirmation that Lethington was denying that Mary attended to her ailing suitor. Two letters Cecil recently received from Berwick had alerted him to this rumored behavior. On the 18th Bedford related that the bearer of Lennox's letter reporting on Darnley's convalescence claimed she risked her health to visit him during his illness, and on the 23rd Randolph stated enigmatically that the greatest and fairest often visited the ailing Darnley. It is noteworthy that Bedford, Randolph, and Cecil never used the word *nurse* in these documents. Indeed, in Randolph's dispatches of the 7th and the 15th, written after he left Stirling on the 6th, he failed to refer either to her *nursing* or to her attendance on Darnley. The news he forwarded on the 23rd about her visits to Darnley was from others' reports and not from personal observation.[20]

Randolph's dispatches reporting that she was favoring Darnley and contemplating marriage to him probably caught Elizabeth and her councilors by surprise. They did not confirm Throckmorton's final instructions until 2 May. Their concern about Guise influence on Mary was seemingly more significant for the fears that it aroused in them about her completing a foreign Catholic marriage than for its actual effect on her decisions. Cecil probably met Francis, the Grand Prior, and Elboeuf when Elizabeth entertained them at her court as they returned overland to France in 1561 and 1562. Any discussions Cecil and Elizabeth might have held with them neither diminished the secretary's firm belief in the existence of a Guise conspiracy to destroy Protestantism nor the queen's opinion that Mary's uncles were the ones mainly responsible for her assumption of England's royal arms. Some foreign diplomats were predicting that the Guises would choose Mary's next husband, an opinion expressed by Randolph, who had greatly criticized Elboeuf in his dispatches. In 1563 partly in response to Lorraine's attempts to match Mary with the archduke, Elizabeth had agreed to reopen marriage negotiations with the Austrian prince.

In 1564 Randolph did report troubling gossip to Cecil. Many Scots, he claimed, believed that when their queen invited Mary to wed any appropriate Englishmen, she actually meant Darnley; the ambassador had also heard that they believed Mary preferred Darnley to the other English candidates. Despite these and other rumors, Elizabeth relied on her ambassador's assurances that her cousin would never marry beneath the rank of prince and ennobled Dudley to make him more acceptable to her. In September 1565 two months after Mary wed Darnley, Cecil was still complaining about the inequality of the match, and when Mary was her prisoner, Elizabeth continued to accuse her of enticing her English subject to Scotland and marrying him without her permission.

Throckmorton's initial instructions on 24 April directed him to warn Mary to wed Leicester rather than Darnley, but if she must choose a foreign prince, she could marry Condé. Apparently, this Huguenot's name surfaced because after his wife died in 1564, Elizabeth's advisors heard that Lorraine was recommending him to his niece. Following discussions with Paul de Foix, the French ambassador, Cecil dropped this option from Throckmorton's final instructions, dated 2 May, which ordered him to inform Mary that she was free to marry any English nobleman except Darnley. However, only if she wed Leicester, whom Elizabeth regarded as if he were her own son and whose virtues she esteemed, would she permit an inquiry into Mary's English succession rights or a publication of her claims to the throne.

After receiving Lethington's negative messages from London on 3 May about both her inheritance claims and the Spanish marriage, Mary planned on the 15th to grant Darnley the lordship of Ardmanoch and the earldom of Ross and to knight 14 men, nominated by Lennox, and scheduled on the 16th to advance Darnley to the dukedom of Albany. When Throckmorton reached Stirling on the 15th and found the gates closed to him, he retired under protest to await her summons to an audience, as he still hoped to prevent Darnley's ennoblement. Later that day, Mary explained to Throckmorton that she informed Elizabeth as soon as she had decided to marry Darnley, but she promised to delay the ducal ceremony until after receiving further communications from her cousin.

Mary then sought her privy council's approval for her decision to wed Darnley, but without the presence of Moray, who had left court greatly offended by her marital plans. Upon gaining the council's agreement, Mary invested Darnley with the earldom and knighted the appropriate candidates. Despite the council's official action, some of its assenting members, including Lethington, were privately opposed to her plans. He later complained to Archbishop Beaton that she had advanced Darnley to great honors without the advice of her friends or her subjects and had received only ingratitude from him.

Throckmorton believed she was either a victim of love or cunning and recommended that Elizabeth incarcerate Darnley's mother and invite Anne, dowager duchess of Somerset, to court. As she was the mother-in-law of Catherine Grey, who was still under arrest for marrying Hertford, observers might view this royal treatment of the duchess as a move toward recognizing the Grey succession claims.

Mary's wedding preparations included dispatching messengers to the continent concerning Darnley's candidacy. As Francis's widow, she appropriately sought his mother's permission before remarrying. Both Catherine and Philip accepted her choice primarily because Darnley was neither Spanish nor French. Since she and Darnley were related in the second and fourth degrees of consanguinity, Mary also sent William Chisholm, bishop of Dunblane, to Pius IV to request a dispensation. Although unenthusiastic about his niece's plans, Lorraine assisted Chisholm in obtaining the dispensation, which was issued in September after the wedding but was backdated to May. It was not unusual for individuals to wed before a dispensation arrived or even to request one retroactively.

Three interpretations have attempted to explain Darnley's successful courtship. First, some writers have suspected that Elizabeth permitted him to join Lennox because she secretly endorsed his candidacy, but she was consistently hostile to her claimants' marriages and routinely enforced the statute forbidding them to wed without royal permission. Until Catherine Grey's death in 1568, she remained under arrest, and in August 1565 when her sister Mary secretly wed Thomas Keyes, a royal sergeant-porter and a widower with several children,

Elizabeth ordered them separated and incarcerated. Because Randolph's initial instructions promised Mary any suitable English noblemen, she could and did argue that Elizabeth offered Darnley to her, but later communications do not validate this claim. In short, Mary's protests against a union with a social inferior and her well-known attempts to wed a foreign prince caused the English to underestimate the value to her of Darnley's lineage.

A second reason given for her marriage to him is one that modern scholars unanimously reject but that many contemporaries could accept. In June rumors spread that he bewitched her. Among the evidence cited were the bracelets that contained sacred mysteries.

Third, as noted earlier, most biographers claim Mary fell in love with the young man, almost exactly three years younger than she, but while she was supposedly becoming enamored with him, Lethington was in London discussing both the Spanish and English alliances, either of which she would have accepted given the right circumstances. In May she promised Throckmorton to delay granting Darnley the dukedom, an act scheduled to precede the marriage. Then on 15 June she sent to England Moray's friend, John Hay, principal master of requests, with instructions to promise Elizabeth she would "embrace all reasonable means" to please her. Mary ordered Hay to inform Elizabeth that she had suspended the wedding for "a convenient season" and to recommend a meeting of Scottish and English commissioners to discuss her marriage.[21] While awaiting Hay's return, she continued to favor Darnley, perhaps hoping the threat of an alliance with him would prompt her cousin to concede her succession rights, making it possible for her to marry Leicester. Later Mary assured Randolph that she wed Darnley because he had a claim to the English throne and Leicester did not. Even Knox believed that she selected him because of his lineage, and Godfrey Goodman, the seventeenth-century bishop of Gloucester, wisely opined: "No sooner did Queen Mary see the Lord Darnley but she instantly fell in love with him, and the rather because, next after her own title, his title was next to the crown of England."[22]

If all the facts known about Darnley were limited to the information Mary had in early 1565, he might be judged an acceptable choice. The son of Lady Lennox, whom many Catholics esteemed, he was a native Englishman and was reared as a Catholic. If English experts denied Mary's succession rights because of her foreign birth, her union with him erased that technicality. After her and his mother, he held the best hereditary claim. Her child by him, furthermore, would have an English father. Finally, their marriage would negate concerns that Elizabeth might name him as her heir if Mary rejected Leicester or that Darnley might become a dangerous rival to Mary by converting to Protestantism and marrying into a prominent English family.

In May 1565 Mary could have found reason, however, to be concerned about Darnley's rash behavior and inability to handle extreme stress, if Randolph's hostile report can be believed. He related that Darnley kept to his chamber, only emerging for the ennoblement on the 15th, and that when he learned Mary was delaying the ducal ceremony, he threatened to strike Bellenden, the bearer of the bad news. Until he possessed that title, Darnley realized she might refuse his suit. It is interesting that Randolph's account assumed a formal relationship that kept Mary from personally revealing the postponement to Darnley.

On 6 July Hay arrived with a negative response from Elizabeth, who had also demanded that Lennox and Darnley return to England. With her other options defeated, Mary ordered final arrangements for her wedding to Darnley. Two weeks later she ennobled him as duke of Albany, and on the 22nd the first of the three obligatory marriage banns was announced; on the 28th Mary had him proclaimed king and early the next morning, a Sunday, they were wed. She had, after all, married a prince, even if only by her own creation.

Lennox and Atholl escorted Mary, who was dressed in a black mourning gown and wore a black hood on her head, into Holyrood chapel between 5:00 and 6:00 a.m. and then fetched the groom. Following trumpet fanfare, John Sinclair, future bishop of Brechin, officiated at the service. After exchanging their vows, Henry placed three rings, the middle a valuable diamond, on her finger. Following prayers and blessings, he kissed her and departed before the nuptial mass, perhaps another conciliatory gesture to those wanting her to wed a Protestant.

Reaching the chamber where he awaited her, she briefly resisted changing her costume out of respect for her first husband. Preparing then to retire to another room to don a brightly colored outfit, she asked each man to take a pin from her gown. As sixteenth-century garments contained component parts that were usually laced together, she obviously had hers pinned for ease in changing into another outfit to signal her departure from widowhood. Afterwards, she threw the traditional handfuls of money to the crowds outside the palace and attended a banquet. Buchanan composed masques for the three-day wedding festivities: the *Pompa Deorum, Pompae Equestres*, and *Ad Salutem in Nuptiis Reginae*.

On her wedding day Mary denied the petition of the Kirk's General Assembly to abolish the mass at court but promised that its members could continue to worship as they pleased and confirmed that only parliament would make religious changes. Unlike many of her contemporaries, she seems to have genuinely wished that people of differing faiths could live unmolested together. Earlier on 1 July when she and Darnley attended the Protestant baptism of her godson, the child of Agnes Fleming, Lady Livingston, and William, sixth Lord Livingston of Callendar, the brother of Mary Livingston, the queen stayed to hear the minister's sermon.

THE CHASEABOUT RAID

Having left court to organize opposition to her authority, Moray joined Châtelherault in recruiting other supporters, among them Argyll and William Kirkcaldy of Grange. As expected, the Hamiltons eagerly defended their succession rights against the Lennox–Stewarts' challenge. Moray also distrusted Darnley, who will be addressed hereafter either as king or by his first name Henry to highlight his new status, which was to have grave repercussions for the queen, his wife. Randolph encouraged Moray's animosity to Henry by repeating his alleged remark to Lord Robert that the earl controlled too much territory. In a sense if the king did express this belief, he was answering the question Moray, himself, posed during the Leicester negotiations. At that time he had wondered, in the event that Mary married someone other than Leicester, how that husband would treat Moray, knowing he had preferred a different suitor. Buchanan later explained another motive for the rebellion: "Many were of the opinion that it was more equitable that the people should choose a husband for a girl, than a girl should choose a king for a whole people."[23]

Mary reacted with fear and official remonstrations to Moray's desertion. She and Darnley had a scare on 1 July as they rode from

Perth to Livingston's home at Callendar for her godson's baptism. Rumors that Moray and Argyll were planning to abduct them and incarcerate them at Lochleven, referred to as the Raid of Beith, greatly alarmed Mary and Darnley. Afterwards, Mary granted her half brother three separate safeguards to appear before the privy council, and when he failed to respond, she had him put to the horn, declaring him an outlaw on 6 August.

Perhaps to prevent the rebels from defining their struggle as religious, Henry sat on a throne at St Giles' church on the 19th, listening to Knox's sermon. This ploy backfired since Knox's comparison of the king to Julian the Apostate and the royal couple to Ahab and Jezebel was so offensive that the privy council ordered him to abstain from preaching for 20 days. Henry, nevertheless, decided to continue his Protestant pretensions and attended the sermon of John Craig, Knox's colleague at St Giles, in September.

To suppress the rebellion Mary gathered support from Moray's enemies, recalling Bothwell and Sutherland from exile and liberating Huntly's heir. While the rebels assembled at Ayr, she ordered a muster and pledged her jewels for the soldiers' pay. In September Henry and she sent Francis Yaxley, a former client of Lady Lennox, to Philip to request aid against the rebels. Yaxley obtained 20,000 crowns for them but died when shipwrecked on the return voyage. Lennox also recruited allies. His wife's renunciation of her claim to her deceased father's estates meant that Morton, the guardian of Archibald Douglas, eighth earl of Angus, would aid the queen. The 14 mostly Protestants, whom Lennox selected for knighthood in May, likewise possessed relatives willing to join her forces.

In late August with 12 earls and 21 lords in a broadly based coalition, Mary, having just recovered from a fainting attack, left Edinburgh with Henry to pursue Châtelherault's and Moray's army. The rebels evaded them but met a hostile reception upon entering Edinburgh, since Erskine, recently ennobled as the earl of Mar, turned the castle's guns on them. Learning that her larger army was returning, they retreated to Dumfries in what is known as the Chaseabout Raid. The insurrection fizzled out in October when the raiders, except for Argyll secure in his mountainous retreat, fled to England. Indicating a disdain for challengers to lawful authority, Elizabeth permitted them asylum but refused them assistance.

MARITAL DIFFICULTIES

Meanwhile several disagreements between Mary and Henry began to surface. She not only failed to appoint his father as the realm's lieutenant general but also pardoned Châtelherault on 1 December for his role in the Chaseabout Raid on the condition that he dwell in exile for five years. That Henry was expected to sign letters under the great seal permitting his family's old enemy to move to France probably increased his aggrieved feelings. Henry's major concern, however, was her refusal to seek a parliamentary grant to him of the title and powers of king matrimonial, which her former spouse Francis II had enjoyed, and which, given early modern gender relationships, surely he and his network of male relatives and friends thought was his due or right as her husband. Evidently, Mary had anticipated that Henry would seek to destroy the Hamiltons and replace Châtelherault as her Scottish heir presumptive. In resisting Henry's demands for regal power, she risked antagonizing him but must have hoped, unrealistically as it turned out, to keep under control her youthful spouse, who although utterly inexperienced in governance matters, seems to have harbored more dynastic ambitions than she had realized. Several contemporaries, including Leslie, later commented on his youthfulness, unstable personality, and rash behavior, perhaps hinting at a certain immaturity for even a 19-year old man. Disappointed by her reluctance to empower him, Henry consequently disappeared on long hunting trips, forcing her to order an iron stamp with his signature to process official documents.

Randolph suspected they were having marital problems, noting that Henry remained mostly at Fife hunting after she became ill in mid-November. When Lennox wrote his wife in December that Mary was pregnant and that their son was in good health and favor, he was either personally deceived or more likely withholding news about their estrangement. Mary had conceived probably in late September, but the major symptom of her November illness was a recurrent pain in her side, which Randolph claimed she usually suffered at that time of year.

On 23 December Randolph related that she no longer favored her consort, that her attendants addressed him as the queen's husband rather than king, and that contrary to recent practice her name preceded his on coins and documents. These assertions were only partially true, but they do indicate Randolph was aware of the council's decision to create a new coin, the Mary Ryall, which carried her name before Henry's. Some writers, citing Randolph, have argued that their estrangement prompted its issuance, but public business rarely reflected shifting personal feelings. In 1565 the decision to mint the Ryall was prompted by a quest for profit, as it was valued at 30 shillings while its bullion value was only 22 shillings.[24] It is significant that three of the councilors making the decision were Henry's relatives: Atholl, Morton, who replaced Huntly as lord chancellor, and Patrick, third Lord Ruthven. The documentary placement of Mary's and Henry's names, moreover, did not change: *rex* continued to precede *regina* in the privy council register, for example. Meanwhile, Randolph noted other evidence of Henry's and Mary's estrangement, observing that Henry revealed his true faith by attending mass on Christmas Eve while Mary played cards until almost daybreak. Immediately after Christmas, Henry departed for Peebles to hunt only returning to court in mid-January.

The king's celebration of Christmas mass; the queen's selection of four Catholics to preach public sermons, among them John Black, a Dominican friar, and the royal couple's urging of the courtiers to attend services at Holyrood may have been hints that she intended to seek a statute restoring the mass for all Catholics at the parliament scheduled to meet in March. On 1 February 1566, Candlemas Day, some individuals did agree to worship with them but others, including Bothwell, declined their invitation. It is noteworthy that these efforts to encourage their presence at mass occurred during the visit to Scotland of two Catholic envoys, Clernault de Villemont from the cardinal of Lorraine and John Thornton from Archbishop Beaton. The royal couple may have hoped to impress these visitors with their success in recruiting new converts to their faith. They could also have planned to provide information about the additional Catholic worshipers to Nicholas d'Angennes, seigneur de Rambouillet, who arrived on 4 February to invest Henry in the Order of St Michael.[25]

Elaborate festivities celebrated Henry's installation on the 10th. Disguised in male attire, Mary and her ladies presented gifts to Rambouillet and his attendants during a banquet that evening. At a later supper the royal couple and Riccio joined others in performing in a masque. On the final evening, according to the reports of Rambouillet's attendants as translated by Sir William Drury, captain of

Berwick Castle, Henry enticed the Frenchmen to become drunk. They claimed that he was an alcoholic and that Mary had departed in tears from a merchant's house after arguing with him about his drinking. It is possible that his decision to plot the death of Riccio was unnerving the young man, as Randolph seems not to have identified drunkenness as one of his vices, although Knox did later claim that he was partial to wine.

Henry's installation may have raised issues that clinched his determination to move against Mary and Riccio. After investing Henry, when Rambouillet asked what arms should be emblazoned on the armorial, the council replied that since he did not possess the crown matrimonial, he should bear only his noble arms and not those of Scotland. This response as well as the council's earlier approval of Randolph's petition to omit the king's name from his passport home could have been the immediate reasons Henry turned against his wife. He may have believed that if he possessed the crown matrimonial he would be able to force absolutely the recognition of his royal status.

Henry was also disturbed by the rumors, which he may have initially believed, that Riccio was the father of the child Mary was carrying. Born in 1534 near Turin, Riccio belonged to a poor, noble family of Piedmont, which formed part of the duchy of Savoy. After serving at the Savoyard court, he became the secretary of Robert Solaro, marquis of Moretta, and accompanied him to Scotland in 1561 to discuss Mary's union with the duke of Ferrara. On Lorraine's recommendation and with Elboeuf's support, Mary persuaded Riccio to remain in Scotland when Moretta returned home. According to James Melville, she needed him to sing basso with three chamber musicians who took the other parts. In late 1564 Riccio replaced Raulet as her secretary for French affairs after he departed for France to join the cardinal of Lorraine's household.

It was not until May 1565 when Moray lost favor that Randolph began complaining about Riccio's undue influence at court. Wholly supportive of the Leicester match for Mary, Randolph accused Riccio and others, including Atholl, Ruthven, Balfour, and Bellenden, of promoting her marriage to Darnley. Because the ambassador, like most of his contemporaries, assumed that women were incapable of sustained personal initiative or autonomous political action, he sought to identify the male advisor with the most input into her governmental decisions. Later in 1565 noting Mary's estrangement from her husband, Randolph mainly condemned Riccio for the other royal policies he deplored, although he also blamed Balfour. By early 1566 rumors about the influence of these two officials had even reached France.

James Melville recalled that when he warned both Riccio and Mary that Scotsmen did not take kindly to foreigners wielding so much influence, she denied that Riccio spent more time with her than had Raulet or that he meddled in her business except for French writing and affairs. That Melville remembered this exchange with her is interesting because of later occurrences in England. In 1574 at the death of Raulet, who had resumed these secretarial duties during her captivity, she confided to Archbishop Beaton that as her secretary was dead, her enemies could no longer suspect that he was greatly influencing her opinions.[26] Women's reputations were more susceptible to gossip than men's, however, and Randolph's repeated accusations in 1565 lent credibility to Riccio's alleged importance to her. Indeed, James Melville later noted that in letters written to him and his brother Robert Melville, Throckmorton accused his countryman of deliberately causing political discord in Scotland.

Henry apparently believed that Mary's failure to seek the parliamentary grant of the crown matrimonial for him diminished his manhood and deprived him of the headship of his household. His feelings of inadequacy made him receptive to the gossip blaming Riccio for his powerlessness. Given social and legal practices, it was far from absurd for him to reach this conclusion. Normally after marrying, early modern women ceased to have legal *personae* and generally their husbands controlled their movable property and even their rents from inheritable estates. Husbands also had custody of their wives and could decide their places of residence. A later English publication summed up contemporary beliefs about spousal relationships:

> I would counsel women not to presume to command their husbands, and admonish husbands not to suffer themselves to be ruled by their wives; or in so doing I account it no otherwise than to eat with the feet, and travel with the hands, to go with their fingers, and to feed themselves with their toes.[27]

As good reputations were the keys to people's social standing, their enemies sometimes gossiped about their sexuality to sully their honor. Because female honor was considered fragile and once besmirched almost impossible to retrieve, numerous women sued slanderers in Kirk sessions or other courts to clear their names from sexual defamation. Few aristocratic women sought legal remedies, but they did sometimes adopt deep religious demeanor partly to protect themselves from slander. Female rulers often formed political alliances with ecclesiastics to forestall such gossip albeit sometimes unsuccessfully. In 1543 Sadler heard that James V had harbored suspicions about Mary of Guise's intimacy with Cardinal Beaton. Twenty years later, the exiled Bothwell repeated rumors circulating in France that Mary had been Lorraine's whore. Believing that Francis was impotent, some evil tongues even claimed that her uncle planned to impregnate her.

Since their contemporaries interpreted wives' adultery as evidence of their husbands' failure to maintain household authority, female immorality dishonored the men, called cuckolds, as well as the women. The cuckolded husband, a name derived from the cuckoo's practice of laying eggs in other birds' nests, was expected to perform acts of prowess to recover his reputation; indeed, the honor code permitted all men to defend their reputations with swords. It was best for a man to maintain secrecy about his wife's adultery. If knowledge of it became widespread, however, he needed other men to witness the violent acts that would restore his honor, since male networks confirmed and validated masculinity. Thus, Henry planned for his allies to attack Riccio in Mary's presence to signal her disgrace and his vindication.

Men could only with difficulty distinguish personal honor from their family honor, as this trait descended to them through their collective blood inheritance. Therefore, Lennox probably promoted his son's decision to murder Riccio and usurp his wife's throne. George Buchanan later claimed that Lennox had actually advised Henry to seek out two of the co-conspirators, his cousin, the sixth Lord Lindsay, and Morton. Nisbet, Lennox's master of the household, was also one of the assassins. Randolph certainly believed that both Lennox and his son conspired against Mary. Frequently at court during the winter of 1566, the earl served as one of the parliamentary lords of the articles on 7 March, two days before the attack on Riccio, and was elsewhere in the palace when it occurred.

Many of the assailants, including Morton, Ruthven, and George Douglas, postulate of Arbroath, were relatives of Henry's mother, Margaret Douglas, countess of Lennox. As Scottish women, who took their husband's titles but not their family names, were considered more a link to their in-law's kindred than a part of it, Henry normally would have sought Stewart assistance. Scotsmen, in fact, usually supported others with their surnames even if only distantly connected. Since Mary was also a Stewart, and since individuals with the same surname were not expected to fight against each other, her husband turned to his Douglas kin for assistance.

During the Order festivities, if not before, Henry began conspiring with them to murder Riccio and take his wife captive. On 13 February Randolph predicted both Riccio's death and the usurpation of Mary's crown, and by the 25th shortly before departing, he learned that the bands would soon be signed. The king had likely agreed orally to the conspiracy before witnessing the wedding of Huntly's sister, Jean Gordon, to Bothwell in a Protestant service at Holyrood Abbey chapel on the 24th. Earlier, perhaps at Mary's behest since Jean was a Catholic, Archbishop Hamilton, by virtue of his authority as papal *legate a latere*, issued a dispensation permitting her to marry in a Catholic ceremony the earl, who was related to her in the double fourth degree of consanguinity. Delighted with the match, Mary presented the bride with 11 ells of cloth-of-silver lined with taffeta for her gown. For five days the duplicitous king participated in the celebrations, including lavish banquets and tournaments.

In early March he signed two bands, the first with his relatives and associates for Riccio's murder. It is possible, as Mary later claimed, that the motive of the signatories for removing her from the queenship was that she, as was her right after she reached her 25th year, would revoke some of the grants made to them during her minority. Additionally, Randolph passed on the absurd rumor that she would give to Riccio the chancellorship held by Morton. In the second band, which referred to Riccio's death and was endorsed by Moray and the other noblemen with him, the king promised to pardon Moray and the Chaseabout raiders, who were mostly at Berwick, and to support the Protestant faith. In return, they pledged to assist him in obtaining the crown matrimonial and to petition Elizabeth for the release of his mother, imprisoned because of his marriage. Ironically, eight months after these men rebelled against Mary because she wed Darnley, they agreed to empower him as king and aid him in usurping her realm. Aware of these bands, Bedford and Randolph at Berwick informed Elizabeth that Moray would soon return home. The date parliament was to meet scheduled the timing of the attack. On the 7th the king refused to accompany Mary to the opening of parliament, which among its other business, restored Huntly and Sutherland to their earldoms and ordered the raiders to appear on the 12th for the forfeiture of their lands.

Two days later about 7:00 p.m. the assault commenced as the queen, who was six months pregnant, supped in a small room just off her bedchamber on Holyrood's second floor. The following account is based mostly on Mary's letter of 2 April in which she described the events to Archbishop Beaton.[28] It differs in some particulars from Ruthven's apologia which was written on 23 March; however, a rehearsal of her statements is important because they reflect her recollections of the conspiracy that form the context for some of her later actions.

Seated at the center of the supper table, Mary was attended by Lady Argyll, Lord Robert, Arthur Erskine, master of the horse, Robert Beaton of Creich, Balfour, and other domestic servants, including Riccio at the sideboard. Meanwhile, the conspirators assembled, Morton, Lindsay, and his followers securing the courtyard gates and Ruthven and other murderers gathering in the king's apartments on the first floor.

Henry emerged from the secret stairs to her lodgings, entered the chamber, and sat beside her on the royal chair. Soon thereafter to her amazement appeared Ruthven, who was pale and gaunt from a serious illness that took his life three months later. Dressed in armor with a sword drawn and accompanied by Douglas of Arbroath and two others, Ruthven, reputedly a sorcerer, reassured Mary after she ordered him under pain of treason to depart that no harm would come to her and that he wanted only to speak with Riccio. She quizzed Henry about this intrusion, but he denied all knowledge of it. She then promised Ruthven that she would see that justice was done if Riccio, hiding behind her, had committed some crime. As more accomplices, including Makgill, rushed in shouting the Douglas war cry, Ruthven ordered Riccio to depart with him. In the ensuing tumult the assailants overturned the table, prompting the quick witted Lady Argyll to grab a falling candle to prevent total darkness from descending upon them. Andrew Ker of Fawdonside held a loaded pistol to Mary's breast; Douglas of Arbroath wounded Riccio over her shoulder with Henry's dagger; they dragged him from the room and stabbed him some 56 times, leaving the king's weapon in his body.

Upon returning, Ruthven explained that Riccio was killed for counseling her to restore Catholicism, refusing to pardon the Chaseabout raiders, maintaining friendly relations with Catholic powers, and appointing the traitors, Bothwell and Huntly, as her councilors. In extreme fear for her life, Mary responded defiantly that if she died or her child perished, European princes would avenge their deaths. Ruthven assured her and later Bothwell and Huntly, who were elsewhere in the palace, that no harm would come to them.

Her husband foiled her chance for escape when Simon Preston, Edinburgh's provost, and other citizens arrived to check on her safety. The conspirators kept her from the window while Henry reassured them all was well. When Huntly and Bothwell heard that their enemies, Moray and the other raiders, would reach Edinburgh the next day, they fled through a window. Subsequently some others escaped, among them, Atholl, Sutherland, John, fifth Lord Fleming, brother of Mary Fleming, Livingston, and even Balfour, whom Mary claimed the assassins meant to hang. Besides Riccio, they also murdered John Black, the Dominican friar.

That night and the next day, the 10th, she was confined to her chamber with only limited access to her attendants while Henry kept his promise to the raiders and issued a proclamation proroguing parliament. At 8:00 p.m. that evening when Mary claimed she was having a miscarriage, Morton sent her a midwife and other women to assist her. Later, after the raiders reached Edinburgh and supped at Morton's house, Moray visited Mary, who graciously received him and heard him mendaciously deny knowing anything about Riccio's murder.

The next morning she convinced her weak-willed, youthful husband, whom she dominated with her stronger personality, that he was the assailants' dupe, pointing out that a guard stood near his door as well as hers. She also warned him about diplomatic problems if he agreed to religious changes. Leslie later reported that the king had been so blinded with ambition that he had not foreseen the evil intent of his cunning allies and almost too late realized that he was their pawn and in as much danger as the queen. Undoubtedly, Mary also took care to persuade him the child she carried was his. Endowed with a malleable personality, perhaps even a cowardly one, and separated from the influence of his father, the young king fell under the control of his older, more experienced wife.

Later that day Mary granted pardons to the conspirators, who were planning to incarcerate her at Stirling while her husband ruled her realm. This was a huge concession on her part. Even drawing a sword in the monarch's presence constituted a capital offense, but Mary was willing to appease them, as her cooperation offered evidence of her wifely submission. When Henry requested to be left in control of the palace's security, they agreed and departed for Morton's residence.

Mary sent a message through John Stewart of Traquair, captain of her guard, to Arthur Erskine to bring horses at midnight for their journey. The royal couple's escort also included Anthony Standen, the king's servant, Traquair's brother William, and her attendant, Margaret Carwood. Mary's mode of escape is difficult to credit because of her pregnancy, but in her letters to Archbishop Beaton and Charles and Catherine, she claimed that Bothwell and Huntly arranged for her to be let down from the palace walls in a chair with ropes and other devices. They then hurried to their horses and successfully escaped imprisonment. Undaunted by this narrow escape, Mary planned to ride southeast to Dunbar, her fine artillery castle, call on her lieges for support, and secure her kingdom.

6

CONFRONTING ADVERSITY, MARCH 1566–MAY 1567

About midnight on the evening of 11 March, they left Holyrood on horseback: Mary mounted behind Erskine; Traquair took Carwood; Standen rode with Henry; and William Stewart brought up the rear. They hastened to Seton Hall, the home of Mary Seton's brother, George, fifth Lord Seton, and the grand master of the queen's household since 1563. The previous July during happier times, the royal couple had stayed at his mansion, which stood nine miles from Edinburgh. Resuming their flight, they reached Dunbar Castle, located on the North Sea southeast of Edinburgh. After conferring with Huntly, Bothwell, Seton, Fleming and others, Mary summoned her lieges to Haddington on 17 March.

As she approached Haddington, the rebels retreated from Edinburgh, permitting her access the next day with a force of about 8,000, composed mainly of her lords' retainers. Avoiding Holyrood, she occupied private homes before removing to Edinburgh Castle. Having decided for security reasons to establish her lying-in room at the castle, she ordered new lodgings constructed in it with her and her husband's monogram displayed above the doorway. By custom arras would have been hung on the confinement walls and windows except for one to let in some light.

By condemning Riccio's murderers but pardoning the Chaseabout raiders, Mary split the confederates' unity. Following the council's summons to 60 fugitives to appear before it, Morton, Ruthven, Lindsay, and the others, fled south toward England while the principal Chaseabout raiders submitted to Mary and were pardoned. Meanwhile, Henry denied involvement in the murder. A proclamation on 20 March at Edinburgh's Mercat Cross declaring his innocence prompted his former allies to send Mary copies of the bands he signed. In May she admitted in a letter to the duchess of Guise that his betrayal had changed her from a contented, satisfied person to one oppressed with troubles and perplexities.

Mary rewarded her loyal supporters with the rebels' offices: Huntly obtained Morton's chancellorship and after she knighted Balfour, a councilor since 1565, he assumed Makgill's post as clerk register. James Melville later recalled performing Lethington's secretarial duties until his reconciliation with Mary, which occurred in September. When Joseph Riccio arrived with Mauvissière in April, she defiantly appointed him to his late brother's secretarial post. In June at Berwick, Randolph heard that Leslie had the chief management of her affairs.

CHILDBIRTH ARRANGEMENTS

That Mary was increasingly thinking about her unborn child is proven by her communications with Elizabeth. In her letter from Dunbar on 15 March revealing Riccio's murder, she apologized for not writing with her own hand, but admitted she was exhausted from covering 20 miles on horseback in a five-hour period and was also indisposed because of her pregnancy. In April she confessed she had grown so large she could not stoop over and that physical overexertion made her ill.[1]

Treating pregnancy as a disease, physicians diagnosed women fearful of surviving their confinements as melancholic. Modern demographers have concluded that the mortality rate in childbirth was no greater than that of the victims of infectious diseases; even so many expectant mothers prepared for their deaths. That Mary had her will drawn up by Mary Livingston, her jewelry custodian, and Carwood, her bedchamber attendant, indicates she began arranging for her demise as her due date drew closer. None of the copies she reportedly retained for herself or sent to her executors and to France is extant but an inventory on which she indicated her jewelry beneficiaries is available. She gave one item to Bothwell, three to his countess, and the most, 26, including her wedding ring, to Henry. Altogether she bequeathed 253 pieces to 60 persons with the proviso that they go to her infant should he survive her. Biographers have viewed these gifts as measures of her esteem for the recipients, but she must have designated most, if not all, to individuals because of their rank and relationship to her. She gave three diamond rings to her husband's parents despite her estrangement from Lennox since Riccio's murder. The 14 gifts destined for the Maries and their families were less valuable than the 14 bequeathed to the Guises. Perhaps, she offered some out of affection but pinpointing which ones is impossible.

As contemporary understanding of reproduction was limited, she must also have been concerned about her child's well-being. Following the assault on Riccio in her presence, observers treated her request for a midwife seriously because they believed that a sudden shock could cause a miscarriage. James Melville remembered that Mary's attendants feared she would lose the baby she was carrying.

Midwives entreated pregnant women to curtail physical activities, display moderation in their activities, and avoid riding on horseback because the movement might dislodge the fetus. In 1561 Catherine de' Medici advised her pregnant sister-in-law, Margaret of Savoy, that if she must travel she should journey in a chair but only for short distances. Husbands were also admonished to be solicitous over the health of their pregnant wives.

Clerics frightened parents by warning that a wrathful God interfered with nature to cause sinners' children to be born with deformities, such as missing digits. Expectant mothers were also admonished to monitor the objects they observed; their viewing a creature with excessive hair, for example, might cause their fetuses to develop that trait. This possibility could partially explain Mary's astonishment at the sickly appearance of Ruthven in her supper room. She might have been more concerned about her child's condition than her intruder's health.

After entering her lying-in lodgings in early June to await delivery, she depended only on women attendants, since childbirth was an all-female affair. If she had harbored fears that witnessing the attack on Riccio would harm her infant, they were misplaced. Between 10:00 and 11:00 a.m. on Wednesday, 19 June, after a long, difficult labor in which she was assisted by Margaret Houston, her midwife, she was delivered of a healthy son. As midwifery was often associated with witchcraft, the supernatural was sometimes evoked during childbirth. Reportedly, Margaret Fleming, countess of Atholl, futilely attempted to cast Mary's suffering upon Margaret Beaton, Lady Reres, who later became the prince's wet-nurse. To celebrate his birth Mar fired the castle guns and the citizens lit the customary bonfires.

A tradition repeated in the Herries Memoirs claims that when Henry, a castle resident, visited her, she showed him the child in the presence of witnesses and announced that he was his "own" son. She may have uttered this remark but the other claims of Herries, who was absent at the Anglo–Scottish border, are improbable. It is unlikely that she stated it would "be the worse for him [their son] hereafter," since she would not have alluded to Riccio's death. She did not predict that he would be the first monarch to unite Scotland and England; those were the words of someone writing with hindsight.[2]

In letters to Charles IX and to the cardinal of Lorraine that same day, Henry announced his son's birth and requested that the king serve as his godfather. For the second godfather Mary selected the duke of Savoy. She sent James Melville to relate news about the prince's birth to Elizabeth, who had previously agreed to act as his godmother.

On the 22nd Henry Killigrew reached Edinburgh Castle with instructions to convey Elizabeth's congratulations to Mary and to discuss Border violence, which may have increased because of the nearby presence of Morton and the other rebels. Having declined to replace the ousted Randolph with a resident ambassador, Elizabeth sent Killigrew on special assignment. He twice saw the prince, whom he judged had a good appearance and was endowed with well proportioned head, hands, and feet. He also visited with Mary, who spoke to him in a soft voice with a cough. While at Edinburgh Killigrew heard that Leslie managed Scotland's affairs and that Bothwell had great credit with the queen.

Following the usual practice of remaining secluded after childbirth for about one month, Mary stayed in the lying-in apartment for 35 days. Adopting the Judaic tradition that reproduction rendered women unclean, the Catholic Church required new mothers to undergo a purifying rite called churching before resuming social relationships. No record exists of her ceremony but it would have occurred at Edinburgh before she left for Mar's Alloa Castle on the north coast of the Forth.

As hereditary Lord High Admiral, Bothwell provided water transportation for her journey but did not accompany her on this five-week
retreat with Mar and Moray. Arriving by land, Henry stayed for two
days and issued a joint proclamation with her on 28 July, announcing
the holding at Jedburgh of a justice ayre, a special court to try criminal matters on the Borders. After reaching Alloa to convey his
monarch's congratulations on Mary's successful delivery, Mauvissière
concluded that she and Henry had reconciled.

Between 13 and 19 August the king and queen, along with Moray,
Huntly, Bothwell, and Atholl, hunted at Meggetland in Peeblesshire
near Ettrick Forest. Disappointed with the sport, they issued a joint
proclamation, demanding the punishment of deer poachers. Upon
reaching Edinburgh on the 20th after resting a night at Traquair, Mary
gave Henry a newly reconstructed and costly bed of violet-brown
velvet and other valuable items. Two days later Mary removed their son
to Stirling, the place she selected for his christening. Henry then traveled with her to Perthshire, stopping at Drummond Castle near Crieff
on the 30th before returning to Stirling to monitor preparations for the
ritual. Since the Roman Catholic Church taught that the deceased who
were not cleansed of original sin were excluded from paradise, the
faithful often had their infants christened shortly after their birth. That
new mothers remained in lying-in rooms meant that fathers and
godparents usually arranged the christenings, but Mary decided that
her son was healthy enough for his ritual to be delayed until October,
allowing her the opportunity to orchestrate a gala affair. Ultimately,
her illness and the belated arrival of Savoy's proxy caused it to be
deferred until December. That in 1562 her aunt by marriage, Margaret
of Savoy, postponed her son's christening to prepare a festive occasion
may have inspired Mary to make similar plans for her child's first
sacrament.

Having already accompanied Mary from place to place, Henry
remained at Stirling when she departed for Edinburgh with Moray and
Argyll on 6 September to raise funds for the christening. After witnessing the annual audit of the crown revenue at the Exchequer on the
11th, she borrowed £12,000 from some merchants, which she planned
to repay with a special tax. Monarchs often relied on procedures such
as these to finance events occurring before the tax revenue could be
collected.

Mary had earlier assigned another task to Bishop Chisholm, who was at Paris *en route* to Scotland from his mission to obtain the papal dispensation for her marriage to Darnley. She sent Chisholm back to Pius V to request funds for the Catholic religion in Scotland, including her son's christening. The agreeable pope not only advised Charles and Philip to provide assistance to Mary, whose masculine spirit he lauded for escaping Riccio's murderers, but he also authorized his nuncio, Vincent Laureo, bishop of Mondavi, to deliver to her 20,000 crowns in five installments.[3]

A few weeks after entering France *en route* to Scotland in late July, Laureo dispatched to Mary with the first payment John Beaton, the archbishop's brother whom she had sent to greet the nuncio. After receiving her welcoming message, Laureo was surprised to learn from secret intelligence when he reached Paris in October that she had only reluctantly authorized his visit to her realm. In December she wrote, explaining that her subjects would receive him but only on some business other than religion without clarifying what that business was. These mixed signals prompted Laureo to request Chisholm, returning from his latest papal mission, and Edmund Hay, a Scottish Jesuit and a French subject, to determine from her whether he could safely enter Scotland. Meanwhile, he stayed at Paris with the remaining funds.

Following the Exchequer audit, Mary journeyed to Stirling to find, according to Philibert du Croc, the French ambassador, a discontented husband, who declined accompanying her to Holyrood on 23 September. His negative attitude probably resulted from his realization, as he observed the lavish christening preparations, that since Elizabeth was to serve as their child's godmother, he would have to endure the public slight of her proxy because she still refused to recognize his royal status.[4] Feeling marginalized, he confided to his father who was visiting his grandson at Stirling, that he planned to go into exile probably to France.

On the 29th at Holyrood Mary received Lennox's letter from Glasgow, requesting that she prevent his son's departure. At 10:00 p.m. that evening, Henry appeared at the palace gates, refusing to enter until she dismissed certain councilors, probably Moray and Lethington. She greeted her husband, conducted him to her bedchamber, and remained with him that night. The next day following her instructions, Leslie announced to the privy council the king's decision to go abroad. Also summoned to the meeting, du Croc officially warned Henry that abandoning Scotland would adversely affect his and the queen's honor. Mary requested Henry to explain why he wished to leave the realm. While holding his hand, she further asked if she had offended him in anyway. He responded negatively and departed for Glasgow, remarking that she would not see him for awhile.[5]

On 1 October Mary informed Lennox of this exchange, assured him that she was attempting to treat his son in a reasonable manner, and promised that she would never deal with him otherwise.[6] In a later discussion with du Croc somewhere between Edinburgh and Glasgow, Henry admitted he longed for his previous relationship with her and confessed he was apprehensive about being slighted at the christening.

JUSTICE AYRE AT JEDBURGH

While the Stirling preparations continued, Mary turned her attention to the Borders. It remained a lawless area despite her on-going efforts to administer justice there, which the gratified Randolph had once praised. In June Killigrew discussed Border violence with Mary, who agreed to summon her wardens of the marches to confer about the disturbances. Then, as noted above, Henry and she proclaimed a justice ayre at Jedburgh.

The clans that lived in fortified houses in the buffer zone, the 121-mile frontier between Scotland and England, were organized for war. In this poverty-stricken area with its high rugged terrain, they mostly eked out a living raising cattle, horses, and sheep, often supplementing their incomes by raiding and stealing goods and livestock, especially cattle. Clan allegiance to their surnames took precedence over other loyalties, and the Scottish and English Borderers had more in common with each other than with their compatriots in the settled communities to the north and south of them, which they regularly raided.

As the justice clerk, Bellenden cooperated with local officials in preparing the dittays or indictments. At least fifteen days before the justice ayre was scheduled to begin, sheriffs were notified to secure the attendance of those accused of murder, arson, rape, and theft. Wealthy individuals could purchase remissions in advance for their crimes and then pay compositions to the designated official at the justice ayre.

Assizes or juries, usually composed of 15 men, decided the other defendants' culpability. On 10 October, the day after reaching this town some 40 miles southeast of Edinburgh, Mary met with the council to regulate prices and prevent merchants from taking advantage of the justice ayre's many participants. Having followed her there, du Croc remarked that he never saw her subjects honor her so much. Although originally planning to accompany her, Henry remained at Glasgow.

Earlier on the 8th while chasing criminals in upper Liddesdale as lieutenant general of the marches, Bothwell encountered John Elliot of the Park, a notorious thief and murderer. In a hand-to-hand skirmish after receiving some serious wounds, the earl managed to kill Elliot. For medical treatment his aides carried him to the Hermitage, a royal castle in his keeping. On the 15th or 16th Mary and some of her councilors rode the 50 miles round-trip to the Hermitage to discuss Border problems with him. The presence of Moray, usually identified as Bothwell's enemy, indicates she was pursuing crown business rather than personal interests. After two hours, they returned to Jedburgh since the Hermitage lacked adequate housing for them.

PREPARING FOR DEATH

For some time Mary had been ailing and by the 17th she was extremely sick. Believing that physical overexertion and emotional distress caused sickness, some blamed her condition on the Hermitage visit while others cited her grief at her husband's indifference. Traveling 50 miles on horseback in one day was unusual but not an impossible feat for an intrepid horsewoman like Mary.

On the 17th and 18th she suffered her chronic side ache, diagnosed by Dr Arnault Colommius as a spleen malfunction, and vomited 60 times. On the next two days she lost her sight and consciousness several times. Fearing death, the 23-year-old queen confessed her sins to Leslie, swore she accepted the fate God had appointed her, and summoned her councilors, including Huntly, Moray, and Bothwell, who had just arrived on a horse litter. She begged them to be loving to each other, cease oppressing Catholics, care for her son, and execute her will deposited at Stirling. Assuring du Croc of her deep faith, she recommended her son to Charles and Catherine.

Late on the 24th Colommius vigorously massaged her numb and cold limbs for four hours. At 6:00 a.m. she became unconscious, appearing dead with her mouth clinched shut, her limbs stiff, and her eyes closed. He again massaged her limbs, this time for three hours, poured wine in her mouth, and administered a clyster or enema. After vomiting blood, she slowly recovered her sight and speech. On the 28th her husband arrived, stayed one day, and departed for Stirling.[7] When he heard of her illness, Marc' Antonio Barbaro, the Venetian ambassador in France who had probably never seen her but was relying on his predecessors' views, lamented the possible death of the most beautiful princess in Europe.

Mostly endorsing in some form the humoral theories of Galen, a Graeco-Roman physician, early modern medical practitioners blamed the imbalance of their sick patients' sanguine, choleric, phlegmatic, and melancholic humours as the immediate cause of their symptoms. When Mary's spleen malfunctioned, creating her melancholic condition, it reportedly failed to fulfill its primary function of absorbing excessive black bile from the blood and the liver, permitting hot vapors to corrupt her body and interfere with the digestive system. Physicians usually identified one of the following for the imbalanced conditions: a bad environment, including emotional problems and excessive exercise, divine punishment, or the *maleficium* of witches. The physicians did not attempt to cure diseases; that was God's domain. Their more mundane goal was alleviating symptoms with purges, bloodlettings, vomits, and massages. They also advised cold-and-dry melancholic people to eat moist foods, sleep in warm beds, and moisten their bodies.

Modern diagnoses of Mary's illness include epileptic seizures, hemorrhages from a gastric ulcer, as well as the more likely problem, acute intermittent porphyria. It is a rare metabolic disorder caused by an inherited enzyme deficiency, the symptoms of which usually emerge after puberty. In the 1960s when Ida Macalpine and Richard Hunter investigated the madness of George III, Mary's direct descendant, they discovered that his urine turned a reddish color, a sign it contained abnormal metabolites. Viewing the discoloration as proof he suffered from porphyria, they examined a descendant of his and another of George I, his great-grandfather, both of whom tested positive for the disease. They next turned to the clinical observations of Mary's son while king of England by Dr Theodore Turquet Mayette, who noted his patient's urine also turned reddish in color. Most of Mary's recurrent symptoms, like James's, were identical to those of individuals suffering from this disease: abdominal colic with nausea, insomnia, coma, temporary paralysis, convulsions, soreness, and limb malfunctions (these occurred in England), mental shifts from depression to excitement, and difficulty in swallowing.[8] Since no record indicates that her urine changed color, the evidence remains inconclusive, but the goal here is not to prove a particular diagnosis but to emphasize that she suffered a chronic, debilitating malady that left her crippled before she was 40 years old.

Porphyria is still incurable, but modern doctors alleviate its symptoms with a high carbohydrate diet and drugs. Mary's diet may well have exacerbated her condition. The contemporary wisdom was that patients, including pregnant women, needed additional protein to overcome their maladies. Church officials routinely issued licenses for them to eat meat during fast periods.

In November when her health improved, Mary toured the Borders with Moray, Huntly, Bothwell, Alexander, 5th Lord Home, Lethington, and 500 horsemen before turning northward toward Craigmillar. Their journey led them through a strip of English territory where Sir John Forster, warden of the middle march, met them and escorted them to Halidon Hill from which they could hear the distant salute of Berwick's ordinance. On the 20th they reached Craigmillar, the seat of Simon Preston, which was separated from the capital by an extensive royal park.

Before arriving, she learned that Henry had informed the French and Spanish monarchs, Lorraine, and Pius V that her faith was insincere. His betrayal greatly troubled her. Instead of modeling herself after Mary Tudor as Pius IV requested, she was attempting to soften Protestant response to her son's Catholic christening by granting the Kirk's General Assembly control over appointments to the lesser benefices.

From Craigmillar on 2 December du Croc wrote Archbishop Beaton that the queen, who was still being treated for melancholy, had repeatedly said she wished she were dead. After reporting the king's recent visit there for one night only, du Croc doubted that the two could be reconciled because Henry would not humble himself as he should and because she suspected he was plotting against her whenever she saw him conferring with anyone. In January she later informed Beaton that she had ordered an investigation into rumors that Henry wanted their child to be crowned so that he could rule Scotland as his regent.[9]

Aware of Mary's marital difficulties, her councilors initiated a conversation with her about a divorce probably shortly after Henry's brief visit. In English captivity in 1569, Mary referred to this discussion in a protestation, drawn up at Robert, fifth Lord Boyd's advice and said to have been in conformity with Huntly's declaration to Leslie. It was sent to Huntly for his and Argyll's endorsement but was intercepted and forwarded to Cecil.[10] According to the protestation, Moray and Lethington entered Argyll's chamber to discuss obtaining pardons for Morton and his allies. Concluding that Mary would grant them if they could assist her in gaining a divorce, they consulted with Huntly and then Bothwell, who joined them in raising that issue with her. She maintained that she might agree to a divorce but worried that it would prejudice her son's succession. Despite Bothwell's reminder that he had inherited his family estates after his parents' annulment, she remained unconvinced. To her assertion that she opposed any action that would besmirch her honor, Lethington replied that they would recommend only measures that parliament could approve.

In his 1570 *Defence* of Mary, Leslie claimed that at Craigmillar she had categorically denied wanting a divorce. Leslie also revealed that unbeknownst to the queen, Moray and Bothwell signed a band at Craigmillar and inscribed indentures at various places with Morton and others, agreeing to Henry's demise. Leslie placed much of the blame for the king's assassination on Moray, who was not at the murder scene. Leslie claimed that the earl planned the king's death before leaving Edinburgh. It is noteworthy that Leslie failed to note Argyll's and Huntly's presence at Craigmillar probably because he did not wish to implicate in the murder the captive queen's two trusted allies in the Scottish civil war. In a manuscript dated in 1580, Leslie did add Argyll but not Huntly to the list of Craigmillar conspirators.[11]

In Marian studies the queen's marital difficulties have usually dominated discussions about the Craigmillar stay, but most of her activities there dealt with her son's christening. She appointed Simon Preston to raise the tax approved by a convention on 6 October to cover the ceremony's costs and undoubtedly consulted with him about the collection procedures.

CHRISTENING FESTIVITIES

On 10 December shortly after the earl of Bedford, Elizabeth's deputy for the christening, reached Scotland, Mary departed for Stirling. Although she had already postponed the ceremony for two months, she waited a few more days for the arrival of Moretta, Savoy's proxy, before holding it in his absence on the 17th. Since the Protestant Bedford would not participate in a Catholic service, Lady Argyll represented Elizabeth. Jean de Luxembourg, count of Brienne, acted for Charles IX and du Croc substituted for Moretta. The godparents sent lavish gifts: a bejeweled golden font from Elizabeth, a pearl and ruby necklace and earrings from Charles, and a large bejeweled fan belatedly from Savoy. Later, Lethington reassured Elizabeth that because of Stirling's narrow lodgings, Bedford's housing equaled that of the French ambassador, who normally enjoyed the best quarters.

Held at the vesper hour the christening was a full Catholic service except that Mary forbade John Hamilton, archbishop of St Andrews, to anoint her infant's lips with his spittle because he was rumored to be syphilitic. Between two rows of lords and gentlemen carrying candles, Brienne brought the prince into the Chapel Royal. Then in processed Atholl with a large wax candle, Hugh Montgomery, third earl of Eglinton, with the salt, Robert, third Lord Sempill, with the cross, and James, fourth Lord Ross, with the ewer and basin. Attended by various bishops, including Crichton, Leslie, and Chisholm, the archbishop received the prince from Brienne and handed him to the countess to hold at the font while he baptized him with the names of Charles James. After a trumpet fanfare, heralds proclaimed the prince's names and titles three times.

Elizabeth sent Lady Argyll a precious ruby for acting as her proxy, but since the countess was a Protestant, the Kirk later required her to do penance for participating in the ceremony. Bedford stood outside the chapel with Argyll, Bothwell, and Moray, who were dressed respectively in expensive red, blue, and green attire purchased by Mary for the occasion. Although Henry did not attend the service, he lingered in the castle, sending three requests to meet with du Croc, who declined the invitations because of his estrangement from Mary.

At the entertainment, which constituted a full-scale Renaissance triumph, status dictated the seating arrangements. That evening Mary supped at a table seated between the English ambassador and the French proxies while the prelates and others ate nearby. To signal religious reconciliation, Protestant Argyll and Catholic Seton carried white staffs into the room. The banquet ended with dancing and music. Altogether, the spectacles celebrating the prince's christening utilized the literature of four languages, Latin, French, Italian, and Scots.[12]

On the 19th, Bastian Pagez, a French valet of the queen's chamber, produced Buchanan's Latin entry, *Pompae deorum rusticorum*. For the food service Pagez disguised singing waiters as nymphs and satyrs and decorated a moving stage with laurel. After the 12 satyrs led into the dining room the stage carrying the six nymphs and the food, the nymphs handed the dishes to the satyrs for delivery to Mary and her guests, who sat at a replica of King Arthur's Round Table. When the satyrs wagged their tails with their hands, they offended the Englishmen who were aware of an old French claim that they possessed tails, but Bedford soothed their ruffled feelings. On Stirling's Esplanate was staged the main attraction, an assault on a burning fort by actors disguised as Highlanders and Moors. Sitting under a canopy, the queen and the ambassadors observed the spectacle that ended with fireworks.

Later she completed several official acts. To appease the Protestants she gave £10,000 to the Kirk but offended them by restoring Hamilton's ecclesiastical authority. After the Kirk's General Assembly protested that he planned to utilize these powers to establish Catholic courts, she rescinded the grant. Some writers have claimed that she empowered him so that he could annul Bothwell's marriage and hers with the king, but the archbishop as papal *legate a latere* already possessed the authority to end the earl's union, and since the twelfth century, only the pope or his commissioned legate could nullify a royal marriage. Bedford also understood that Hamilton intended to erect Catholic courts to compete with the new commissaries.

To please Bedford and Moray, Mary pardoned Morton and 75 others involved in Riccio's murder but only on the condition that they remain seven miles from court for two years. The gratified Bedford informed

Cecil that his and Moray's petition would have failed without the assistance of Bothwell, Atholl, and others. James Melville later recalled having advised the queen to pardon them. Monarchs as God's earthly representatives, he had opined, approached nearest to His nature when exhibiting their readiness to forgive. In July after Mauvissière petitioned Mary on behalf of his government for their restoration, Morton complained he would rather not have to rely on French assistance for his relief. It is possible that Cecil pressed Bedford to obtain Morton's pardon because he believed the Scotsman would join in a conspiracy with Bothwell to assassinate Henry and destabilize Mary's rule. Some evidence indicates, however, that Bedford attempted to reconcile the royal couple. Elizabeth seems also to have been concerned about the presence both of armed men on her side of the Borders and of so much dissension in an adjoining realm.[13]

At his queen's behest Bedford demanded the punishment of John Adamson, a Protestant minister who composed a poem published in France that celebrated James as the prince of Scotland, England, and Ireland. For his offense Adamson spent six months in prison; Elizabeth thus clarified that agreeing to serve as James's godmother did not alter her succession stance.

His birth did apparently prompt her to plan an inquiry into the validity of Henry VIII's will, a decision she communicated to Mary through Bedford and Robert Melville. The gratified Mary promised on 3 January 1567 to send councilors to discuss the investigation with Elizabeth's advisors and expressed the hope the inquiry might occur before the end of the present English parliament, which had uttered prejudicial comments about her claims. Elizabeth did not intend to seek legislative action on this issue and on 2 January dissolved this acrimonious parliament, which futilely petitioned her to marry and name her successor. She probably planned to appoint commissioners to investigate the legality of the will. If they deemed it invalid, their decision would eliminate a major impediment to Mary's claims but would not constitute the legislative recognition of her as heir presumptive that she desired. The king's death seems to have ended all discussion about this inquiry.

During the christening festivities, Mary confided to du Croc, who found her on her bed weeping on 22 December, that she had a side ache and a swollen breast, which was injured on her horse when departing Edinburgh. Henry's health was also worrisome. At Glasgow he developed an illness that contemporaries identified as smallpox but that a later study of his skull claims was syphilis, although doubts remain about whether it is his skull. Mary sent a physician to examine him to discover when she could safely visit him since he was reputedly suffering an infectious disease. Meanwhile, she celebrated the Christmas season at the homes of David, second Lord Drummond, and Sir William Murray of Tullibardine and returned to Stirling to be with her son by 1 January.[14]

MURDER OF THE KING

About the 18th or 19th January a murder conspiracy was afoot at Whittingham, the home near Dunbar of Morton's cousin, William Douglas. Shortly after Morton arrived there on the 10th, Bothwell and Lethington conferred with him about killing the king. At his murder trial in 1581 Morton recalled that since Bothwell and Lethington lacked Mary's written approval, he refused to sign the band for Henry's death, which Balfour reportedly prepared and endorsed along with Huntly, Argyll, Bothwell, and Lethington. In 1580, as an English captive, Mary instructed Archbishop Beaton to request Balfour, then in French exile, to send her a copy of the band, indicating her belief that he played this role in the conspiracy. She also informed Beaton that she felt unable to trust Balfour, but that he ought to be humored in case a need for his service arose. Balfour later sent her a version of the band without his signature.

In 1583 Archibald Douglas, a brother of the above William, informed Mary about events following the Whittingham meeting. Morton had sent Archibald, apparently unaware of the band, with Bothwell and Lethington to Holyrood, which Mary had reached with James on the 14th, to fetch a written statement from her consenting to Henry's death. Returning from their private audience with her, Bothwell and Lethington instructed Archibald somewhat enigmatically: "Shew to the Earl Morton that the Queen will hear no speech of that matter appointed unto him."[15]

Given the concern for her honor that Mary expressed at Craigmillar, they surely did not ask her to provide Morton with written permission to kill her husband. As Morton was prohibited from attending court, perhaps they suggested she summon him to an audience so that he could discover the extent of hers and Henry's estrangement. If so, there are at least three reasons for her negative response. Preparing to leave for Glasgow, she probably lacked time to see him; she may have shrunk from meeting a rebel whom she had reluctantly pardoned, or she may have indicated that she hoped to reconcile with her husband. If she admitted this goal to them or if they surmised that this would be the result of her visit, she unwittingly speeded up their murderous time-table. On the 20th, perhaps the day before her departure, she reported to Archbishop Beaton that Henry and his father would injure her if their "power were equivalent to their minds," for her husband was "occupied and busy enough to have inquisition of our doings, which, God willing, shall always be such as none shall have occasion to be offended with them, or to report of us anyway but honorably."[16] Both this letter and her October message to Lennox, promising to treat his son reasonably, explain why she went to Glasgow; she was protecting hers and his honor.

Having primary responsibility for treating their families' and their villagers' sicknesses, early modern women's control over informal med-icine was substantial. Growing herbs for medicinal purposes and acquiring the knowledge to use them loomed large in their education. If wives failed to attend to their husbands' medical needs, they breached marital etiquette and besmirched their own and their family's honor. Catherine de' Medici taught Mary the proper behavior when she nursed not only Mary and her own children but also Henry II. Another lesson Mary learned from her mother-in-law was that she should bear patiently her husband's slights. Henry's conspiracy against Riccio was more serious than the French king's philandering, but a certain level of marital violence was condoned. It was not, for example, a dishonorable act for a man to whip his wife unless he seriously injured her. While a queen regnant would surely be exempt from her husband's physical abuse, she could, as Mary had discovered, be victimized by his attempts to imprison her.

As Mary set off with mounted guardsmen and a horse litter, Bothwell and Huntly accompanied her as far as Callendar, the home of Livingston. After one night there, she resumed her westward journey while Bothwell, who planned to suppress crime on the Borders, returned with Huntly to Edinburgh. On the 25th Bothwell arrived at Jedburgh and on the 27th was at Liddesdale.

Thomas Crawford of Jordanhill, Lennox's gentleman, greeted Mary at Glasgow, and, according to his later unverified testimony, related to her that her indisposed father-in-law was reluctant to meet her because of the manner in which she spoke to his servant at Stirling. Mary reportedly responded that if Lennox were innocent, he had nothing to worry about and then commanded Crawford's silence.

Entering Glasgow, she visited Henry at the castle and attended to his needs; they became reconciled, and he agreed to accompany her to Edinburgh. On the 27th with him in the horse litter, she began the return trip, reaching Edinburgh about the 31st.

Unwilling to expose their son at Holyrood to her ailing husband, she suggested that he convalesce at Craigmillar. When he objected to residing at this fortress perhaps aware that it had served as a royal prison, James Balfour urged him to go to the more accessible Kirk o'Field, which lay near the Canongate. On the south side of its quad-rangle of houses was the Old Provost's Lodge, an unoccupied residence belonging to Balfour's brother, Robert. Mary moved Henry to the building's upper floor and ordered her servants to transfer to it from Holyrood some rich furnishings and the velvet bed she gave him. She slept there on the 5th and the 7th; on the latter date he wrote his father that she was a loving, attentive wife. Perhaps, he was gratified by her arranging for him to take a medicinal hot bath, a treatment that soothed the symptoms of her illness. He might well have been pleased that she scheduled his removal to Holyrood on the 10th. Sometime during their days at Kirk o'Field, as recalled by James Melville, Henry confided to Mary that Lord Robert warned him to leave the lodge or he would lose his life. When she confronted her half brother about this conversation, he denied having made that dire prediction to her husband.

On the 9th, Shrove Sunday, Moray departed to visit his ailing wife. That same morning Mary witnessed the wedding of Christian Hogg and Pagez, the producer of her son's christening triumph, and prom-ised to attend a masque celebrating the occasion at Holyrood that evening. At 4:00 p.m. along with Huntly, Argyll, Bothwell, and Gilbert Kennedy, fourth earl of Cassilis, she enjoyed a farewell supper for Moretta, hosted by James Hamilton, bishop of Argyll, at John

Balfour's Canongate house where the Savoyard had resided since arriving on 24 January.[17] At 9:00 p.m. she returned to Kirk o'Field for a two-hour visit with Henry and then keeping her promise to Pagez, departed for Holyrood after giving her husband a ring and promising to spend the following evening with him. While exiting according to the later account attributed to Claude Nau, she observed with surprise that Nicholas Hubert alias French Paris, her valet of the chamber and formerly Bothwell's servant, was covered with gunpowder, apparently, unbeknownst to her, from delivering it to the lodge. Later in his book, *Martyr de la Royne d'Eccosse*, published at Paris in 1587, Adam Blackwood denied her complicity in the murder, citing as one of his proofs her astonishment at Paris's filthy condition.

After hearing the massive explosion about 2:00 a.m. on the morning of the 10th and learning that Henry was dead, Moretta briefly delayed his departure. One and one half days later, he left in the company of Chisholm and Hay, stopping in France *en route* to Savoy to inform Charles and Catherine of the murder. Moretta's testimony represents what some believed occurred. When Henry became aware of suspicious noises outside his chamber, he escaped through a window overlooking the garden. Assassins then strangled him with his shirt sleeves and destroyed the part of the house where he slept, intending to have it appear that he was killed in the descent. Moretta described Mary as very fearful and repeated rumors that Moray was the instigator of the murder.[18] Actually, the explosion destroyed the whole building. According to Lorraine's client, Clernault de Villemont, an underground mine that sounded like the firing of 25 or 30 cannons in volley caused the blast. Villemont also revealed that the greatly distressed queen had been on good terms with her husband.

In her letter to Archbishop Beaton, written the 10th but dated the 11th, Mary likewise related that the lodge was in ruins. She and some others believed that Henry was still asleep when the gunpowder exploded, but he more likely escaped through a window, as Moretta later asserted. His body and that of his valet, William Taylor, still attired in their night clothes, displayed no visible marks even though they were found some 40 yards away in a garden on the other side of the town wall. Conspirators probably grabbed them as they descended, smothered them, and dumped them there. Also, according to Moretta, some women heard him cry, "O, my brothers, have pity on me for the

Plate 1 James V and Mary of Guise, King and Queen of Scotland. Hardwick Hall, The Devonshire Collection (The National Trust)

Plate 2 Francois II c.1553 by Francois Clouet, Musee Conde, Chantilly,
France/The Bridgeman Art Library

Plate 3 Henry Lord Darnley and his younger brother Charles, by Hans Eworth. © Leeds Museums and Art Galleries (Temple Newsam House) UK/The Bridgeman Art Library

Plate 4 James VI of Scotland and I of England holding a bird of prey, c.1580 by Arnold Bronckorst, Scottish National Portrait Gallery, Edinburgh, Scotland/The Bridgeman Art Library

Plate 5 A miniature, by an unknown artist, traditionally said to be of Bothwell, Scottish National Portrait Gallery, Edinburgh, Scotland

Plate 6 Mary Queen of Scots in white mourning, 1560 by Francois Clouet, Bibliotheque Nationale, Paris, France Giraudon/The Bridgeman Art Library

Plate 7 Mary Queen of Scots, miniature by Nicholas Hilliard. Victoria & Albert Museum, London/The Bridgeman Art Library

Plate 8 The execution of Mary, Queen of Scots, 1587. ©Bettmann/CORBIS

Plate 9 Mary's effigy on her tomb in Westminster Abbey. © Dean and Chapter of Westminster

love of Him who had mercy on all the world," fueling the speculation he was addressing his Douglas relatives.[19] Mary confided to Beaton that she believed the murderers had planned to kill her, recalling that she had only by chance gone to Holyrood that night. She surely spent most of the 10th personally inquiring about Henry's assassination, instructing her household about disposing of his remains, and preparing messages announcing his demise. She commissioned Villemont, for example, to carry her notification of his death to Archbishop Beaton.

Then on the morning of the 11th, Shrove Tuesday, before beginning the widow's customary 40-day seclusion, she witnessed the marriage of John Stewart and her attendant, Margaret Carwood, whose wedding dress she purchased for £125. Her attendance at this religious ritual has been characterized as showing her disdain for Henry's memory, but no gala festivities celebrated the occasion. Not only had she ordered the court into mourning but also, according to Moretta's testimony to de Silva in London, she donned a widow's thick black veil. Leslie even claimed that questions were raised about the appropriateness of a queen's mourning a husband, who was a private man and one of her subjects, but noted that despite these concerns, she decided to follow traditional protocol for honoring a royal spouse.

While departing for Edinburgh Castle, the residence Mary chose for security reasons, she received Archbishop Beaton's dispatch of 27 January, relating that Don Frances de Alava, the Spanish ambassador in France, informed him of rumors that a dangerous conspiracy was directed at her. By 17 February de Alava and Margaret Farnese, duchess of Parma, regent of the Netherlands, had alerted de Silva about this apparent threat to Mary.

Meanwhile the council sent a magistrate accompanied by surgeons to examine the bodies of the king and his valet. The councilors also questioned servants who slept in adjoining buildings and called other witnesses for information. A paper on the 11th written by Alexander Hay, secretary to the council, contains notes concerning the interrogation of three deponents about the crime: two women and a surgeon who reported on the number of men they saw and other events following the explosion. George Buchanan later claimed that Huntly, Bothwell, and Leslie attended this meeting, which was convened by Argyll in his chamber.

No evidence that the councilors continued these interrogations has survived, but on the 12th they did offer £2,000 and a pension to anyone identifying the murderers. On that same day Mary's household began arranging Henry's burial. They had his body embalmed and laid in state at Holyrood for three days before having it interred on the 15th in the royal vault near James V. A night funeral service without Psalms or music was held, following the custom Protestants had introduced into Scotland to avoid all hints of the Catholic tradition of praying for the dead.

For her son's safety Mary placed him in the custody of Huntly and Bothwell at Holyrood on the 16th before moving from the castle to Seton with her ladies, Archbishop Hamilton, Argyll, and Lethington to receive, according to James Melville, some purgations. In fact, she seems to have suffered a physical and emotional breakdown after her husband's death. Blaming the environment for her disease, her physicians hoped Seton's air would restore her fragile health. Leslie claimed that she wanted to continue depending on candlelight but her doctors ordered the windows open to let in the light. Other evidence attests to her persistent illness. Her letters were mostly in Scots, which she was as yet unable to write and were, therefore, dictated. She also failed to correspond with her relatives as usual.

Between 19 February when she returned to Edinburgh and 23 March when this mourning period ended, she moved back and forth between the castle and the hall. In late February the gossipy Drury at Berwick reported that Argyll, Huntley, and Bothwell dined with her at Tranent and that she competed with Bothwell in an archery match. Since she was observing Lent as well as mourning her husband's death, Drury's claim, based on spies' reports, is absurd. George Buchanan later repeated these rumors, substituting golf for archery.

On 8 March when Killigrew condoled with her in a dark chamber at the castle, he reported that he could not see her face, which must have still been hidden by her thick black veil, but that she exhibited profound grief in her voice and manner. The limited visibility he described has fueled the speculation that an attendant disguised as Mary met with the ambassador presumably because she was too ill to see him. This deceit seems unlikely: Mary had visited with Killigrew the previous June when she was also unwell, and he would have been somewhat familiar with her subdued voice. Locating a six-foot female attendant who could speak with her accent would surely have constituted a great challenge for Mary's staff. If Mary had instructed a servant to substitute for her at this audience, she would have breached diplomatic protocol, taking a chance on gravely offending her royal cousin, whom Killigrew represented. Apparently, noting no irregularity in Mary's behavior or appearance, the ambassador handed over some official documents to her.

Shortly after Henry's assassination, rumors began to spread about his killers' identities. On 16 February an anonymous writer placed a placard on the Tolbooth door blaming Bothwell, Balfour, David Chalmers, and Black John Spens. Others accused Mary's servants, Pagez, John Francisco de Busso, Francis Sebastien, John de Bordeaux, and Riccio. Steeped in hierarchical notions and convinced that a nobleman must have been involved in a prince's murder, many named Bothwell. In early March an offensive placard displayed her as a mermaid–siren with a crown on her head and Bothwell as a hare with the Hepburn crest, crouching in a circle of swords. On the 14th the council charged with slander in absentia James Murray, her comptroller's brother.

It is impossible given the flawed evidence to identify definitively the ringleader of the murder and the tasks his co-conspirators completed. Conflicting information is scattered in chronicles, memoirs, and the statements of those later convicted, many of whom were threatened with torture and placed on bread-and-water diets. Certainly, Morton, Balfour, Bothwell, and his followers were involved but so were others. The assailants seem to have been so disorganized that the disparate groups moving around the lodge were unaware of each other's presence. That the explosion failed to kill Henry also indicates inadequate, hurried planning. The knowledge that Mary was reconciling with the king may have prompted the haste, since they would soon be sleeping together in the same residence.

Even so, it seems reasonable to assert that Balfour organized the plot: he composed the band for Henry's death, offered his brother's lodge for the king's convalescence, and stored the gunpowder in his Canongate and Kirk o'Field houses. Bothwell and his followers delivered and fired the gunpowder while Morton dispatched his allies, including Archibald Douglas and Ker of Fawdonside, to ensure Henry's death.

In depositions taken in 1575 before an official of Paris at the instigation of Leslie to obtain evidence supporting Mary's petition to

Gregory XIII for a divorce from her third husband, an interesting story about his involvement in the king's murder was revealed. A deponent, Cuthbert Ramsay, who was a brother of Lord Dalhousie, recalled having spoken with John Hepburn, a servant of Bothwell and one of the king's murderers, both in prison and at his execution. Hepburn had confided to Ramsay that he had saved Bothwell's life at Kirk o'Field. Apparently, the earl had decided to investigate the reason for the delay in the explosion of the train of gunpowder. When he neared the gunpowder, it suddenly caught fire, and reacting quickly, Hepburn had pushed him away from the danger.[20]

Citing contemporary rumors as well as the Casket Letters, writers have often linked Henry's murder to Bothwell's later abduction of Mary as though the two events formed steps in a long-term conspiracy. Since this theory depends on the knowledge of hindsight, it is useful to separate the two crimes, first identifying the assassins' motives and then the abductor's goals. Henry's murder was partly the result of his victims' reaction to the bloodfeud he initiated when he led Riccio's armed killers into Mary's chamber, frightening her attendants and others present at the palace. Relying on a kin-based justice system and a customary code of honor, the injured party or their relatives either retaliated with violence or demanded compensation. When the king denied participating in Riccio's murder, he left the victims with only the option of force to redeem their honor. His later public denial of involvement, furthermore, antagonized the perpetrators, his former allies, making it possible for them to unite with the victims against him.

Avenging Riccio, as some observers assumed, were Riccio's brother Joseph and various Catholic members of the queen's household. Besides Riccio, the next most aggrieved individual was Balfour, whom Mary believed the armed intruders intended to hang. The king's killing place belonged to Balfour's brother, Robert, who was present during the explosion to restore the family honor. Rumors also named Bothwell, who fled the palace in the belief that Henry planned to surrender him to Moray. Although he was declared innocent at his murder trial, the accusations against Bothwell and his adherents are surely accurate.

In their depositions and confessions, furthermore, some of Bothwell's accomplices who were executed for the murder, for example, John Hay the younger of Tallo, James Ormiston, and French Paris, claimed both Huntly and Argyll were also endorsers of a band to kill Henry. In his *History of Scotland* George Buchanan identified Huntly as one of the principal perpetrators. Writing after Huntly died in 1576, John Knox's secretary, Richard Bannatyne, asserted that both Huntly and Argyll were the king's assassins. At his trial for Henry's murder in 1581, Morton claimed Archibald Douglas admitted to being present at Kirk o'Field with Bothwell and Huntly. Finally, a statement drawn up in 1582, listing the offences committed by Esmé Stuart, duke of Lennox, James VI's former principal minister, included a claim that the duke had restored to their honor and heritage those forfeited for the king's murder; among the names on its margin was Huntly's (obviously for his heirs).

The reason for Huntly's endorsing the band was that he had escaped Holyrood after Riccio's death in the belief that Henry meant to turn him over to Moray. If Argyll, who, of course, was not at Holyrood, also signed the band to kill Henry, as is likely, he would have done so to defend his personal reputation and his family's honor. Although estranged from his countess, he was surely offended that armed murderers had charged into the small chamber, threatening the well-being of his wife and its other occupants. For anyone to assault the earl's kinfolk or affinity was to insult him as the head of his kindred. An armed attack like the one his countess was forced to witness would have been viewed as a much greater blow to his honor than any physical or emotional damage actually inflicted on her.

The names of Lethington and Morton also frequently appeared alongside Huntly's and Argyll's in the above documents. Henry's betrayal alienated Lethington, as it did the other Riccio conspirators, but the king's treatment of Mary further angered the secretary. Executed for Henry's murder in 1581, Morton and his allies either signed the band or became assassins because Henry publicly denied involvement in Riccio's death. They may also have felt disdain for his manhood. He had stood by while they restored his honor by completing the murder with his dagger.

In April 1566 William Henrisson, a secretary of Archbishop Beaton, delivered a letter from Mary to de Silva in London. During their conversation, Henrisson reported his recent audience with Elizabeth during which she asked if Henry drew his dagger during the attack on Riccio. When she learned he had not, she said she was not surprised, recalling he failed to put his hand to his knife when he was in England. Perhaps she was belittling his courage, as one proof of noble honor was the visible readiness to defend it with violence even for trivial matters.

Immediately after the king's assassination, rumors accused the absent Moray of the crime, but he was probably not one of the conspirators. Like Henry, Moray was a Stewart and may have been disinclined to participate personally in another Stewart's death. It is true he was a Chaseabout raider but he had been reacting to concerns that Mary's new husband would damage his political and economic standing and jeopardize the Protestant religion. At least by Riccio's death most individuals understood that Henry had little influence with Mary. The king did, moreover, keep his word to Moray and the other raiders when he dissolved the parliament summoned to forfeit their estates. Without blemishing his honor, Moray could, therefore, refuse to sign the band for the king's murder. In this context, the comment in French Paris's confession that Moray would neither help nor hinder the conspiracy seems to ring true. If Moray did know about the plan to kill the king, as he surely must have, he obviously did not feel honor bound to warn Henry of the danger. In April as Moray was planning to go abroad, he drew up a will, naming Mary as his daughter's guardian, apparently not yet committed to charging his half-sister with her husband's death. George Buchanan was later to claim that the underlying motive for Moray's decision to attack her honor was his own exculpation.

On 23 March after emerging from seclusion, Mary ordered a requiem mass and a dirge for Henry. She next faced mounting pressure to bring someone, principally Bothwell, to trial for her husband's assassination and to combat rumors that she colluded in his death. Traditionally, writers, who have doubted that she was innocent of the murder, have claimed either that she aided and abetted it or that she at least knew about it. Those who believe she conspired against him have erroneously pointed to her restoration of Hamilton's ecclesiastical powers, permitting him to grant Bothwell's divorce. Next, they have contended that she returned Henry to the lodge to make him vulnerable to the plot, but she preferred Craigmillar for his convalescence. Finally, they have cited contemporary rumors as well as the Casket Letters, which contain her alleged confessions of love for Bothwell. Surely forgeries, the Letters will be briefly discussed in Chapter 7.

Another larger group of writers, believing that she must have at least known a conspiracy was afoot, have cited other evidence. They have referred to the so-called coded language at Craigmillar that should have alerted her to the danger, but she seemed forthright enough when she demanded, while discussing a divorce from her husband not his murder, that her reputation must remain unsullied. They have also pointed to Morton's claim that after the Whittingham conference, he sent Bothwell and Lethington to obtain from her a warrant for Henry's death. No transcript of that conversation is available, but Morton denied receiving her written permission to kill the king.

These writers have further argued that because so many people knew about the conspiracy, a hint of it must have reached her or intuitively she must have guessed its existence. The number involved should not be cited as proof that she became aware of the plot. She could have known about it only if someone revealed it to her. To provide a perspective for the allegation that she must have guessed something was brewing, no one has ever claimed that she knew about the Riccio assault, which attracted over 100 conspirators. The royalty, furthermore, did not often welcome the bearer of bad news. In 1562, for example, when Arran alerted Mary that Bothwell planned to abduct her, she agreed to have both earls incarcerated. In his letter to her in 1583, cited above, Archibald Douglas denied scheming to kill the king but admitted failing to warn her that most of her nobility were angrily disposed toward him. Even brave individuals would have hesitated to reveal information to her that might well draw upon them the wrath of so many noblemen.

Determining whether she could have realized that a conspiracy against her husband was afoot must involve a consideration of her state of mind. She seems to have been so fearful that Henry was scheming with his father against her that she did not seem to be aware of, or at least sense, his political vulnerability. In January as she planned to fetch him from Glasgow, she ordered investigations into rumors about his machinations to usurp her throne, and after his death in February she believed that the assailants had also targeted her. As she entered mourning seclusion, she probably viewed Beaton's message concerning a rumored plot against her as confirmation of her concerns that the villains meant to harm her as well as Henry.

Only twenty-four years old that February, Mary had already undergone numerous life-threatening experiences: the forcible attempts by

Henry VIII and Somerset between 1543 and 1548 to remove her to England, the poisoning conspiracy in France in 1551, the bloody attacks at Amboise in 1560, the Scottish rebellions during her personal reign, 1562 and 1565, several abduction scenarios, the Châtelard incidents in 1563, and the assault on Riccio in 1566. It is no wonder that she viewed the explosion at Kirk o'Field as a foiled attack on herself.

ABDUCTION AND RAPE

While writers have paid little attention to how her fears that the conspirators also meant to kill her might have affected her emotionally, they have sometimes argued that Bothwell planned her husband's murder as a prelude to abducting her. An assessment of his personality is an important consideration in determining whether this was his motive for plotting against the king. In fact, Bothwell seems to have been more adept as a fierce, opportunistic combatant than as a patient conspirator with long-term schemes. In 1566 Robert Melville described him as courageous but of little help in policy discussions. Since he was more physical than mental in his problem-solving capacity, it seems uncharacteristic for him to have invented this complicated assault on Henry; other reports do indicate that he favored an attack on the king in the open fields. A second trait of Bothwell's, which partially explains the mermaid–hare cartoon, was his lechery. He had promised, for example, to marry a Norwegian woman named Anna Throndssen, whom he deserted after living with her for a few months in Flanders. The daughter of Christian Throndssen, an admiral at the Danish court, she apparently bore him a son named William. In 1563 Randolph commented on the earl's lustful reputation while he was in England awaiting permission to go to France. Warning about the dangers Bothwell posed to women, Randolph pleaded that Bothwell not be sent to Dover Castle, which stood near the residence of the ambassador's still youthful sister and her daughters.

Although the cartoonist's motives can never be fully known, three additional reasons besides Bothwell's lechery can be offered to explain why he and others validated the rumors linking the queen to the earl. First, Mary increasingly turned to him for advice especially about the Borders; without negative criticism, du Croc noted her reliance on him at Jedburgh. Second, it was common knowledge that she imprisoned him in 1562 for plotting to abduct her. Finally, the easiest way to besmirch a female ruler, especially a widow, since women with marital experience were viewed as sexually insatiable, was to charge her with illicit relations with a male advisor. Had Bothwell not been available, the cartoonist would have named some other councilor, perhaps, as odd as it may seem, even Bishop Leslie. Clerics were a favorite target of sexual rumors; gossip earlier linked Mary of Guise to Cardinal Beaton and Mary, herself, to her uncle, Lorraine.

Before emerging from seclusion, Mary made a decision that helped to perpetuate her dynasty but ultimately enabled the usurpation of her crown. She transferred her son from Bothwell's and Huntly's care at Holyrood to Mar's custody at Stirling. On 19 March she discharged Mar, whose father had served as one of her guardians, from the captaincy of Edinburgh Castle, and on the 29th provided instructions for his governance of James at Stirling. To safeguard her son she ordered Mar to prevent anyone from entering the castle with more than two or three attendants.

Rumors claimed she transferred Edinburgh Castle to Bothwell, already the keeper of Dunbar Castle, but instead she assigned Edinburgh to James Cockburn of Skirling, her comptroller who later assisted her in England. Those who believe incorrectly that Mary granted Edinburgh to Bothwell to permit his abduction of her have overlooked the significance of her removing James from his custody. That Bothwell readily relinquished control of the prince supports the conclusion that he had not yet settled on an abduction plan although seizing her may have crossed his mind.[21]

While still in seclusion Mary also agreed to Lennox's request of 20 February for parliament to try his son's murderers. On 26 February, five days after she informed him that she had summoned parliament to meet, he requested a change in procedures for two reasons. He wanted an earlier trial than could be held in parliament, which required a 40-day notice, and had concluded that punishing murderers was not a parliamentary matter. He requested instead that the crown imprison the men listed on the placards and try them for murder. Since parliament's original jurisdiction in judicial matters usually involved treason accusations, Lennox probably realized that some members might question whether the death of his son, who lacked the crown matrimonial,

was a treasonable act. On 1 March Mary asked Lennox for greater speci-
ficity, pointing out that many names appeared on the often
contradictory placards. Although he had asked her to arrange an early
trial, he did not respond to her request until the 17th, over two weeks
later, when he repeated eight names from the placards with Bothwell
and Balfour heading the list.

Over a month had elapsed from the beginning of Lennox's correspondence with Mary, all of which was in Scots, until her re-entry into
public life on the 23rd. Five days later she met with her privy council.
Noting that Lennox had responded to their request for information
about the king's killers, the queen and her council, with Huntly,
Argyll, Bothwell, Lethington, but not Balfour in attendance, decided
that the accused earl and the other suspects, who were not named,
should be tried for murder. Since he knew that the anonymous placards
could not be introduced into a criminal trial and that Lennox had
obtained no other evidence against him, Bothwell welcomed the
opportunity to clear his name. As the law stipulated a 15-day notice,
the council set the trial for 12 April as a private rather than a crown
process in the justiciary court where an assize would determine
Bothwell's fate. Ironically, the parliament Mary had originally summoned to try Henry's killers met two days later.

The crown had jurisdiction over murder, arson, rape, and theft, as
noted in the above discussion of the Jedburgh justice ayre. Because
public and private justice overlapped in Scotland, however, it was actually the victim's paternal relatives, the agnatic group, who usually
initiated proceedings against the accused. In fact, the normal procedure
until the seventeenth century was for the injured party or his kin to
advance the prosecution by means of criminal letters passed under the
signet of the court of session.[22]

Lennox had gone directly, however, to Mary and through her to the
privy councilors, whose advice she solicited for the appropriate measures to adopt when a nobleman made a criminal charge against another
nobleman. Although he initially named eight men, the council had, in
fact, by leaving seven of the accused nameless, reduced Lennox's challenge to one person, another earl, Bothwell. The council's usual method
was to mediate noble disputes, promoting measures for keeping the
peace rather than ordering a trial for one of the aggrieved parties. Even
in 1589 during her son's reign, for example, the council issued an order

to suppress the quarrel between Francis Stewart, fifth earl of Bothwell, a nephew of the Bothwell the queen married, and Alexander, sixth Lord Home, even though in the course of their on-going bloodfeud Bothwell had by then killed three members of the Home family. Usually, to prosecute a powerful earl, royal officials had either to obtain his permission for the trial or to build a military and political alliance against him that could successfully bring him to justice. Only in the late sixteenth century was the crown's advocate transformed from an official acting mainly in civil cases on behalf of the monarch into a public prosecutor.

In preparing for the trial, Lennox started toward the capital with 3,000 armed retainers, following the usual noble practice of surrounding the courts of justice with armed allies. On the 11th realizing he could not collect a force larger than or even comparable to Bothwell's, he unsuccessfully pleaded for the postponement of the trial that on 26 February he had pressured Mary to expedite. He then abruptly left the realm. Various writers have claimed she instructed him to bring only six attendants, but the council order does not confirm this charge. The confusion probably arose from a law that prohibited the accused from having more than four attendants and the accuser more than six at the trial, a restriction that did not apply to the troops milling outside the courtroom. In obtaining retainers for the trial, Bothwell, the hereditary sheriff of Edinburgh, possessed a distinct advantage over Lennox, who had only recently returned to Scotland after a 20-year absence to resume control of his estates that lay near Glasgow. For legal proceedings as well as for military confrontations, the nobleman with the lesser force normally retired from the conflict.

At 6:00 a.m. a few hours before the trial was scheduled to begin, Drury's messenger, John Selby the younger, provost-martial of Berwick, arrived to petition Mary on behalf of Lennox to delay the proceedings. At first Bothwell denied Selby permission to see the still sleeping queen. When Selby returned about 9:00 a.m., Bothwell and Lethington took his message inside Holyrood and about one-half hour later, replied, surely mendaciously, that she had not yet arisen and advised him to return after the trial.

Bothwell was clearly interested in expediting the legal process. At 12:00 p.m. only he was tried in the justiciary court. As the other suspects, left unidentified by the privy council, were commoners, their status would have prevented them from being included in a nobleman's trial in any case. Argyll, the justice general, chose to preside despite usually relinquishing this duty to his justice depute. Although the trial lasted until 7:00 p.m., the assize's verdict was a foregone conclusion mainly because the accuser Lennox failed to appear with any evidence. The assize could only find the defendant guilty if the accused confessed to the crime or if eyewitness testimony was introduced. Unlike English law, Scottish law did not permit the admission of circumstantial evidence on the major charge. While the assize may have felt some concern about the number of Bothwell's retainers in Edinburgh, it unanimously acquitted him for lack of proof and not because of threats or because of special friendship. His armed troops could have, however, frightened away witnesses who might otherwise have volunteered information against him. Following the verdict, Bothwell posted his arms on the doors of the Tolbooth, St Giles' Church, and other places, offering personal combat to anyone challenging the decision.

After learning of Henry's death, Elizabeth and her councilors advised Mary to see that justice was done, but they lacked an appreciation of crown limitations. Scottish monarchs routinely took advice from their privy councilors on matters such as this, attempting to govern by consensus. Untrained in the law, they lacked expertise in the minutiae of legal issues.[23] Although, according to Thomas Craig, Mary commented wisely on questions of equity and justice, she was not conversant on the intricacies of criminal procedures as were her councilors, particularly Bellenden, the justice clerk.

Lennox might well have had more success in bringing his son's murderers to justice had he initially accused only the commoners in the hope, as did later occur, that during their trials they might reveal damaging information against Bothwell. The proof Lennox offered the council, rumors repeated on anonymous placards some of which slandered the queen, was totally inadequate. They did not constitute compelling evidence for Mary to attempt to remove Bothwell from the privy council, which had other compromised members, among them Balfour, her clerk register, and Argyll, her justice general. Even if she had not confirmed Argyll's life appointment to his hereditary position in 1558, she would have found it difficult to replace this powerful earl, who had access to great resources and who in peerage rank came after only Châtelherault and Huntly.

If the murder verdict against Bothwell that Lennox sought had actually been achieved, Mary would have been unable to enforce it unless her father-in-law had successfully raised more troops than his opponent. Lacking a royal army, she depended on noblemen's lieges for assistance.[24] Most of the earls who could have aided her against Bothwell were either compromised or accessories to Henry's death. Morton, who was involved in Riccio's assassination, was executed for Henry's murder in 1581, and Moray and Châtelherault, who surely would not have been interested in assisting the Lennox–Stewarts, were on the continent. In short, there were hardly any powerful noblemen she could summon, as she had, for example, when she called upon Huntly and Bothwell to aid her against the Chaseabout raiders. Surely, Lennox left Scotland because he had exhausted the reservoir of military support available for revenging the death of his son who had made so many enemies in less than two years as king.

Two days after Bothwell's acquittal, a parliament that lasted five days was held. In the procession Argyll carried the crown, Bothwell the scepter, the earl of Crawford, the sword. Mary assented to statutes annulling all acts contrary to the Protestant faith and took the Kirk under her special protection, publicly confirming she would not attempt to legalize Catholicism. The fallout from Henry's death had ended that goal. Other statutes returned his family estates to Cardell, confirmed Moray's and Morton's restoration, and ratified grants to them, as well as to Huntly, Bothwell, Lord Robert, and Lethington.

On the 19th after parliament was adjourned, Bothwell decided to strike for royal power. Having invited the parliamentary lords and bishops to a supper at Ainslie's Tavern in the Canongate, he asked them to sign a band declaring his innocence in the king's murder and, if the queen would humble herself enough to marry him, one of her subjects, promising to prevent any disruption of that union. Although extant lists vary, approximately 24 of the astonished men endorsed it: among them Archbishop Hamilton, Leslie, the earls of Argyll, Cassilis, Huntly, Morton, Sutherland, and Crawford, and Lords Seton, Fleming, and Herries. Only Eglinton escaped the tavern without subscribing. Many of the endorsers later renounced their action and signed bands to remove her from Bothwell's control. James Melville even recalled that Herries advised her not to marry Bothwell. It was not unprecedented for lords to agree to a proposal when confronted by someone with a strategic advantage and then to change their minds at a convenient opportunity. In France in 1558, for example, Moray approved Mary's marriage contract with Francis, surely aware that it had the potential for making Scotland a permanent French protectorate, but in 1559 joined the Congregation and challenged her mother's authority partly because of his hostility to French rule in Scotland. In 1567 some individuals might have agreed to the band because they believed it would never be implemented. Bothwell was still married to Huntly's sister and Mary would surely deem him an unworthy suitor.

News of the band having reached Lennox *en route* to England, he wrote his wife on 23 April that Bothwell would seize Mary. Why no one informed Mary of this possibility can best be explained by James Melville's later admission that they believed she would confront Bothwell with their accusation and were afraid of his reaction. This expectation seems reasonable, since Mary questioned Lord Robert about his alleged claim that it was unsafe for Henry to remain at Kirk o'Field.

On the day the Ainslie band would be signed, Mary retreated to Seton for a short rest. Then on the 21st she left for Stirling to visit James with an escort of about 30 individuals, including Huntly, Lethington, James Melville, and her household servants. When departing on short trips, she often moved with a small train, as in February 1564 when she traveled to Dunbar with a company of 20. While at Stirling she wrote to Bishop Laureo, expressing concerns about Elizabeth's mistreatment of Scottish travelers, promising on returning to Edinburgh to send him an express messenger, and requesting he inform Pius V that she would do nothing inconsistent with her devout purpose to die in the Catholic faith. These were not the sentiments of a woman who was planning to marry her abductor in a Protestant wedding. Unbeknownst to Mary, the bishop had abandoned his mission after conferring with Hay and Chisholm about Henry's murder and had left Paris. On 23 April the day before her abduction, he was at Lyons and in May reached Mondovi, where in June he received her letter, written in French by her own hand. Arriving with her letter was a message dated 4 May from du Croc, warning that she would marry Bothwell. She never, of course, sent Laureo the promised express messenger.

On 23 April Mary departed for Edinburgh but becoming ill, decided to rest at a private home before proceeding to Linlithgow. A porphryia attack could last for months, like the chronic illness she had suffered since October. The next day the 24th, as she reached "Foulbriggis," which lies just west of Edinburgh between two bridges, one crossing the Almond and the other Gogar Burn, Bothwell approached her with 800 armed horsemen.[25] Warning it was dangerous to go to Edinburgh, he seized her bridle and escorted her for safe keeping to Dunbar, one of the best examples of artillery fortifications in Scotland. As he possessed this large force, she surely discouraged her attendants from resisting; a strong cultural convention, moreover, held that it was dishonorable for a gentlewoman to fight back on a personal, physical level in public.

Four of the deponents at Paris in 1575, who were asked for information to support Mary's petition for a divorce from Bothwell, swore that they were at Edinburgh when James Borthwick, her messenger, arrived with her plea for help. The burgh's inhabitants quickly collected their armor and rushed out of their portes, but all they could accomplish was firing their cannon twice at the riders as they sped by on their way to Dunbar.[26] Bothwell then replaced her ladies with one attendant, his sister Janet Hepburn, the widow of Mary's half-brother, Lord John, who died in late 1563.

Some writers have criticized Mary for not shouting for assistance on the journey to Dunbar, citing this failure as evidence of her desire to be abducted. That she did not seek aid depends on the evidence of chroniclers, who did not witness the abduction, although they were probably correct, but for the wrong reason. Armed horsemen surrounded her, shielding her from contact with bystanders as she rode toward Dunbar. Even in the unlikely event that some observers could have heard her cries over the pounding of horses' hooves, they would have been unable to organize a rescue party in time. Others in her train, like James Melville, who later recalled that Bothwell boasted he would marry his royal captive whether she would or would not have him, would surely have summoned aid if they had not feared the reprisals of this powerful earl who could rally thousands of lieges for support.

Bothwell botched the arrangements for murdering the king with gunpowder, which required much planning and coordination, but he pulled off the abduction without a hitch. James Melville also recalled that after the still married earl seized Mary, he compelled her to become his bedfellow. In his old age, Melville might not remember all these events clearly, but the sexual violation of his queen would surely not be one he would forget. Probably, Bothwell raped her and threatened to use her sexually as his wife until she consented to marry him. Leslie, who was not present at the abduction, confirmed the earl's use of force against her.

Even so Bothwell attempted to soften news about the violence by pretending that governmental business continued as usual perhaps to forestall rescue attempts. Clearly, he directed his captive's various activities; between 26 April and 1 May he provided several charters for her to sign. Meanwhile, his adherents, among them Captain William Blackader, who was to be arrested and executed in June for his share in Henry's murder, spread rumors eagerly repeated by her enemies that she agreed to the abduction to invent an excuse for marrying Bothwell.

James Melville's view was different: he claimed she had to marry Bothwell because he forced her to lie with him and ravished her. Shamed by the emotional and physical assault, she reacted like many other early modern victims who believed their ravishment polluted them: she decided to marry the rapist and to suppress all references to the sexual violation. Unwilling to dishonor her family by revealing the rape and eliciting charges that she was immensely immodest or that she deserved to be attacked because she had not lived virtuously enough, she chose to act politically foolish and to brave religious censure. As she must have known, many people would disbelieve a woman who claimed she was raped; church courts sometimes punished both the accuser and the attacker, although the rapist's penalty was usually more severe. Rape is still the most under-reported crime, but it was even more under-reported in her society because of the value placed on female chastity. In characterizing male ideas about women's virginity as "ridiculous," Montaigne referred disparagingly to a contemporary who argued that ladies should embrace death rather than "submit to the outrage of their chastity."[27]

Mary may not have discussed the assault with her confessor, Roche Mamerot, a doctor in theology and a French Dominican, who entered her household about 1563. After learning she intended to wed Bothwell, the disappointed cleric left Scotland. To de Silva in London he explained that two or three Catholic priests reassured her that she could wed Bothwell because he and his wife were too closely related. Mamerot also claimed that Mary viewed her union with him as a way of settling religion in Scotland. Had he remained at her court, Mamerot would have witnessed the queen's great despair at becoming Bothwell's wife and would have been called upon once again to comfort a woman wishing herself dead. When de Silva asked if Mary had colluded in her husband's murder, Mamerot swore that she was a devout Catholic and knew nothing about his death. Until the question of her marriage with Bothwell arose, he maintained that he had never seen a woman act more courageously or virtuously.

7

Seeking Refuge,
1567–69

On 6 May as a public sign that Mary was under his control, Bothwell led her by her horse's bridle into Edinburgh's almost impregnable castle, ensuring that she could neither escape nor be rescued before publicly repeating her promise to wed him. It had been 12 days since he took her to Dunbar and raped her, forcing her to agree to marry him. For security reasons two days after arriving at Edinburgh, he transferred the castle from the control of Mary's appointee, Skirling, to Balfour, whom Bothwell gravely misjudged since the new captain would soon betray him.

That Bothwell was in the awkward position of planning his royal wedding while his wife was ending their marriage supports the argument that his abduction of the queen was opportunistic. On 26 April two days after Mary's capture, Lady Bothwell petitioned Edinburgh's commissary court for a divorce on the grounds that her husband committed adultery at Haddington with her sewing-maid, Bessie Crawford, and on 3 May the suit was granted. In contrast to the Catholic Church's policy of allowing couples to remarry only if the union was deemed invalid from its inception, the Kirk usually permitted divorce with the possibility of remarriage in the presence of adultery or desertion.

Although aware that Bothwell was planning a Protestant wedding, Mary asked Archbishop Hamilton on 27 April to inquire into the validity of the earl's marriage. On 7 May by virtue of his authority as papal *legate a latere*, Hamilton nullified Bothwell's alliance with Jean Gordon on the grounds that they were related in the double fourth degree of consanguinity, thus ignoring his dispensation of that impediment in 1566. Technically, however, his decision was justifiable. The earlier dispensation was a dead letter, as it had not been published and executed according to its terms because the Bothwells were wed in a Protestant rather than a Catholic ceremony.

On 7 May the same day Hamilton pronounced the nullification, apparently at Mary's request to ease her conscience, Bothwell instructed John Craig to publish the banns, a demand the preacher refused until the queen sent a signed order requiring his compliance. Denouncing the marriage in his sermon, Craig published under protest the first of the three obligatory banns on Sunday, the 11th.

Motivated by a variety of beliefs, individuals had been attaching placards on the Tolbooth door charging Mary with colluding in the abduction. Some of the anonymous authors undoubtedly thought women secretly desired to be ravished. In 1564 speaking more generally of women's nature and not specifically about rape, Randolph succinctly stated that after many refusals, women were usually willingly drawn to that which they desired. Prevailing attitudes about the remarriage of widows reinforced the collusion theory. Widows who were also mothers were accused of neglecting their children to feed the insatiable sexual appetites aroused by their previous marital experiences. In fact, bereft of a husband's and sometimes even a brother's protection, widows were extremely vulnerable to rape. It could be argued that Henry's murder, followed by the departure of Moray, the relative who was most capable of assisting Mary, made her vulnerable to the ambitions of bold soldiers of fortune like Bothwell.

Others assumed that she colluded in her abduction because she needed the assistance of a strong husband in governing her realm's many factions. This was an argument presented in the official notification of their marriage to the French crown, but it was a problematic allegation at best. Factions posed no greater threat to her in 1567 before Bothwell seized her than in 1565 when Moray challenged her marriage to Darnley. Even if Bothwell were of sufficient social status to become her husband, she had no incentive to relinquish her realm to him since she was already relying on his advice and that of Lethington, whom de Foix compared favorably to Cecil.

Still others viewing Bothwell as an unworthy bridegroom claimed his success depended on evoking the supernatural, referring, for example, to the magical assistance of Janet Beaton, a niece of Cardinal Beaton and the widow of Sir Walter Scott of Buccleaugh. These suspicions took on greater validity when a suitor, like Bothwell, appeared to have no chance to win his bride by ordinary means. Even he conceded his unworthiness in a letter to Archbishop Beaton, admitting that Mary could have wed men of greater birth and estimation although none of them would have been more affectionately inclined to honor and serve her than he.[1]

A further complication concerning abductions generally is that upon release, hostages often face accusations that they collaborated with their captors. Even Christians in early modern England's West Country charged their country folk, whom Barbary pirates seized and kept in captivity, of returning home as Islam's spies.

Despite rumors that Mary welcomed the abduction, as late as 12 July the privy council was still accusing Bothwell with violently seizing her and naming him the king's chief murderer. This official position undoubtedly reflected what had actually occurred. Mary had been well aware that if she consented to remarriage only three months after her husband's death, many would deny she had affection for him and doubt he was the father of any child she might be carrying. More importantly, as her foremost priority was James's well-being, she would have shrunk from presenting him with so unworthy a stepfather as Bothwell. The queen also understood that ignoring the long-held tradition of obtaining the consent of relatives and friends to a proposed marriage would not only besmirch her honor but also that of her kinship and lineage. Indeed, in May 1566 when the dowager duchess of Guise sought her advice about the possibility of marrying Jacques de Savoy, duke of Nemours, a nobleman with whom the queen was acquainted, Mary replied positively, noting particularly that the alliance would be of great advantage to her aunt's children by her previous marriage.

On 12 May the day after Craig published the banns, Bothwell decided he could safely escort Mary to Holyrood Palace. *En route*, they stopped at the Tolbooth to permit her to assure Huntly, the lord chancellor, and the lords of session that she was not a captive. While there, she granted a remission to Bothwell and others for her abduction and for all other crimes whatsoever, words that clearly encompassed the king's murder. To the list of those pardoned, Balfour added his name.

That evening she ennobled Bothwell as the duke of Orkney and the lord of Shetland. It is noteworthy that she neither advanced him to the kingship nor to the dukedom of Albany, the title formerly held by the king's younger son and his heirs and the one she had bestowed upon Darnley. Later, James VI granted the Orkney title, reduced to an earldom, to Mary's illegitimate half brother, Lord Robert. Hereafter, Bothwell will be referred to as Orkney to highlight his unique position in the Scottish aristocracy, since the only other dukedom was a French peerage held by the exiled Châtelherault. On the 14th Mary and Orkney signed their marriage contract, which Archbishop Hamilton, Leslie, Huntly, Fleming, Lindsay, Bellenden, among others, witnessed; on the 15th Adam Bothwell, bishop of Orkney, married them in a Protestant service in Holyrood's Great Hall. She wore a black gown decorated with gold braid, which she later exchanged for a yellow outfit. The wedding banquet lacked the usual festivities at least partly because of the haste with which the ceremony was arranged. Some protestors placed on the palace gates the words, *Mense malas maio nubere vulgus ait* (Wantons marry in the month of May).

Afterward on her wedding day, an extremely depressed Mary met with du Croc, who had refused to attend the ceremony. In reporting their conversation to Catherine de' Medici on the 18th, he explained that Mary had asked him to excuse the formality between her and her husband, since if she seemed unhappy, it was because she could not rejoice and she wished herself dead. The sympathetic ambassador also repeated rumors he had heard that when closeted with Orkney on the 17th, she was overheard screaming for a knife to stab herself. Du Croc further revealed that he was refusing to recognize the duke as Mary's husband and advised Catherine against responding to Orkney's letters that Chisholm would bring to her. In June confirming Mary's continuing depression, du Croc learned from Lethington that since her marriage she had shed endless tears. Leslie also recalled that after the illegal ceremony, he had a conversation with the depressed queen who wept and showed many signs of repentance.

One of the most mortifying experiences of Mary's life must have been the duty of sending out announcements, dictated by her husband, explaining why she wed so soon after the king's death and without prior communication with her relatives. Hinting at Bothwell's control over her, Robert Melville had informed Cecil on 7 May that the contents of a recent letter to Elizabeth derived more from the counsel of those about Mary than from herself. She lacked, he remarked, her usual wise advisors. Although absent in Fife while writing this letter some 13 days after Mary's abduction, Melville, like others knowledgeable about her habits, would have realized that she was Bothwell's captive. For almost two weeks on the day Melville wrote, the usually accessible queen had been seen in public only once: when Bothwell led her from the castle at Dunbar to the one at Edinburgh.

Chisholm delivered the official marriage announcement to Charles and Catherine in late May. He was required to inform them of Orkney's loyal service to the crown, to attribute his earlier disfavor to the jealousy of Mary's other subjects, to point out her nobility's support for the alliance, and to claim that she could no longer rule alone because of the realm's many factions. Chisholm's instructions also contain the only contemporary assertion that Bothwell courted her before the abduction. After obtaining the Ainslie band, he supposedly began from afar to reveal his intentions to her, but as she was then at Seton and left the next day for Stirling, this claim seems contrived and even preposterous. At the abduction, as James Melville recalled, Bothwell's vow to wed her whether she would or would not have him, indicates he had probably not yet proposed to her. Finally, Chisholm's instructions ignored the rape, admitting only that Bothwell's actions were rude.[2] After conveying the above information to Charles and Catherine, Chisholm explained that the wedding, which he had attended, took place out of necessity rather than by free choice.[3] Meanwhile Robert Melville took the official explanation to Elizabeth.

The response abroad was mostly negative. Michael Bonelli, Cardinal Allesandrino, assured Laureo that Pius V would decline to communicate with her again until he could discern some sign of improvement in her behavior and religious life. Many Catholics condemned the Protestant wedding; if she had converted Bothwell to her faith, she might have mollified some of her critics who could anticipate that he would assist her in re-establishing Catholicism in Scotland. Despite Orkney's Protestant beliefs, Elizabeth also deplored the union because she viewed him as a French ally who might send James to France for his upbringing.

Even before the wedding some endorsers of the Ainslie band were conspiring against Bothwell. On 1 May at Stirling, Atholl, Morton, Argyll, Mar and others signed a band to free her and to protect her son, whom they believed Bothwell would attempt to seize to coopt a possible competing center of authority. Some, like Kirkaldy of Grange, even feared he might have the prince murdered. Instead of challenging him immediately, they delayed, seeking to attract greater numbers. Another band subscribed after the wedding carried the names of 12 earls and 14 lords and offered a pardon to Balfour in exchange for his promise to deliver Edinburgh Castle to them.

On 28 May Orkney summoned lieges to convene at Melrose in the Borders on 15 June ostensibly to deal with criminals there but more likely to raise forces for combating the growing threat of the confederate lords. When he learned they were planning to surprise him at Holyrood, he took the queen on 6 June to Borthwick Castle, about 12 miles south of the capital. Four days later with 1,200 troops, the confederates, including Atholl, Morton, and Mar, threatened Mary and Orkney at Borthwick.

Learning of their advance, Orkney quickly slipped away, and about midnight on the 11th dressed in men's clothing, Mary joined him at a prearranged rendezvous and returned with him to Dunbar. The disguise offered her not only a means of protection but also an opportunity to travel more easily than usual, since it permitted her to ride astride on a man's saddle. Surely, she kept the appointment because she already suspected that she was pregnant. She also probably did not wish to surrender to the rebel leaders, particularly Morton who was implicated in Riccio's death.

Balfour had meanwhile been permitting the confederates peaceful access to the capital. On the 11th they proclaimed at its Mercat Cross their intention of rescuing the queen, securing the prince's person, and avenging the king's murder. The next day they issued a proclamation that charged Orkney with forcing the queen to marry him and summoned allies to help them bring him to justice for ravishing her and for killing the king.

Because Balfour promised, but ultimately failed, to support Orkney and Mary with the castle guns, they left the safety of Dunbar prematurely, still raising troops as they marched northward. On the 15th their army confronted the confederates at Carberry Hill about seven miles from Edinburgh. Hoping to avoid bloodshed, du Croc attempted to end the dispute by promising Mary if she abandoned her husband, he would arrange for her restoration to power, an offer she turned down. About evenly matched, neither army was eager for battle but as the day wore on, her soldiers began wandering off. When Orkney characteristically called for single combat to settle the dispute, several men accepted his challenge, but he declined to meet them, claiming their status was inferior to his. Although Lord Lindsay then volunteered to fight him, the duke eventually gave up the attempt, fled southward to the Borders, tried futilely to recruit another army, and then moved northward to his duchy. Short of funds he resorted to piracy and managed to collect and equip six ships. Upon learning that a Scottish fleet was pursuing him, Orkney set sail in September for Scandinavia, where he was captured and then released to Frederick II, king of Denmark and Norway, who placed him in prison.

IMPRISONMENT AT LOCHLEVEN

Following Orkney's departure, Mary surrendered to Grange, who led her by her horse's bridle into the confederate camp amidst shouts that she was a whore and the murderess of her husband and should be burned. Labeling her a whore was doubly significant. Protestants also denounced Catholic Rome as a harlot, the whore of Babylon. Displaying banners depicting Henry's corpse lying under a tree with his son kneeling and praying to the Lord for vengeance, they lodged her, still dressed in tattered clothes, in the provost's house in Edinburgh. Then after briefly stopping at Holyrood, Lindsay and William, fourth Lord Ruthven, the future first earl of Gowrie, obeyed an order from the confederate lords and moved her late on the 16th to Lochleven, a lake-moated castle. Its castellan, William Douglas, the uterine half brother of Moray, lived at Lochleven with their mother, Margaret Erskine, who still begrudged Paul III's refusal to grant the dispensation that would have permitted her to wed James V. Initially, Mary's jailers confined her in the small Glassin Tower in the courtyard, but in August they transferred her to the main tower or keep's third (solar) floor, which was divided into two rooms.

Keeping her secluded, her captors refused to permit either Nicholas de Neufville, seigneur de Villeroy, or Throckmorton access to her when they reached Scotland on special assignment. Throckmorton remained in Edinburgh from 12 July to 30 August, communicating with her through Robert Melville. Like du Croc who departed for home in June, Throckmorton noted that Balfour met daily with Morton, Atholl, Home, and even Lethington, who had joined the confederates on 6 June and then accompanied them to Carberry Hill. According to Richard Bannatyne, Lethington later claimed he decided to support Mary's rebels because he wanted to bring the king's principal murderer, Orkney, to justice and to remove the queen from her unhappy marriage with him.

Throckmorton's instructions directed him to inform Mary that Elizabeth desired her freedom but required she divorce Orkney. Both he and Melville tried unsuccessfully to convince her to repudiate him to gain her release. On 17 July Throckmorton revealed that she declined the divorce because she was seven weeks' pregnant and did not wish to forfeit her honor by bearing an illegitimate child. Concerned for her well-being partly because he was denied access to her, he responded that this dishonored status was deplorable, but it was a better option than dying. He continued to fear for her safety, especially after learning that the privy council had been discussing the political advantages of her death. He later claimed that her captors had spared her life only because he conveyed his monarch's strong warning not to harm her, an assessment validated by Robert Melville. Indeed, on 23 June as Elizabeth was planning to send Throckmorton to Scotland, she had reassured Mary in writing of her support, promising to accomplish whatever she could for Mary's "safety and honor" and pledging to be a "good neighbor" and "dear sister" to her. She also said she would omit nothing in furthering the "tranquility" of Scotland.[4]

It was unlikely that Mary knew the precise duration of the pregnancy that prevented her from agreeing to a divorce. In fixing on seven weeks, she was claiming that conception occurred subsequent to the wedding, thereby implicitly denying the pre-marital rape. About a week after revealing her condition to Throckmorton, she suffered a miscarriage, which her secretary, Nau, later reported was of twins. In July Robert Melville noted that she had gained weight; twin fetuses would have caused her condition to become noticeable sooner than was the normal case. If she were bearing twins, her pregnancy must have been more advanced than seven weeks, since her midwife could have detected them only if she were about three months along. In that case conception must have occurred by late April about the time of the abduction. That her discharge was examined carefully enough to discern twins was not unusual, as midwives routinely inspected the afterbirth for abnormalities.

It is possible that her miscarriage prompted a visit from Lady Moray. On July 26 Throckmorton noted that recently Mary, recovering from two fits of ague, sorrowfully met with her and sadly parted from her. In June 1564 when Lady Moray's nearly two-month old son died, Mary, who had been present at his birth, condoled with her. At the end of July rumors claimed that Mary was still bedridden.

Threatened by Lindsay and her other captors, the ailing queen had already agreed to abdicate. On 24 July she signed a statement claiming that her illness made it impossible for her to reign, designating the absent Moray as her son's regent, and until his return, appointing Morton as his deputy. In the unlikelihood her half brother would refuse this office, she named a council, including Châtelherault and Lennox. Five days later, Bishop Hepburn officiated at James's coronation. In August as Mary's health was improving, Moray reached Lochleven, lectured her for her mistakes over a two-day period, and assumed the regency.

Earlier on 29 June Mary's allies, a mixture of Catholics and Protestants, including Archbishop Hamilton, Argyll, Huntly, Lethington, Fleming, Herries, and Boyd, had signed a band at Dumbarton to free her. But discouraged because Moray maintained control of her, most of them had by mid-September acquiesced in his regency. They surely remained somewhat concerned, however, about the restricted access to her at Lochleven. Instead of moving her to Stirling where she could interact with her child under Mar's supervision, Moray instructed his relatives to keep her closely confined at Lochleven, permitting, for her only exercise, walks around the island's limited grounds. For someone of royal status she possessed inadequate clothing and attendants, the latter never numbering more than 12. On 17 July a month after her capture when she was still pregnant, she lacked a cleric, an apothecary, a valet, and an embroiderer to draw designs for her sewing, one of her few leisure employments.

During her almost eleven-month captivity, she dispatched secret messages pleading for assistance and searched for a means of escape, despite her reported chronic side ache, a swelling in her arm, and a serious fall in February 1568. Three months later on 1 May, the day before her liberation, she sent Elizabeth a reminder of her promise of assistance when the ring she gave Mary was returned. Since her enemies had confiscated her possessions, Mary continued, she hoped that Elizabeth would agree to help her without recovering the gem.

ESCAPE, DEFEAT, AND FLIGHT TO ENGLAND

The next day aided by William Douglas's brother, George, and his cousin, Willie Douglas, she escaped from Lochleven. Disguised in shabby clothes, she traveled with Willie in a stolen boat to the shore where George awaited her with horses. They met Lord Seton, accompanied him to his Castle of Niddry near Winchburgh, and then journeyed to Hamilton House, a few miles from Glasgow. On the 4th she notified Moray that she had repudiated her abdication. In the next few days she attracted a large number of warriors to support her restitution: 9 earls, 9 bishops, 17 lords, 12 abbots, 14 commendators, numerous lairds and their followers, totaling in all about 6,000 men. Many must have joined her army because they were appalled at Moray's treatment of her. Her supporters continued to be a broad mixture of Catholics and Protestants. Indeed, following her captivity in England, the Scottish civil war and Marianism more generally were never synonymous with Catholicism. She continued to have many Protestant adherents.

With Argyll serving as her lieutenant general, the army began escorting Mary toward Dumbarton Castle, which Fleming had controlled since 1565, but unfortunately for her and her allies, Moray was nearby at Glasgow holding a justice ayre. On 13 May with Grange's brilliant tactical assistance, Moray's smaller force of 4,000 defeated her army at the village of Langside. Her overconfident supporters misjudged Moray's intentions, assuming that since his army was smaller than theirs, he would permit them to pass on to Dumbarton. Because of their superior numbers, Mary's allies had also anticipated victory if Moray unexpectedly chose to engage them in battle. James Melville recalled that having just gained her freedom after almost a year in close confinement, Mary was more interested in reaching the safety of Dumbarton than in challenging Moray in battle. Cecil also remarked that her forces were stopped in flight past Glasgow.

Her behavior following the defeat lends credence to their opinions. Having witnessed the conflict from the hillside and seen scores of soldiers killed or captured after Argyll fell ill possibly from a mild stroke or heart attack, the frightened queen fled in disguise southward, reaching Dundrennan Abbey in Galloway by the 15th. Later, she explained to Elizabeth that Moray's soldiers had stopped pursuing her straggling troops and had turned to prevent her from reaching Dumbarton. She also criticized the misguided method of her allies who defended themselves in a disorderly fashion and marched in a confusing manner. This experience made her realize how warfare diminishes the authority of queens regnant. Having relinquished the command of her army to her warriors, she was forced to rely on their strategies for her defense.

Unable to reach Dumbarton, Mary decided to seek refuge in England over the protests of her adherents, who surely reminded her of the 18-year English captivity of her ancestor, James I. To Richard Lowther, deputy governor of Carlisle, she wrote, explaining that she was being forced into exile and requesting permission to enter England. Enclosed with the message was the ring from Elizabeth, which Robert Melville retrieved for her. On the 16th without waiting for a reply, Mary boarded a fishing boat at a small bay called Abbey Burnfoot and disembarked on the Cumberland side four hours later at a place then called Ellensport. Fleming, Herries, Lords Livingston and Boyd, George and Willie Douglas, and nine or so others moved with her to Workington Hall, where Lowther with 400 horsemen greeted her and then escorted her to Carlisle in the absence of Henry, ninth Lord Scrope, the warden of the west marches. Having reached Carlisle by 18 May without funds or a change of clothing, Mary requested assistance from both Elizabeth, who was surprised to learn of her arrival, and Catherine, who soon would be unable to aid her since France was on the brink of another religious conflict: Condé declared war on the crown in August.

With hindsight it is clear that the flight to England was a blunder, but Mary had few options. Even a France on the brink of another civil war was a better destination, but traveling there on the fishing boat was impossible: she had no French fleet to defend her against pirates or other enemies and the uncertain weather made sea voyages perilous at any time. Recalling Elizabeth's sympathetic messages when she was at Lochleven, relying on their kinship, an important impulse in this society, and recognizing the significance of the ring, an assurance of aid sent to her by her good sister, Mary seems to have thought, incorrectly as it turned out, that her cousin would assist her in recovering her throne. It is also true that the losing faction in Scottish struggles usually sought refuge in England.

After reaching Carlisle with Scrope on the 28th to become Mary's guardian, Sir Francis Knollys, vice-chamberlain of the royal household, reported that she fled to England because she lacked a secure refuge in Scotland or safe passage to France. Indeed, eight days before he arrived, she wrote to Cassilis, explaining that "for the safety of my body finding no sure access nor place within my realm to retire," she was constrained to depart for England. She further informed him that within a few days she planned to leave for France to obtain aid against her rebels.[5]

Her flight left her allies with certain psychological and strategic disadvantages in the ensuing civil war, but she could not have anticipated that Lethington and Grange, who replaced Balfour as captain of Edinburgh Castle in September 1567, would join her forces in 1569 or that the struggle on her behalf would survive without significant foreign aid until 1573. She did know in 1568 that her supporters were somewhat unreliable. The Hamiltons, led by the archbishop during Châtelherault's exile, had challenged her authority in 1559–60 and again in 1565; Argyll, the losing general at Langside and probably an endorser of her husband's murder band, had been a Chaseabout raider. Huntly, one of her most trusted supporters, had not only conspired against Henry but had also joined Archbishop Hamilton and Argyll in signing the Ainslie band. From her perspective, their present loyalty must have been gratifying, but as they were all descendants of her Stewart ancestors and related to the Hamiltons through the female line, they possessed reversionary interests to the regency that her half brother controlled and, indeed, also to the royal succession.

If Mary had remained in Scotland, she would have had to respond to the belief of many of her subjects that she needed the aid of a husband to rule the realm. At Lochleven when she was still pregnant, Throckmorton learned that plans were underway to marry her to a Campbell or a Hamilton to consolidate her political position. Entering either of these unions would have diminished her authority; with English or French aid, however, she might avoid another Scottish alliance and retain governmental flexibility. Her noblemen's views seemed to have accorded with Sir Anthony Weldon's later remark in his chronicle of the English kings that he had omitted Queen Mary and Queen Elizabeth because he would have nothing to do with women. Indeed, in September 1567, de Silva reported to Philip that the Scots hate the rule of kings but despise even more the governance of a woman.

The wives of Scrope and Knollys, Mary's first guardians, were Elizabeth's maternal relatives. Margaret Howard, Lady Scrope, was one of Norfolk's sisters and the cousin of the English queen, whose maternal grandmother was a Howard. One of Elizabeth's favorite ladies was Catherine Carey, Lady Knollys, who was the daughter of Mary Boleyn Carey, the queen's maternal aunt. When Lady Knollys became seriously ill while her husband served as Mary's guardian, a post he reluctantly accepted, Elizabeth refused either to send his wife to him or to release him from his duties so that he could attend her. She died on 15 January as he was transferring Mary to the control of George Talbot, sixth earl of Shrewsbury.[6]

Even before Knollys reached Carlisle, his duty to secure the Scottish queen had begun. Having learned that Thomas Percy, seventh earl of Northumberland, was attempting to gain access to her, Knollys wrote to him, but before sending the letter, encountered the earl *en route* to Carlisle and complained to him about his actions. Northumberland, who, of course, would be one of the important rebel leaders in the Northern Rising of 1569, responded that he sought only to protect Mary from enemies who might follow her into England and then retired from the scene. In fact, Mary, herself, expressed concerns that Moray might cross the border and attempt to capture her.[7]

Knollys and Scrope offered interesting observations about the Scottish queen. Noting that she was a pleasant woman with an eloquent tongue, discreet head, stout courage, and a liberal heart, she was, they also believed, impervious to flattery and undaunted by the plain speech of persons she deemed honest. They judged her to have a high opinion of her worth, citing her claim that no one but God could judge her and her prediction that she would revenge her wrongs with her enemies' blood. Her ready wit impressed them: they discovered that she understood her allies' motivations, some joining her for her sake, some for the French cause, and others for the Hamilton claim. Then, there were the opportunists.

Mary sent Herries and Fleming to Elizabeth on 28 May with three requests. She asked for a private meeting with her good sister and her aid in restoring her regal authority, but if her cousin could not help her, she required a passport for Fleming so that he could seek assistance for her in France. She also reminded Elizabeth that it was the rebels she asked Mary to pardon who forced her into exile. In the next few days Elizabeth and her councilors came to an agreement on three issues concerning Mary and her requests. First, responding to Knollys's warning that she might escape on horseback if she remained housed so close to the frontier, Elizabeth decided to transfer her to a residence farther away from the border. Second, she decided she would not meet with Mary until after a hearing was held in England to settle the Scottish disputes. Third, she declined to provide Fleming with a passport to seek aid from Catherine and Charles because a major English priority was preventing renewed French involvement in Scotland.

In June Elizabeth dispatched Henry Middlemore, Throckmorton's cousin who had served as his secretary in France, on a dual mission. He carried with him her correspondence for Mary at Carlisle and for Moray in Scotland, as well as Cecil's instructions with additional explanations. On the 14th Middlemore delivered Elizabeth's letter to Mary, which promised that she would be as careful of her cousin's life and honor as any parent would be. The English queen also explained that it would damage her honor if she invited Mary to court before her acquittal of the crimes charged against her. Responding emotionally to Middlemore, Mary protested that she had expected a better welcome than this from Elizabeth to whom she wished personally to reveal matters that she had never told anyone else. He tried to assuage her concerns by pointing out that once she was declared innocent, Elizabeth would see that she was restored to her regal dignity. If, furthermore, his queen were to meet with Mary before the hearing, he explained, her Scottish adversaries would not view Elizabeth as a neutral judge. It was also Middlemore's duty to convey the news that his queen wanted her to be located closer to her court. Expressing a strong disinterest in moving farther from Scotland, Mary asked him if she would have a choice in the matter or if she would be forcibly taken like a captive to another residence. Also concerned about the delays in hearing from Herries, she asked Middlemore if Elizabeth were holding him as a prisoner. Middlemore denied, of course, that either of them was his government's captive.

On 14 June before departing for Scotland, Middlemore sent a report about his discussion with Mary to Cecil along with a note from her to Elizabeth. Mary wrote that she regretted her confidence in requesting her cousin for assistance had been so misplaced. She asked Elizabeth's permission to seek aid elsewhere and reminded her of her audience with Moray in 1565, when he was an English refugee. Middlemore then left to deliver Elizabeth's letter to Moray, which informed him about the inquiry and ordered him to refrain from attacking or injuring Mary's allies.

Although the privy council originally recommended that Mary be housed at Tutbury in Staffordshire, a royal castle of the duchy of Lancaster, she refused to move to that location. Under protest she finally agreed to go to Bolton, Scrope's castle in Wensleydale. On 13 July claiming that she preferred relocating to Dumbarton or to France, Mary commenced the two-day journey to Bolton, a walled structure in a mountainous area of Yorkshire described by Knollys as desolate and wild. Just before their departure, more of her servants and attendants reached her, including Mary Seton with wigs for the queen's hair, which had been clipped for the incognito flight from Langside. These newcomers, including Lady Livingston who arrived in August, increased Mary's household to 30 gentlefolk and 45 domestics; the number of the latter, referred to by Knollys as the baser sort, grew to 60 at Bolton. In addition, another 30 allies, among them, Skirling and Lord Claud Hamilton, commendator of Paisley, the fifth and youngest son of Châtelherault, resided in town at their own charge.

At Bolton Mary installed procedures as though she were holding court. She ordered erected in her great chamber a canopy or cloth of state made of satin figured with gold, which arrived from Scotland along with some of her clothes and furnishings. The canopy was a symbol of high social rank, usually indicating some degree of royal status. Noting that she hunted and hawked daily, Knollys predicted that preventing her from pursuing these sports, which brought her such pleasure and delight, would greatly depress her.

Among Mary's retrieved possessions were her sewing materials, making it possible for her to resume the needlework that she greatly enjoyed. One of her English guards, Christopher Norton, later described an encounter with her at Bolton. His recollection indicates that she customarily joined other members of her guardians' household in their leisure moments at dinnertime. While Knollys and Scrope played chess and Lady Scrope stood by the fireside, Mary sat at the window knitting. Deciding to warm herself at the fire, she asked Norton to hold her sewing for her. When Knollys's chess game was over, he noticed Norton assisting the queen with her sewing and warned him to stop watching her, for she would make a "fool" out of him.[8]

As Mary's guardian, Knollys contended with many of the same problems that were to plague his successors. Her uncertain status did make his duties somewhat more awkward than theirs, however. Under his charge she was neither completely free nor yet entirely a prisoner. He struggled daily with preventing her household from increasing in size, with acquiring sufficient funds to purchase provisions, and with finding sufficient quantities of them. That she was winning support in the community for her personal cause and for her faith also deeply concerned him. Then, too, her secret correspondence and numerous visitors, especially Francis Montmorin, seigneur de Saint-Herem, a French envoy, complicated his supervision of her. Finally, he was forced to respond to claims that he was treating her too leniently.

Imprisoned with few occupations beyond her daily exercise, Mary wrote numerous letters. By 22 October four months after reaching England, she had addressed more than 20 to Elizabeth concerning several issues. Mary asked her to prevent Moray's forfeiture of her friends' estates at a pretended parliament and charged him with stealing her jewels. She denied she was guilty of any wrongdoing and repeated her desire for a meeting with her good sister. Other letters to Elizabeth referred to the plague at Edinburgh Castle where many of Mary's allies were imprisoned, to Border violence, and to arrangements for the inquiry in England to settle the differences between her and her subjects.

In treating Scottish problems Cecil, among other Englishmen, advocated his realm's feudal superiority, which he justified with documentary evidence. He claimed that it was appropriate for an investigation concerning the dissension between Mary and her subjects to occur in England because its rulers had the right to settle disputes over the Scottish crown, as could be proved by many records and precedents.

When Herries finally returned from court, reaching Bolton on 24 July, he briefed Mary about the proposed inquiry. Like Middlemore before him, Herries gave assurances to Mary that following her acquittal, the English queen would restore her cousin to her regal authority in Scotland. In her letters, as for example, one written on 22 June, Elizabeth was less specific, promising only that when Mary was found innocent, her English cousin would aid and honor her and do nothing to harm her. After consulting with Herries, Mary informed Elizabeth that she would consent to the inquiry under two conditions: she must maintain her royal rank in it, as she would not allow her subjects a status equal to hers, and its purpose must be limited to arranging her restitution. She would not accept anyone as judge over her except God. Attempting to appear conciliatory, she offered to establish English Protestantism in Scotland at her return.

In September after her attendance at prayer services fueled rumors of her conversion to Protestantism, she explained at a meeting in her great chamber that she remained a faithful Catholic. To Knollys' protest concerning her dissimulation, she responded:

> Why would you have me to lose France and Spain and all my friends . . . by seeming to change my religion, and yet I am not assured that . . . my good sister will be my assured friend to the satisfaction of my honor and expectation?[9]

That same month she confided to Elizabeth of Valois in Spain that her Protestant captors were trying to convert her but that she would never change her religion. If she made concessions, it was only because she was a prisoner. Later in December she confessed to Pius V that as Elizabeth had denied her a priest, she listened to a minister praying in English. She pleaded for his pardon and absolution and promised to be an obedient member of the Roman Catholic Church.

THE INQUIRY INTO MARY'S RESTITUTION AND THE CASKET LETTERS

From the outset Moray viewed the inquiry as her murder trial, believing that only if she were declared innocent of complicity in the king's death would the English demand her restitution. Prompted by a strong dislike of rebels against legitimate authority, Elizabeth seemed initially to promise through intermediaries more favorable treatment to Mary than she ultimately delivered. Elizabeth could not, moreover, control the behavior of her councilors, many of whom were satisfied with Moray's regency. Mary later complained that throughout the inquiry English officials conspired with her brother and his allies against her.

At York on 4 October Norfolk, Thomas Radcliffe, third earl of Sussex, and Sadler opened the tribunal. Representing Mary were a mixture of Protestants and Catholics: a cousin of Châtelherault, Gavin Hamilton, archdeacon of St Andrews and commendator of Kilwinning, Bishop Leslie, Lords Livingston, Boyd, and Herries, Sir John Gordon of Lochinvar, and Skirling. Leslie had accepted the appointment reluctantly because he believed that the proceedings not only would fail to hasten her restitution but would also actually increase her estrangement from her half brother. Attending Moray were Morton, Lindsay, Maitland, Bishop Hepburn, and Robert Pitcairn, commendator of Dunfermline. Although technically representing the two-year old king for whom he served as regent, Moray was, in fact, the Scottish ruler and possessed a distinct advantage over the other participants, who had to wait for instructions from Elizabeth or Mary when new issues were raised.

With Moray also were Makgill, the clerk register, Henry Balnaves, a lord of the session, and Buchanan, whose motives for supporting Mary's opponents are unclear. It is usually alleged that the king's death outraged Buchanan because his ancestor served as chamberlain to an earlier earl of Lennox. At the Scottish council's request, Buchanan prepared a book of articles for the inquiry.

On the first few days they read their commissions, took oaths, and heard Herries's denunciation of Mary's ill treatment. On the 8th Moray condemned her support for Orkney, an evil and ambitious man, claimed she abdicated because she was weary of ruling, and interpreted

her defeat at Langside as God's will. Moray and his associates emphasized her sexual liaison with Orkney because it offered a motivation for
their later charge that she was an accessory to the king's death and
because many contemporaries viewed fornication not only as more
criminal than murder but also as inevitably leading to murder. Knollys
believed that Lethington hoped to prevent this accusation and to
obtain an agreement that would restore her authority with certain limitations. Preferring that she remain an English prisoner, Moray secretly
had some evidence revealed about her to the English commissioners to
gauge their response.

On the 11th Norfolk, Sussex, and Sadler reported to Elizabeth that
Lethington, Buchanan, Makgill, and Balnaves presented to them
without the knowledge of Mary's representatives some documents
deposited in a foot-long silver and gilt casket with the Roman F under
a crown in several places, obviously a gift from Francis to Mary. These
are the Casket Letters, which include eight French epistles, allegedly
written by Mary to Bothwell, two contracts of marriage for them, one
undated and one signed in April prior to his trial, and a French love
ballad of twelve unequal verses. As transcripts of the letters have neither subscriptions (Mary's signature) nor addressees, and only one of
them has a date, the presumption is, as Leslie maintained, that the
originals, which have disappeared, also lacked these identifying items.
Not only are the originals of these no longer extant, but neither are
the originals and copies of two other documents described by the commissioners: Mary's request to the noblemen that they sign the Ainslie
band and her admission to engineering a quarrel between Henry and
Lord Robert.

Before discussing the employment of the Casket Letters at the
inquiry, the question of whether they were forged will be addressed by
examining several topics: the practice of forgery in Britain, the official
version of how the confederates obtained the documents, the question
of whether Edinburgh Castle held Bothwell's correspondence, the contents
of Letter II, the most damaging of the eight letters, and the speculation
that Balfour was their author. Finally, it will follow Moray's references
to them in 1567 to his introduction of them in the inquiry in 1568.

The documents were almost certainly forgeries, perhaps some parts
entirely invented and others distortions of actual messages composed
by Mary to Henry or other recipients. It is highly unlikely that she

would have written down in any language her illicit passion for Bothwell or any other lover. Aware from childhood that her correspondence might be intercepted, she used ciphers to communicate sensitive material. In 1563 she complained to Randolph that someone had opened up her dispatches, and in 1569 she explained to Elizabeth that even if she had imagined the foolish remarks in the Casket Letters, she would never have put them in writing.

In early modern Britain forgeries often for political reasons were not an aberration. Richard Bentley even admitted, for example: "The greatest part of mankind are so easily imposed upon in this way, that there is too great an invitation to put the trick on them."[10] As previously noted, Mary of Guise had a letter from Châtelherault forged and her daughter probably invented one from Lorraine. In July 1569 after Grange joined Mary's party, he even falsified an order from Moray to obtain Lethington's release from confinement.

How the Casket Letters were discovered depends partly on Morton's declaration in December 1568. Supposedly, on 19 June 1567 shortly after the Carberry Hill confrontation, Orkney sent his servant, George Dalgleish, a tailor, to retrieve the casket with his documents at Edinburgh Castle. Both Leslie in his *Defence* of Mary and Buchanan in his *History of Scotland* asserted that Balfour, the castle's captain, released the casket to Dalgleish. The next day, 20 June, according to Morton, his men captured Dalgleish, confiscated the casket but waited another day before breaking its lock and in front of witnesses removing its documents. The date, 21 June, on which Morton said he first viewed the casket's documents is interesting because nine days later on 30 June, he and some other confederate lords issued a summons against Orkney for murdering the king and taking the queen by force.

It is puzzling that Dalgleish did not immediately return the casket to the duke, who was attempting to raise troops on the Borders. Since Orkney was short of funds, it is even more puzzling that he ordered Dalgleish to fetch only these documents, most of which were allegedly written by Mary. Surely he could have used some of her jewels which were at the castle to finance a challenge to the confederates' control of her. Although Dalgleish's accusers asked him about the king's murder for which he was convicted and executed, they neglected to inquire about the casket probably because it had never been in his possession.

The evidence that Balfour had betrayed Orkney also raises doubts about whether the duke sent Dalgleish to him for the casket. After Balfour refused to turn the castle guns on the confederates in May 1567, Orkney planned to replace him as its keeper. James Melville recalled assuring him that he was fortunate to be in the duke's bad graces because their alliance had made him one of the rebels' prime targets. Leslie later confirmed that Balfour had become Orkney's enemy. Why then, only one month later in June, would Orkney trust Balfour as the captain of the castle to permit Dalgleish to obtain the incriminating documents? And even if he did, why would Balfour surrender the casket that Orkney so clearly valued?

It is highly unlikely that Bothwell would have deposited his personal correspondence in the crown archive at the castle. His only known residence there in 1567 was from 6 to 12 May after he abducted Mary. He would normally not have carried his documents with him but would have kept them secured either at the places he acquired them or at Crichton or Dunbar. Furthermore, he could have received at Edinburgh (the town not the castle) only one of the two Casket Letters, usually labeled as I and II, that Mary allegedly sent him there after reaching Glasgow about 22 January 1567. When he was arrested, French Paris, her supposed letter-bearer, admitted delivering both of them to Bothwell at Edinburgh. It is possible, but unlikely, that Paris could have found Bothwell there with Letter II (which was written before Letter I) on the 24th, the day he left for Jedburgh to pursue Border criminals. However, Paris would have arrived too late at the capital about the 26th to give Bothwell Letter I. After confessing, Paris was summarily executed but not before publicly retracting these admissions.[11]

The most damaging to Mary's honor of the eight Casket Letters is Letter II. At 3,300 words it is the longest of the epistles, has a rambling style, and is structurally disjointed, but states in unequivocal language that she loved Bothwell and loathed her husband. In addition, it has several asides, including allusions to Henry's bad breath and the assembling of a bracelet. Some statements are inaccurate, for example, her inability to see Lennox, who was said to be closeted in his chamber but was actually at another residence. From her enemies' point of view, however, Letter II confirmed her adulterous passion for Bothwell, which provided her with a strong motivation for colluding in Henry's murder. Thus, two of the weapons Moray used in attempting to destroy Mary's reputation were her sexuality and her literacy, especially her ability to write.

On the assumption that these documents were forged, previous historians have identified Buchanan, Lethington, or Archibald Douglas as their author, but Balfour, who later claimed that Mary asked him to kill her husband, seems a more likely suspect. Even if he were not the forger, information about Balfour's life is useful because he played such a pivotal role in the king's murder and in later negotiations about it. It would be ironic if Balfour invented these letters, which may have gone through several drafts, to focus blame on Mary and her third husband in order to deflect attention away from himself.

Educated individuals in early modern Britain gained experience in creating fictional letters because their tutors regularly assigned them epistle-writing tasks, but Balfour, especially, possessed more training and more opportunities than many of his contemporaries for forging documents attributed to Mary. A legal expert skilled in preparing briefs and reports, he served since 1565 as her clerk register, whose duties, according to privy council guidelines, included assisting the lord chancellor in receiving the letters the queen sent to her councilors. Besides having occasion to study her handwriting, his positions as lord of session, as chief of the four commissaries of Edinburgh, and as captain of Edinburgh Castle, offered him access to evidence he could easily plagiarize. These legal experiences would also have taught him the value of documentary evidence even of a fictional nature in judicial proceedings.

While he obviously possessed extensive legal and governmental experience, less information is known about his vernacular skills beyond his native tongue. His biographers, among them David M. Walker, a noted legal expert, could only speculate about his formal education. Balfour probably attended St Andrews University in 1539 or 1540 and the University of Wittenberg in 1544. Occasionally, he was identified as maister, a title indicating he probably earned a master of arts. He became a fine Latin scholar, but French, the apparent original language of the Casket Letters, was not included in university studies. It was a language educated Scotsmen often chose to learn, however, because of Franco-Scottish cultural and political connections.

If Balfour had not already begun on his own volition to acquire an understanding of French, he was given ample opportunity to do so as a result of joining the murderers of Cardinal Beaton at St Andrews in 1546. With some limited English aid, these men, the Castilians, controlled the castle until July 1547 when a French fleet arrived and forced their surrender. Their conquerors impressed Balfour, a few of his relatives and, among others, John Knox, to serve as galley slaves. Sometime in 1548 or 1549 Balfour either escaped or was freed. Knox later recalled that his own imprisonment lasted 19 months.

Balfour's biographers failed to note whether they found any French documents in his handwriting. They have, however, revealed some important evidence about his language skills in the *Practicks*, which they believe is justifiably attributed to him, although he had assistance in assembling the materials. A pre-eminent record of Scottish law, the *Practicks* is the earliest collection of rules and propositions enunciated in the Auld Laws, the Acts of Parliament, and the decrees of the session and the council. Its existence has led David Walker to exclaim that "Balfour may have been a scoundrel but he deserves our gratitude."[12]

A section at the end of the *Practicks*, entitled "the constitutiounis of Francois King of France, annis 1543, 1547," offers evidence of Balfour's French skills. Between May 1579 and December 1580 following political disputes with Morton who was then James VI's regent, Balfour joined the Hamiltons in France. During his exile, he reportedly met on more than one occasion with Henry, third duke of Guise, and Esmé Stuart, sixth seigneur of Aubigny, the future duke of Lennox, in the company of Archbishop Beaton and Bishop Leslie. Balfour was also said to have advised Lennox to confer with Lord John Hamilton, commendator of Arbroath and the third son of Châtelherault, before departing for Scotland. It could have been during this sojourn that Balfour collected the French laws cited in the *Practicks*. Almost certainly, he could read French, and if he could not write it, he could have employed a scribe. It is also possible that the original version of the Casket Letters was in the Scots language. The only extant French versions are apparently translations from a Latin or Scots rendition. This issue will be revisited later in this chapter in a discussion of the English inquiry concerning Mary's return to Scotland and in a section in Chapter 8 on the Letters' publication.

Some of Balfour's activities after the king's death support the speculation that he was desperate enough to create these Letters. He demonstrated concerns about his criminal status by ensuring that his name was on the list of pardons Mary granted in May 1567. Besides obtaining Morton's goodwill in June by informing him that Dalgleish had possession of the casket, Balfour won Moray's favor when he returned to Scotland in August to become the king's regent. For turning Edinburgh Castle over to him, Moray gave Balfour the priory of Pittenween, a pension out of the Priory of St Andrews, a lump sum of £5,000, and income from lands in Fife for his son, Gilbert. Moray also appointed Balfour president of the court of session and continued him on the council when he resigned the position of clerk register. At the parliament in December 1567, he served as a member of the lords of the articles. While most of Moray's concessions to Balfour were undoubtedly rewards for surrendering this strategic castle, the regent's continued favor raises the possibility that Balfour maintained some kind of hold over him. When damaging information surfaced in 1569 pointing to Balfour's share in the king's murder, some officials ordered his arrest, but Moray's somewhat mysterious and indirect interference in the proceedings led to his liberation.

Although Balfour attempted to keep his political options open, supporting Mary's petition for a divorce from Orkney in 1569, for example, he enjoyed the regent's protection from criminal prosecution until James Hamilton of Bothwellhaugh assassinated Moray in 1570. After Lennox became regent, Balfour encountered some difficult times and supported the Marian party, but in 1572 he gained protection from Morton, who succeeded Mar as regent. Only when confronting political problems in 1578 did Morton turn against Balfour, who fled to France. Following Morton's fall from power, Balfour returned home and won James VI's favor perhaps for offering to provide evidence about the former regent's complicity in Henry's murder. Although before Balfour's death from natural causes in 1583, he still faced some legal problems, he seems never to have been convicted of the king's assassination, one of Orkney's few non-noble allies to escape that plight.[13]

Regardless of who actually wrote the letters, the first extant references to them, which Morton later claimed he obtained in June 1567, are in the dispatches of de Silva to Philip. On 12 July he reported that Jacques Bochetel de la Forest, the French ambassador, revealed he knew of some incriminating letters in Mary's own hand. A few weeks later on 2 August, de Silva related that while in England *en route* to Scotland, Moray described to him one of the letters Mary allegedly wrote.

After discussing her imprisonment with Moray, de Silva concluded that his manner of speech and the difficulties he perceived about his sister's restoration indicated that although expressing a desire to help her, he was unlikely to do so. When de Silva explained that her confessor denied she had any knowledge of Henry's death, Moray responded that he knew differently and revealed he had heard of a letter containing three sheets of paper, written with her own hand and signed by her, in which she explained she would go to Glasgow to fetch her husband, attempt to poison him on the return, and if she failed, take him to a house where he could be blown up. Moray seems to have been describing Letter II but with significant differences: it was composed after, not before, she went to Glasgow and lacked explicit references to Henry's murder. Either Moray's source gave him incorrect information or he was deliberately exaggerating the contents of Letter II to the ambassador of a Catholic monarch.

No extant evidence indicates Moray referred to the letters again until December 1567 when he faced challenges to his regency. On the 4th the privy council recommended that parliament justify the conduct of the lords in opposing and imprisoning Mary because of the private letters that she wrote and subscribed to Bothwell, the king's chief murderer, which proved she aided and abetted that crime. Parliament subsequently endorsed this request but referred only to letters written by her to Bothwell, omitting the word subscribed. It also passed acts of attainder against Orkney and other named traitors who had not appeared to answer the charges of murder against them.

Moray's next extant statement about the Casket Letters, some six months later, relates to preparations for the proposed English inquiry. In June 1568 copies of these documents that Moray identified as Scots translations of the French originals were presented by his agent, John Wood, to Elizabeth. Moray hoped to discover from her whether they might be introduced as evidence into the inquiry, which he labeled a trial. It is odd that he chose to send Scots versions to Elizabeth because he knew she was at least as fluent in French, if not more so, than in his native tongue. He, himself, had an understanding of French and surely could read the letters if they were in that language. In October 1565 when he was a Chaseabout raider, Elizabeth permitted him an audience with her but insisted that he communicate in French rather than in

Scots because their conversation occurred in the presence of de Foix and Mauvissière.

Moreover, as she would appoint her councilors to evaluate the documents, if Moray thought they needed to be translated, why not English rather than Scots? The regent's inexplicable decision about the language in which he forwarded them raises the possibility that the originals were in Scots, or mostly in Scots, and that he was waiting to learn if they could be utilized at the inquiry before troubling to have them rendered into French. If so, Mary could not have composed them because she was not then able to write in Scots. Less than a month after sending the translated copies to Elizabeth, Moray indicated that her response, which is not extant, pleased him and that he should be ready to participate in the hearing as soon as she named the place and time.

On 14 October 1568 at York, Moray stated his intention to attach an Eik or additional evidence to his case during a subsequent session. Mary's representatives were aware of Moray's private discussions with the English commissioners, but their replication on the 16th responded only to his official comments. They stated in this document that an assize acquitted Orkney of murder and that most of the nobility, including some of her opponents at the English inquiry, approved the marriage. The confederates, they alleged incorrectly, did not appear to oppose the alliance until they began plotting with Balfour and others to capture her and Orkney at Borthwick Castle. Then at Lochleven, Lindsay so frightened the imprisoned queen that she was forced to abdicate, but once liberated, she revoked her renunciation of the throne.

On the 22nd because Elizabeth decided she needed to confer with individuals from both sides, Lethington, Makgill, Herries and Leslie journeyed to her court. On that same day, Sussex warned Cecil that if Moray charged Mary with Henry's murder, she would deny it and accuse her brother and his colleagues of complicity in it. He believed Moray would forego defaming her if she agreed to surrender her crown, confirm him in the regency, and remain in England. On the other hand, Sussex continued, her supposed allies, the Hamiltons, whose leader Châtelherault reached London in September, were charging her with misgovernment, demanding Moray surrender the regency, and requesting the appointment of a council to rule on her behalf. They were willing, Sussex explained, for the prince to be reared in England

and might even be persuaded to change their opinion concerning Mary's release and accept her continued exile. After asserting that neither side cared for the mother or the son, Sussex judged that it would be best for the English if Mary were retained as their prisoner.

Meanwhile, two events occurred that provide insights into Mary's future. The first was the October death in childbirth of her sister-in-law, Elizabeth, queen of Spain. In June after arriving in England, Mary had notified Elizabeth of her exile and her political problems. At that time, John Baptista Castagna, archbishop of Rossano, the papal nuncio to Spain, informed his correspondents that these queens were brought up together and loved each other very much. Mary had hoped that one of Elizabeth's two daughters by Philip would marry James. After learning of her demise, Mary lamented the loss of her dear sister and friend. The death of Elizabeth, like that of her Guise uncles, meant that Mary's contacts abroad were increasingly with distant connections rather than with personal friends and acquaintances, making it more difficult for her to understand or to discover how deeply committed they were to assisting her in gaining her freedom.

The second event concerned a possible English marriage for Mary. Whether or not observers believed she was involved in her husband's death, they viewed her, although still Orkney's wife, as a valuable commodity on the marriage market. Knollys even suggested to Henry Carey, first Lord Hunsdon, his brother-in-law, that she wed his son, George Carey, but the candidate she favored was Norfolk, a descendant of Edward I and Edward III, an extremely wealthy landowner, and the only English duke. Lethington seems to have proposed the marriage to Norfolk in October as a step toward gaining her restitution. The possibility of the alliance led Mary to seek a divorce from Orkney. Although she never met Norfolk, she had ample opportunity at Bolton to discuss the likelihood of their marriage with his sister, Lady Scrope. The duke's subsequent courtship of Mary occurred within the context of two conspiracies against Elizabeth and led to his execution in 1572.

After conferring with the Scottish representatives, Elizabeth decided to reopen the inquiry at Westminster and to enhance the commission membership: to Norfolk, Sussex, and Sadler, she added the ailing Henry, earl of Arundel, who did not appear until December, Leicester, Edward Fiennes, Lord Clinton and Saye, Cecil, and Sir Nicholas Bacon. On 25 November when they reconvened the hearings in Westminster

Hall's painted chamber, they were joined by Northampton, Bedford, William Herbert, first earl of Pembroke, and Sir Walter Mildmay. On the 26th Moray privately submitted his Eik, accusing Mary of conspiring to murder her husband. On the 29th Lennox also presented a bill of supplication charging Mary with aiding and abetting his son's death.[14] Two days later, Herries responded to the Eik, a copy of which had been delivered to Leslie and him. He claimed that Moray and his associates had invented this charge against Mary in 1567 out of fear that they would lose their estates since she would have soon been 25 years old, the age for Scottish monarchs to revoke grants made during their minorities.

Mary's representatives then began to question the tribunal's procedures and goals. On 2 December they complained to the English commissioners about Elizabeth's receiving Moray at court on 13 November although she refused to meet with Mary and indicated they planned to request that their queen be allowed to defend herself personally. On the 3rd at Hampton Court, they petitioned Elizabeth in writing to allow Mary to participate in the inquiry. On the 4th before they were scheduled to hear Elizabeth's response to their request, they reminded Leicester and Cecil that Mary had been informed these proceedings would result in her restitution and in the establishment of safeguards for Moray and the confederates in Scotland. If these were not the inquiry's intentions, and if Mary were prevented from answering for herself, they must decline further participation. Afterward, Elizabeth explained to the Scottish commissioners that she would not allow their queen to appear at the inquiry, first because while she remained defamed by the accusations, her presence there would dishonor both her and Scotland, and second, if Mary wished her crown restored, she must be found innocent of complicity in Henry's murder. The disappointed commissioners departed and subsequently withdrew from the proceedings. It is interesting that Bertrand de Salignac de la Mothe-Fénélon, the French ambassador, sent to his government in December a copy of an opinion of English civilians who believed that Mary should have been permitted personally to answer the charges against her.

In the absence of his half sister's commissioners, Moray read out on the 6th Buchanan's book of articles, accusing her of aiding Henry's murder and of colluding in Bothwell's abduction.[15] On the next two days, Moray introduced into evidence the Casket Letters, various confessions of the king's convicted murderers, and other manuscripts. No witnesses were called to testify, and no one questioned the validity of the facts alleged in the documents, also made available in English transcripts. On the 9th the commissioners did attempt to judge whether the handwriting in the French Letters matched that in Mary's dispatches to Elizabeth. The most pressing issue for the English commissioners, even if, as Leslie later alleged,[16] they believed the documents were invented, was how much importance they should attach to the decision of Mary's brother and his colleagues to accuse her under oath of enabling her husband's murder because of her passion for Bothwell. Trial evidence whether flawed or not had credibility because it conveyed what the accusers believed had occurred and was sufficient to cast doubts on the defendant's character and honor. Moray's defamation of his sister undoubtedly highlighted for Elizabeth and the English commissioners the unlikelihood of persuading him to endorse a plan for Mary's restitution.

At Hampton Court on the 14th and 15th, Elizabeth had a transcript of the entire proceedings, including the book of articles, read to the privy council and six principal noblemen, Northumberland, Shrewsbury, Warwick, Charles Neville, sixth earl of Westmorland, Henry Hastings, third earl of Huntingdon, and Edward Somerset, third earl of Worcester. After initially involving only three of her subjects in the inquiry, Elizabeth had by stages increased the number made privy to the accusations against her cousin. On the 16th in the presence of her councilors, she explained to Leslie, Boyd, Herries, and Hamilton of Kilwinning that her honor would not permit her to meet with their queen until she was proved innocent of the charges.

Four days later as Sussex predicted, Mary, who had received information about the Eik, sent messages to her representatives, charging Moray and his allies of accusing her of a crime that they committed. She also requested copies of the evidence allegedly in her hand but which was forged. Leslie and Herries delivered her response to Elizabeth on Christmas Day.

On 10 January Cecil made a noncommittal statement on behalf of Elizabeth about the inquiry's results: she decided that the plaintiffs had proved nothing against Mary that caused her to think ill of her and that the defendant had proved nothing against Moray that impugned his honor. Declared neither guilty nor innocent, Mary remained an English prisoner while the half brother who had defamed her returned home with a loan of £5,000. After she again requested to see the evidence against her, Elizabeth agreed to forward it to her but only if Mary promised in advance to respond to the accusations, a pledge she refused to make.

Aware of repeated attempts to persuade the Scottish queen to renounce her throne, Arundel protested to Elizabeth that a person who possessed a crown could hardly persuade another to give hers up because her subjects would not obey her. That, he said, might be a new doctrine in Scotland, but he did not think it was wise to teach it in England.[17] George Buchanan also noted Elizabeth's concern that the example of dethroning Mary in Scotland might pass on to neighboring kingdoms. Mary's final answer to the suggestion that she abdicate was that the last words she uttered would be as the queen of Scotland.

In the meantime the English officials had begun the process of moving her to Tutbury Castle, which was controlled by Shrewsbury, the wealthiest peer in England who had recently accepted appointment as her custodian. When Knollys learned in October that Cecil expected him and Scrope to escort her to Tutbury, he protested that they lacked authority or friends in that district and worried about security during the move and about furnishing the castle. He also revealed Mary's claim that they would have to bind her hands and feet and force her to go. Heeding his complaints, Cecil ordered provisions transferred to Tutbury from the Tower of London and recommended that Knollys request Elizabeth Hardwick, countess of Shrewsbury, for additional items. Sussex also supplied Knollys with information about places to stay on the journey and the names of gentlemen who would receive them. To encourage Mary to go willingly, Elizabeth wrote, explaining that they were preparing a more honorable residence for her. Whether it was illegal to move her to a more secure fortification and to retain her against her will, as the Scottish queen claimed, depends on one's point of view. An English tradition dating at least from the reign of Henry VII, who imprisoned the Yorkist prince, Edward, earl of Warwick, justified this action under certain circumstances: "Unless he acts through evil intention, one prince may without sin keep prisoner another prince or a lord on whose account he fears an insurrection within his own territory."[18]

8

NEGOTIATING RESTITUTION, 1569–84

On 26 January 1569 having borrowed and leased numerous horses and carts, Scrope and Knollys moved southward with the ailing queen, who protested this forcible change in her residence during the winter. Following stops at Ripon, Weatherby, and Pontefract, they rested at Rotherham until the 30th. Scrope and Knollys permitted the seriously ill Lady Livingston to halt at Rotherham but forced Mary, who was suffering her chronic side ache, to resume the journey. Aware of her sickness, they lingered two nights at Chesterfield before proceeding to Wingfield, a Derbyshire home of her new custodian, George Talbot, earl of Shrewsbury.

On the 3rd they reached Derby and on the 4th entered Tutbury, the Staffordshire castle near the Derbyshire border, which was in Shrewsbury's keeping. Mary later described her prison as an extremely old hunting lodge built of timber and plaster that sat in a walled enclosure on top of a hill where it was exposed to the winds and inclement weather. The lodge was built so low that one side of it did not rise higher than the huge rampart of dirt behind the wall that enclosed it. The sun, therefore, was prevented from reaching that side of the building, leaving its chambers cold, moist, and moldy.

Besides serving as constable of Tutbury and possessing Wingfield, Shrewsbury owned five more mansions situated near each other: Sheffield Castle, which was separated from its lodge by an extensive park, in Yorkshire, Buxton Hall in Derbyshire, and Rufford Abbey and

Worksop Manor in Nottinghamshire. Elizabeth Hardwick, Shrewsbury's much married second wife, as he became her fourth husband in 1568, also owned in Derbyshire Chatsworth the seat of her second, deceased spouse, Sir William Cavendish, and Hardwick Hall her paternal home. Between January 1569 and November 1570, Shrewsbury housed Mary for about eight months at Tutbury, five months at Wingfield, six months at Chatsworth, and six weeks at Coventry during the threat of the Northern Rising. Thereafter while under his charge, Sheffield Castle served as her primary residence although she spent brief periods at its lodge, Buxton, Chatsworth, Worksop, and Wingfield.

As Tutbury Castle was a leaky, drafty structure with small and incommodious rooms, Shrewsbury normally used it as a hunting lodge. When Leslie, Boyd, and Herries arrived to confer with Mary, the earl refused them accommodations, and Elizabeth rejected Mary's subsequent appeal for them to stay at the castle. Ultimately, Herries returned to Scotland while Boyd and Leslie momentarily found lodgings at Burton-on-Trent, some three miles away.

Because of his wife's recent death, Knollys lingered at Tutbury only long enough to acquaint Shrewsbury with Mary's daily routine. From the outset her new custodian grappled with problems similar to those that troubled Knollys. Shrewsbury's long-term concern was the cost of providing for his prisoner. The crown approved a weekly allowance of £52 for a household of 30, the inadequacy of which he complained bitterly, especially after its reduction to £30 in 1575. He also found it difficult to comply with his instructions to prevent Mary's communication with strangers, to monitor her correspondence, and to reduce her household from 60 to 30 members. An additional nine men were allowed to care for her ten horses that were soon culled to six. Initially, he encouraged her outdoor exercise in the good hunting areas near Tutbury, hoping it would distract her from escape attempts.

Although a prisoner, Mary maintained her residence as a court. Over a dais in her grand chamber hung her canopy of estate with the embroidered motto, *En Ma Fin Est Ma Commencement* (In my End is my Beginning), probably referring to the Phoenix bird, her mother's *impresa*. She dined on silver and slept on fine linen, often never retiring to her bedchamber before 1:00 a.m. Turkish carpets covered the floors of her two rooms; gilt chandeliers lighted them, and her chairs were upholstered in crimson and cloth-of-gold. During bad weather, she embroidered, a task rendered less tedious by her use of various colored threads. Despite orders to limit her interaction with his household, Shrewsbury permitted her, Lady Livingston, and Mary Seton to pass the time sewing with his wife daily.

In addition, Mary sought other indoor activities, sending for turtle-doves, Barbary fowls, and red partridges to keep in cages and for lap dogs. She also read and studied religious material, such as the prayers at the holy altar of Dr Allen Cope, which she obtained in 1577, but her favorite pastime seems to have been sewing. She employed embroider-ers to copy onto canvas for her needlework the birds, beasts, and fish in her designs from the emblem and fable books of editors, such as Claud Paraden, Conrad Gesner, Pierre Belon, and Gabriel Faerno. Some of her creations were presented as gifts, the ones to Elizabeth presumably to win concessions on the strictness of her captivity. In 1574 Mary sent her a skirt of crimson satin lined with taffeta and worked with silver thread that took three months to complete, and in 1575 she forwarded to her three nightcaps or headdresses.

At Oxburgh Hall, Norfolk, on loan from the Victoria and Albert Museum, are three large hangings or curtains, two by Lady Shrewsbury and one by Mary. About ten by seven feet in size, the queen's curtain is in green velvet with scrolls couched in gold and has appliqued on it some 37 canvas panels containing emblems rendered principally in cross-stitch with silk thread. On the center panel is an emblem with a hand holding a sickle descending from the sky to prune a vine and dis-playing the motto, Virtue Flourishes by Wounding. It is flanked by two trees, the left with Francis II's and Mary's monogram and the right with the Scottish royal arms. Some writers have claimed it predicted the removal of the unfruitful Elizabeth to make way for Mary, but as this is a traditional Christian design representing resignation to suf-fering, it was more likely a reference to her captivity.[1]

When in February on his way to Ireland, Nicholas White stopped at Tutbury, he observed the many colors of Mary's embroidery thread, and noted that in her theoretical discussion about the relative merits of sewing, carving, and painting, she selected the latter as the most com-mendable. She was probably not clarifying her personal preference since there is little evidence in her records about painting but much about embroidering. Greatly impressed by her personally, White reported to Cecil, "She hath an alluring grace, a pretty Scottish accent, and a searching wit, clouded with mildness." He warned Cecil to limit access to her, for "Fame might move some to relieve her, and glory joined to gain might stir others to adventure much for her side."[2] Since he described her hair as black, it either darkened as she aged or her custom of wearing colored wigs misled him. As he counted 50 in her household, she had apparently persuaded Shrewsbury of the inadequacy of 30 servants.

When Cecil questioned the appropriateness of White's visit, Shrewsbury defended it with the explanation that he and Knollys's brother, Henry, who departed in March, were witnesses to their conversations. Shrewsbury's role never ceased troubling him; while realizing he must guard her closely, he believed that in some sense he was her host and that it was important he not appear to be greatly limiting her activities. This diffidence ultimately raised suspicions that he had succumbed to her alluring charm. After he removed her to Wingfield on 16 April, the number visiting and living with her increased to 80, and she seems to have enjoyed more freedom there than at Tutbury.

THE NORFOLK COURTSHIP

In May Leslie journeyed to London to discuss Mary's restitution with Elizabeth. While there he also consulted with some noblemen who favored the Stewart succession in England. Willing to support Mary's marriage to Norfolk, they originally sought the downfall of Cecil, one of her most outspoken opponents, although they later abandoned that goal. The hostility to Cecil arose from the premise that his non-noble origin made him an upstart councilor, unlike Norfolk, whose nobility won him recognition as a natural leader. They favored Mary's alliance with the duke because they viewed it as a step in securing Protestantism in Britain. Most of those involved, including Norfolk, were Protestants. Leslie recorded a meeting with Norfolk, Arundel, a Catholic and the father of Mary Fitzalan the duke's first wife, Pembroke, and Leicester, who required that Queen Mary answer some questions before they could agree to advance her restitution. When Leslie forwarded them to her at Wingfield, she responded as follows:

she pledged to refer her cause to Elizabeth to whom she would give surety concerning her good sister's title to the crown and to substitute a league with England for the one with France. As to whether England's religion would be imposed in Scotland, she cited her instructions to Leslie. Finally, she replied cautiously concerning the union with Norfolk, whom she had agreed to marry without having met him since he was the most eligible noble Englishman and would be able to assist in her restitution and in the recognition of her rights to the English crown. As marriage to him would displease her Catholic friends, she wondered what she would gain in return for losing their support, and she expressed reservations about both Elizabeth's attitude and Norfolk's well-being, recalling her second husband's fate. After eliciting positive responses to the marriage from John, Lord Lumley, and Throckmorton, the optimistic Leslie even began to hope that Cecil might support it.

With these discussions underway, Mary turned to Scotland's leaders for assistance. In July at Perth, Boyd introduced two of her requests at a convention. The estates subsequently denied her petition to share equally with James in Scotland's governance and rejected her plea for a divorce from Orkney. They also condemned her letter proposing the divorce, since she styled herself in it as queen. At the meeting, Lethington argued for the divorce while Makgill spoke vociferously against it.

In England Norfolk continued to pursue his marriage plans without informing Elizabeth, although she had heard rumors about them. When Leicester admitted to her in September that Norfolk hoped to wed Mary and to obtain the recognition of her succession rights, which had gained momentum from Catherine Grey's recent death, Elizabeth angrily chastised the duke about his intentions. Suspecting that Mary had drawn Shrewsbury into this conspiracy, Elizabeth instructed two noblemen: the earl of Huntington, a Yorkist claimant to the throne by virtue of his descent from Margaret Pole, countess of Salisbury, and Walter Devereux, Viscount Hereford, to assist Shrewsbury in preventing his prisoner's escape.

After they returned her on 21 September to Tutbury, a more defensible structure than Wingfield, Elizabeth considered appointing Huntington as Mary's sole guardian but finally decided to associate him with Shrewsbury as joint custodian. She demanded her prisoner's close confinement, the reduction of her household to 30, and, too late, a search of her chambers for evidence to implicate her in the Norfolk conspiracy. Before leaving Wingfield, Mary had instructed her attendants to burn many of her documents. Despite the surveillance, she managed to send letters out secretly, some to de la Mothe Fénélon, complaining about her circumstances and asking for assistance, a plea that led Charles to protest to Elizabeth about her harsh treatment.

Before Mary's transfer to Tutbury, Norfolk left court without Elizabeth's permission for Kenninghall, his principal seat. Suspecting he planned to rally support for the marriage, Elizabeth recalled him, alerted Shrewsbury of the possible danger his absence posed, and on the duke's return ordered him incarcerated in the Tower on 11 October. She also retained Pembroke, Arundel, and Lumley at court and placed Throckmorton in detention but permitted Leicester to remain at liberty, perhaps because he confirmed the marriage rumors to her.

In November Norfolk's Catholic allies in the North, Westmorland, the husband of his sister, Jane Howard, and Northumberland became restless about the delays in arranging Mary's marriage and in ratifying her English rights. Leslie, Norfolk, and Mary warned the earls against taking action, perhaps fearing for her safety if a rebellion to release her occurred without adequate armed support. When Elizabeth summoned them to court, nevertheless, they rang the bells backward at Topcliffe, Yorkshire, gathered a large force for a rebellion, later called the Northern Rising, and raised a banner depicting Christ's five wounds, a traditional Catholic symbol. On 14 November at Durham Cathedral, they destroyed the prayer books and heard mass before moving south to Tadcaster. Shrewsbury reassured Cecil on the 21st that having learned the rebels were 54 miles away, he had increased his guard from 40 to 100 men, although the earls had probably already decided they could not successfully storm his castle. Their destructive behavior at Durham and their banner signaling their rebellion, sometimes identified as the last feudal outburst against the Tudor monarchy, were protests against the supremacy of the Protestant faith in England, as legislated by Elizabeth and her parliaments. In short, the earls' rising was more a reaction to the decline of their local power in the conservative catholic North than to the unresolved succession issue.

On the 25th Mary was transferred to the walled city of Coventry and housed first at Bull Inn and then at a private home near

St Michael's Church. Meanwhile, the rebels declined to push further southward and in December their forces dispersed. As the two north-ern earls fled to Scotland, English troops invaded that realm the next spring, destroying many villages and laying waste the Borders. Westmorland escaped abroad, but the Scots captured Northumberland and returned him to England, where he was tried for treason, con-victed, and beheaded. Mary had great sympathy for the conspirators. Upon hearing a premature rumor in June 1569 about the capture of Northumberland to whom she had sent a ring, she wept so deeply that her face was swollen for three days, and following his flight to Scotland, Mary authorized relief payments to Anne, his countess, and his allies.[3]

After returning Mary to Tutbury in early January 1570, Shrewsbury was relieved to learn that Elizabeth had decided to restore him as her sole custodian. It was not that Shrewsbury relished serving as Mary's jailor but that he feared the besmirching of his honor if Elizabeth determined he was inadequately fulfilling his duties. Even at Tutbury he continued to feel uneasy about Mary's activities, believing correctly that various plans were afoot to free her. Wearing Norfolk's diamond ring about her neck, Mary corresponded secretly with him about their marriage and her liberation.[4]

When Elizabeth learned that Hamilton of Bothwellhaugh had assassinated Moray on 23 January 1570, she ordered Leslie restricted to the bishop of London's palace on general grounds of suspicion. During questioning he denied having dealings with her northern rebels and disputed the claim that the book he recently had published defending Mary's honor and supporting her English succession rights, was inju-rious to Elizabeth's estate. Mary protested Leslie's detention because as her ambassador at the English court, she believed he should be immune from arrest. She also assured Archbishop Beaton she did not know in advance about her brother's murder but planned to grant a pension to his assassin.

Following Leslie's release, he joined her at Chatsworth in June, where Shrewsbury had transferred her at the end of May partly because of Tutbury's coldness and dampness and partly because of the scarcity in the surrounding area of provisions, such as fuel. Chatsworth, where Shrewsbury housed Mary until 13 June when they departed for Wingfield, was a spacious house with footpaths within its walls where she could exercise. She complained to Leslie that she feared her enemies might persuade Elizabeth to replace Shrewsbury about whose strictness she had otherwise been complaining with a Puritan, especially Huntington, who might inflict personal injury on her, perhaps even poison her. She viewed Huntington as her main threat because of his Yorkist claims. When Leslie departed for London, he carried letters for her to numerous correspondents.

In February 1570 Pius V excommunicated Elizabeth, hoping to encourage English Catholics to make greater efforts to liberate Mary. Despite the issuance of the bull, *Regnans in excelsis*, Elizabeth continued to explore the possibility of Mary's restitution but only under certain conditions: she must not wed anyone other than a native Scotsman without Elizabeth's permission, must ratify the Treaty of Edinburgh, and agree not to challenge Elizabeth's or her heirs' rights to the throne. In addition, Mary must conclude a league with Elizabeth that was guaranteed by Scottish hostages, the cessation to her, until her rebels were returned, of Dumbarton and Hume Castles, and the removal of the almost four-year-old James to England. Finally, Mary must maintain Protestantism in Scotland and keep the king's party in office.[5]

Mary deplored these stipulations, especially the one requiring her son's removal to England about which she even communicated with her still hostile mother-in-law, Lady Lennox. She may have been concerned that, as she was later warned in 1574, if the English obtained both her and her son, the Stewart dynasty might be doomed to extinction. Mary also protested surrendering the two strongholds to Elizabeth, but after receiving Leslie's and Lethington's advice to agree to these demands, she reluctantly accepted them. Lethington pressed her to gain her freedom even if it meant conceding harsh conditions because he believed that her life was in danger as long as she remained a prisoner.

Mary had continued considering various escape schemes and communicating in cipher with Norfolk. In January 1570 she assured him of her constancy, pointing out that "Our fault were not shameful; you have promised to be mine, and I yours; . . . As you please, command me, for I will, for all the world, follow your commands." Her concerns about the conditions Elizabeth demanded before agreeing to her restitution prompted Mary in April to ask Norfolk to aid her forces in Scotland.[6] After she requested Charles IX to send troops to liberate her, he dispatched Monsieur de Poigny to Elizabeth and to Mary, calling for her restitution. When Poigny departed from Mary, he, too, carried various letters to her correspondents.

In August while negotiations for Mary's restitution were underway, Elizabeth instructed Shrewsbury to permit her to ride abroad and exercise for her health and freed Norfolk when he agreed to abandon the Scottish marriage. Noting that Charles, Catherine, and sundry princes had requested she arrange Mary's return to Scotland, Elizabeth decided to dispatch Cecil and Mildmay to Chatsworth in October to confer with Mary about the treaty. Scottish commissioners, among them Morton, arrived in England in early 1571 to consult with Mary's agents, Livingston, Leslie, and Alexander Gordon, bishop of Galloway.

At the outset of these discussions, which were terminated in March after Elizabeth discovered that the Scottish commissioners lacked authority to change the king's status, Mary promised to reject the Norfolk marriage and to cease seeking aid for her liberation from her friends abroad. Nevertheless, suspicious of Elizabeth's intentions, partly because of the inquiry's unfavorable results and the treaty's delay, Mary kept her options open and authorized Lord Seton to seek Alva's assistance in June. Confirming her suspicions, Lethington warned Mary in August that Elizabeth did not intend to enter into any accord with her. Mary also urged Archbishop Beaton to propose a French invasion of Scotland, but after learning that Elizabeth was considering marrying Henry, duke of Anjou, Mary decided that her best hope for assistance lay with Spain.

Along with Norfolk she had begun plotting with Roberto di Pagnozzo Ridolfi of Florence, an influential Catholic banker in England who had recently cleared his name after somewhat compromising dealings with Northumberland and Westmorland. Mary and Norfolk dispatched Ridolfi to Alva, Pius V, and Philip with requests for financial and military aid. Since Mary and Norfolk mostly communicated with Ridolfi through intermediaries, Leslie and the ducal secretary, William Barker, it is not certain what their specific instructions were. Norfolk did meet with Ridolfi but Leslie and Barker worked out the details with him.

In Mary's instructions, which Ridolfi drew up for her in March 1571, she offered Philip and Alva either Dumbarton or Edinburgh

Castle as a base for their expedition. She also requested Pius V to free her from Orkney, expressing her grief at the abduction and declaring she was forced to consent to the marriage against her will.[7] This plea was likely the reason Pius issued a brief in July, authorizing Archbishops Hamilton and Beaton and William Gordon, bishop of Aberdeen, to begin nullification proceedings.

Her letters to de la Mothe Fénélon and to Archbishop Beaton prove Mary's principal concerns were gaining restitution and assisting her allies in Scotland's civil war. Although her English rights remained important, they were not her highest priority. After the plot was discovered, she explained to de la Mothe Fénélon that seeking aid for her Scottish allies was not equivalent to inciting an English rebellion. A confirmation of this assertion can be found in her March instructions to Lord John Hamilton, her envoy to the duke of Alva. She directed Lord John to inform Alva that she was seeking assistance from all Christian princes for her realm of Scotland.

In contrast, Leslie and Ridolfi understood Philip required a greater incentive for invading Britain than her recovery of Scotland. Ridolfi's instructions on Norfolk's behalf held out the possibility of gaining the English throne and restoring the island to Catholicism. The duke reportedly promised to raise considerable forces but required money, arms, and additional troops to establish Mary, his future wife, as England's queen. He also requested that Alva send an army to England and Ireland to link up with Catholic rebels. The churchman, the secretary, and the diplomat-financier thus concocted intrigues beyond their capacity to implement.

Shortly after Ridolfi's departure for the continent, Lennox, who had succeeded Moray as regent, sent soldiers for a surprise assault on Dumbarton Castle. After they seized the castle on 2 April, the earl had his old rival, Archbishop Hamilton, one of its residents, tried and executed for Moray's murder. At Dumbarton Lennox also discovered documents detailing Mary's communications with Alva, which he revealed to Cecil.

Having received the intelligence that a plot was underway for Mary's escape to Scotland, Elizabeth instructed Shrewsbury to institute strict orders to secure her and to reduce the number in her household to 30. He reported progress on 4 May in expelling some of Mary's attendants and noted she was sickened at the loss of Dumbarton Castle to Lennox. She had also heard of Archbishop Hamilton's death. New rules were imposed on the servants remaining with her. They had to depart her chambers between 9:00 p.m. and 6:00 a.m.; only Andrew Beaton, the master of her household, could wear a sword, and all must have a license to leave the castle.

In April Cecil, recently ennobled as Burghley, had ordered the arrest of Charles Bailly, one of Leslie's secretaries, when he returned from the Netherlands with copies of the reprint of the bishop's manuscript defending Mary's honor and with some ciphered letters. Burghley incarcerated Bailly in the Marshalsea, confiscated his manuscripts, and ordered his spy William Herle to contact the prisoner. After winning Bailly's confidence, Herle became his messenger, carrying to Burghley some ciphered letters from Ridolfi and others that were addressed to Leslie. Burghley had them copied before forwarding them to the addressees.

Following further questioning and at least the threat of the rack, Bailly revealed the information he could remember from having aided Ridolfi in encoding the documents, making it possible for Burghley to read them. In May Burghley detained Leslie in the bishop of Ely's palace. Leslie later reported to Henry III that he had "suffered terrible injuries in England,"[8] which apparently caused the fearful bishop to implicate Mary, Norfolk, and himself in the Ridolfi plot and to describe one of her gifts to the duke, a cushion embroidered with the pruning emblem that she sent to him before the Northern Rising. Fearful of bodily harm, the frightened bishop proved willing to admit to any statement, no matter how outrageous. He even charged Mary with colluding in the death of her first husband, with poisoning the second one, and with plotting to do away with the third. Toward the end of 1571, Elizabeth had Leslie transferred to the Tower and ordered the expulsion from England of Guerau de Spes, the Spanish ambassador, for assisting Leslie's and Ridolfi's communications with Alva and Philip.

Although greatly concerned about a possible invasion of England, Elizabeth and her councilors were also unhappy about Mary's plans for Philip's interference in Scotland. They had not repulsed France from that realm with the intention of permitting another power's intervention there. As Sussex predicted in 1568, the best scenario was to keep Mary their prisoner and leave Scotland to the rule of her son's regents who were friendly to England. During her captivity the Northern Rising was the only English rebellion favoring Mary's cause, and the Ridolfi conspiracy was the most serious plot on her behalf involving foreign powers. Unwilling to accept her captivity complacently, she encouraged schemes that posed no grave threat to Elizabeth but that resulted in her closer confinement and ultimately her execution.

It is also true, however, that it was unrealistic for the English to expect the acquiescence in her imprisonment of a woman who was a queen regnant from her infancy, was reared at the French court, and had already escaped captivity twice. In a letter of December 1571, she defiantly asked Elizabeth what she would do if they changed places. After receiving this message, as well as another from her in January 1572 protesting her imprisonment, Elizabeth did not respond directly to this question, although she had once experienced the fears and worries of captivity. Instead, she replied that she had never refused Mary's reasonable requests and pointed out that she was not a captive but lived in a nobleman's house, waited upon as a queen. The draft of this letter that survives is in Cecil's hand.

In September 1571 after discovering the Ridolfi Plot, Elizabeth had required Shrewsbury to confine Mary to Sheffield Castle, her residence since November 1570, and to reduce her household to 16. Grief-stricken by these orders, Mary composed an emotional letter of farewell to her servants. Among those leaving were the Livingstons, Willie Douglas, and her almoner, Ninian Winzet, a recent arrival who was transferred to the imprisoned Leslie's residence. As Shrewsbury suspected accurately that Winzet was a priest, his employment at Sheffield would soon have ended in any case. Mary arranged passage to France for the Scottish attendants fearful of returning home and pledged her willingness "to endure every kind of misery and suffering, even death, in the cause of my country's liberty."[9]

Meanwhile, de la Mothe Fénélon sent Norfolk 2,000 crowns[10] of which the duke forwarded £600 to an agent to pass on to Grange, still holding Edinburgh Castle for Mary. Instead, the messenger carried the money to Burghley, who had Norfolk's house searched and acquired Mary's ciphered letters to him and her cipher key. Hampered by his loyalties to the crown and to Protestantism that gravely weakened his leadership in these conspiracies, Norfolk was imprisoned in the Tower again in September.

After intercepting a letter to Mary from Ridolfi in which he related his successful visits to Pius V, Philip, and Alva, Burghley placed further restrictions on her household. On 22 November she related to Leslie that she had been detained in her chambers for ten weeks. While continuing to seek help from friends on the continent and requesting Seton to reveal her plight to Alva, Mary reminded Elizabeth that for four years she had been complaining about her good sister's refusal to assist her restitution that caused her to seek aid elsewhere.[11]

In January 1572 as Lord High Stewart, Shrewsbury headed a commission to try Norfolk for treason at Westminster Hall, leaving Sadler as Mary's substitute custodian. After learning about the duke's guilty verdict, Sadler informed Lady Shrewsbury so that she could convey the news to his prisoner. The countess found a grieving and weeping Mary, who had already heard about the verdict; she subsequently decided to observe three days of abstinence weekly to pray for his preservation. In June when he was beheaded after parliament requested his execution, Mary became quite ill. She had rightly been concerned about this parliament's actions. It also demanded her execution and approved a bill to prevent her accession in England on which Elizabeth postponed her decision.

In June Elizabeth dispatched four commissioners, William West, first Lord de la Warr, Sadler, Thomas Wilson, master of requests, and Christopher Bromley, solicitor-general, to charge Mary with attempting to advance her claims to the throne by marrying Norfolk and participating in the Ridolfi plot. Her response to them was that although she recognized no earthly superior, she would be willing to answer Elizabeth's accusations in person.[12]

Two months later European Protestants were horrified by the St Bartholomew massacre in which Catholics slaughtered 2,000 Huguenots at Paris and another 3,000 in the provinces. Concerned about possible French aid to Mary's allies in Scotland, Elizabeth attempted to resolve the question of her captivity. Elizabeth sent Killigrew ostensibly to alert James's governors to the possible danger but actually to negotiate Mary's return home, her murder trial, and execution, relieving the English of responsibility for her fate and preventing future complications if she escaped or gained restitution. Having succeeded Lennox as regent after he was killed in a scuffle engineered by the Hamiltons in 1571, Mar proved receptive to the English proposals. The terms had not been worked out when he died of natural causes in October 1572, however, and they were dropped under his successor, Morton. Between 1574 and 1576, Elizabeth briefly raised the possibility of her cousin's restitution with Morton, again unsuccessfully mainly because he did not want her returned. By then the Scottish civil war was over; in late May 1573 Drury led a force of 1,500 equipped with artillery and seized the last stronghold of Mary's allies, Edinburgh Castle, including its keeper, Grange, who was later hanged, and Lethington, who died somewhat mysteriously.

LESLIE'S DEFENSE AND BUCHANAN'S DENUNCIATION

While English officials were handling issues relating to Mary's captivity, Leslie's and Buchanan's tracts about her involvement in her second husband's murder and about her English succession rights were being published. Outraged by the defamation of her character at the inquiry in 1568, Leslie decided to defend her publicly. In his *Defence of the Honour of . . . Marie Quene of Scotland*, which appeared in 1570 and in revised form in 1571, he denied that she colluded in her husband's death and characterized the undated and unsubscribed Casket Letters as forgeries. (Actually, one of the letters was dated.) He condemned the spite and malice of Moray, whom he charged with actually planning the king's murder. Validating Plowden's and Browne's arguments that the common law rule against alien inheritance did not apply to the crown, he explained that even if they were incorrect, she could still succeed because of England's claim of lordship over Scotland. He also questioned the validity of Henry VIII's will, which was stamped but unsigned by him. Finally, he rebutted Knox's arguments limiting the monarchy to males, claiming instead that the law of nature emerged from the historical process in which many women participated as rulers.

In 1570 Buchanan criticized both the Hamiltons in *An Admonitioun to the Trew Lordis*, which was published that year, and Lethington in *The Chamaeleon*, which remained in manuscript until the eighteenth century. The first printed version of his denunciation of Mary appeared in London in November 1571 after Burghley's discovery of the Ridolfi plot caused Elizabeth to cease opposing the public defamation of her cousin's character. In *De Maria Scotorum Regina* (later entitled *Detectio Mariae Reginis*), which Buchanan prepared in 1568 at the direction of the Scottish privy council, he offered dishonest interpretations and inaccurate facts about Mary's relationships to her second and third husbands, accusing her of colluding both in the king's death and in Bothwell's abduction of her. Appended to *De Maria* was *Actio Contra Mariam Scotorum Reginam*, composed by Thomas Wilson, which emphasized female fickleness and claimed Mary aggressively pursued Bothwell, a mere puppet in their liaison. Finally, the appendix contained three of the Casket Letters in Latin. Burghley probably promoted this first publication of Mary as a murderess in the Latin language to attract a large Catholic readership abroad. Wilson also translated the *De Maria (Detectio)* into a language, identified as Scottish, and added all eight Casket Letters, two editions of which appeared within one month of the Latin rendition. Afterwards, most of the letters were issued in correct Scottish and French.

It is interesting that the French versions of the letters, which were published in 1572, are bad translations of the Scots, which seem to be versions of Buchanan's Latin renditions of the originals. Since the Scottish privy council authorized some of the translations that were published and presumably had access to the actual letters, it is extremely odd that they never appeared in their initial French form. This bizarre publication record lends support to the speculation that the Casket Letters were originally written in the Scots version that Moray sent to Elizabeth in 1568. The last known possessor of the letters was a descendant of Morton. After his death, they disappeared.

Since the Letters were published in various translations in the 1570s and since the transcriptions of them made in 1568 remained in England, the destruction of the original manuscripts, if they were not in French, would seem to be more important to the agenda of Mary's enemies than it would be to that of her friends. Without them her sympathizers could not prove definitively that she was defamed. It is not even clear that any of Mary's commissioners ever saw the alleged originals in England. They were not present when Moray introduced the documents into the inquiry, and Leslie failed to note in his *Defence* that one of them was dated. Meanwhile, the publications of them in the various translations, other than their original versions, continued to taint Mary's reputation for centuries. Surely, if the Casket Letters were actually written in French, they would have had an important enough monetary value for Morton's heir to attempt to preserve or even to market them. Henry VIII's love letters to Anne Boleyn still survive, after all, at the Vatican. But this, of course, is mere speculation.

After John Bateman, Shrewsbury's secretary, delivered Buchanan's denunciatory work to Mary, already in possession of Leslie's favorable treatise, she blamed Cecil for sending it to her. Some of her contemporaries claimed that the public attacks of critics, like Buchanan, whether true or false, irreparably damaged her reputation. When the 64-year-old Buchanan, whom Mary denounced as an atheist, became James's tutor in 1570, the outraged queen protested her enemy's appointment to her young son's household.

HOUSEHOLD MATTERS

In the years following the forced reduction in 1571 of Mary's own household to 16 individuals, some of its members had to be replaced because of deaths. In the summer of 1575 Claude Nau, a Guise client, assumed the office of French secretary, formerly held by the late Pierre Raulet, who had in 1568 rejoined the captive queen's staff.[13] In 1577 the master of her household, Andrew Beaton, the archbishop's brother, died while returning from a mission to the continent to obtain the release from a vow of celibacy for his betrothed, Mary Seton. Andrew had actually succeeded his deceased older brother, John, to this office in 1570. When Seton expressed concerns about marrying Andrew, a younger son of inferior lineage, the queen had reassured her that she would enhance his status before their wedding.

Other members departed because of illness or old age. In 1583 Seton's poor health prompted her to retire to the abbey of St Pierre at Rheims. Even before her departure, Mary had longed for the company of her former Scottish dames of honor and had requested unsuccessfully that either Livingston's or Lethington's widow rejoin her household.

Another of Mary's pressing concerns was obtaining a resident Catholic priest. When she asked specifically for a cleric to administer to her spiritual needs, Shrewsbury inevitably responded negatively. She complained bitterly to English officials about her lack of a priest, pointing out that even foreign ambassadors were permitted to observe the Catholic faith at their embassies. Until Leslie's imprisonment and Winzet's dismissal in 1571, she had, of course, been able to rely on them for spiritual guidance. In fact, Leslie did continue to send her his published treatises.[14]

By 1578 long bereft of a priest, she was requesting Edmund Augier for prayers to say on solemn days and at times of great necessity. Finally, in late 1581 or early 1582, some ten years after Winzet's departure, Henri de Samerie alias Henry de la Rue, a Jesuit priest, joined her household disguised as a physician. Departing after eight or nine months, he returned for brief periods in the summers of 1583 and 1584.

Even without a cleric, she continued to participate in some traditional religious services. At the annual Maundy, celebrating Christ's washing of his disciples' feet, a ceremony Elizabeth also observed, Mary gave to some poor women, the number equaling her age, one and one-half yards of woolen cloth, two yards of linen cloth, and 13 pence in coin. In addition, she bestowed six pence to the elderly in the nearby town. Since an English farm laborer in the 1560s might hope to earn £3 a year, these were generous offerings.

Besides seeking to continue some religious traditions and to employ appropriate staff, she also attempted to acquire clothes suitable for her royal status and fine items for her chambers. In 1574 she requested that Archbishop Beaton forward patterns of dresses of cloth-of-gold and silver and of silk like those worn at the French court. She also required some Italian headdresses, veils, and ribbons as well as a crown of gold and silver, similar to ones formerly created for her. In 1576 Mauvissière asked Walsingham's permission to send Mary four boxes of wearing apparel and clothes and two boxes of preserves that had arrived for her. Moreover, she ordered a bed and six great candlesticks in 1577 and some gold articles for tokens and New Year's gifts for her servants in 1579.

In 1575 as some individuals had requested portraits of her, she instructed Beaton to send her four set in gold. Two years later, Nau noted that an artist, who was not identified, was painting her portrait. In all only 50 images of her are extant, a small number when contrasted to the 250 images of Elizabeth. In France the master artist, Francis Clouet, had painted Mary: his rendition of her in white mourning, *en deuil blanc*, is the most well known of her early portraits, and a number of copies were derived from it. The surviving Scottish images are limited to engravings on medals and coins or sketches in crude drawings. It is not known when she sat for the exquisite English miniaturist, Nicholas Hilliard. As he was in France until at least August 1578, he was not the artist painting her in 1577, and it is possible that he rendered her miniatures from French models, although his work has the appearance of having been taken from life. The famous Sheffield types, the original of which is reportedly at Hardwick Hall, are standard Jacobean portraits. Among other extant English images of her are drawings of her execution and memorials in martyrologies.

In addition to obtaining portraits and other items from France, Mary attempted to recover her jewels from Scotland. While serving as regent, Moray seized many precious items, including a huge diamond called the Great Harry given to her by Henry II as a wedding present. Having learned Moray was selling off her jewels, Mary petitioned Elizabeth to prevent him from disposing of them. In 1568 Elizabeth did ask him to refrain from marketing them, a somewhat disingenuous request since she had recently obtained from him the magnificent set of large pearls Catherine gave to Mary as a wedding present and ultimately collected a rather extensive inventory of the gems. When Moray died in 1570, his widow refused to surrender the remaining jewels, even seeking Burghley's protection against anyone who might attempt to recover them. After succeeding Moray as regent, Lennox gathered an assortment of Mary's gems from her friends by threatening their imprisonment unless they relinquished them. Following the fall in 1573 of Edinburgh Castle, the depository of Mary's other jewels, Morton, then her son's regent, collected them and ignored her request for those dating from her French marriage. A confiscated letter by Grange to Mary, which was written two days before his death, probably assisted Morton in obtaining them. It declared Grange's devotion to her and revealed where all her jewels were kept. Morton later also acquired the ones Lady Moray still retained.

FRENCH DOWER INCOME

The repossession of her jewels would have been a welcome boon to Mary, helping to offset the loss of dower funds her French servants and relatives had been siphoning off. Without naming a particular individual, she claimed in 1574 that someone was forging her documents to seize her funds illegally. The shortages caused great concerns. She relied on this income to pay her household wages, to support the defense of her castles until 1573, to provide pensions for those leaving her service and for Catholic refugees, and to take care of her personal needs.

While in Scotland she never obtained the total amount due her, but her English captivity compounded the collection woes. From her prisons, she had difficulties communicating with her French council, which was convened by Archbishop Beaton as chancellor until 1573 when he reluctantly relinquished this office to Gilles, sieur du Verger, President of Tours. It was only in 1573, five years after Mary reached England, that Elizabeth permitted her to confer with a French advisor. Du Verger visited with her then and again in 1577. Sometimes Mary's councilors ignored her long-distance instructions; she often criticized, for example, the uncooperative attitude of her treasurer, René Dolu, sieur d'Ivoi in Berry, who traveled to England in 1576 but failed to obtain permission to consult with her. Two years later, she complained to Mauvissière about the denial of her recent request for the visit of one of her treasury commissioners. In 1581 Mary blamed her problems on the lack of good management in France and on Elizabeth's refusal to allow her staff access to her. That year she replaced Dolu with Anthony Arnault, sieur de Chérelles, whose brother Jean was employed at the French embassy.

In late 1582 Elizabeth permitted Mary to meet with two of her French councilors who happened to be Nau's brothers-in-law. *En route* to Scotland in September 1582 to confer with King James, Albert Fontenay, secretary of her council, stopped by to discuss his mission with her. Jean de Champhuan, sieur du Ruisseau, her chancellor, also met with her at that time to audit the dower accounts. Since Elizabeth began accurately to suspect that du Ruisseau was discussing the plans of Henry, third duke of Guise, to liberate his cousin, Mary, the English queen instructed Shrewsbury to delay momentarily du Ruisseau's departure. After returning to the English court in October, he elicited permission for Mary to consult annually with a French advisor, a promise that was apparently kept in 1583 but retracted thereafter, according to Mary's complaint in September 1585.

Du Ruisseau's appointment to Mary's French council actually represented a change in the nature of its membership. By the early 1580s, Catholic refugees from Britain had gained considerable influence over Mary's French officers, who were mainly men of lesser social status than her earlier appointees. The institution had changed from an administrative unit with the goal of preserving and investing her funds into an arm of her household intent on coordinating political activities, a development that reflected her interest in utilizing her revenue for Catholic goals.

Two prominent refugees associated with her business affairs were Thomas Morgan and Charles Paget. In 1572 Shrewsbury had ordered the arrest of Thomas Morgan, a Welshman who had served as his secretary for three years, for aiding Mary's secret correspondence and for warning her about court intrigues against her. Imprisoned for ten months at the Tower, he fled to Paris in 1575 and had gained the positions of cipher clerk for Archbishop Beaton and of receiver of her dower revenues by 1581. Paget, another Catholic exile and a brother of Thomas, third Lord Paget, became Morgan's close ally and also won appointment as Beaton's secretary. Morgan and Paget exchanged letters frequently with Nau and Gilbert Curle, Mary's other secretary in England, and conspired successfully to undermine her trust in Beaton's loyalty. In 1584 Paget complained to Mary, for example, that Beaton was attempting to discredit him and Morgan with Guise. That Mary's relatives misused her dower income and rights was also worrisome. While depending on her uncle, Lorraine, to oversee her transactions, she complained bitterly about his disposition of her assets. In 1574 when he assured her that her affairs were managed with great integrity, she noted that he had given away several offices and seignorial rights and forbade her councilors to authorize his expenditures or grants without her approval. Even so after he died that December, she lamented to Beaton that God had taken away her father and her uncle at one stroke.

Although Henry III, her brother-in-law, was ostensibly her friend, he emerged as a formidable opponent. In 1576 Henry granted his brother the duke of Alençon, an augmented dukedom of Anjou that contained the county of Touraine, which formed part of her dower. She had no choice but to yield the property when Henry agreed to substitute estates of comparable value. Instead, he released to her only the county of Vermandois and later some estates in the villages of Senlis and Vitry. Her cousin, Catherine, countess of Montpensier, however, obtained claims to the estates in Senlis and Vitry and initiated a lawsuit to protect her rights there. Mary became so strapped for funds that she had to borrow money from Norfolk's son, Philip, earl of Arundel, and even Nau, her secretary. At her death the French government owed her about eight years of her annual dower revenue of 60,000 livres.

In 1584, furthermore, Henry sent an envoy, Sieur Maron, sénéschal of Poitou, to petition Mary on behalf of the royal favorite, Anne, duke of Joyeuse. When William Waad, clerk of the council, escorted Maron to Sheffield for a meeting with Mary, Shrewsbury initially prevented the knowledgeable Nau from participating in their discussions because Elizabeth's instructions permitted the Frenchman access to her solely in Waad's presence. After extended debate, Shrewsbury finally allowed Maron also to inform Nau about Joyeuse's request but only in Mary's and Waad's hearing. The duke possessed property that owed her dower estates 30,000 crowns in fees and duties, which he wished her to waive. She granted Joyeuse's petition, explaining that she did so with the hope that he would provide her with a better hearing at the French court than she presently possessed.

CHRONIC AILMENTS

While protecting her dower income and struggling with life in captivity, she continued to suffer her chronic illness, which, even if it were not porphyria, mirrored most of its symptoms. In May 1569 she complained about a new on-going problem that prevented her from writing: a weakness in her right hand that later extended to her arm, which she described as a rheumatic attack in 1585. In May 1569 about the time the weakness of her hand first appeared, she took pills the physicians prescribed to treat her spleen and developed symptoms, including convulsions, similar to those manifested at Jedburgh. The aches in her side and head and a weakness of her hand continued to trouble her until at least early 1570. Visiting her in December 1569, Leslie described her disease: she had a distillation from her head into her stomach that weakened her so that she could not eat; she often vomited phlegm. Also disturbing her was a great inflammation in her left side under her ribs, which spread so far in every direction that the physicians were unsure whether it began in the stomach, the spleen, or the womb. Having endured insomnia for 12 days, she alternated between pensiveness and hysteria. Her melancholy, he also reported, led her to pray to God for deliverance from this life rather than remain in so much anguish and misery.

In mid-1571 she vomited blood and developed a fever. That December, a physician reported that her disease originated from the drying up of the melancholic humour and had worsened because she lacked outdoor exercise. He observed a swelling in her left side, frequent discharges from the brain, a great disability in the stomach that disturbed her sleep, and constant vomiting. Over the years these symptoms continued to plague her, Lady Shrewsbury noting in 1578, for example, that Mary blamed her chronic weakness and ailments on lack of exercise. She also suffered other maladies, a head full of rheum and swollen eyes in 1572, the tertian fever and a catarrh in the face in 1575, and a very bad dry cough in 1579. Another chronic problem afflicted her in 1581, a weakness in her legs that interfered with her walking and required her attendants to carry her in a chair. Despite the severity of her attacks, her captors occasionally questioned whether she was as sick as she claimed.

In February 1577 her illness prompted her to draw up a will, which survives in draft form only. In it, she referred to the dangers that might befall her in captivity, perhaps her fear of being poisoned. Attempting to protect herself from this problem, she had the preparation of her food monitored closely and had ordered a unicorn's horn and a half-pound of mithridate both of which were regarded as poison antidotes. In her will she went on to request burial with Francis and to bequeath her rights to the Scottish and English crowns to her son if he converted to Catholicism. Otherwise, she granted them to Philip II or to a member of his family. In 1576 she had exchanged gifts with Philip: he sent her a ruby ring and she gave him a book of gold. Although she did not specify the member of his family who might inherit her rights, she may have meant Don John of Austria, whom rumors had repeatedly said she might wed. Finally, she named Henry III and the dukes of Lorraine, Guise, and Mayenne as her son's protectors.[15]

Despite the physicians' claims that the exercise, such as hunting, that delighted her would improve her health, Elizabeth and her council forbade her horseback riding after discovering the Ridolfi plot. Mary sorely missed outdoor sports not just for relieving her illness but also for helping her to pass the time. In late 1572 Shrewsbury eased the rules enough to permit her to walk on the castle leads or in its vicinity but only under close guard. He was relieved to discover in February 1575 after an earthquake damaged her bedchamber that the problem was not the frightened queen's possible escape but her falling down. In February and May 1581 Mary explained to Elizabeth that to recover her health she needed to exercise on horseback or to be allowed to ride because she could no longer walk. Finally in late 1581, Elizabeth agreed to alter the restrictions enough to permit her prisoner to ride in a coach two or three miles out of Sheffield Park, as long as Shrewsbury was careful to prevent strangers from approaching her. In January 1582 he reported that she was so weakened by sickness that she had not yet taken advantage of this new privilege.

Mary's chronic ill health led Elizabeth to grant permission for her to receive medical treatments at Shrewsbury's Buxton baths, where by 1572 he had erected a square mansion with four stories, a battlemented roof, a great chamber, and 40 bedchambers.[16] It stood between St Anne's Well and three ancient hot baths with water of 82 degrees fahrenheit. Some of the evidence about Mary's visits is obscure, but she was certainly at Buxton an average of five or six weeks about seven times between 1573 and 1584. Some writers have claimed that she met both Leicester and Burghley at the baths, but she explained to Mauvissière in 1580 that she had less liberty there than at any other English mansion and that during her stay, all other clients were refused admission. That same year, Shrewsbury noted that during her residence she left the hall only one evening to take the air under close guard. From the beginning of his custodianship, Shrewsbury had to promise to meet his own friends in places other than the houses where she was in residence. The belief that she became acquainted with Leicester at Buxton may stem from the misreading of letters referring to his visits there. In one in 1577 Nau mentioned that he had personally returned from the baths; probably Mary sent him to confer with Leicester, who had recently arrived there.[17]

After discovering the Ridolfi plot, Elizabeth and her privy councilors attempted to restrict Mary's interaction with her English subjects, even Shrewsbury's children. In February 1578, for example, when Elizabeth momentarily considered transferring her prisoner to Huntington's custody from concerns that she could no longer trust Shrewsbury, she issued specific instructions for the move to Ashby-de-la-Zouch, Huntington's seat in Leicestershire. In a draft letter to Shrewsbury and Sir Henry Neville, who were to act as Mary's escorts on the journey, Elizabeth required them to utilize private houses but warned them against permitting the owners to see her.

Mary's interest in going to Buxton baths was for medicinal reasons not for recreation or cleanliness. Early modern Europeans rarely bathed to remove dirt and sweat because they feared that when the hot water opened up their pores, evil vapors would enter their bodies. In 1580 Shrewsbury learned, for example, that after Elizabeth's physicians prescribed a bath for her, she had caught a cold and was ill for two days. Instead of bathing, individuals changed their linen, which absorbed their sweat, rubbed away bodily odors with perfume, and washed their face and hands with cold water for civility, not for cleanliness. Mary chose to use wine rather than perfume for washing. Concerns even existed about how to treat dirty hair. In 1542 the duchess of Guise recommended that her daughter, who was pregnant with the future Scottish queen regnant, either wash her hair once a month or cut it short because greasy hair would cause her to catch a cold. The duchess confided that she cut hers every six weeks. In captivity Mary's hair turned completely gray before she was 40 years old. Thereafter, she seems to have kept it cut short and to have worn wigs.

For the medicinal baths that became popular in the mid-sixteenth century, physicians instituted a special regimentation. They recommended that their patients bathe between May and September, the sunniest months, and advised them to rest two or three days after reaching their destinations before beginning their treatments, which optimally should continue for at least a fortnight. For protection from the water's adverse effects, patients exercised, were purged, and said a set prayer before bathing, usually in the mornings and again in the evenings for two or three hours. Following immersion, they sweated in their beds with the aid of two bladders of hot water.

Beginning in 1572, Mary repeatedly petitioned to visit Buxton, since she had long believed bathing lessened the severity of her symptoms. She had probably ordered the construction of the bathhouse that still stands near Holyrood Palace, and she had also arranged for Henry's medicinal bath shortly before his death. The waters, she claimed, eased her side ache and her rheumatism while other topical aids, such as rubbing ointments, which she ordered in 1575, for example, were ineffective. Even when she injured her back in a fall from her horse at the start of her 24-mile ride to Buxton in July 1580, she insisted on continuing the journey. Following her last visit in July 1584, she confided to Mauvissière that she had recovered the use of her hand and that the water had soothed her nerves and dried up the harmful bodily fluids she suffered for lack of exercise. Before leaving, she wrote with a diamond on the window pane:

> Buxtona, quae calidae celebraris nomine Lymphae
> Forte mihi post hac non adeunda, Vale
> (Buxton, which is celebrated because of your tepid waters Perhaps I shall never visit again, farewell.)[18]

POSSIBLE MARRIAGE TO DON JOHN

In 1574 after returning from Buxton, she corresponded with Archbishop Beaton about rumors that she might wed Archduke Charles, Leicester, or perhaps Don John, whom her allies especially favored because of his tremendous naval victory over the Turks at Lepanto in 1571. Although 15,000 Christians perished, Turkish deaths numbered some 30,000 and 113 of their galleys were destroyed while another 117 were captured. It was the "biggest battle of the sixteenth century."[19] In October 1574 Nicholas Ormanetto, papal nuncio to Spain, proposed to Ptolemy Galli, cardinal of Como, two other candidates besides Don John: the duke of Anjou and Alençon and the recently widowed duke of Savoy. Ormanetto favored Don John because he was well suited to rule England as Mary's husband and to assume the regency of the Netherlands, where William the Silent, prince of Orange, with English aid was challenging Spanish rule. Ormanetto warned that Mary should be married before her English accession, since otherwise she might act independently in selecting her husband. Catholics abroad believed that her governance of England, if she were assisted by an appropriate Catholic husband, would result in the pacification of the Netherlands and the conversion of Britain to Catholicism.

In her surviving correspondence, Mary made infrequent, non-committal references to marrying Don John, a reticence that is striking when compared to her enthusiasm about the Norfolk match. An intriguing aspect about the possibility of her union to Don John was her decision in 1575 to seek an annulment of her third marriage. If she had a bridegroom in mind, it was likely Don John, who arrived in the Low Countries as their governor-general in 1577. Although Mary suffered from a chronic illness that caused her to draft a will, from time to time her health improved enough for her to contemplate marriage, which she viewed as a vehicle to win her freedom from the English captivity that she believed contributed greatly to her sickness.

In January 1575 she appointed Leslie, who moved to Paris after his release from prison in 1574, as her ambassador to Gregory XIII. Before departing for Rome, Leslie initiated proceedings for her annulment. In April Leslie discussed these plans with Antonio Maria Salviati, the papal nuncio to France, and in August he witnessed depositions taken from several Scotsmen, some of whom were at Edinburgh in 1567. Leslie planned to transmit this evidence, establishing that Orkney was Jean Gordon's husband and that at least one observer stated Mary colluded in his abduction of her, to Rome for Gregory's final decision. Mary's letter in October to Gregory, committing herself and all her business to him and requesting aid for herself, a devout Catholic oppressed with many failures, may have been an oblique reference to these hearings.[20]

Evidence that Gregory acted upon her petition has not survived, but subsequent events indicate he favored the annulment. In late 1575 Leslie traveled to Rome to confer with him about these depositions and to handle other business. There he met with several English Catholic exiles, including William Allen, the future cardinal, and Robert Persons, a Jesuit priest, who were framing an enterprise for two invasions of England, one in the south and one at Liverpool, which lay about a day and a half's journey from Sheffield Castle. They planned to free Mary, place her on the English throne, and wed her to a Catholic prince of the pope's choosing. Most English refugees, including Allen, favored Don John as her husband. With some reservations, Philip approved the scheme, although he demanded that Don John first pacify the Low Countries.

The next surviving evidence of Mary's concern for Don John dates from 1577 when he was serving as regent of the Netherlands. In her letter to Archbishop Beaton in January, she reported that the English erroneously suspected her of communicating with the prince. Two months later she predicted that if Don John landed in England with or without her consent, her captors would treat her more harshly. That summer rumors spread in England that when Lord Seton left to visit a spa in the Netherlands, he actually went there to confer with Don John about marrying the Scottish queen. In November Mary implored Beaton to relay to her any information he might discover about Don John's plans to invade England. By then Elizabeth had expelled Antonio de Guaras, the Spanish envoy, because he had secretly forwarded Mary's letters abroad, perhaps to Don John, himself.

That Mary hoped the prince would invade England in 1577 is proved by her letter to Paget in 1586. In it, she wondered whether Sir Francis Drake's raids on Spanish territory and Elizabeth's aid to the Dutch rebels would finally cause Philip to attack England. It would have been better, she opined, if he had done so when Don John was regent, since France and Scotland were well disposed to help English Catholics at that time. She recalled Don John's belief that the only way to appease the Netherlands was to have a friendly English ruler.[21] His mission had ended with his death on 1 October 1578 from typhoid; rumors circulated that his demise greatly troubled Mary, who ate very little for two days after hearing about it.

DEATH OF ORKNEY, HER THIRD HUSBAND

That same year the duke of Orkney died at the Danish fortress of Dragsholm, which is located on an island some 58 miles west of Copenhagen. In George Buchanan's *History of Scotland* in 1582, he stated publicly for the first time that the duke suffered from mental illness.[22] It was rumored that as he lay dying, he confessed that he, along with Moray and Morton, were parties to the king's murder but that Mary was not involved. Actually in 1576, two years before his demise, she had received information about this alleged confession. Having learned that it was written at Malmö and that several Danish dignitaries witnessed it, she instructed Beaton to determine if it were valid because if it were, it might be useful in combating her enemies' accusations. Since her husband died at Dragsholm and some of the alleged witnesses were no longer alive in 1576, it seems likely that a friend attempting to aid her forged the document.

SCOTTISH POLITICS AND THE TREATY OF ASSOCIATION

In 1579 the year after Orkney's demise, Esmé Stuart, sixth seigneur of Aubigny, moved from France to Scotland. Since the king's grand-mother and his aunt, Margaret, countess of Lennox, had died in 1578, Aubigny was hoping to secure the earldom of Lennox for himself. His father John was the brother of her husband, Matthew, earl of Lennox. The impressed 13-year-old James, whose minority had ended in March 1578, not only granted his 37-year-old cousin the earldom in early 1580 but also raised it to a dukedom the next year. With his assistance, James ordered the arrest of Morton for knowing about and concealing the murder of his father. The jury having found him guilty of treason and murder, Morton was executed on 2 June 1581. Under Lennox's influence, the crown's policy became pro-Guise and pro-Catholic.

Although Mary had demonstrated an interest in her son's welfare, sending him gifts, inquiring about his health, and worrying that Morton might inflict physical harm upon him, she remained unwilling to concede her crown to him. In 1579 she had dispatched Nau to him with her letters, but as she directed them to her son rather than to the king, Morton had refused her secretary's request for a royal audience. Nau succeeded in communicating with her allies, who reassured him that James understood his filial duty. Mary remained concerned about her son's well-being during Morton's regency and informed Archbishop Beaton that she wanted Philip to send forces to Ireland, which could then cross over to Scotland and remove James to Spain.

In 1581 Mary attempted to take advantage of Lennox's rise to power to reopen negotiations for her association with her son as joint ruler of Scotland. This association would resolve the Catholic princes' problem of how to address James, would relieve her of having to accept the validity of her abdication, and would offer her an opportunity to seek more favorable living conditions perhaps even her freedom. In 1581 Mary obtained Henry III's and Catherine's approval for her joint rule with James, and Cecil even discussed French support for it with Bernardino de Mendoza, the Spanish ambassador. Subsequently, Henry continued to instruct his English diplomats to press for Mary's association with James and to petition Elizabeth for her liberty.

In November Elizabeth sent Robert Beale, a clerk of the council, to discuss with Mary the treaty of association with her son. Although her illness complicated the negotiations, Beale obtained Mary's promise to recognize Elizabeth as the rightful English monarch and to refrain from negotiating with foreign powers or English rebels. Further talks were delayed because of political developments in Scotland.

In August 1582 some nobles led by the earl of Gowrie kidnapped James in what became known as the Ruthven Raid, imprisoned the duke of Lennox, and then in December forced his retirement to France. In June of the next year after James escaped the raiders at St Andrews, James Stewart of Bothwellmuir, the second son of Andrew, second Lord Ochiltree, a Protestant who had competed with Lennox for the king's favor, assumed great influence in the government. As a descendant of the first earl of Arran by his first wife, Stewart had claimed the earldom of Arran in 1581 on the basis that the deceased Châtelherault and his heirs sprang from an irregular marriage.

THE THROCKMORTON PLOT

Meanwhile, Mary had been considering more than one method for escaping imprisonment. The delays in arranging the joint rule with James troubled her. Although Elizabeth permitted the negotiations to resume in 1583, sending Beale to Mary in April and again with Mildmay in June, the English queen decided to cancel them in August in response to the on-going political developments in Scotland. Mary's second option for liberation which she had pursued since 1582 was to obtain aid from Lennox. That year the duke sent two priests, William Crichton and William Holt to Guise, Allen, Persons, Philip, and Gregory with plans for an invasion of Scotland with forces that would move south to liberate Mary. Guise greatly offended Paget and Morgan by failing to include them in a Paris meeting about this conspiracy in 1582, and their bitter protests revealed a serious split among the English Catholic exiles. The complaint of the overlooked pair that politics was a task for lay people not priests was supported by Mendoza, who agreed that priests could not be trusted to take part in enterprises such as this.

After Lennox's death in 1583, England rather than Scotland became the focus of the enterprise amidst rumors that Philip, whose fourth wife, Anne of Austria, died in 1580, might wed Mary. Attempting to reconcile the English exiles, Guise invited Paget and Morgan to discussions with Allen and Persons concerning attempts to free Mary. While a Spanish army of 20,000 would invade Lancashire to raise the Catholic north and liberate her, Guise would lead a force of 5,000 to Sussex to link up with allies there to overthrow Elizabeth. Although these plots were unrealistic as events later showed, Mary clung to them as they seemed to offer some hope of gaining her freedom.

To aid his two accomplices in England, Mendoza and Francis Throckmorton, a wealthy gentleman who served as Mary's secret messenger, the duke of Guise sent Paget to confer with various interested conspirators. In September at Petworth, the Sussex home of Henry Percy, eighth earl of Northumberland, the brother of the executed earl, Paget met with Northumberland, Lord Paget, his brother, and others concerning possible invasion ports and the likelihood of a supportive Catholic uprising.

Walsingham had meantime been building up a vast spy network while serving as a principal secretary; the queen had advanced him to this position after moving Burghley to the post of Lord High Treasurer. In November 1583 when Walsingham heard of the plot to invade England from his spies, he had Throckmorton arrested. Under intense interrogation including reportedly the employment of the rack, Throckmorton implicated both Mary and Mendoza in the enterprise. He was tried and convicted in May and executed in July. The following January Elizabeth demanded Mendoza's expulsion and broke off diplomatic relations with Spain, thus depriving Mary of that embassy's support. In addition, the crown imprisoned several prominent Catholics, including Northumberland and Lord Henry Howard, Norfolk's brother and the accomplice of Mendoza since 1579. Some observers suspected that Lord Henry hoped to wed Mary who seemed to favor him. She addressed Lord Henry as her brother-in-law and his nephews, Norfolk's offspring, as her children. In a letter to Mauvissière in early 1584 after lamenting Lord Henry's and Throckmorton's treatment, Mary warned the disbelieving ambassador about a mole in his embassy.

Actually, Walsingham not only employed a spy there from early 1583 to the end of 1585 but also received copies of 40 letters from Mauvissière's clerk, Nicholas Leclerc, sieur de Courcelles. Disheartened by the discovery of the enterprise and by the delays in arranging the joint rule with James, Mary confessed to Burghley in March 1584 that the association was the only thing in the world that could comfort her and that her captivity had so depressed her she thought she could no longer bear it.

Subsequently in May and June, Waad and Beale reopened discussions with her at Sheffield about the association and obtained her pledge to ratify the Treaty of Edinburgh, to suspend all dealings with foreign powers, and to refrain from communicating with papists and Jesuits in England. Citing her ill health, she assured them that if granted more freedom, she would not try to escape. Her attempt to associate with James in the governance of Scotland eventually ended in failure but that occurred after Shrewsbury was no longer her custodian.

THE SHREWSBURYS' MARITAL PROBLEMS

The earl's marital difficulties with his countess caused him to request replacement as Mary's guardian in 1584. An event that formed the backdrop to his domestic discord was the marriage his countess secretly arranged ten years earlier for her daughter, Elizabeth Cavendish, with Charles Stewart, fifth earl of Lennox, Mary's brother-in-law. As the Scottish queen and her mother-in-law were reconciled, rumors circulated, which were probably untrue, that Mary promoted this match. The fears she shared with Lady Lennox that their enemy, Morton, might harm their beloved James had drawn them together. Lady Lennox assured her that she had been deceived about Mary's complicity in her son Henry's death and exchanged tokens with her, including a diamond ring that Mary proudly wore. When in the autumn 1575, the young countess gave birth to Arbella, Mary sent her infant niece a gift for which Lady Lennox wrote a letter of thanks, signing off as her loving mother and aunt.

As Arbella's father died in 1576, followed by her grandmother

Lennox in 1578 and her mother in 1582, she was left to the care of Lady Shrewsbury, her ambitious grandmother, who began to promote her native-born granddaughter as Elizabeth's successor. Irate about her schemes, Mary accused Lady Shrewsbury in 1584 of even hoping to match Arbella with James.

By then the Shrewsburys, whose marital problems began in 1577, were living apart. One of her ladyship's servants, Marmyon, described their quarrels as "civil wars," called their house a "hell," and revealed that the earl blamed his wife and him for passing on falsehoods that led Elizabeth to reduce his allowance for maintaining Mary.[23] Lady Shrewsbury and her two sons, Charles and William Cavendish, also accused the earl of having had an affair with his Scottish prisoner that produced at least one child.

Horrified by these allegations, Mary complained about them in several letters to Mauvissière. She denounced as liars all who said she had a dishonorable relationship with Shrewsbury and speculated that her enemies meant to prevent her marriage to Philip and to defraud her and her son of their English succession rights. Swearing that there was nothing that she would not do to clear her honor, she explained that she hoped Elizabeth would retain Shrewsbury as her custodian, since replacing him might seem to confirm the gossip. Despite this controversy, Mary continued to maintain in her household Lady Shrewsbury's granddaughter, Elizabeth, the child of Frances Cavendish and Sir Henry Pierrepont.

Existing as vivid evidence of her loathing for her former companion, is Mary's unsent letter to Elizabeth, sometime called the Scandal Letter, probably written in late 1583, relating some rude comments of the countess and her two sons about Elizabeth. Mary reported that they described Elizabeth as vain and a lover of flattery. She also pointed out that in 1578 after Lady Shrewsbury predicted Elizabeth would succumb to the serious illness she was suffering, the countess even offered to help liberate Mary if the English queen died. Since throughout her captivity the fearful captive worried that some English guard might kill her at her cousin's death, she had probably been grateful for this promise of freedom. Finally, Mary claimed the countess described Elizabeth as a physically deformed nymphomaniac, whose lovers included Leicester and Sir Christopher Hatton. It is not possible to determine whether Lady Shrewsbury made these comments or whether

Mary was merely trying to impeach the countess's honor to raise doubts about her and her sons' defamation of her. That Mary never sent the letter probably means that she realized besmirching Lady Shrewsbury's character would not clear her own name and that repeating the malicious gossip to Elizabeth might only incense her. Monarchs often did not, as she well knew, reward the bearer of bad news. The letter stands as evidence, however, of Mary's outrage at being accused of illicit sexual relations with Shrewsbury. In 1586 she was still complaining to the French embassy about the countess's wickedness.

Disillusioned by his role as Mary's custodian, Shrewsbury sought permission in 1584 to discuss his financial and marital problems with Elizabeth personally. On 20 March the crown issued instructions for Sadler to replace Shrewsbury as her custodian and to move her to Wingfield. Among the orders was one permitting her to take air on foot or by coach but not to go far from the residence. Sir Henry Neville and Shrewsbury were to assist Sadler in moving her to Wingfield until Melbourne Castle in Derbyshire, her final destination, was ready to receive her. These provisional plans were not implemented and perhaps were not even communicated to Sadler and Neville. Five months later in August, the 77-year-old Sadler agreed to become her temporary guardian, expecting to relinquish the position upon Shrewsbury's return or as soon as another keeper for Mary could be found. In preparing for Sadler's arrival, Walsingham instructed Shrewsbury to transfer Mary to Wingfield because the elderly Sadler, who was used to fresh air in his own house, might suffer from the stuffiness of Sheffield where she was then in residence. Walsingham thus unwittingly validated Mary's charges that her confinement was adversely affecting her health. Hoping to avoid the cost and trouble of that move, Shrewsbury responded that he would take her to the lodge where Sadler would "find as good and open air" as at any of his houses.[24]

9

FAILING ENTERPRISES, 1584–86

On 25 August 1584 after a seven-day ride from Standen, his Hertfordshire home, Sadler reached Sheffield and learned the unwelcome news that Shrewsbury was bowing to orders and planning to remove Mary to Wingfield. The disappointed Sadler wrote Walsingham that he preferred remaining at Sheffield because it was more defensible than Wingfield and because he was too exhausted to resume traveling so soon. On 2 September after exchanging messages with Walsingham, Sadler decided to obey the initial instructions and assisted by John Somer, his deputy custodian who was also his son-in-law, he joined Shrewsbury in transferring Mary to Wingfield.

During the journey Mary conversed with Somer, whom she had met when he served as Throckmorton's aide in France. After blaming her bad health on her captivity, she wondered whether she should rely on her son or Elizabeth for her liberation:

> For if I should leave my son, who is to me more than anything in this world, and trust to the queen, my good sister's favor, which I cannot get, I might so be without both; and then what should become of me?

When Somer asked her what diplomatic strategies Elizabeth should adopt, Mary recommended that she negotiate an offensive and defensive league with Scotland and comprehend France in it out of respect for the auld alliance. Since Scotland was too impoverished to maintain a monarch adequately, Elizabeth should grant a pension to James in return for which he would aid her in resolving England's Irish problems. Following that island's pacification, Elizabeth could stop promoting wars in France and the Spanish territories, and then, somewhat unrealistically Mary predicted, even her Guise relatives would become England's friends.

She admitted when he turned to James's future marriage that she was aware of suitable brides in the Catholic noble families of Florence and Lorraine and also in the Protestant royal family of Denmark. To his inquiry about a Spanish marriage, she responded that if James could have the Low Countries, it would be a good match, a sentiment that recalled her earlier efforts to marry the Spanish prince whom she hoped would be appointed regent there.

Answering Mary's question about whether he thought she might try to escape, Somer opined that it was natural for prisoners to seek freedom. She disagreed for her "heart" was so great that she would "rather die in this captivity with honor, than run away with shame." If the treaty of association provided for her liberation, however, she wanted to visit her son but only for a short time because she could not "abide" the sight of her old enemies. Unless Elizabeth granted her an allowance enabling her to reside in England, she would live off her dower in France where she would have nothing more to do with governance and would remain unmarried for she had a son who was a man. Her goal was to end her days in freedom.[1]

The return home from France of a young Scotsman, Patrick, master of Gray, the future sixth Lord Gray, raised Mary's expectations about the treaty of association. After residing as a Catholic refugee in France and gaining the friendship of Beaton and Guise, Gray escorted the late duke of Lennox's young heir Ludovick to Scotland in November 1583. Successfully ingratiating himself with James, who was then seventeen, Gray ostensibly became James Stewart, earl of Arran's confederate while secretly working against his authority.

In the summer of 1584 when Mary sent Fontenay to Scotland again to explore James's feelings about the treaty, her representative reassured her of her son's support and also revealed he had forged a letter from France to indicate to James and Gray that Philip and Henry approved of the association. In a postscript to Nau, however, Fontenay questioned Gray's dependability and related some troubling comments about James's attitude toward Mary. He had noted, he explained to his brother-in-law, that while James expressed filial and dutiful love for his mother, he seemed uninterested in her personally, never inquiring about her health, about her treatment as a captive, about her servants, or about her recreation.

When learning that James was planning to dispatch Gray on a mission to England that autumn, Mary also named him as her envoy to negotiate the treaty of association and instructed him to assure Elizabeth that no differences of opinion existed between her and her son and that they were both committed to the joint-rule of Scotland that it would establish. She also complained about the mismanagement of her French finances, noting Beaton had not forwarded the 10,000 crowns for James or the 12,000 crowns for the maintenance of his guard that she requested. The 6,000 crowns he had received, she related, came from Spain.

With orders to counter the Shrewsbury slanders and to monitor Gray's negotiations, Nau reached London in mid-November following the Scotsman's arrival in late October. Nau's first task was accomplished some two weeks later when Lady Shrewsbury and her sons swore before Elizabeth and her councilors that they knew Mary was chaste, that they never heard of her having a child in England, that the rumors concerning her affair with the earl were false, and that they had not spread them.

Meanwhile, Gray was maintaining an independent course in English negotiations. His instructions from James Stewart, earl of Arran, did not refer to the association, and English councilors soon discovered that Gray would not insist on including Mary in the proceedings. He proposed an Anglo-Scottish defensive and offensive league that left James in sole command of Scotland. When Mary wrote to Gray that her son should recognize his obligations to her by accepting her joint-rule with him, the envoy's reply that his instructions did not include that issue came as an unpleasant surprise to her. He promised to correspond with James about it and to inform her of his response.

She was so eager to gain the greater freedom that the proposed treaty with her son seemed to promise, that in late November she sent word to Elizabeth that she would agree to further concessions: she would renounce her right to the English crown and deny the validity of the papal bull in so far as it was interpreted in her favor. She also pledged to refrain from entering into any agreement that might endanger England and pledged not to leave the realm without Elizabeth's license.

After discovering Gray's betrayal, Mary futilely requested Elizabeth's permission to send Nau to meet with James and pleaded for a less stringent confinement. Emphasizing that her health required regular exercise, Mary asked to go eight to ten miles beyond Chartley and for additional horses so that her guards could ride with her to enable her to move at a faster pace. Because of her chronic illness, the symptoms of which were then mainly a weakness or swelling in her right arm and hand and in her left foot and leg, which had become shorter than her right leg, she also petitioned for more servants to assist her. She could no longer turn herself over in bed.

She sent several dispatches to James pleading for a clarification of his intentions unaware that his councilors were advising him to reject the treaty with her. In January 1585 his privy council concluded in his presence that the association would disadvantage him and his realm. In March James accepted this advice, and in May English and Scottish commissioners began negotiations for the Treaty of Berwick that was finally ratified in July 1586. This defensive and offensive Anglo-Scottish league that excluded Mary ended all hopes of her restitution and resulted in his becoming Elizabeth's pensioner. By 1602 he had received from her £58,500. Initially, Mary characterized her son as a usurper of her crown but eventually blamed traitors around him, especially Gray, for his betrayal. She also assumed inaccurately that Walsingham had corrupted Gray with hints of English aid in ruining James, earl of Arran, who had served as Scotland's lieutenant general since February 1585. Elizabeth's agreement to release Arran's enemies, the Ruthven raiders, who had been banished to England, did, however, contribute to Arran's loss of power in late 1585.

ENTERPRISES

While seeking the association, Mary promised Elizabeth to eschew agreements unfavorable to England, but as usual she kept her options open. In October 1584 the same month that Gray reached London, she requested Allen to expedite Guise's enterprise. The invaders should not, she confided, worry about her well-being, as she could not give her life for a better cause than the liberation of the oppressed of the Catholic Church.[2] Upon learning that Walsingham had gained custody of Father Crichton, who was captured in September on his way to Scotland, bearing evidence about the enterprise, she sent him denials that she ever had any contact with the priest. As Walsingham was still obtaining information from his spies in the French embassy, he knew she was a party to that conspiracy.

Events were underway in France that caused the enterprise's leadership to shift from Guise to Philip and his regent in the Netherlands, Alexander Farnese, duke of Parma. Six months after the death in June 1584 of Henry III's brother and heir, the duke of Anjou and Alençon, Philip and Guise signed a secret treaty at Joinville to prevent Henry of Navarre, the heir presumptive who was a Protestant, from succeeding the childless Henry III as king of France. Civil war broke out in the spring of 1585, distracting the Guises from the enterprise.

At this time Mary still distrusted Beaton. In January 1585 seemingly contradicting her charge to Allen the previous November to promote the enterprise, she instructed the archbishop to refrain from all political activities. She had resolved, she explained, to use peaceful means to obtain her liberation. Undoubtedly, she meant to deceive him. Diplomatic rumors claimed that if Beaton were informed about the enterprise, he would reveal it to Henry III, who was a supporter of Mary's association with James but was not a party to the Guise schemes for invading England. Earlier in a letter of February 1583 to Mendoza, Mary even accused the allegedly ambitious archbishop of attempting to obstruct the duke's plans.

Besides encouraging her suspicions about Beaton, Morgan became involved in intrigues with a fellow Welshman, Dr William Parry, who toured the continent in 1582 with a license to travel for three years. As one of Walsingham's spies, Parry sought to debate with various Catholic exiles whether or not assassinating Elizabeth was justified. Allen and Persons avoided him but Morgan allegedly approved the scheme. While Parry may have had an authentic Catholic conversion, he could also have been a double agent.

Back in England in 1584 he not only reported on Catholic conspiracies to Elizabeth but also conversed about assassinating her with

Edmund Neville, a returned Catholic exile. Later that year, as a member of parliament, Parry gained notoriety by denouncing a bill that required Jesuits and seminary priests to leave England within 40 days or be treated as traitors. In February 1585 Walsingham learned about Neville's and Parry's earlier conversations and ordered the doctor's arrest. He discovered in Parry's possession a letter from Cardinal Galli, relating that Pope Gregory granted the "Indulgence and remission" of his sins that he requested for completing his "service and benefit public," presumably Elizabeth's assassination.[3]

Parry was convicted and executed although he denied his guilt and identified Morgan as the author of the plot. Elizabeth demanded Morgan's extradition from France, but Henry placed him under house arrest on 9 March and had him transferred to the Bastille five days later. It is unlikely that Mary was involved in the Parry conspiracy. When Mauvissière sent her a copy of the cardinal's letter, she responded that the doctor was unknown to her. Since Parry's plot contained no specific plans for her liberation, she was probably stating the truth to Mauvissière, even though she deemed him a blunderer because he rejected her warning that someone in his household was leaking information.[4]

In March 1585 parliament passed the Act for the Safety of the Queen's Person, which was based on the Bond of Association that Burghley and Walsingham drafted the previous October in reaction to William the Silent's assassination in July, as well as to Throckmorton's conspiracy. The bond obligated its endorsers to respond to a murderous attack on Elizabeth by killing not only the perpetrators but also the claimants to the throne and their heirs for whom the traitors acted. Thousands of Englishmen subscribed, swearing to avenge all assassination attempts against her. The major differences between the bond and the statute were that the latter exempted the claimants' heirs, unless they were involved, and authorized a state trial rather than a private assassination. This was the statute by which Mary would be tried and executed.

When informed about the bond, she realized that she was the intended claimant and denounced it as a conspiracy fomented by her public enemies to obtain pardons for murdering her under the pretext of preserving their queen's life. Mary, herself, endorsed it in January 1585, officially repudiating attacks against Elizabeth. In a letter dated in March, Mary assured Elizabeth that she had nothing to do with Parry's schemes and predicted that if her cousin's life were taken, the new associates (signatories of the bond) would assassinate her. Another concern of Mary's was that as a prisoner she would be extremely vulnerable to attack in the event of Elizabeth's death whether by natural causes or foul play. This concern gained momentum after Sir Amyas Paulet took charge of her in April 1585; she feared that when Elizabeth died, her new custodian or another bond signatory would kill their prisoner before she could escape from captivity. Indeed, Guillaume de l'Aubespine, baron of Châteauneuf-sur-cher, Mauvissière's successor, later confirmed that Mary's would-be liberators well understood that they must free her first before attacking Elizabeth. Otherwise, Paulet or his agent would kill her.[5] Meanwhile, Mary's friends on the continent, like her agent, Sir Francis Englefield in Spain, were claiming that Elizabeth and her councilors were secretly working to take her life.

REMOVAL TO TUTBURY AND PAULET'S CUSTODIANSHIP

By the time Paulet succeeded Sadler as her custodian, Mary had changed residences. Shortly after arriving at Wingfield, Sadler commenced plans to remove her to Tutbury, where he could more easily monitor her communications. He and Somer not only needed to order repairs, such as window glazing, but also to furnish the royal castle. They could no longer utilize Shrewsbury's household effects except for some plate he loaned to Mary. Besides supervising these arrangements, their concerns about the queen's health and the decision to await Nau's return from London delayed their departure until January 1585.

To furnish Tutbury Walsingham transferred to it Lord Paget's confiscated belongings. Because some had been sold and those that arrived were fewer in quantity and of lesser quality than anticipated, Sadler and Somer had to request additional sheets, blankets, lined wall hangings, silver vessels, and floor coverings. They ordered these items well before the move, but Mary's rooms were still inadequately furnished at her arrival. Two months after entering Tutbury, she lacked Turkish carpets to lay around her bed and under her seat in the dining chamber where the plaster floor although scattered with rushes was exceedingly cold. In April a shipment with plate and the hangings, which needed lining, did reach Tutbury, but without the three Turkish carpets for her bedchamber. Finally, as to her horses, which Shrewsbury had provided, Elizabeth would bear the charges for four coach horses and two geldings but not for the ten others Mary required.

Sadler seemed satisfied with her Tutbury accommodations: she had a fair dining chamber, 36 feet long, with a cabinet that had a chimney, and a bedchamber, 27 feet long, with two beds, a pallet, and a closet. In addition, she possessed a room for a close-stool and suitable servants' quarters. Disagreeing with his assessment, Mary complained her lodgings consisted of two wretched small rooms and some closets that were suitable only for a close-stool. From the 16 members allowed in 1571, her household had increased to 48, half of them women and children some of whom were quite young. At least from late 1584 Mary had acquired the services of Camille de Préau, a Jesuit priest, probably without Sadler's knowledge as to his true vocation. De Préau may have arrived secretly with Father Samerie the previous summer, intending to remain when his colleague departed.

While assisting with the housing arrangements, Somer reported on her diet. She ate capons, rabbit, partridge, various other wild fowl, and venison in season and especially liked mutton. Because Wingfield was so far from the sea, it was impossible for her to obtain the good seafood, such as the plaice, turbot, sole and lobster that she enjoyed. Throughout her imprisonment, Mary continued the hierarchical arrangements for dining that she utilized in Scotland. She was served, for example, 16 dishes at the first and second courses while her master of the household and her chief officers were served 10 dishes at the first and second courses.

Her ill health continued to cause concerns. Even during the journey to Wingfield in September 1584, she suffered from a swelling in her left leg. In the next few weeks, her left foot became swollen and by early November she was bedridden with swellings in her right arm and hand and left foot and left leg. Sadler noted that insomnia further weakened her condition. By the end of November her health had improved except for her sore foot, which, he thought, she could rest on a pillow in the coach during the journey. Her sickness plus her promise to cooperate in the move at Nau's return led Sadler to postpone their departure. On 13

January 1585 about two weeks after Nau's arrival, they began the 16-mile trip, spending that night at Derby and entering Tutbury on the 14th. The coach ride may have further aggravated her problems. In February she was bedridden for six days with chronic pain in her side and hips and could walk only with assistance.

While planning the transfer, Sadler pleaded for release from the custodianship. He described the country as a cold and miserable place with foul weather that prevented the exercise necessary for his health, thus unwittingly validating Mary's claims about her captivity's adverse effects on her physical well-being. In October 1584 Elizabeth had appointed a reluctant nobleman, John, second Lord St John, of Bletsoe, Bedfordshire, to succeed Sadler, but on 4 January citing St John's ill health, she replaced him with Paulet, her former French ambassador who was originally scheduled to serve as St John's deputy. For personal reasons Paulet did not reach Tutbury until 17 April.

The instructions of her new guardian, which were dated 4 March, permitted Mary for the first time officially since the Ridolfi Plot to take air either on horseback or on foot for up to two miles from the castle. It is likely, however, that Shrewsbury had occasionally allowed her to do some limited horseback riding; in an October 1584 note is the information that when Mary exercised, the earl's soldiers were always at hand to lead her horse through difficult terrain.

Whether or not Sadler was aware of Paulet's instructions granting Mary the privilege of horseback riding within two miles of the castle is unknown. Chafing from lack of exercise while awaiting his replacement, Sadler sent for his hawks and falcons to help pass the time. He decided to permit Mary to join him because she took great delight in the sport. On 22 March, consequently, he had to respond to Walsingham's charge that he had taken her riding six or seven miles from Tutbury. Sadler explained that he allowed her to join him on two or three occasions only and traveled no more than three miles from the castle. When furthest away from it, 40 or 50 servants on horseback, some armed with pistols, accompanied him. Sadler further groused that if he had known he must continue in this office so long, he would have refused it as others had, apparently a gibe at St John. Somer also assured Walsingham that had she attempted to escape she would have placed her life in great jeopardy.

Sadler left two days after Paulet's arrival and Somer departed in May. Mary dreaded Paulet's custodianship because she feared that, as a Puritan, he might inflict personal injury on her. She was also aware that when he served as English ambassador to France, he condemned the activities of her Guise relatives. In their first interview, she confided that she believed he was ill-affected toward her, but as she had recently learned of his good qualities, she was content to have him serve as her guardian. It was not long before their disagreements led her to describe him as one of the most bizarre and cruel (*bizarres et farouches*) persons she had met and to avow that he was fitter to be in charge of criminals than of someone of her rank and quality.[6]

Paulet was soon corresponding with Walsingham about Mary's claims that he was treating her and her household too rigorously. For security reasons, he confirmed, he prohibited her coachman from leaving Tutbury without his permission and from eating with his staff, since he preferred to keep the two households separate. He also admitted forbidding her attendants to walk on the walls overlooking the gates to prevent them from observing those entering and departing the castle but emphasized he allowed them to accompany her abroad. Most of his comments concerned his removal from the great chamber of her cloth of estate with the arms of France and Scotland. He explained that he believed it was inappropriate for a canopy with foreign insignia to hang in the governor's dining room and that she had supped under it only once at which time Sadler had eaten at the lower end of the chamber, a familiarity Paulet deemed inappropriate. He later reminded Walsingham that a cloth of estate continued to hang in her personal dining chamber and that since she had been taking physic for several days and planned to follow a diet that would keep her confined in her bedchamber for about six weeks, she would not have an opportunity to eat in his great chamber for some time.

In May he justified forbidding de Préau, whom he suspected was a Catholic priest, from distributing alms to the town's poor because he believed Mary was using the funds to win local friends. Mary protested that her only goal was to encourage the paupers to pray for her better health. Later, when she went to watch her new greyhound chase a deer in Stockley Park, less than one mile from the castle, Paulet further angered her by denying her almoner permission to accompany her because she had to pass through the town to reach the park.

Paulet's duties also included monitoring her correspondence. From October 1584 until January 1586, Walsingham intercepted all her secret communications and sent them to Paulet to decide which to distribute to her and her household. Paulet delivered to her reports from her French council, unimportant letters from Scotland, and unciphered messages from Mauvissière, Beaton, and other officials. The cessation of her secret correspondence made even more unpleasant her incarceration at Tutbury, which she described as a dungeon fit only for the worst criminals.

After suffering from Tutbury's damp and cold for several months, she began to insist that Elizabeth order the repair of its lath and plaster walls that were riddled with cracks. In August Mary complained to Mauvissière that she had hoped her special diet would restore her health, but for 15 days she suffered chills, especially in one thigh, and sciatica. Paulet commented insensitively that her crippled legs made his supervision of her easier. He blamed her illness on her emotional state but did admit that her lodgings were extremely cold even in August.

When she requested the repairs to Tutbury, she made other demands of Elizabeth, who returned mixed responses. She agreed thereafter that Mary could remove to another dwelling to permit the regular cleansing of Tutbury, that she would have access to a dining hall and a gallery in her temporary residence during Tutbury's renovation, that she could distribute alms but only with Paulet's knowledge, and that she could ride a mile or two from the castle. Since Paulet's instructions had permitted his prisoner this last privilege, Mary's request may have been an allusion to his strict supervision of her. He later defensively informed Walsingham that at least three times when Mary had gone into the little park one-half mile away, she had ridden from it into another park, traveling in all almost two miles. Elizabeth offended Mary, however, by refusing to permit annual visits from her councilors, Fontenay and Chérelles, although the latter was allowed to meet with her in early 1586. She also denied Mary's request for the attendance of a Scottish noblewoman, Margaret Fleming, the widowed countess of Athol, who assisted her at James's birth. Finally, Elizabeth was undecided about whether to permit her French embroiderer to return home, possibly from concerns that he might act as Mary's messenger.

REMOVAL TO CHARTLEY AND THE BABINGTON PLOT

Rather than repair Tutbury, Elizabeth found her cousin another prison. Over the protests of Robert Devereux, second earl of Essex, she ordered Mary transferred to his moated manor at Chartley, which was 12 miles from Tutbury. Walsingham questioned whether Mary might reject Chartley because of the water but she was so desperate for a different prison that she sent assurances she had no objection to the moat. The move on Christmas Eve required four carts to carry her books and apparel. To transfer Mary, ailing from a weakness in her right arm, Paulet had the assistance of Richard Bagot, his new deputy.

This journey may have further aggravated her physical condition. In late January after asserting that she was feeling better, Paulet reported that she walked haltingly, had a diseased hand, slept little, and ate less. In early February he noted that she had been bedridden for a month with painful swellings in her limbs that prevented her from walking without assistance. On the 17th she suffered a severe, painful attack in her side that lasted for seven or eight hours. Showing unusual sympathy, he repeated her servants' testimony that they had never seen her condition so grave and even judged as reasonable her request for a softer bed, but he also warned that her sickness increased household expenses since she kept four fires going continuously in her chambers.

While she was still at Tutbury, meetings were underway that were to culminate in the Babington plot. In October 1585 Gilbert Gifford, whose family home lay near Tutbury, visited Morgan at the Bastille and impressed him with his alleged loyalty to Mary. Two months later Gifford disembarked at Rye with a recommendation to her from Morgan, who hoped he would be able to re-establish their secret communications. The port's searcher took Gifford to Walsingham, who recruited him as one of his servants, appointing him to spy on the queen of Scots. Perhaps Walsingham was reacting to heightened fears concerning the political divisions in France. Earlier that year, noting the growth in the political power of Mary's Guise relatives, he had warned Sadler, who was still her custodian at Tutbury, to guard her closely.

Some historians have questioned Morgan's trustworthiness mostly because he sent Gifford and other unreliable persons to Mary with good references. Confined to prison and at odds with some of her other allies, he was likely unaware of the success of Walsingham's spies in infiltrating Catholic households even Allen's seminaries. Later in 1591 the cardinal, who was not Morgan's friend, denied he had purposely betrayed Mary or the "common cause"[7] but also claimed that he was involved in double-dealings that prompted many to suspect he cared more for his advancement than for God's service.

After leaving Walsingham, Gifford met with Trianou Cordaillot, secretary to Châteauneuf, to establish procedures for delivering her secret messages. A brewer, dubbed the honest man, was recruited to collect her secret letters, place them in a cork tube, slip them through a barrel's bung-hole, and then surrender them to Gifford for display to Paulet and delivery to Thomas Phelippes with whom Gifford lodged in London. Phelippes was already an acquaintance of Paulet, having assisted him at Paris in decoding intercepted letters in 1578. Either in London or at Chartley, Phelippes deciphered Mary's correspondence for Walsingham, who retained the copies; his clerk, Arthur Gregory, counterfeited the seal, and Gifford's servant took her original ciphered messages to the French embassy. When Châteauneuf received packages for her, these same procedures were followed only in reverse order. Mary obtained her first letter via this route on 16 January 1586 from Morgan, who had written it in October 1584.

An interesting and important secret letter that she received in April 1586 was from Persons, who composed it in late 1584. After deploring their failure to liberate her, he warned against fostering an invasion because if English soldiers captured her after an unsuccessful escape attempt, her imprisonment would become more difficult and might result in personal injury to her. He recommended the strategy that worked in Scotland: she should slip out of her residence in disguise at night with one or two servants and await the arrival of some designated individuals to assist her in leaving England secretly. After also relating that Parma had inquired about whether she planned to remarry, Persons recommended that she hold out some hope to the duke, who might then follow his own interests and aid her.

In late May Mary responded to Persons' letter, explaining that she might well have followed his recommendations had she received them at Wingfield, where Sadler permitted her more liberty than she had previously enjoyed. At Chartley not only was she watched too closely to escape the building with her attendants but she was also in poorer health. As for Parma, she asked Persons to assure him that she would be greatly beholden for any service he rendered her.[8]

Deeply disappointed by James's failure to approve the treaty of association and by the delays in launching the enterprise, Mary decided to make an invasion of England more attractive to Philip and Parma, who were combating Leicester's military support of their rebels in the Netherlands. In May she wrote Mendoza at Paris that she planned to cede her English succession rights to Philip if by her death James had not converted to Catholicism and that she wanted the Spanish king to take her under his protection. She requested that they keep this bequest secret because otherwise she would lose her French dower, receive even worse English treatment, and become irrevocably estranged from her son whose heretical views were sorely troubling her. Philip had hitherto worried that aiding Mary would advance Guise interests in England. When he learned she was adopting him as her heir and privileging her faith over her love for her son, he agreed to undertake the protection of her person and interests and promised financial support as soon as Mendoza could arrange to deliver funds to her.

Despite making this bequest to Philip, Mary continued to hope for James's accession in England. In July only two months later, she repeated to Châteauneuf rumors she had heard concerning secret articles in the Treaty of Berwick, which reportedly promised the English throne to her son. That her progeny should succeed in England if she, herself, could not, she explained, was the chief reason she had been able to endure her captivity. If she were deprived of that hope, there was no extremity, even a dishonorable one, which she might not venture to win release from her misery.[9]

On 20 May the same day she informed Mendoza she was bequeathing her English succession rights to Philip, Mary also sent a message to Paget concerning James's religious and political views. If her son failed, she explained, to support the enterprise to free her, she wanted Catholic lords in Scotland to seize him and deliver him to Philip, who should then convert him to Catholicism. While James was absent from his realm, she thought the prudent and loyal Lord Claud Hamilton should serve as regent. He had, she continued, greater influence than his older brother, Lord John.

Besides channeling Mary's letters through Walsingham's hands, Gifford also encouraged Anthony Babington, a young well-to-do Derbyshire gentleman, to participate in a plot to free Mary. As Babington had served as Shrewsbury's page in the 1570s, the young man might have met her but they would have had little contact since their households were mostly kept apart. Later in 1580 while touring France, he became conversant with Morgan and Beaton, and after returning home with their recommendations, acted as Mary's secret messenger for two years, probably in 1583–84.

In the spring of 1586 Babington learned about a number of Catholic plots against Elizabeth. On 30 and 31 May fresh from a mission to France concerning the raising of armed forces to invade England, John Ballard, a priest, consulted with Babington, an acquaintance of his, about employing those troops to liberate Mary. Besides seeking to raise an invasion force, Ballard had been meeting with English Catholics to discuss their fomenting an uprising against Elizabeth and had traveled to Scotland to sound out Mary's allies, including Lord Claud, about aiding their captive queen. Ballard also revealed a regicide vow of John Savage to the horrified Babington, who initially shrank from involvement in a conspiracy to kill Elizabeth. Earlier at Rheims, Savage had sworn to assassinate the English queen, but after reaching home and entering Barnard's Inn, he had failed to act upon his vow. Babington soon became reconciled to Elizabeth's assassination and attended several meetings in June with Gifford, Ballard, Savage, and other friends to ascertain if these schemes could be combined into one venture that would end in the liberation of Mary and the death of Elizabeth. Soon wearying of the plotting, however, Babington decided to seek Walsingham's permission to travel abroad and actually met with him three times between 25 June and 13 July. Walsingham refused to grant him a passport and by hinting at secret goings-on with Mary attempted unsuccessfully to elicit information from him about the plans to free her.

Mary's communications with Babington had resumed on 25 June, when at Morgan's urging, she asked the young man to forward any secret correspondence of hers he still possessed. On 6 July three days after the second of his three sessions with Walsingham, Babington received Mary's letter and sent her the requested messages along with a plan for achieving two goals: first, he would lead ten gentlemen and

100 followers to release her from captivity, and second, six persons would commit the "tragical execution" of Elizabeth, "the usurper." Later in the text, he repeated that Mary's deliverance needed to be first, for "thereupon dependeth our only good."[10]

In her reply on 17 July extant only in a deciphered copy, she first described the armed forces both local and foreign that were necessary for achieving her liberation and recommended that Babington seek Mendoza's assistance in raising and supplying them. Next, she requested that as soon as the six gentlemen completed their task, messengers immediately rush to alert her so that she could gain release from her prison before Paulet could act against her.[11] Finally, she suggested various plans for her liberation. In sharp contrast to Babington's design, Mary's proposal provided for him and his allies to execute Elizabeth before, not after, liberating her. The importance of this altering of the sequence of events will be discussed in more detail below. While she did not specify her final destination once she gained freedom, Mary did inform Châteauneuf in late July that her physicians had recommended she receive medical treatment at some very hot baths in Italy.

Although a few days after responding to Babington, Mary rode on her horse to a nearby park to kill a deer with her crossbow and to chase after her hounds, she still could not walk alone. A month earlier desperate to cure her lameness, she had taken a special physic that kept her secluded in her chamber for several days. It not only failed to ease her symptoms but also made her weak and faint. Because she had long claimed her captivity caused her chronic ailments, it was not surprising that in July 1586 she would approve generally of Babington's plot although it included Elizabeth's murder. Mary believed her strict confinement had greatly diminished the quality of her life physically and socially and felt tremendous disappointment at James's rejection of his filial duty to assist her in alleviating the conditions of her captivity. Consequently, she began to commit somewhat reckless acts: she consented to Babington's plot despite the threatening Bond of Association, facilitated Philip's invasion of England by pledging to grant him her English succession rights unless James converted to Catholicism, and initiated plans to have her son delivered to the Spanish king for religious indoctrination. She made these secret offers knowing that if they were publicized she risked English, French, and Scottish reprisals.

Mary's response to Babington's letter was in Curle's rather than her own handwriting. She sent Babington Curle's ciphered rendition of his English translation of Nau's polished French version of her dictated statements. After Phelippes received and deciphered it, he recopied the ciphered letter in order to add at least one part: a postscript requesting the six assassins' identities. Walsingham forwarded this recopied message with the postscript to Babington, who obtained it on the 19th. That all historians agree that Phelippes created the postscript has led some scholars to make the unlikely claim that he invented the entire text. Her apparently disjointed composition has also attracted attention. As noted, her ciphered letter envisioned three phases: Babington was to obtain sufficient armed forces; next the six gentlemen were to proceed; and then her liberators were to act. In a later paragraph, she explained some concerns:

> And to take me forth of this place . . . before well assured to set me in the midst of a good army . . . it were sufficient cause given to that Queen in catching me again to enclose me forever in some hole.[12]

This statement indicates that she took seriously Persons' warning about the danger to herself if the invasion forces failed to free her.

Since Mary ignored the six gentlemen's role in this comment and assumed that during her escape attempt Elizabeth would still be living, some writers have claimed that all the brief references to the assassins in her letter were, like the postscript, forged insertions. Because the drafts of her letter were destroyed, the question of whether the original French did refer to the six gentlemen is impossible to determine definitively. Some of Phelippes's statements to Walsingham after deciphering it can be interpreted to mean he believed Mary had approved of regicide, but it is difficult to understand why she did not refer explicitly to the assassination in her 27 July 1586 encoded message to Mendoza or in any other extant comment about the plot.

Her ciphered letter to Babington, as copied by Phelippes, makes its first allusion to Elizabeth's death in the form of a brief question: "By what means do the six gentlemen deliberate to proceed?" It can be found at the beginning of her letter in a list that sets out various matters that needed to be considered before she went on to elaborate upon them individually. It is the only item in the list that is a complete sentence and is the only issue raised there on which she did not subsequently expound: she later discussed plans both for the raising of troops and her liberation but offered no strategies for murdering Elizabeth. Her other references to the six gentlemen's task were limited to requests that messengers should notify her immediately when the deed was done. She advised Babington to station four men at court, who could speedily bring her the news of Elizabeth's death, permitting her opportunity to escape from prison before Paulet could learn of his queen's execution and retaliate against his captive. No explanation was given as to how those messengers could inform her while Paulet still kept her closely watched. Mary's liberation strategies, moreover, were not structured as mere hasty responses to message bearers arriving at top speed to announce Elizabeth's death. The schemes she elaborated required advanced planning and careful timing. In one scenario, for example, she proposed that her liberators arrive at midnight and set adjoining buildings on fire to distract Paulet and his soldiers while she escaped.

That her first reference to the six gentlemen in the ciphered letter was in the form of a question and that she failed subsequently to offer strategies for the men's task make it possible to suggest that Phelippes purposely inserted the reference into the text in the form of an inquiry, hoping to elicit details from Babington about his plans for the regicide. Keeping in mind Phelippes's postscript asking the assassin's identities, it can be surmised that after copying over Mary's long letter in cipher, he realized that while he had inserted a question in the text about the six gentlemen's deliberations, he had neglected to solicit their names. To obtain that vital information, he created the postscript rather than undertake the arduous task of recopying the entire letter to include that question.

An interesting aspect of Mendoza's role in this conspiracy is that he learned about Elizabeth's proposed murder but not from Mary. On 21 July, two days after Phelippes deciphered Mary's letter, Gifford departed for France. There he met with Mendoza ostensibly to arrange the assembling and arming of the invasion forces required for Mary's escape. In discussions with the ambassador, Gifford revealed that six men would murder Elizabeth before the other conspirators freed Mary, thus conveying information from her ciphered letter that Phelippes recopied rather than from Babington's message. When predicting to

Philip that if Elizabeth were assassinated first, Parma would aid her killers, the gratified ambassador explained that he had heard of earlier English schemes to murder Elizabeth but that none of them had proposed to commit this act before Mary's liberation.

Socialized to accept the honor code of the early modern network of dynastic families, Mary most likely would have shrunk from approving regicide. A ruler's violent death showed disrespect for the royal hierarchy that God had created and jeopardized the lives of her noble counterparts. Even tolerating public criticism of another monarch could be viewed as breaching royal protocol. In 1570 Mary complained to Elizabeth about a minister at Lichfield who criticized her in a sermon, pointing out her disbelief that a prince would permit evil to be spoken of another prince in her realm. Elizabeth subsequently promised to punish the cleric.

Like most hereditary monarchs, Mary maintained that only God could judge her and her activities. Since in July 1586 she also expressed concerns to Châteauneuf and to an unknown correspondent that if she were still an English prisoner when Elizabeth died, her life would not be safe in Paulet's hands, it is extremely unlikely that she would have consented that same month to her cousin's assassination as the initial step in her own liberation. In a document summarizing the events of 1586, Châteauneuf agreed with Mary's analysis.

Earlier in 1581, Mary had complained to Archbishop Beaton about Walsingham's rumored assertion that she would leave no stone unturned to escape, implying apparently that she would approve any dishonorable act to gain her freedom perhaps even murder. She had also predicted that Walsingham would use his opinion of her evil nature to restrict further her activities. Probably confirming her assessment of his character, Walsingham instructed Phelippes to add certain brief phrases to her ciphered letter to Babington when recopying it to create evidence for the charge that she had specifically assented to Elizabeth's assassination as a prelude to gaining her freedom. If so, it was Phelippes's textual insertions that created her letter's disjointed structure.

In his edition of this correspondence Conyers Read dismissed the importance of the disjointedness with the quip, but "if we argue that every inconsistent thing a woman has ever written is, ipso facto, a forgery, we shall have to reject many interesting and valuable historical documents," failing, however, to identify the other female inconsistencies in question.[13] His biased analysis appears even more invalid when compared to the equally biased comment of Antony Perrenot, cardinal of Granvelle, Philip's regent in Madrid during his absence in Portugal. In 1582 Granvelle indicated he admired the epistolary skills of Mary's correspondence. After reading her message about the enterprise, he surmised that she employed a very intelligent secretary. It was impossible to explain with greater clarity than she had in her lengthy letter the manner in which the business should be conducted, the extent of financial support that would be necessary, and the number and kind of armed forces that would be required.[14]

Mary's recent biographers, including those who have generally written favorably about her, such as Antonia Fraser and John Guy, have either failed to note or at least to consider seriously the inconsistencies in Mary's letter. Accepting the extant decoded version as a true reflection of her intent, their reading of it in association with Babington's letter provides adequate proof for them that the references to the six men's design meant Mary did approve of Elizabeth's assassination as a prelude to her own release from prison. Earlier sympathetic writers also failed to understand the significance of the placement of Elizabeth's death before Mary's liberation.[15] This altered sequence of events did not make sense given Mary's fears that her guardian would kill her or could not protect her if Elizabeth died first either peacefully or violently.

Even if, as is being argued here, Mary did fail explicitly to approve the six gentlemen's task, the Statute for the Safety of the Queen's Person still applied to her because Babington was conspiring on her behalf to assassinate Elizabeth. To enforce this statute against Mary, Walsingham and the other councilors realized that their major hurdle was persuading Elizabeth to assent to her captive's death. Although Walsingham had amassed extensive data linking Mary to various invasion schemes, he used his spy network to manipulate her and her allies into agreeing to a conspiracy that included Elizabeth's demise. He surely realized that this was the only evidence that would induce his queen to permit her cousin's execution. To convince Elizabeth that Mary had approved of the plot's every detail, including regicide, Walsingham must have ordered Phelippes to add brief phrases to the letter that could be read as specifically confirming that consent.

Indeed, on 19 July after recopying Mary's ciphered message to Babington, Phelippes predicted that the letter would inspire their queen. In discussions of Mary's trial and execution in Chapter 10, the question of whether Phelippes inserted passages into her letter will be revisited.

ARREST OF THE BABINGTON PLOTTERS

On 4 August Ballard was arrested and tortured so severely he could not stand during his trial. By the 14th nearly all the other conspirators, including Savage and Babington, were in custody and probably fearing torture had begun confessing their parts in the scheme. They were tried in mid September, found guilty, and executed a few days later.

While these events were underway, Paulet received new instructions concerning his prisoner and her household. First, pretending to have arranged a stag hunting party, he should escort her to a nearby residence and confine her there for several months. *En route* he should have her secretaries, Curle and Nau, arrested and sent to London under strict guard. Next, Paulet should confiscate her documents at Chartley and seal them in bags for delivery to London. Finally, he should reduce the number of her 47 or so servants; ultimately, he permitted her to retain ten men, seven women, and Pagez's young son.

The dwelling Paulet chose was Tixall, Sir Walter Aston's seat three miles from Chartley. Their original departure date of 11 August having been postponed to the 16th, Mary looked forward to the sport and rode happily toward Tixall. She soon discovered the ruse which, when followed by Curle's and Nau's arrest, upset her so much that she demanded to be returned to her quarters. After realizing they were taking a different route, she dismounted but unable to walk sat on the ground weeping. Then supported under each arm by her servants, she knelt under a tree and prayed God to have pity on her and her people and to pardon her for her offences, claiming she wanted nothing but "the honor of His holy name."[16] Remounting, she rode to Tixall and disappeared into her chambers. On the 22nd Paulet requested and obtained permission to return to Chartley, a more defensible structure than Aston's residence. Emerging from Tixall's gate on the 25th, Mary tearfully explained to the waiting paupers that she had nothing for them and that she was also a beggar since everything had been taken from her. To the gentlemen she denied being involved in any conspiracy against their queen.

At Chartley she learned that Barbara Mowbray, Curle's wife, had delivered a baby and that Paulet had sent de Préau away. When Paulet refused to let his chaplain conduct the christening rite to permit her as the godmother to name Curle's daughter, Mary astounded him by sprinkling her with water, saying, "I baptize thee in the name of the Father and of the Son and of the Holy Ghost," and calling her Mary.[17] After discovering that her papers were missing, she swore she possessed two things they could never take from her, her English blood and her Catholic faith.

Elizabeth was meanwhile approving the relocation of her prisoner to Fotheringhay, a royal castle in Northamptonshire in the keeping of Sir William Fitzwilliam. Walsingham and Burghley sent Mildmay to report on its condition and required Paulet to determine how much of Chartley's furnishings should be transferred to it. Having earlier requested removal from Essex's manor house, Mary was pleased to learn that her next residence would be Fotheringhay. As it was only 84 miles from London, she hoped to be permitted to speak to Châteauneuf. Also delighted to leave Staffordshire, Paulet requested replacement as her custodian.

On 10 September before their departure, while suffering pains in her neck, unable to use her hands, and scarcely able to walk, the outraged queen was forced to witness Paulet confiscating more of her property. He seized from her cabinet over £100 in coins, from Curle's closet 2,000 crowns intended as his wife's dowry, and from Nau's chamber gold and coins worth over £1,400, earmarked to pay for the costs of her funeral and of her servants' transportation home after her death. Retaining £500 for household expenses, Paulet forwarded the remainder to London and later took additional money from her quarters. These were not to be his last unpleasant acts. After her trial and conviction, he humiliated the queen by removing the cloth of estate from her chamber and depriving her of the support and presence of her priest and the master of her household.

10

ENDING CAPTIVITY

On Wednesday, 21 September, Mary's servants carried her to the coach for the ride to Fotheringhay, which they reached on Sunday, after four stops: Burton in Staffordshire, Hill Hall Castle near Abbots Bromley, a property of the earl of Huntington, the Angel, a Leicester hotel, and Roger Smith's manor in Rutlandshire. A stone castle with a double moat, Fotheringhay, where her trial and execution took place, was destined to be her last prison. Following those events, the book ends with brief discussions of Buchanan's theory of revolution, of James's memorial for her at Westminster Abbey, and of her status as a Catholic martyr.

After settling in at their new quarters, Paulet attempted to persuade Mary to confess her involvement in the Babington plot. He argued that she would receive better treatment if she admitted her offences instead of leaving the determination of her guilt to the royal commissioners, who would shortly arrive to interrogate her. Proclaiming her innocence, she protested that the only superior authorities she recognized were God and the Church.

On 11 October along with other officials, the commissioners began arriving at Fotheringhay, although six of the 48 who were appointed did refuse to attend and participate. On the 12th Mildmay, Paulet, and Edward Barker, the royal notary, delivered to their prisoner Elizabeth's letter authorizing the trial. She explained to Mary that she was subject to English laws, as she resided in England under its queen's protection.

Aggrieved that Elizabeth was commanding her to undergo a trial as though she were her subject, Mary again swore she was innocent and complained about the confiscation of her documents and her lack of counsel.

The next day, the 13th, when a number of the commissioners, including Sir Thomas Bromley, the lord chancellor, and Burghley, informed her that neither her prerogative nor her captivity could exempt her from trial by the common law, she again refused to prejudice her rank by responding to their charges, but as she was innocent, she agreed to defend herself before parliament. Finally, she requested a list of the commissioners' names, which was afterwards released to her, and promised to inform them presently whether she would appear at the trial.

When they later returned to her apartment, although she did not object to any of the commissioners named, she still denied their right to judge her. She complained that their authority derived from the Statute for the Safety of the Queen's Person, which had been enacted to entrap her. Christopher Hatton, the royal vice-chamberlain, warned Mary that if she were innocent, she would besmirch her reputation by declining to answer the charges, and Burghley then revealed that the proceedings would commence the next day even if she refused their jurisdiction. Later that evening, she resolved to speak to them again before the trial.

The next morning, the 14th, when they re-entered her chamber, she repeated that as a foreign, anointed queen, she was not subject to their laws or their monarch. Since she cared more for her honor than her life, she continued, she was persuaded by Hatton's argument to participate in the hearing but would answer only to the allegation that she had plotted Elizabeth's death. Then dismissing them, she promised to join them in the great hall after dining, as she felt feeble and ill and needed to drink a little wine. One explanation for her decision to respond to this charge is that it was the only one of which she was truly innocent. This limited defense supports the contention that the references to the six men in the Babington letter were forged insertions.

At the upper end of the chamber in which the trial was conducted stood Elizabeth's dais of estate and a table holding the documentary evidence. At the table were positioned the crown's representatives, including Sir John Popham, attorney general, Sir Thomas Egerton, solicitor general, and two clerks to record the proceedings. The commissioners were arranged along both sides of the room. When she appeared at 9:00 a.m. supported under her arms by Andrew Melville, master of her household, and Dr Dominique Burgoyne, her physician, she wore a black dress with a long train and a pointed widow's cap with a long white gauze veil.

After she was seated on a velvet chair near the dais, Bromley opened the proceedings, accusing her of conspiring to murder Elizabeth, usurp her realm, and disrupt religious matters and the public peace. She protested that as she was an absolute queen and had come voluntarily to England seeking the aid that had been promised, she would refuse to prejudice herself, her allies, or relatives by responding to his charges. Only to the untrue claim that she sought Elizabeth's death would she answer, not as a subject but as an innocent declaring to the world her blamelessness. After he pronounced her protestation illegal, she asserted that she lacked political ambitions because her captivity had ruined her health, leaving her with at most three years to live. To Burghley's pointed reminder that she had once borne England's arms, she explained that she had been obeying Henry II's orders. That Burghley could not resist referring to this earlier behavior, although she had not repeated it since 1560, indicates some of the lingering outrage he and his associates felt. Mary next displayed the ring Elizabeth sent to her in Scotland with a promise of assistance. Finally, the commissioners instructed the clerks to record her protestation and Bromley's response.

When questioned about Babington's plot, she denied knowing him or communicating with him. After copies of her letters to him were read, she accused her enemies of tampering with her ciphers and requested to see the originals. Furthermore, she had not been in contact with Ballard, as they claimed, and charged Walsingham with manipulating the evidence. Declining to respond to her accusation directly, Walsingham replied defensively:

> I call to God to witness that as a private person I have done nothing unbeseeming an honest man, nor, as I bear the place of a public man, have I done anything unworthy of my place. I confess that being very careful for the safety of the queen and the realm, I have curiously searched out all the practices against the same.[1]

Following an hour's recess, the trial resumed at 2:00 p.m. During this session, Nau's and Curle's depositions concerning her communications with Babington and a copy of Paget's letter about Guise's enterprise were read. She surmised that her secretaries had confessed under fear of death, although she admitted that Nau was capable of taking bribes to give false information and of enticing Curle to follow his lead. As for Guise's enterprise, its goal was her liberation not Elizabeth's murder. Burghley also reproached her for employing Morgan after he plotted with Parry to assassinate Elizabeth, but she insisted she knew nothing about that conspiracy and denied that the imprisoned Morgan was her servant, although she admitted supplying him with funds.

At the opening of the trial on the 15th, she reminded the commissioners that she was appearing before them voluntarily and that their authority derived from the Statute for the Safety of the Queen's Person. She also reminded them that if it had been in force in 1554, when Wyatt had rebelled against Mary Tudor on Elizabeth's behalf, it would have required the death of their future queen. Her protestation having once again been recorded, they introduced copies of her communications with Paget, Allen, and Mendoza, which called for an invasion of England. She repeated that the goal of the enterprise was her liberation and charged her captors with punishing her for her religion. Burghley denied penalizing individuals for their faith and accused her of scheming to send James to Spain and to give her alleged succession rights to Philip. The English should be sorry, she retorted, for separating her son from his mother in their treaty and for making him Elizabeth's pensioner. Again, she asked for a parliamentary hearing, and then as she departed, she pardoned the commissioners for their rude behavior.[2]

Believing that the commissioners had condemned her before they arrived, she assured Paulet that she possessed a clear conscience and was prepared to die. At the end of October, she took physic several times and was bedridden for five or six days, an indication that this ordeal may have adversely affected her health.

At the proceedings, which followed contemporary rules for English treason trials, only copies of Mary's correspondence were produced and her judges declined to question her secretaries in her presence. In obedience to Elizabeth's request, the trial was prorogued and reopened on the 25th in the Star Chamber at Westminster. There, Curle and Nau confirmed the validity of their depositions and admitted burning

Babington's letter and the drafts of her responses to him. It is note-worthy that both secretaries made independent statements contradicting their official testimony. Earlier in September Nau sent a private message to Elizabeth denying that Mary was a party to the assassination plot and later, in 1605, repeated that denial to James. In 1609 Curle swore on his deathbed to his confessor that none of the "calumnies and imputations put in print" about her were true.[3] In 1586, nevertheless, the commissioners pronounced Mary guilty and sentenced her to die.

Pressure mounted for Elizabeth to agree to the death penalty. On 12 November when a parliamentary deputation requested Mary's speedy execution, Elizabeth asked them to reconsider since she was loath to pursue this severe penalty. Two days later, they repeated their original recommendation, undoubtedly holding the same opinion as Thomas Sackville, first Lord Buckhurst, who declared to Elizabeth that "every hour of her life did greatly endanger your death."[4]

Meanwhile, responding to Châteauneuf's written request, Elizabeth temporarily postponed the publication of Mary's death sentence. She decided, however, to proceed with informing Mary of her decision to accept the commissioners' verdict. Elizabeth issued instructions on the 16th, requiring Buckhurst and Beale to convey that information to her captive. Four days later, the two messengers recommended to the Scottish queen that she begin preparations for her demise and made the offer to her, which she declined, of the spiritual services of Dr Richard Howland, bishop of Peterborough, or Dr Richard Fletcher, its dean. Joining Buckhurst and Beale in imparting this news to her were Paulet and his new deputy custodian, Sir Dru Drury, who privately referred to Mary as a serpent in his queen's bosom. Some two weeks later, Elizabeth permitted the death sentence to be published.

Earlier on 22 November, Paulet and Drury revealed to Mary that their queen had commanded them to remove from her chamber the cloth of estate with her royal arms and explained that she was a "dead woman, incapable of dignity."[5] Mary defiantly ordered a crucifix hung in its place.

When informed of Mary's death sentence, James and Henry dis-patched envoys to plead for clemency for her. Despite his estates' recommendation that he prepare for war if she were executed, James and his agents, William Keith, Robert Melville, and Grey, who joined

Archibald Douglas, the Scottish resident ambassador in England, refrained from threatening military retaliation. James's poverty and concern about the English succession led him to protest Mary's treatment cautiously and circumspectly, and Walsingham had, furthermore, informed him that she bequeathed her English rights to Philip. Her intentions were also reiterated in a letter to Sixtus V on 23 November that was made public. The subsequent plea of Pomponne de Bellièvre, the French envoy, that Elizabeth should permit Henry to ransom Mary met with no success; concerned about domestic disturbances, the king could not insist that Elizabeth release her captive to him.

On 19 December Mary wrote to Elizabeth about the commissioners' recommendation that she prepare for the end of her "long and weary pilgrimage." After pardoning everyone for the wrongs done to her, she requested that her servants be allowed to witness her death and her constancy to His Church. As to her remains, she wished to be buried in holy ground in France near some of her predecessors, especially her mother at Rheims. She promised to return to Elizabeth the ring she received from her and asked permission to send one with her last goodbyes to her son. Her dying benediction was:

> In the name of Jesus Christ, and in respect of our consanguinity, and for the sake of King Henry VII, your grandfather and mine, and by the honor of the dignity we both held and of our sex in common do I implore you to grant these requests.[6]

She also noted that Paulet alleged he was obeying Elizabeth's instructions when he removed her dais but that she had since learned he was following privy council orders. She was thankful that Elizabeth was not the source of that "wickedness," which served "rather to vent their malice than to afflict me, having made up my mind to die." Because Paulet feared that this emotional letter might cause Elizabeth to postpone the execution, he momentarily delayed sending it. In January, he refused to forward to her another of Mary's messages.

In preparing for death she also composed letters to Beaton, Mendoza, and Guise in which she denied plotting Elizabeth's murder, described her secretaries' confessions as false, and hoped that her death would testify to her willingness to die for the restoration of Catholicism on the island. In her message to Beaton, more particularly, she indicated a softening in her earlier distrustful attitude toward him, referring to him as the principal and the oldest of her servants and signing off as his affectionate and good mistress. To Mendoza, furthermore, she presented a large diamond given to her by Norfolk.

On 17 December, following orders, Paulet delighted Mary by sending to her du Préau, whose spiritual assistance she valued in preparing for death. In January, however, Paulet and Drury displayed their vindictiveness with petty acts reminiscent of the removal of her dais. On the 21st when without explanation they denied both du Préau and Melville access to her, she greatly condemned and deplored their wickedness. Three days later, they forbade Jean Landet, her butler, to carry the customary rod before her dinner. On the 29th it is no wonder that some predicted that a comet flashing across the sky heralded her doom.

Elizabeth reluctantly signed the death warrant on 1 February but gave it to Davison without orders for delivering it. Shrinking from publicly executing another monarch and recalling the vigilantism of the original Bond of Association, she instructed Walsingham and Davison to inform Paulet that she believed if he were truly zealous in her service, he would discover some means to shorten Mary's life. He, of course, refused the assassin's role. Ironically, in two different conversations with Mary in late January he defended himself from her charge that he might secretly kill her, protesting that she had no right to suspect him, an "honest man and a gentleman," of such "butchery."[7] While Elizabeth hoped that Paulet would act as an endorser of the bond, Mary feared that he might do so and prevent the public execution by which she could prove to the world that she had prepared well for her death.

On 4 February realizing that Beale was meeting with Henry Grey, sixth earl of Kent, and Shrewsbury concerning her execution, Paulet hesitated before permitting Burgoyne to gather herbs from the garden to treat her illness. Three days later Shrewsbury, Kent, Beale, Paulet, and Drury requested to see her. Although resting, she arose and received them at the foot of her bed. After they read the warrant for her execution, which the privy council had ordered acted upon without Elizabeth's knowledge, Mary explained that she had not believed her good sister would consent to her death. After thus indicating an understanding of Elizabeth's difficult position when advised by her most trusted councilors to order the execution of another monarch, Mary went on to confess that she was pleased that God would permit her to shed her blood for Him. They denied her plea for her priest's return, offering instead Peterborough's bishop or dean, both of whom she rejected. She explained that when Shrewsbury was her custodian, she had heard their preachers' sermons during one Lent and rejected their faith. The outraged Kent responded: "Your life will be the death of our religion, as contrary wise your death will be the life thereof."[8] Finally, the earls dismissed as invalid her vow that she had not conspired to kill Elizabeth because she swore it on a Catholic New Testament. Challenging their judgment, she declared that it was more likely to be true if sworn on a Catholic book.

After they departed, she called for an early supper. Near the meal's end, she drank a toast to her weeping servants and commenced the final preparations for her death. First, she asked for the inventory of her goods and jewels on which she wrote the names of the recipients of the articles. Second, she sent a letter to du Préau, still detained with Melville in another part of the castle, requesting his pardon and absolution for her sins and seeking advice about the prayers appropriate for her to say before her death.

Third, she drew up her will, naming Guise, Beaton, Leslie, and de Ruisseau as executors. After testifying to her Catholic apostolic faith in her will, she requested funeral services at St Pierre in Rheims and at St Denis in Paris and arranged for an annual obit. Then, she bequeathed her dower funds, which she expected to be collected for a year after her death, to her relatives, servants, and several charities, including the Foundling Hospital at Rheims, her scholars, four mendicants, and some hospitals. Hoping that Henry III would assist her executors, she informed him of the bequests.

These tasks accomplished, at 2:00 a.m. her feet were washed in imitation of Christ before his crucifixion. After resting on her bed for a few hours, she rose about 6:00 a.m. to pray for awhile before her maids dressed her. According to Robert Wingfield's report to Burghley, she wore a gown of black satin with a train, a petticoat of crimson velvet, a pair of purple sleeves, Spanish leather shoes, and a linen veil that fell from her head to the ground. Around her neck was hung a pomander chain and an *Agnus Dei* and at her waist was attached a pair of rosaries. To her assembled household, she read her will and distributed some small amounts of money before returning to her prayers.

Between 8:00 and 9:00 a.m. Sir Thomas Andrews, sheriff of Northamptonshire, arrived to escort her to the great hall. As her attendants declined to enable her execution, two of Paulet's soldiers supported her under each arm as she moved haltingly behind the sheriff. At the hall's entry Melville knelt tearfully to converse with her as she approached. With tears in her own eyes, she told him to testify to the world "That I do die a true woman to my religion and like a true woman of Scotland and France."[9] Also awaiting her were Kent, Shrewsbury, Paulet, Drury, the dean, and others. To her requests that a certain sum of money be forwarded to Curle, that her bequests be given to her servants, and that they be permitted to return home, Paulet responded that he would attend to those arrangements for her.

After the earls rejected her plea for her priest, she begged them to permit her servants to witness her execution, a concession they initially denied from concerns that her attendants might superstitiously dip handkerchiefs in her blood, as children had done, for example, at Northumberland's execution. Finally, the earls agreed she could select some of them to accompany her, and she chose seven attendants: Melville, Burgoyne, Jacques Gervais, her surgeon, Pierre Gorion, her apothecary, Didier, her porter, and two ladies, Jane Kennedy and Elizabeth Curle.

At the hall's upper end stood a railed scaffold, twelve feet wide and two feet high, hung with black cloth, on which were placed a stool, a cushion, and a block about one-foot high covered in black cloth. Still supported by the soldiers, she moved calmly, almost cheerfully into the room and sat down on the stool in front of about 300 spectators, who observed that her diseased body was somewhat swollen and that she had a double-chin. To her right stood the earls and to her left the sheriff. Beale then read the warrant for her execution. Displaying her religious constancy, she refused the dean's exhortation to repent her faith or to listen to his prayers. First sitting and then kneeling, she held up a crucifix and prayed in Latin from the Office of the Blessed Virgin Mary with her servants until he had finished. Turning from Latin to English, she pleaded for the well-being of Christ's oppressed Church, her son, and Elizabeth.

When Kent beseeched her to leave off her Popish "trumpery" and receive Jesus Christ into her heart, she confessed that she hoped to be saved "by and in the blood of Jesus." She further prayed that God would "avert his wrath from this island and that he would give unto it grace and forgiveness of sins." Pardoning her enemies and desiring the saints to intercede for her, she kissed her crucifix, crossed herself, and asked Jesus Christ for absolution.[10]

Mary's English prayer can be viewed as her last speech, a customary part of the contemporary ceremonial drama of death. Those facing imminent demise, whether by natural causes or execution, routinely attempted to demonstrate by their comments and demeanor that they had prepared well for a Christian death following the *ars moriendi* tradition. An integral part of the condemned's atonement was, moreover, an expected public admission of all offenses against the crown and the request for royal pardon, but Mary finished her prayer without this confession and plea. Clearly, this omission and her serenity in her final hour must have deeply impressed all spectators. Walsingham, himself, had considered her last speech important enough to list among his duties in preparing for her execution the need to designate a specific person to heed it. Given her society's death customs and beliefs, her last speech offers further support for the contention that Phelippes did, indeed, add the references to the six gentlemen to her Babington letter probably because Elizabeth might otherwise have refused to sign the death warrant.

To modern observers, Mary's declaration of innocence may seem to carry with it an element of sophistry or deception. She not only approved a plot that involved Elizabeth's assassination but also promoted foreign invasions of England, which, if successful, would surely have led to her cousin's removal as queen and possibly her death. In these conspiracies, believing herself to be imprisoned illegally, Mary seems to have focused on her liberation, leaving to others the issue of Elizabeth's demise.

Her prayers over, she pardoned at their requests, her executioner, Bull, and his assistant. After her weeping maids helped her to stand up, Bull and his assistant aided them in removing her outer garments, leaving her dressed in a black kirtle and the red petticoat; red, of course, was the color of martyrdom of the Catholic Church. She joked that "she never had such grooms before to make her unready, nor to put off her clothes before such a company." After exhorting her attendants to cease weeping, as she was leaving her sorrows behind, she knelt again, lifted her hand with the crucifix to heaven, and with her eyes covered by a

Corpus Christi cloth, she knelt on the cushions with the assistance of the executioners. Extending her neck, she placed her head on the block, holding out her arms to either side, signaling that she was prepared to die. As long as she could speak, she said, "*In manus tuas domine commendo spiritum meum*" (Into thy hands, O Lord, I commend my spirit). The first stroke of the axe plunged into the back of her head; the second cut it off except for a sinew; using the axe as a saw, the executioner completed his task. When, as he cried "God save the Queen," he lifted up her head by its auburn tresses, it fell forward from the wig she wore, revealing her grey hair. The dean said, "So perish all the Queen's enemies," and Kent exclaimed that such an "end" should "happen to all the Queen's and Gospel's enemies." For a further 15 minutes, her lips moved silently "up and down" during which time her little Skye terrier was discovered hidden under her bloody dress.[11] The next morning du Préau said a mass for her.

The world's reaction was mixed. Attempting to distance herself from the execution, Elizabeth ordered Davison fined and imprisoned for delivering the warrant without her permission. The courts of France, Spain, and Lorraine dressed in mourning and held funeral services in her honor. Philip became more fully committed to sending an armada to collect Parma's army in the Netherlands for an invasion of England. Although James protested the execution, many people believed he was more concerned about his succession rights and a promised English pension than his mother's life, but he did order his court to go into full mourning for one year.

At Fotheringhay surgeons embalmed her body shortly after her death, but it was not until August that she was buried and a heraldic funeral was held for her. Elizabeth decided to have her interred in the choir of Peterborough Cathedral near Catherine of Aragon's grave. On the evening of 30 July carrying torches, William Dethick, garter king of arms, five other heralds, and 40 horsemen escorted her body to the cathedral where it was immediately buried. On 1 August, Lammas Day, an effigy rather than a coffin was carried in the funeral procession of some 300, a small number for a royal occasion, in which Bridget Hussey, countess of Bedford, acted as chief mourner.[12] William Wickham, bishop of Lincoln, the conductor of the Protestant service, admitted in his sermon that he was unacquainted with Mary but that he learned "she took her death patiently, and recommended herself wholly to Jesus Christ."[13]

CONTROVERSY OVER QUEENS REGNANT

In life and death she was and remains the center of controversy. Her accession and that of the other two queens regnant in the British Isles intensified sixteenth-century debates over the locus of sovereignty. Representing the humanist opposition to women rulers, Buchanan validated the theory of popular sovereignty that justified the revolutions against Mary of Guise and her daughter. In *De Jure Regni Apud Scotos* and in *Rerum Scoticarum Historia*, published in 1579 and 1582 respectively, although both dated from about 1567, he manipulated Scottish history and customs, which he identified with natural law, to prove his case. Claiming that monarchs were subject to their realm's laws, he argued that they must carry out the will of a majority of the people, who possessed the right to restrict regal authority. Identifying as elective the Scottish monarchy, allegedly founded by Fergus I in 330 BC, Buchanan was able to claim that the coronation oath represented a pact between rulers and their subjects. If monarchs acted tyrannically, as had Mary, whose alleged licentiousness led her to aid and abet her husband's murder, the people had the right to revolt against them. For the most recent historical exercise of that right before Mary's reign, Buchanan cited the murderous rebellion against James III in 1488.

In the 1580s several Catholic writers, including Mary's clients, Ninian Winzet and Adam Blackwood, responded with publications defending divine-right theories of monarchy. In some ways, however, the most interesting reaction was that of James, who demanded in 1584 that all who possessed copies of Buchanan's *De Jure* or *Historia* must hand them over to the privy council to be censored or incur a fine of £200. Ironically, in condemning the slanderous comments about his mother, he also denounced the theory that justified the revolution enabling his accession.

Scholarly debate continues about whether or not he was responding to the deceased Buchanan's work in *The True Law of Free Monarchies*, which was published in 1598 during his struggle with those Presbyterians who espoused the popular sovereignty theory. As James's assertion that kings were answerable only to God relied on scriptural evidence, which was not essential to Buchanan's arguments, *The True Law* as a whole cannot be said explicitly to refute his theory. Some scholars do believe, however, that his view of Scottish history and his approach to fundamental laws were intended to counter Buchanan's version of natural law. Denying that the Scottish monarchy was elective, James insisted that Fergus I had conquered the realm and that James III was assassinated by a few murderers and not removed from office by the majority exercising their right of rebellion. Furthermore, as the kingship was hereditary, it was impossible for the coronation oath to represent a pact between the monarch and his subjects. As they were God's agents, kings were obligated to rule according to the law but were responsible only to God for their actions. A patriarchal analogy expressed his understanding of natural law: as children must obey their fathers, subjects must obey their monarchs.

HENRY VII'S CHAPEL AT WESTMINSTER ABBEY

The attitude of James toward his mother was somewhat ambivalent during her lifetime, but after his accession to the English throne in 1603, he honored her memory as a step in the process of validating his dynasty's legitimacy. Although he failed to order the destruction of Fotheringhay Castle as legend claims, he did finalize arrangements to transfer her remains from Peterborough Cathedral to Westminster Abbey while leaving his father's body undisturbed at Holyrood chapel. First in 1606, however, James had Elizabeth buried in the north aisle of the chapel of Henry VII at the Abbey under a white marble tomb holding a recumbent figure of her, valued at £785. Beneath her coffin lies her half-sister Mary. Six years later, his mother's tomb, which cost £2,000 and which displays a white marble, recumbent effigy of her with her hands raised in prayer, was completed in the south aisle of the same chapel.

It is appropriate that the remains of these three British queens regnant should together occupy the chapel of their ancestor, Henry VII. Although provided with a humanist education like their male counterparts', their subjects still doubted their ability to rule and demanded they heed the advice of male councilors. Even Mary's son James stated in the *Basilikon Doron*, his advice book for his heir Henry which was published in 1599, that when his grandfather, James V, died, he left a "double curse behind him to the land, both a woman of sex, and a new borne babe of age to reign over them." Although he also described

Buchanan's and Knox's works as "infamous libels," thus condemning their outrageous statements about his mother, his belief that women were the "frailest sex," may have influenced his decision to accept his councilors' recommendation to reject the treaty of association with her.[14]

These three female monarchs responded to dynastic expectations with different degrees of success. Mary Tudor is often viewed as a failure partly because she could not bear children at what was then considered an advanced age for a first pregnancy. Having learned from her Guise relatives the importance of marriage for the advancement of family goals, Mary Stewart wed Darnley to strengthen her English succession claims and gave birth to a male heir, but partly because she lost her throne to that son, she, too, is deemed a failure. Most contemporaries and subsequent writers have condemned her third, forced marriage that fostered the discord that led to her captivity, but it is a fact that rebellions were directed against not only all three of her unions but also that of Mary Tudor because their subjects anticipated that their husbands would gain control of their realms. Having the advantage of learning from their experiences, Elizabeth ultimately chose to ignore contemporary expectations about marriage, thereby avoiding sharp factional divisions on that issue among her advisors and possibly rebellions against her authority. Her decision kept her from bearing children, but partly because of her longevity, her choice proved wise and her reign is deemed a success.

More particularly, it is also appropriate that Mary's and Elizabeth's tombs lie in precise symmetry on the north and south sides of Henry VII's chapel. Too much emphasis has focused on their personal rivalry that supposedly arose from differences in their personal make-up, one exhibiting masculine self-control and the other demonstrating feminine passion, but their disagreements derived from dynastic and religious issues much larger than their individual characteristics. Elizabeth, who never departed England's shores, slowly and reluctantly agreed under pressure from her advisors, especially Burghley, to seek for defensive purposes the pacification of the British Isles under essentially Protestant rule. By contrast, through her marriages, Mary hoped to attach Scotland and ultimately England to a Catholic continental empire governed by either the royal families of France or Spain. This was a goal she learned in her childhood education and experience in France.

By placing their tombs in the same chapel, James sought to achieve dynastic reconciliation, since Elizabeth was the godmother that his mother chose for him. It is noteworthy that godparents' duties in the sixteenth century were not limited to supervising their godchildren's religious education but also involved aiding them in achieving their political and social aspirations, especially in the absence or the death of their biological parents. In 1581 Mary reminded James that Elizabeth was his second mother, godmother, and kinswoman. In 1592 some years after Mary's death and the defeat of Philip's Armada, although Elizabeth's relationship with James still had to endure difficult periods, her message to him reflected a sense of her duty but not exactly as his mother had intended:

> You know my dear brother, that, since you first breathed, I regarded always to conserve it my womb it had been you bear. Yes, I withstood the hands and helps of a mighty king to make you safe, even gained by the blood of many my dear subjects' lives. I made myself the bulwark betwixt you and your harms when many a wile was invented to steal you from your land, and making others possess your soil.[15]

Mary not only gave him an hereditary claim to England but also selected Elizabeth as his godmother, making it possible for her in some sense to view him as her son.

MARTYRDOM?

From the moment of Mary's death, Catholics began to recognize her as a martyr to their cause while Protestants, like Burghley, denied that the English punished individuals for their faith. Others have argued that Mary's early flirtation with Protestantism and her political scheming prevented her from achieving martyrdom status. For the validity of Burghley's claim, it will be helpful briefly to consider the life of Norfolk's heir, Philip, earl of Arundel.

Along with other Howards, the government suspected Arundel was involved in Throckmorton's plot. After the earl converted to Catholicism in late 1584, he worried about his fate and without royal permission attempted to seek sanctuary abroad with William Allen.

When Arundel was captured, the Court of Star Chamber ordered him to pay the exorbitant fine of £10,000 and imprisoned him at Elizabeth's pleasure. In 1588 still in captivity, he was accused of urging a priest to say mass for the Armada's success. Although he admitted only to praying for Catholicism and for himself, he was condemned as a traitor and remained a prisoner in the Tower until his death in 1595. Lacking any firm evidence except his attempted flight and his prayers, his government incarcerated him for ten years during which time he was not permitted to see his wife or child. Can it truly be said that Catholics were not being punished for their faith? In 1970 he was canonized.

When considering whether Catholics may view Elizabethan victims as martyrs, the judgments of Catholics and the condemned's preparation for death should have more credibility than the opinions of Protestants. In the early 1580s on the continent, Catholic authors, such as Richard Verstegan, extolled Mary's commitment to her faith and in various publications after her death described her as a martyr to their religion. From her first communion to her execution, only briefly did Mary personally flirt with Protestantism. That she was willing to support the Scottish Protestant establishment was a decision she made in association with her six Guise uncles, three of whom traveled with her to her realm. Although Mamerot, her confessor, deserted her after she married Bothwell in a Protestant service to protect her honor, the Frenchman testified to her previous religious constancy. As an English prisoner, she held out the possibility of converting to the Church of England in negotiations to obtain her freedom, but by 1570 she had won the sympathy of Catholic leaders abroad. On 9 January of that year, Pius V avowed his "paternal affection" for her and praised her "burning zeal" for their faith.[16] Afterward, she behaved as a loyal Catholic, repeatedly demanding a resident priest for her household, aiding religious refugees abroad, and calling for the return of Catholicism to Britain. Finally, in despair at her son's betrayal and refusal to accept her faith, she bequeathed her English succession rights to Philip, who commended her for privileging her religion over her son.

In 1587 her faith aided her in preparing for a Christian death to the outrage of the dean of Peterborough and the earl of Kent, who challenged her to convert to their religion. Had she complied, they would have eagerly welcomed her into their church. Mary relished Kent's earlier claim that her life would be the death of his religion, since she interpreted his words to mean she was dying for hers.

Catholics unanimously condemned her execution, and soon after her translation to Westminster Abbey, her bones were rumored to work miracles. Henry Clifford, the contemporary biographer of Jane Dormer, an English Catholic who wed Don Gomes de Figueroa, duke of Feria, and moved with him to Spain, referred to Mary as a dying saint and martyr.[17] So did others.

Although through the centuries that have passed, biographers have sometimes presented her life within a romantic framework, both sixteenth-century sympathizers and critics often interpreted her life as tragic. Michele Surian, the Venetian ambassador in France, predicted in 1569 that someday the English and their monarch, instigated by Moray, would find the means to kill Mary because she had treated Elizabeth as a bastard when she assumed her arms and style. And so, he said, "her life, which till now has been compounded of comedy and tragi-comedy, would terminate at length in pure tragedy."[18] And so it did.

It was not a tragedy stemming ultimately from the disappointment of romantic love affairs gone sour. It was a tragedy largely rooted in the gender relations of early modern Europe through which she was forced as queen to negotiate her rule. She made two decisions that ignored the advice of her councilors, one to marry Darnley, and the second, to seek refuge in England, which contributed greatly to her tragic ending. When she chose to wed Darnley, she gave him the trappings of royal office but not the power, which most people, including her husband, expected he would wield. She had depended on her experience and his youthful status to help her retain her regal authority, but she underestimated the influence of his male relatives and allies, who urged the ambitious young man, a claimant to her throne, to take charge of his household and, therefore, the realm. His ambition for power led him to plan Riccio's death, which culminated in his own murder and made Mary vulnerable to abduction, forcible marriage to Bothwell, and then imprisonment.

After escaping Lochleven and facing defeat at Langside, her advisors and friends begged her to remain in Scotland. Clearly, she should have done so, but prevented from reaching the safety of Dumbarton, she would have had to place herself in the power of either the Hamiltons or the Campbells, one of whom she would have been expected to marry and who, like her second husband, would have demanded control of her realm. Argyll could certainly have protected her from Moray in his mountainous retreat, for example, but there she would have lost independence of authority and action.

Unlike many of her contemporaries, Mary, herself, viewed the end of her pilgrimage on earth as a triumph, not as a tragedy, and she believed that her suffering was part of God's plan for her. She approached death calmly, having defended her honor at the trial, and looked forward to eternal salvation. It was with this expectation that she prepared herself to die bravely and serenely. It seems appropriate to close here by letting her speak for herself. The following, which is part of "Meditation in Verse" written originally by her in French in 1573, seems to capture her feelings in 1587:

> So, when, my Savior, from captivity,
> Thy clemency and goodness set me free,
> And when I turn to bid a last adieu
> To woe and grief and sickness, then I sue
> That Thou wilt grant me this one favor yet,
> That never shall my weeping soul forget
> Thy grace and mercy, and Thy boundless love,
> Which Thou hast ever sent me from above.

And finally,

> I plead no merit. Witness, on my part,
> Thy Passion, deeply graven in my heart.[19]

When she composed this piece, she could not have anticipated, of course, that a public execution would liberate her. Because of her chronic, debilitating illness, she may have supposed she would die in prison of natural causes, although she feared then and continued to fear until shortly before her death, that she would suffer private assassination. The bloody execution that she sought in 1587 allowed her to prove publicly and courageously that she died a true woman to her religion and a true woman of Scotland and France.

NOTES

1 INTRODUCTION

1 The Scottish spelling for her name is used because her importance in British and continental diplomacy stemmed from her status as queen regnant. Although as a child, she learned to use the French spelling of her name, she never ceased to identify herself with her native land and with her Stewart relatives.

2 Antonia Fraser, *Mary Queen of Scots*, New York: Delacorte Press, 1969; New York: Delta, 1993, 2001.

3 Michael Lynch (ed.), *Mary Stewart in Three Kingdoms*, London: Blackwell, 1988.

4 Jenny Wormald, *Mary, Queen of Scots: Politics, Passion and a Kingdom Lost*, New York: Tauris Park, 2001; *Mary Queen of Scots: A Study in Failure*, London: George Philip, 1988.

5 *The Register of the Privy Council of Scotland*, (ed.) J.H. Burton, *et al.*, 14 Vols, Edinburgh: H.M. General Register House, 1877–98.

6 James MacKay, *In My End is My Beginning: A Life of Mary Queen of Scots*, Edinburgh: Mainstream, 1999.

7 Susan Watkins, *Mary Queen of Scots*, New York: Thames and Hudson, 2001.

8 John Guy, *The Life of Mary Queen of Scots: My Heart is my Own*, London: Fourth Estate, 2004; *The Memoirs of Sir James Melville of Halhill*, ed. Gordon Donaldson, London: Folio Society, 1969, p. 64.

9 Guy, *Mary Queen of Scots*, pp. 226–7 (for my discussion, see Chapter 4, note 18); see also pp. 282, 366, for other examples.

10 Alison Weir, *Mary Queen of Scots, and the Murder of Lord Darnley*, New York: Random House, 2004; Claude Nau, *The History of Mary Stewart From the Murder of Riccio Until her Flight into England*, ed. Joseph Stevenson, Edinburgh: William Paterson, 1883. Another popular work appearing in 2004 is Jane Dunn, *Elizabeth & Mary: Cousins, Rivals, Queens*, New York: Knopf, 2004.

11 Gordon Donaldson (ed.), *Scottish Historical Documents*, Edinburgh:

Scottish Academic Press, 1970, p. 68, quoted from *Acts of the Parliament of Scotland*, vol. I, 492–3.

12 *The Warkis of Schir David Lyndesay* (Edinburgh, 1574), New York: Da Capo Press, 1971, p. 108 (see Chapter 2). *The Political Works of James I*, ed. Charles McIlwain, New York: Russell and Russell Reprint, 1965, p. 34; David Calderwood, *The True History of the Kirk of Scotland from the Beginning of the Reformation unto the End of the Reign of King James VI*, ed. Thomas Thomson, 8 vols, Edinburgh: Woodrow Society, 1843–49, vol. I, p. 57; *Selected Sermons of Hugh Latimer*, ed. Alan Chester, Charlottesville, VA: University of Virginia Press for the Folger Shakespeare Library, 1968, p. 34.

13 A.N. McLaren, *Political Culture in the Reign of Elizabeth I: Queen and Commonwealth, 1558–1585*, Cambridge: Cambridge University Press, 1999, pp. 1–2, 26.

14 Roger Mason, "Imagining Scotland: Scottish Political Thought and the Problem of Britain, 1560–1650," ed. Mason, *Scots and Britons: Scottish Political Thought and the Union of 1603*, Cambridge: Cambridge University Press, 1994, p. 6.

15 *Calendar of Documents Relating to Scotland and Mary Queen of Scots*, ed. J. Bain, *et al.*, 13 vols, Edinburgh: H.M. General Register Office, 1898–1969, vol. I, pp. 270, 510, 517. (Hereafter *CSP Scot.*)

16 Margaret Christian, "Elizabeth's Preachers and the Government of Women: Defining and Correcting a Queen," *The Sixteenth Century Journal*, 24, 1993: 561–76.

17 Julian Goodare, "Scotland," in B. Scribner, R. Porter, and M. Teich (eds), *The Reformation in National Context*, Cambridge: Cambridge University Press, 1994, pp. 95–111; Michael Lynch, *Edinburgh and the Reformation*, Edinburgh: John Donald, 1981, pp. 214–23.

18 These can be accessed through a variety of printed catalogues. Most, but not all, are at the Public Record Office, the British Library, the National Library of Scotland, and the Bibliothèque Nationale de France. An example of the misuse of diplomatic records is the oft-quoted allegation that in 1560 Mary ridiculed Elizabeth's intention to marry her "horse-keeper." Her alleged remark survives in Robert Jones's letter to Throckmorton, the English ambassador in France. He reported that Lord Robert Dudley, Elizabeth's master of the horse, asked whether he knew about Mary's comment, which Cecil had recently repeated to Dudley. Jones admitted he knew nothing about

her quip but lacked any evidence denying she had said it. A reading of Jones's dispatch indicates that Dudley was less concerned about Mary's description of him as a "horse-keeper," a somewhat accurate, although simplistic, rendering of master of the horse, than about her claim that Elizabeth would marry him. See P. Yorke (ed.), *Miscellaneous State Papers from 1501 to 1726*, 2 vols, London: Strahan and Cadell, 1728, pp. 163–4.

19 *Lettres, Instructions et Mémoires de Marie Stuart, Reine D'Écosse*, ed. Alexandre Labanoff, 7 vols, London: Dolman, 1844.

2 SCOTTISH BEGINNINGS TO 1548

1 Robert Lindsay of Pitscottie, *The Historie and Cronicles of Scotland from the Slauchter of King James the First to the Ane Thousand Fyve Hundreith Thrie Scoir Fyftein Zeir*, ed. A.J.G. MacKay, 3 vols, New York: Johnson Reprint Corporation, 1966, vol. I, p. 358.

2 An English crown was worth 5 shillings.

3 *Lettres, Instructions et Mémoires de Marie Stuart Reine D'Écosse*, ed. Alexandre Labanoff, 7 vols, London: Dolman, 1844, vol. II, p. 2.

4 Lindsay, *Historie*, vol. I, 407; *John Knox's History of the Reformation in Scotland*, ed. W. Croft Dickinson, 2 vols, Philadelphia, PA: Philosophical Library, 1950, vol. I, ix, p. 39, made a similar claim, which was likely a rumored expectation that was transposed on to James. Knox's and Lindsay's writings remained in manuscript until after their deaths, Knox's first appearing in an incomplete and suppressed version in 1586–87 after Lindsay composed his in the 1570s.

5 Quoted by Elizabeth Bonner, "The French Reactions to the Rough Wooings of Mary Queen of Scots," *The Journal of the Sydney Society for Scottish History*, 6, 1998: 13. For the speculation about the disease, see Roger Mason, "Scotland, Elizabethan England, and the Idea of Britain," *Transactions of the Royal Historical Society*, 6th series, vol. 14, 2004: 283.

6 Calderwood, *The True History of the Kirk of Scotland from the Beginning of the Reformation unto the End of the Reign of King James VI*, ed. Thomas Thomson, 8 vols, Edinburgh: Woodrow Society, 1843–49, vol. I, 57.

7 *The Warkis of Schir David Lyndesay* (Edinburgh, 1574), New York: Da Capo Press, 1971, p. 108. All quotations have been put in modern English except verses in Lowland Scots.

8 *The State Papers and Letters of Sir Ralph Sadler*, ed. A. Clifford, 2 vols, Edinburgh: Constable, 1809, vol. I, p. 87.

9 Ibid., pp. 253, 263.

10 Ibid., pp. 285, 347.

11 *Calendar of Letters, Despatches, and State Papers Relating to Negotiations Between England and Spain*, ed. G. Bergenroth, *et al.*, 13 vols, 2 supplements, London: Longman, 1862–1954, vol. IX, p. 47.

12 *Two Missions of Jacques de la Brosse, An Account of the Affairs of Scotland in the Year 1543 and the Journal of the Siege of Leith, 1560*, ed. Gladys Dickinson, Edinburgh: Edinburgh University Press, 1942, pp. 29, 39.

13 Sadler, *Papers*, vol. I, pp. 86, 265.

3 FRENCH UPBRINGING, 1548–61

1 Joachim du Bellay was not aboard, although his later poem quoted by Alphone de Ruble, *La Première Jeunesse de Marie Stuart*, Paris: Bibliothèque Nationale, 1891, pp. 15–16, referred to a similar voyage.

2 Biographers usually accept the 13th as the date of Mary's arrival because of questions raised about a letter of Henry II's by W.M. Bryce, "Mary Stuart's Voyage to France in 1548," *English Historical Review*, 22, 1907: 43–50, but M.N. Baudoudin-Matusek, "Mary Stewart's Arrival in France in 1548," *Scottish Historical Review*, 69, 1990: 90–5, discovered the draft of another of the king's letters confirming her arrival on the 15th at St Pol de Léon after 18 days at sea.

3 *Lettres du Cardinal Charles de Lorraine (1525–1574)*, ed. Daniel Cuisiat, Geneva: Librairie Droz, 1998, p. 116.

4 Baudoudin-Matuzek, "Mary Stewart's Arrival," pp. 94–5.

5 *Lettres de Catherine de' Medici*, ed. H. de la Ferrière-Percy, *et al.*, 11 vols, Paris: Imprimerie National, 1880–1943, vol. I, lvi, pp. 556–7.

6 Armand Baschet, *La Diplomatie Vénitienne: Les Princes de l'Europe au XVIe Siècle*, Paris: Plon, 1862, p. 486.

7 *The Autobiography of Michel de Montaigne*, ed. M. Lowenthal, Boston, MA: Houghton Mifflin, 1935, p. 83.

8 Anatole de Montaiglon (ed.), *The Latin Themes of Mary Stuart Queen of Scots*, London: Warton Club, 1855; see also *Queen Mary's Book: A Collection of Poems and Essays by Mary Queen of Scots*, ed. Mrs. P. Stewart-MacKenzie Arbuthnot, London: Bell, 1907: 41–83.

9 *The Memoirs of Sir James Melville of Halhill*, ed. Gordon Donaldson, London: Folio Society, 1969, p. 43.

10 De Ruble, *Première Jeunesse*, p. 96.

11 She seems to have obtained her information from a letter of Politianus, which was printed in a volume of his epistles at Paris in 1523 with a commentary by Franciscus Silvius. For an inventory of her library, which no longer exists, see Julian Sharman (ed.), *The Library of Mary, Queen of Scots*, London: Stock, 1889, p. 31.

12 Cuisiat, *Lettres*, p. 154, dates her birth in 1551 and her older brother Henry on 31 December 1549. According to Mack P. Holt, professor at George Mason University, who surveyed reference books, including ones online, concerning these birth dates, the consensus is that she was born in 1552 and he in 1550.

13 Marguerite Wood (ed.), *Foreign Correspondence with Marie de Lorraine, Queen of Scotland from the Originals in the Balcarres Papers, 1548–57*, 2 vols, Edinburgh: Scottish History Society, 1923–5, vol. II, p. li.

14 B. Weber (ed.), *The Marriage of Mary, Queen of Scots, to Francis the Dauphin of France, MDLVIII*, Greenock: Grian-Aig Press, 1969.

15 *The Poems of Sir Richard Maitland of Lethingtoun, Knight*, New York: A.M.S. Reprint, 1973, II, pp. 55–60.

16 George Buchanan, "Epithalamium upon the Marriage of Mary Queen of Scots to the Dauphin of France, afterwards Francis the Second," in I.D. McFarlane (ed.), *Renaissance Latin Poetry*, Manchester: Manchester University Press, 1980, II, pp. 140, 145–6, 151, 225.

17 William Fraser, *The Lennox*, 2 vols, Edinburgh: Privately Printed, 1874, vol. I, p. 469.

18 Gordon Donaldson (ed.), *Scottish Historical Documents*, Edinburgh: Scottish Academic Press, 1970, p. 116.

19 Ibid., pp. 120–4; Clare Keller, *Scotland, England and the Reformation, 1534–1561*, Oxford: Clarendon Press, 2003, pp. 202–3, noted that the commissioners failed to reach an accord in the treaty on the Scottish religious settlement because of disagreements about what it should be.

20 She probably did not write "Verses on the death of Francis II." See Arbuthnot, *Mary's Book*, pp. 85–8.

21 Henry Layard (ed.), *Despatches of Michele Suriano and Marc' Antonio Barbaro, Venetian Ambassadors at the Court of France, 1560–1563*, Lymington: Huguenot Society of London, 1891, pp. 8, 11.

4 RETURNING HOME, 1561–63

1 PRO SP/12/23, no. 14, often cited for a second visit of Darnley to France, records only that he and his parents sent her letters of condolence. Rumors in Britain claimed he was in France, but no indisputable evidence exists that he was there.

2 H. de la Ferrière-Percy *et al.* (eds), *Lettres de Catherine de' Medici*, 11 vols, Paris: Imprimerie National 1880–1943, vol. I, pp. 585, 592.

3 Henry Layard (ed.), *Despatches of Michele Suriano and Marc' Antonio Barbaro, Venetian Ambassadors at the Court of France*, Lymington: Huguenot Society of London, 1891, p. 20.

4 She was also in correspondence with other noblemen, such as Morton and Cassilis. See BL, Add. MS. 23108, ff.13, 16 and Add. MS. 1940, f. 65.

5 Layard, *Suriano and Barbaro*, p. 33.

6 George Buchanan, *The History of Scotland from the Earliest Period to the Present Time*, ed. J. Aikman, 6 vols, Edinburgh: Blackie, 1855, vol. II, pp. 382–3.

7 The piece attributed to her, which ends "*Qui as nourri ma jeune enfance*," was the creation of Meusnier de Querlon in the eighteenth century. Quoted in Imbert de Saint-Amand, *Women of the Valois Court*, New York: Scribners, 1895, p. 200.

8 Layard, *Suriano and Barbaro*, p. 34.

9 *Songs and Sonnets of Pierre de Ronsard*, ed. Curtis Page, Boston, MA: Houghton Mifflin, 1924: pp. 84–5.

10 "Estrait des Memoires de Messire Michel de Castlenau," in Samuel Jebb (ed.), *De Vita & Rebus Gestis Serenissimae Prìncipis Mariae Scotorum Reginae, Franciae Dotarie . . .*, Londini: Woodman & Lyon, 1725, p. 455. He used the N.S. 17 February. He also claimed that they remained at Calais six days.

11 A.A. MacDonald, "Mary Stewart's Entry to Edinburgh: An Ambiguous Triumph," *Innes Review*, 42, 1991: 101–10, for the sources.

12 BL, Cott. MSS. Calig. BX, f. 158; PRO, SP 52/6, no. 81.

13 Buchanan, *Scotland*, vol. I, p. 408.

14 No systematic study of Scottish abductions has been done. For evidence, see, for example, Maureen M. Meikle, who accused the Homes and Turnbulls of this practice in "Victims, Viragos, and Vamps: Women of the Sixteenth Century Anglo–Scottish Frontier," in John Appleby and Paul Dalton (eds), *Government, Religion, and Society in Northern*

England, 1000–1700, Stroud: Sutton, 1997, pp. 177–9; Rosalind Marshall identified Sir Alexander Stewart, grandson of Robert II, as an abductor–husband in *Virgins and Viragos: A History of Women in Scotland from 1080 to 1980*, London: Collins, 1983, p. 20; Robert Agnew named Alexander M'Kie as an abductor–husband in his edition of *The Correspondence of Sir Patrick Waus of Barnbarroch, Knight*, 2 vols, Edinburgh: Ayr and Galloway Archaeological Association, vol. I, p. xxx. Most cases did not go to trial but one did in 1616, see *Ancient Criminal Trials in Scotland: Compiled from the Original Records and MSS. with Historical Illustrations*, ed. Robert Pitcairn, 3 vols, Edinburgh: Bannatyne Club, 1833, vol. III–ii, p. 402. According to *The Practicks of Sir James Balfour of Pitendreich*, ed. Peter G.B. McNeill, Edinburgh: Stair Society, 1963, p. 510, a man convicted of rape could not wed his victim because lower-class men might violate wealthy women or, indeed, filthy women might violate gentlemen. But if the rapist were not convicted, he could marry his victim with the king's license and with her parents' consent.

15 For example, a conspiracy in 1567 involved the poisoning of the earl of Sutherland and the forced marriage of his 15-year-old heir, Alexander, the 12th earl with Barbara, the 32-year-old heir of George Sinclair, fourth earl of Caithness.

16 Sara Mendelson and Patricia Crawford, *Women in Early Modern England*, Oxford: Clarendon Press, 1998, pp. 47–8.

17 The contemporary reference for stepdaughter was daughter-in-law.

18 John Guy, *The Life of Mary Queen of Scots: My Heart is My Own*, London: Fourth Estate, 2004, pp. 226–7, apparently depending on Randolph's dispatch, claims that Bothwell met her at Dunbar in 1564. However, Guy overlooked the last part of the dispatch in which Randolph admitted the rumors of their meeting were false.

19 Boscosel de Chastelard, *Effusions of Love from Chatelar to Mary Queen of Scotland*, trans. Samuel Ireland, 2nd edn, London: Crosby, 1808, p. 17.

5 RULING SCOTLAND, 1563–66

1 *The French Wars of Religion: Selected Documents*, ed. David Potter, New York: St Martin's Press, 1997, pp. 13–17.

2 David Sellar (ed.), *Miscellany Two*, Edinburgh: The Stair Society, 1984, pp. 86–131; W. Tod Ritchie (ed.), *The Bannatyne Manuscript Written in Tyme*

of Pest, 1568, 4 vols, Edinburgh: Blackwood, 1928–30, 1934, vol. II, p. 256.

3   *Register of the Privy Council*. See vol. II for Mary's reign. It seems odd that Bothwell, a fugitive from justice, was included in the rotation.

4   "Letters from Mary Queen of Scots to Sir Robert Melville; And Some Other Papers from the Archives of the Earl of Leven and Melville MDLXV–MDLXVIII," *Miscellany of the Maitland Club Consisting of Papers and Other Documents Illustrative of the History and Literature of Scotland*, 3 vols, Edinburgh: Maitland Club, 1834, vol. III, pp. 180–1.

5   Thomas Craig, *The Right of Succession to the Kingdom of England*, trans. James Gatherer, London: printed by M. Bennet for D. Brown, *et al.*, 1703, p. 84.

6   Alison Weir, *Mary, Queen of Scots, and the Murder of Lord Darnley*, New York: Random House, 2004, p. 38, did cite his comments.

7   The parliament called in 1566 was disrupted and is usually not counted.

8   G.F. Barwick, *A Book bound for Mary Queen of Scots*, London: Bibliographical Society, 1901, p. 10. These Black Acts are not the same as the anti-Presbyterian statues of 1584 that are also called Black Acts.

9   *CSP Scot*, vol. II, 108. In an undated note after her marriage to Darnley, Mary claimed that Leicester sent her a message through Randolph in which he accused Elizabeth of offering him simply to deceive her and distract her from other suitors. See Alexandre Labonoff (ed.), *Lettres, Instructions et Mémoires de Marie Stuart, Reine D'Écosse*, 7 vols, London: Dolman, 1844, vol. I, pp. 295–9.

10 NLS MS 3657, ff. 11r–f.12r.

11 A. Gibson and T.C. Smout, "Food and Hierarchy in Scotland, 1550–1650," in Leah Leneman (ed.), *Perspectives in Scottish Social History: Essays in Honour of Rosalind Mitchison*, Aberdeen: Aberdeen University Press, 1988: 33–9, cited documents from James VI's reign.

12 George Barwick, "A Side-Light on the Mystery of Mary Stuart: Pietro Bizzari's Contemporary Account of the Murders of Riccio and Darnley," *Scottish Historical Review*, 21, 1924: 121–2. For information about her court, see Michael Lynch, "The Reassertion of Princely Power in Scotland and the Reigns of Mary, Queen of Scots and King James VI," in M. Gosman, A. MacDonald, and A. Vanderjagt (eds), *Princes and Princely Culture, 1450–1650*, vol. I, Leiden: Brill, 2003, pp. 199–238.

13 Labanoff, *Lettres*, vol. I, pp. 250–1.

14 Barwick, "A Side-Light," p. 118.

15 *The Memoirs of Sir James Melville of Halhill*, ed. Gordon Donaldson, London: Folio Society, 1969, p. 45; the edition by A. Francis Steuart (ed.), *Memoirs of Sir James Melville of Halhill*, 1535–1617, New York: Dutton, 1930, p. 107, says "properest and best proportioned long man."

16 NLS MS 3657, ff. 18r–20v.

17 Andrew Lang, "New Light on Mary Queen of Scots," *Blackwood's Magazine*, 182, 1907: 24.

18 *Calendar of Letters and Papers Relating to English Affairs in the Reign of Elizabeth, Preserved Principally in the Archives of Simancas*, ed. Martin Hume, 4 vols, London: His Majesty's Stationery Office, 1892–96, vol. I, pp. 412–20. Hereafter *CSP Span*.

19 PRO, SP 52/10, no. 38. The first author to use the word, "nurse," may have been Hilda Skae, *Mary Queen of Scots*, London: Poulis, 1905, 1912, p. 86.

20 PRO, SP 70/77, ff. 1105, 1114–15.

21 Labanoff, *Lettres*, vol. I, pp. 266–75.

22 Godfrey Goodman, *The Court of James the First*, London: Bentley, 1839, p. 76.

23 George Buchanan, *The History of Scotland From the Earliest Period to the Present Time*, ed. J. Aikman, 6 vols, Edinburgh: Blackie, 1855, vol. II, p. 414.

24 Edward Burns, *The Coinage of Scotland*, 3 vols, Edinburgh: Black, 1887, vol. II, pp. 316, 326–48.

25 Thanks to Mack P. Holt, professor at George Mason University, who identified Rambouillet's first name as Nicholas.

26 Andrew Lang, "The Household of Mary, Queen of Scots in 1573," *Scottish Historical Review*, 2, 1905: 352 note; Labanoff, *Lettres*, vol. IV, pp. 216–20.

27 William, marquess of Winchester, *The Lord Marques Idleness*, London: Hatfield, 1586, p. 85.

28 Robert Keith, *History of the Affairs of Church and State in Scotland from the Beginning of the Reformation to the year 1568*, ed. J.P. Larson, 3 vols, Edinburgh: Spottiswood Society, 1844, vol. I, pp. 411–19. Ruthven claimed, for example, that Riccio was armed and that he had not told Mary her secretary was dead. See Patrick, third lord Ruthven, *The Death of Rizzi*, Edinburgh: Goldsmid, 1890.

6 CONFRONTING ADVERSITY,
MARCH 1566–MAY 1567

1 Alexandre Labanoff (ed.), *Lettres, Instructions et Mémoires de Marie Stuart, Reine D'Écosse*, 7 vols, London: Dolman, 1844, vol. II, pp. 334–8.

2 *Historical Memoirs of the Reign of Mary Queen of Scots and a Portion of the Reign of King James the Sixth by Lord Herries*, ed. R. Pitcairn, Edinburgh: Abbotsford Club, 1836, pp. xv, 79.

3 *Calendar of State Papers Relating to English Affairs, Principally at Rome in the Vatican Archives and Library*, ed. J. M. Rigg, 2 vols, London: HMSO, 1926, I, p. 188. (Hereafter *CSP Rome*.) This was probably the French crown or ecu, which was worth about 6 English shillings. In some documents, the money was identified as scudi, which according to Thomas Mayer, *Cardinal Pole in European Context*, Burlington, VT: Ashgate, 2000, pp. XV–3, was about three to a pound or slightly more than 6 shillings each.

4 PRO, 52/10, no. 90.

5 Robert Keith, *History of the Affairs of Church and State in Scotland from the Beginning of the Reformation to the Year 1568*, ed. J.P. Larson, 3 vols, Edinburgh: Spottiswood Society, 1844, vol. I, pp. 448–52.

6 William Fraser, (ed.), *The Lennox*, 2 vols, Edinburgh: Privately Printed, 1874, vol. II, pp. 350–1.

7 John Small, "Queen Mary at Jedburgh in 1566," *Proceedings of the Society of Antiquaries of Scotland*, N.S., 111, 1881: 210–33.

8 Ida Macalpine and Richard Hunter, *George III and the Mad-Business*, London: Lane, 1969, pp. 197–266, and Norman Moore, *History of the Study of Medicine in the British Isles*, Oxford: Clarendon Press, 1908, p. 102, for clinical observations.

9 Keith, *Church and State*, vol. I, pp. xcvi–xcix; Labanoff, *Lettres*, vol. I, p. 398.

10 David Hay Fleming, *Mary Queen of Scots: From Her Birth to Her Flight into England: A Brief Biography*, London: Hodder and Stoughton, 1897, p. 422, n. 88, gives the provenance. For the queen's letter dated 5 January 1569, enclosing the Protestation, see Labanoff, *Lettres*, II, pp. 265–7. See also Lord Hunsdon's letter to Cecil in HMC, *Calendar of the Manuscripts of the Most Honourable the Marquis of Salisbury Preserved at Hatfield House, Hertfordshire*, 20 vols, London: HMSO, 1883–1976, vol. I, p. 390.

11 John Leslie, *A Defence of the Honour of Marie Quene of Scotlande, 1569* (although the imprint is 1569, it was published in 1570.), Menston:

Scolar Press, 1970, pp. 5–6, 38–9, 44–5; for Leslie's 1580 manuscript, see William Forbes-Leith, *Narratives of Scottish Catholics Under Mary Stuart and James VI*, Edinburgh: Paterson, 1885, p. 118.

12 Michael Lynch, "Queen Mary's Triumph: the Baptismal Celebrations at Stirling in December, 1566," *Scottish Historical Review*, 69, 1990: 1–21.

13 In 1568 when Bizari, an intelligence agent for Cecil on the continent, wrote his version of the murders, he blamed Scottish politics and made no reference to an English conspiracy. He also admitted visiting Mary's court in 1564 because Bedford had greatly praised her. See George Barwick, "A Side-Light on the Mystery of Mary Stuart: Pietro Bizari's Contemporary Account of the Murders of Riccio and Darnley," *Scottish History Review*, 21, 1924: 116–22.

14 Keith, *Church and State*, vol. II, p. 496.

15 William Robertson, *The History of Scotland During the Reigns of Queen Mary and King James VI Till His Accession to the Crown of England*, new edition, Aberdeen: Clark, 1847, p. 527.

16 Labanoff, *Lettres*, vol. I, p. 398.

17 Some documents cite the Bishop of Isles, who was John Carswell. Lismore was, however, the cathedral headquarters of Argyll, which was sometimes referred to by its diocesan seat. The Isles, which includes the Isles and Man, is sometimes called Surdreys or Sodor.

18 *Calendar of State Papers Relating to English Affairs Existing in the Archives and Collections of Venice and in Other Libraries in Northern Italy*, ed. H. Brown, 38 vols, London: Lords Commissioners of her Majesty's Treasury, 1864–1947, vol. VII, pp. 389–90. In another statement, he said the whole house was ruined. On his way home Moretta met with de Silva, who wrote to Philip that he believed the Savoyard suspected she was involved in the murder, but de Silva also admitted that Moretta was disappointed that she had not permitted him to see the king's body. Clearly, in France he did not implicate Mary.

19 Labanoff, *Lettres*, vol. VII, p. 108; William Sanderson, *A Complete History of the Lives and Reigns of Mary Queen of Scotland and her Son and Successor, James the Sixth, King of Scotland*, London: Humphrey Moseley, *et al.*, 1656, p. 48, reported that Sir Roger Alston (*sic* Aston) who accompanied James to England made the incredible statement that he and an earl of Dunbar (George Home) were with the king and escaped the house after smelling a lighted match. With sword in hand, Henry sent Alston to protect the prince while remaining to defend himself.

20 *Calendar of State Papers Relating to English Affairs, Preserved Principally at Rome in the Vatican Archives and Library*, ed. J.M. Rigg, 2 vols, London: HMSO, 1926, vol. II, pp. 223–4. (Hereafter *CSP Rome*.)

21 Claude Nau, *The History of Mary Stewart From the Murder of Riccio Until her Flight into England*, ed. Joseph Stevenson, Edinburgh: William Patterson, 1883, pp. clxiii–clxvi, prints a procuratory of Lady Bothwell dated 20 March. Ironically, in the almost certainly forged Casket Letters and Sonnets, she wrote that she would put her son, her honor, and her soul completely in Bothwell's power. See Sarah Dunnigan, *Eros and Poetry at the Courts of Mary Queen of Scots and James VI*, New York: Palgrave, 2002, p. 28, and my review in *Clio: A Journal of Literature, History and the Philosophy of History*, 33, 2004: 83–8.

22 J. Irvine Smith, "Criminal Procedure," in *An Introduction to Scottish Legal History*, Edinburgh: Stair Society, 1958, pp. 432–4; Julian Goodare, *State and Society in Early Modern Scotland*, Oxford: Oxford University Press, 1999, p. 135.

23 Julian Goodare, *The Government of Scotland, 1560–1625*, Oxford: Oxford University Press, 2004, p. 134.

24 Keith Brown, *Bloodfeud in Scotland, 1575–1625: Violence, Justice and Politics in an Early Modern Society*, Edinburgh: Donald, 1986, p. 15.

25 *CSP Scot*, vol. II, p. 341.

26 *CSP Rome*, vol. II, pp. 215–25. Three of the four deponents said she was forced to marry him, but one said he had heard both that she was constrained and that she was willing to wed him. See also, *CSP Scot*, vol. II, p. 362, for a letter of Robert Melville's in which he states that when she requested assistance, the burgh's inhabitants sallied forth through their portes. Sometimes, his letter is read as though she sent the messenger after arriving at Dunbar. That seems an impossible scenario. The author of *A Diurnal of Remarkable Occurrents That Have Passed Within the Country of Scotland Since the Death of James the Fourth Till the Year 1575*, (ed.) T. Thomson, Edinburgh: Bannatyne Club, 1833, p. 109, said that during the abduction she sent to Edinburgh for help but that it was a ruse to conceal her consent.

27 *The Autobiography of Michel de Montaigne*, ed. M. Lowenthal, Boston, MA: Houghton Mifflin, 1935, p. 69

7 SEEKING REFUGE, 1567–69

1 Joseph Stevenson (ed.), *Selections from Unpublished Manuscripts in the College of Arms and the British Museum, Illustrating the Reign of Mary Queen of Scotland*, Glasgow: Maitland Club, 1837, No. 41, pp. 178–9.

2 Claude Nau, *The History of Mary Stewart From the Murder of Riccio Until her Flight into England*, ed. Joseph Stevenson, Edinburgh: William Paterson, 1883, p. 37, later claims that Lethington, who was not Bothwell's friend, and others showed her the Ainslie band and pressured her to marry him.

3 Alexandre Labanoff (ed.), *Lettres, Instructions et Mémoires de Marie Stuart, Reine D'Écosse*, 7 vols, London: Dolman, 1844, vol. II, pp. 31, 44.

4 Leah Marcus, Janel Mueller, and Mary Beth Rose (eds), *Elizabeth I: Collected Works*, Chicago, IL: University of Chicago, 2000, p. 119.

5 Samuel Cowan, *Mary Queen of Scots, and Who Wrote the Casket Letters?*, 2 vols, 2nd edn, London: Low, Marston, 1901, vol. II, p. 337.

6 I wish to thank Robert J. Mueller, associate professor, Utah State University, Utah Basin Campus, for permitting me to read his unpublished manuscript, "Guest or Prisoner? Sir Francis Knollys and Mary Queen of Scots, 1568–1569."

7 BL Cotton MSS, Caligula B, IX, f. 347–8.

8 *Calendar of State Papers Domestic Series, Elizabeth, Addenda, 1566–1579*, 12 vols, London: HMSO, 1855–1872, vol. VII, p. 274. I wish to thank Robert J. Mueller for this reference.

9 *CSP Scots*, vol. II, 210.

10 Quoted in Mark Jones (ed.), *Fake? The Art of Deception*, London: Trustees of the British Museum, 1990, p. 22. Letters were the evidence in many seventeenth-century trials although the accused often disputed their authorship. See Frances E. Dolan, "Reading, Writing and Other Crimes," in V. Traub, M. Lindsay, and D. Collaghan (eds), *Feminist Reading of Early Modern Culture: Emerging Subjects*, Cambridge: Cambridge University Press, 1991, p. 146.

11 Thomas F. Henderson, *The Casket Letters and Mary, Queen of Scots, with Appendices*, 2nd edn, Edinburgh: Black, 1890.

12 David M. Walker, *The Scottish Jurists*, Edinburgh: Green, 1985, p. 48; *The Practicks of Sir James Balfour*, ed. Peter G.B. McNeil, 2 vols, Edinburgh: Stair Society, 1962–63, especially, p. 614.

13 He was forfeited in August 1571, but received a remission for his crimes and a reduction of the forfeiture in 1572. Morton had the forfeiture extended to Balfour's heirs in 1579. Later, King James made legal efforts to protect Balfour's property and before Balfour's death in 1583, he reacquired his lands. See Walker, *Scottish Jurists*, pp. 38–41 and *Oxford Dictionary of National Biography* (www.Oxforddnb.com) for these details.

14 Reginald Mahon, *Mary Queen of Scots: A Study of the Lennox Narrative in the University Library at Cambridge*, Cambridge: Cambridge University Press, 1924.

15 Ibid., appendix, for many of the documents, including the book of articles; see also Gordon Donaldson, *The First Trial of Mary, Queen of Scots*, New York: Stein and Day, 1969, pp. 142–83.

16 Leslie, *The Copies of a Letter Writen Out of Scotland (1572)*, Menston: Scolar Press, 1970, pp. 26–7. He said, "the said English commissioners were yet so moved with that which fell out before them to the manifest proof of the queen's innocence . . . they began to pity her case, and made the earnest request that she might be restored to her crown." Norfolk, he said (p. 17) especially believed her innocent since he wanted to marry her.

17 *CSP Scot*, vol. II, p. 595.

18 Quoted in C.A.J. Armstrong, "An Italian Astrologer at the Court of Henry VII," in E.F. Jacob (ed.), *Italian Renaissance Studies: A Tribute to the late Cecilia M. Ady*, London: Faber, 1960, p. 442.

8 NEGOTIATING RESTITUTION, 1569–1584

1 For examples of her work, see Margaret Swain, *The Needlework of Mary, Queen of Scots*, London: Van Nostrand Reinhold, 1973.

2 HMC, *Calendar of the Manuscripts of the Marquess of Salisbury at Hatfield Hall*, 20 vols, London: HMSO, 1883–1976, vol. I, p. 400.

3 Frederick von Raumer (ed.), *Contributions to Modern History from the British Museum and the State Paper Office*, 2 vols, London: Knight, 1836–7, vol. I, p. 193.

4 Alexandre Labanoff (ed.), *Lettres, Instructions et Mémoires de Marie Stuart, Reine D'Écosse*, 7 vols, London: Dolman, 1844, vol. III, pp. 48–9, for example.

5 *BL, Cott. MSS, Calig.* CII, f. 23.

6   Labanoff, *Lettres*, vol. III, pp. 35, 48–9.

7   William Turnbull (ed.), *Letters of Mary Stuart, Queen of Scotland*, London: Dolman, 1845, pp. 196–7; Labanoff, *Lettres*, vol. III, pp. 221–50.

8   *CSP Scot*, vol. V, 75.

9   Mrs P. Stewart-MacKenzie Arbuthnot (ed.), *Queen Mary's Book: A Collection of Poems and Essays by Mary Queen of Scots*, London: Bell, 1907, pp. 102–5.

10 An English crown was worth 5 shillings.

11 Labanoff, *Lettres*, vol. IV, pp. 40–5.

12 Ibid., p. 326.

13 BL, Royal MSS, 18B, VI, f. 293b.

14 Arbuthnot, *Mary's Book*, p. 106 note.

15 Labanoff, *Lettres*, vol. VI, pp. 352–62.

16 John Jones, *The Benefit of the Ancient Bathes of Buckstone which Cureth Most Greevous Sicknesses*, London: East and Middleton for Jones, 1572. Shrewsbury appointed Jones to a rectory in 1581.

17 PRO SP 53/11, nos 26, 28; BL Cott. MSS. Calig. CVIII, f. 57; Labanoff, *Lettres*, vol. IV, pp. 368–74.

18 John Leader, *Mary Queen of Scots In Captivity: A Narrative of Events*, London: Bell, 1880, p. 584.

19 Richard MacKenney, *Sixteenth Century Europe: Expansion and Conflict*, New York: St Martin's Press, 1993, p. 262.

20 *CSP Scot*, vol. V, 198; *CSP Rome*, vol. II, 215–230.

21 Labanoff, *Lettres*, VI, pp. 312–22.

22 These rumors have been disputed. See Frederik Schiern, *Life of James Hepburn*, trans. D. Berry, Edinburgh: Douglas, 1880; and J. Watts De Peyser, *Mary Stuart, Bothwell, and the Casket Letters, Something New*, New York: Ludwig, 1890.

23 HMC, *Report on the Manuscripts of Lord Middleton Preserved at Wollaton Hall, Nottinghamshire*, London: HMSO, 1911, p. 153.

24 HMC, *Calendar of the Manuscripts of the Most Honourable, the Marquess of Bath at Longleat, Wiltshire. Vol. 5: Talbot, Dudley and Devereux Papers, 1533–1659*, London: HMSO, 1981, pp. 51–2.

9 FAILING ENTERPRISES, 1584–86

1   PRO, SP 53/13, no. 55.

2 *The Letters and Memorials of William Cardinal Allen (1532–94)*, intro. Thomas Knox, London: Nutt, 1882: lxiii–lxiv.

3 *The Intended Treason of Doctor Parrie and Complices Against the Queens Most Excellent Majestie*, London: f. Car, 1585.

4 John Bossy, *Under the Molehill: An Elizabethan Spy Story*, New Haven, CT: Yale University Press, 2001, pp. 175–6.

5 Alexandre Labanoff (ed.), *Lettres, Instructions et Mémoires de Marie Stuart, Reine D'Écosse*, 7 vols, London: Dolman, 1844, vol. VI, pp. 274–93.

6 Ibid. pp. 368–9.

7 Knox, *Letters of Allen*, p. 320.

8 Leo Hicks (ed.), *Letters and Memorials of Robert Persons, 1578–1588*, 2 vols, *Catholic Record Society*, 39, 1942: 246–51, 357–8.

9 Frederick von Raumer (ed.), *Contributions to Modern History from the British Museum and the State Paper Office*, 2 vols, London: Knight, 1836–7, vol. I, p. 309.

10 A.G. Smith, *The Babington Plot*, London: Macmillan, 1936, pp. 35–6 and p. 258 for a discussion of the various texts, which basically agree with each other and are confirmed by his various confessions.

11 Smith, *Babington*, p. 61.

12 Ibid., p. 63

13 Conyers Read (ed.), *The Bardon Papers*, Camden Society, third series, vol. xvii, London: Royal Historical Society, 1909, p. 130.

14 *CSP Span*, vol. III, 382.

15 Samuel Cowan, *Mary Queen of Scots, and Who Wrote the Casket Letters?*, 2 vols, 2nd edn, London: Low, Marston, 1901, vol. II, pp. 240–44, for example, prints both letters, noting the inconsistencies to prove to his satisfaction that the references to Elizabeth's assassination were forged.

16 Samuel Cowan, *The Last Days of Mary Stuart and the Journal of Bourgoyne, Her Physician*, London: Nash, 1907, pp. 159–285

17 *CSP Scot*, vol. VIII, 632.

10 ENDING CAPTIVITY

1 *The Trial of Mary Queen of Scots*, ed. A. Francis Steuart, 2nd edn, London: Hodges, 1951, p. 52.

2 Samuel Cowan, *The Last Days of Mary Stuart and the Journal of Bourgoyne Her Physician*, London: Nash, 1907, p. 228.

3 Henry Clifford, *The Life of the Lady Jane Dormer, Duchess of Feria*, trans. E.E. Estcourt, ed. Joseph Stevenson, London: Burnes, 1887, p. 119.

4 G.R. Batho, "The Execution of Mary, Queen of Scots," *Scottish Historical Review*, 39, 1960: 42.

5 Alexandre Labanoff (ed.), *Lettres, Instructions et Mémoires de Marie Stuart, Reine D'Écosse*, 7 vols, London: Dolman, 1844, vol. VI, pp. 474–80.

6 Ibid.

7 Cowen, *Last Days of Mary Stuart*, p. 268.

8 Ibid., p. 275.

9 Steuart, *Trial of Mary*, p. 196.

10 Ibid., pp. 203–6.

11 Ibid., pp. 204–6.

12 BL, Add. MS. 35,324, f. 14.

13 *Est Natura Hominum: The Scottish Queens Buriall at Peterborough, Upon Tuesday Being Lammas Day, 1587*, London, by A.I. for Venge, 1589; Allan Crosby and John Bruce (eds), *Accounts and Papers Relating to Mary Queen of Scots*, London: Camden Society, 1867, vol. 93, pp. vii–xxii, 28–62.

14 *The Political Works of James I*, ed. Charles McIlwain, New York: Russell and Russell, repr., 1965, p. 34.

15 John Bruce (ed.), *Letters of Queen Elizabeth and King James VI of Scotland*, vol. 16, London: Camden Society, 1849, p. 72.

16 CSP Rome, vol. I, 320; Samuel Cowan, *Mary Queen of Scots and Who Wrote the Casket Letters?*, 2 vols, 2nd edn, London: Low, Marston, 1901, vol. I, p. 219.

17 *Life of Dormer*, Estcourt, p. 175. The fear that she might be canonized led to the following attack: W. Barras, *Proposed Canonisation of Mary Queen of Scots, Cardinal Beaton, and Archbishop Hamilton*, Glasgow: Office of the Scottish Protestant Alliance, 1887.

18 *CSP Rome*, vol. I, 293.

19 Mrs P. Stewart-MacKenzie Arbuthnot (ed.), *Queen Mary's Book: A Collection of Poems and Essays by Mary Queen of Scots*, London: Bell, 1907, p. 110. The French version, taken from Leslie's *Tranquilli Animi Conservatio et Munimentum*, is on p. 166.

FURTHER READING: SELECTED TOPICS

MANUSCRIPT SOURCES

The manuscripts concerning Mary, queen of Scots, can be found in a number of libraries and archives, among them, the British Library, the Public Record Office, the Bibliothèque Nationale at Paris, the National Library of Scotland, the Huntington Library at San Marino, the Folger Shakespeare Library at Washington, D.C., Cambridge University Library, and in the Cecil Papers at Hatfield House. This is by no means an exhaustive list. The most numerous are at the British Library in the Add MSS and the Cottonian MSS Caligula and at the Public Record Office in the State Papers Nos. SP 52 and 70. Readers can access these and other documents at the archives through various calendars and most of the relevant ones have been published and republished.

PRINTED SOURCES

Mary's writings, creativity, and books

Most, but not all, her letters can be found in *Lettres, Instructions et Mémoires de Marie Stuart, Reine D'Écosse*, ed. Alexandre Labanoff, 7 vols (London: Dolman, 1844). Some of them are available in translation in Agnes Strickland, *Letters of Mary Queen of Scots, Now First Published the Originals, Collected from Various Sources, Private as well as Public, with an Historical Introduction and Notes*, new edn, 2 vols (New York: Colburn, 1844); and *Letters of Mary Stuart, Queen of Scotland*, ed. William Turnbull (London: Dolman, 1845). For copies of her creativity, see *The Latin Themes of Mary Stuart Queen of Scots*, ed. Anatole de Montaiglon (London: Warton Club, 1855); *Queen Mary's Book: A Collection of Poems and Essays by Mary Queen of Scots*, ed. Mrs. P. Stewart-MacKenzie Arbuthnot (London: Bell, 1907); Francis de Zulueta, *Embroideries by Mary Stuart & Elizabeth Talbot at Oxburgh Hall* (Oxford: Oxford

University Press, 1923); Margaret Swain, *The Needlework of Mary, Queen of Scots* (London: Van Nostrand Reinhold, 1973); and *Writing Renaissance Queens: Texts by and about Elizabeth I and Mary, Queen of Scots*, ed. Lisa Hopkins (Newark, DE: University of Delaware Press, 2002). See also, *The Library of Mary, Queen of Scots*, ed. Julian Sharman (London: Stock, 1889) and *A Book Bound for Mary Queen of Scots*, ed. George Barwick (London: Bibliographical Society, 1901).

British government domestic publications

Some of the most useful publications are: *Acts of the Parliament of Scotland*, ed. Thomas Thomson and Cosmo Innes, 12 vols (by Queen Victoria's Command, 1814–75); *Calendar of State Papers, Domestic, Edward VI, Mary, Elizabeth I, and James I,* 12 vols (London: HMSO, 1856–72); *The Register of the Privy Council of Scotland*, ed. John Hill Burton, 14 vols (Edinburgh: H.M. General Register House, 1877–98).

Privately printed state papers

Only a sampling is included here: *A Full view of the Public Transactions in the Reign of Queen Elizabeth*, ed. Patrick Forbes, 2 vols (London: Hawkins, 1740–41); *A Collection of State Papers Relating to Affairs in the Reigns of King Henry VIII, King Edward VI, Queen Mary, and Queen Elizabeth . . . Left by William Cecil, Lord Burghley*, ed. Samuel Haynes, 2 vols (London: Bowyer, 1740–59); *A Collection of State Papers Relating to Affairs in the Reign of Elizabeth from 1571–96, Transcribed from Original Papers Left by William Cecil, Lord Burghley, and Reposited in the Library at Hatfield House*, ed. William Murdin (London: Bowyer, 1759); *The State Papers and Letters of Sir Ralph Sadler*, ed. Arthur Clifford, 2 vols (Edinburgh: Constable, 1809); Frederick von Raumer (ed.), *Contributions to Modern History from the British Museum and the State Paper Office*, 2 vols (London: Knight, 1836–7); Robert Keith, *History of the Affairs of Church and State in Scotland from the Beginning of the Reformation to the year 1568*, ed. J.P. Lawson, 3 vols (Edinburgh: Spottiswoode Society, 1844); William Robertson, *The History of Scotland During the Reigns of Queen Mary and King James VI*, new complete edition

(Aberdeen: Clark, 1847); *Miscellany Two*, ed. David Sellar (Edinburgh: Stair Society, 1984); and *The Last Years of Mary Queen of Scots: Documents from the Cecil Papers at Hatfield House*, ed. Alan G.R. Smith (London: Roxburghe Club, 1990).

Diplomatic documents

These must be read cautiously, for diplomats often reported as truth the rumors they heard from their spies without confirming them.

Anglo-Scottish relations

The Hamilton Papers. Hamilton Letters and Papers, Illustrating the Political Relations of England and Scotland in the Sixteenth Century, ed. Joseph Bain, 2 vols (Edinburgh: H.M. General Register House, 1890–92); The Border P pers: *Calendar of Letters and Papers Relating to the Affairs of the Borders of England and Scotland*, 2 vols (Edinburgh: H.M. General Register House, 1894–96); *Calendar of State Papers Relating to Scotland and Mary Queen of Scots, 1547–1603*, ed. Joseph Bain, 13 vols (Edinburgh: H.M. General Register House, 1898–1969). *Foreign Correspondence with Marie de Lorraine, Queen of Scotland from the Originals in the Balcarres Papers, 1548–57*, ed. Marguerite Wood, 2 vols (Edinburgh: Scottish History Society, 1923–5); and *Two Missions of Jacques de la Brosse, An Account of the Affairs of Scotland in the Year 1543 and the Journal of the Siege of Leith, 1560*, ed. Gladys Dickinson (Edinburgh: Edinburgh University Press, 1942).

Other diplomatic correspondence

Calendar *of Letters, Despatches, and State Papers Relating to Negotiations Between England and Spain*, ed. G. Bergenroth, *et al.*, 13 vols, 2 supplements (London: Longman, 1862–1954); Armand Baschet, *La Diplomatie Vénitienne: Les Princes de l'Europe au XVIe Siècle* (Paris: Plon, 1862); *Calendar of State Papers Foreign, Elizabeth*, 23 vols (London: HMS0, 1863–1950); *Calendar of State Papers and Manuscripts Relating to English Affairs, Existing in the Archives and Collections of Venice and in Other Libraries of Northern Italy*, 39 vols (London: HMSO, 1864–1947); *Despatches of Michele Suriano and Marc' Antonio Barbaro, Venetian Ambassadors at the Court of France*, ed. Henry Layard (Lymington: Huguenot Society of London, 1891); *Calendar of Letters and Papers*

Relating to English Affairs of the Reign of Elizabeth, Preserved principally in the Archives of the Simancas, 4 vols (London: HMSO, 1892–96); and *Calendar of State Papers Relating to English Affairs Preserved Principally at Rome in the Vatican Archives and Library*, 2 vols (London: HMSO, 1926).

Scottish chronicles

These, too, must be read with caution, for they were mostly written many years after the events had occurred. *Collections Relating to the History of Mary Queen of Scots*, ed. James Anderson, 4 vols (Edinburgh: Mosman and Brown, 1727–28); *Fragments of Scottish History*, ed. John Dalyell (Edinburgh: Constable, 1798); *The Historie and Life of King James the Sext, Being an Account of Affairs in Scotland from the year 1566 to the year 1596*, ed. Thomas Thomson (Edinburgh: Bannatyne Club, 1825); and *A Diurnal of Remarkable Occurrents That Have Passed Within the Country of Scotland Since the Death of King James the Fourth Till the year 1575*, ed. T. Thomson (Edinburgh: Bannatyne Club, 1833).

Scottish memoirs and histories

Like the chronicles, some of these were written long after the events and need careful analysis. Some also present a biased point of view. *Historical Memoirs of the Reign of Mary Queen of Scots and a Portion of the Reign of King James the Sixth by Lord Herries*, ed. R. Pitcairn (Edinburgh: Abbotsford Club, 1836); Richard Bannatyne, *Memoriales of Transactions in Scotland, 1569–73*, ed. R. Pitcairn (Edinburgh: Bannatyne Club, 1836); David Calderwood, *The True History of the Kirk of Scotland from the Beginning of the Reformation unto the End of the Reign of King James VI*, ed. T. Thomson, 8 vols (Edinburgh: Woodrow Society, 1843–49); George Buchanan, *The History of Scotland from the Earliest Period to the Present Time*, ed. J. Aikman, 6 vols (Edinburgh: Blackie, 1855); Claude Nau, *The History of Mary Stewart From the Murder of Riccio until her Flight into England*, ed. Joseph Stevenson (Edinburgh: William Paterson, 1883); Patrick, third lord Ruthven, *The Death of Rizzi* (Edinburgh: Goldsmid, 1890); Robert Lindesay of Pitscottie, *The Historie and Cronicles of Scotland from the Slauchter of King James the First to the Ane*

Thousand Fyve Hundreith Thrie Scoir Fyftein Zeir, 3 vols, ed. A.J.G. MacKay (New York: Johnson Reprint Corporation, 1966); George Barwick, "A Side-Light on the Mystery of Mary Stuart: Pietro Bizari's Contemporary Account of the Murders of Riccio and Darnley," *Scottish History Review*, 21, 1924; *John Knox's History of the Reformation in Scotland*, ed. W. Croft Dickinson, 2 vols (Philadelphia, PA: Philosophical Library, 1950); *The Memoirs of Sir James Melville of Halhill*, ed. Gordon Donaldson (London: Folio Society, 1969); and John Leslie, *A Defence of the Honour of Marie Quene of Scotlande, 1569* (Menston: Scolar Press, 1970).

Poetry

The most important poetry associated with the Scottish queen is: Boscosel de Chastelard, *Effusions of Love from Chatelar to Mary Queen of Scotland*, trans. Samuel Ireland, 2nd edn (London: Crosby, 1808); *Songs and Sonnets of Pierre de Ronsard*, ed. Curtis Page (Boston, MA: Houghton Mifflin, 1924); *The Bannatyne Manuscript Written in Tyme of Pest*, 1568, ed. W. Tod Ritchie, 4 vols (Edinburgh: Blackwood, 1928); *The Poems of Sir Richard Maitland of Lethingtoun, Knight* (New York: A.M.S. Reprint, 1973); George Buchanan, "Epithalamium upon the Marriage of Mary Queen of Scots to the Dauphin of France, afterwards Francis the Second," *Renaissance Latin Poetry*, ed. I.D. McFarlane (Manchester: Manchester University Press, 1980).

French documents

The most helpful are: *The Marriage of Mary, Queen of Scots, to Francis the Dauphin of France, MDLVIII*, ed. Bernerd Weber (Greenock: Grian-Aig Press, 1969); *Lettres de Catherine de' Medici*, ed. H. de la Ferrière-Percy, *et al.*, 11 vols (Paris: Imprimerie National, 1880–1943); Pierre de Bourdeille, seigneur de Brantôme, *The Lives of Gallant Ladies*, trans. Alec Borwn (London: Elek Books, 1961); *The French Wars of Religion: Selected Documents*, ed. David Potter (New York: St Martin's Press, 1997); *Lettres du Cardinal Charles de Lorraine (1525–1574)*, ed. Daniel Cuisiat (Geneva: Librairie Droz, 1998).

George Buchanan, the Casket Letters, and Darnley's murder

The following are documents cited at the inquiry into whether Elizabeth would return the queen of Scots to her realm in 1568. John Hosack, *Mary Queen of Scots and her Accusers*, 2 vols (Edinburgh: Blackwood, 1870–4); T.F. Henderson, *The Casket Letters and Mary Queen of Scots*, 2nd edn (Edinburgh: Black, 1890); Samuel Cowan, *Mary Queen of Scots, and Who Wrote the Casket Letters?*, 2 vols, 2nd edn (London: Low, Marston 1901); Andrew Lang, *The Mystery of Mary Stuart* (New York: AMS Press, 1970, repr. of 1901); Reginald Mahon, *Mary Queen of Scots: A Study of the Lennox Narrative in the University Library at Cambridge* (Cambridge: Cambridge University Press, 1924); *The Tyrannous Reign of Mary Stewart: George Buchanan's Account*, ed. W.A. Gatherer (Edinburgh: Edinburgh University Press, 1958); and M.H. Armstrong Davison, *The Casket Letters: A Solution to the Murder of Mary Queen of Scots and the Murder of Lord Darnley* (Washington, DC: University Press of Washington, DC and Community College Press, 1965).

Elizabethan records

Elizabeth's letters
Letters of Queen Elizabeth and King James VI of Scotland, ed. John Bruce (London: Camden Society, 1849); *Elizabeth I: Collected Works*, eds Leah Marcus, Janet Mueller, and Mary Beth Rose (Chicago, IL: University of Chicago Press, 2000).

Mary's captivity
Illustrations of British History, Biography, and Manners in the Reigns of Henry VIII, Edward VI, Mary, Elizabeth and James I, ed. Edmund Lodge, 3 vols (London: Chidley, 1838); *Accounts and Papers Relating to Mary Queen of Scots*, ed. Allan Crosby and John Bruce (London: Camden Society, 1867); *The Letters and Memorials of William Cardinal Allen (1532–94)*, intro., Thomas Knox (London: Nutt, 1882); *The Last Days of Mary Stuart and the Journal of Bourgoyne, Her Physician*, ed. Samuel Cowan (London: Nash, 1907); *The Bardon Papers*, ed. Conyers Read (London: Royal Historical Society, 1909), which includes documents

from the Babington Plot; and *The Trial of Mary Queen of Scots*, ed. A. Francis Steuart, 2nd edn (London: Hodges, 1951).

Histories concerning Mary Queen of Scots

Recent biographies

Far too many biographies have been published to cite here. These are among the most recent ones: Antonia Fraser, *Mary Queen of Scots* (New York: Delacorte Press, 1969; New York: Delta, 1993, 2001), which has the best coverage; Jenny Wormald, *Mary, Queen of Scots: Politics, Passion, and a Kingdom Lost* (New York: Tauris Park, 2001); James MacKay, *In My End is My Beginning: A Life of Mary Queen of Scots* (Edinburgh: Mainstream, 1999); Susan Watkins, *Mary Queen of Scots* (New York: Thames and Hudson, 2001); and John Guy, *The Life of Mary Queen of Scots: My Heart is My Own* (London: Fourth Estate, 2004).

Chronology of her early life

Marcus Merriman, *The Rough Wooings: Mary, Queen of Scots, 1542–51* (East Linton: Tuckwell, 2000), which discusses the French alliance and the attempts of English armies to capture the young queen, should be read in association with Norman MacDougall, *An Antidote to the English: The Auld Alliance, 1295–1560* (East Linton: Tuckwell, 2001). James Stevenson, *Marie Stuart: A Narrative of the First Eighteen Years of her Life, Principally from Original Documents* (Patterson, 1886); Alphone de Ruble, *La Première Jeunesse de Marie Stuart* (Paris: Bibliothèque Nationale, 1891); David Hay Fleming, *Mary Queen of Scots from her Birth to her Flight into England* (London: Hodder and Stoughton, 1897); and Jane Stoddard, *The Girlhood of Mary Queen of Scots* (London: Hodder and Stoughton 1908) narrate her early years. Of interest for French strategies are two articles by Elizabeth Bonner, "The French Reactions to the Rough Wooings of Mary Queen of Scots" and "The *Politique* of Henry II: De Facto French Rule in Scotland, 1550–1554," *Journal of the Sydney Society for Scottish History*, vols 6 and 7, 1998, 1999, respectively.

Her personal rule

David and Judy Steel, *Mary Stuart's Scotland: The Landscapes, Life and Legends of Mary Queen of Scots* (New York: Harmony Books, 1987);

Edward Furgol, "The Scottish Iteinerary of Mary Queen of Scots, 1542–6 and 1561–8," *Proceedings of the Society of Antiquaries of Scotland*, 117, 1987; and Peter McNeill and Hector MacQueen (eds), *Atlas of Scottish History to 1707* (Edinburgh: University of Edinburgh, 1996) recount her travels. A.A. MacDonald, "Mary Stewart's Entry to Edinburgh: An Ambiguous Triumph," *Innes Review*, 42, 1991, identifies the Protestant bias present during the entry. Michael Lynch, "Queen Mary's Triumph: The Baptismal Celebrations at Stirling in December 1566," *Scottish Historical Review*, 69, 1990 and "The Reassertion of Princely Power in Scotland: The Reigns of Mary, Queen of Scots and King James VI," in M. Gosman, A. MacDonald, and A. Vanderjagt (eds), *Princes and Princely Culture, 1450–1650* (Leiden: Brill, 2003), discuss her son's christening and her court culture.

Brief comparisons of her rule to her son's can be found in Julian Goodare and Michael Lynch (eds), *The Reign of James VI* (East Linton: Tuckwell, 2000). Gordon Donaldson, *All the Queen's Men: Power and Politics in Mary Stewart's Scotland* (London: Batsford, 1983); and Margaret Sanderson, *Mary Stewart's People: Life in Mary Stewart's Scotland* (Tuscaloosa, AL: University of Alabama, 1987) offer studies of her subjects. Mortimer Levine, *Tudor Dynastic Problems, 1460–1571* (London: Barnes & Noble, 1973) discusses the English succession question. Finally, R.H. Mahon, *The Tragedy of Kirk o'Field* (Cambridge: Cambridge University Press, 1930) examines the death of her second husband.

Her English captivity

Gordon Donaldson, *The First Trial of Mary Queen of Scots* (New York: Stein and Day, 1969) presents information about her trial and the Casket Letters. Katherine Thompson, "All Things to All Men: Mary Queen of Scots and the Scottish Civil Wars, 1568–73," *Journal of the Sydney Society for Scottish History*, 9, 2001, examines the political struggle in Scotland. Andrew Lang, "The Household of Mary, Queen of Scots in 1573," *Scottish Historical Review*, 2, 1905, identifies her attendants and servants. John Leader, *Mary Queen of Scots in Captivity* (London: Bell, 1880); and Patrick Collinson, *The English Captivity of Mary Queen of Scots* (Sheffield: Sheffield History Pamphlets, 1987) examine her years in prison. G.R. Batho, "The Execution of Mary, Queen of Scots," *Scottish Historical Review*, 39, 1960; and Jennifer

Woodward, *The Theatre of Death: The Ritual Management of Royal Funerals in Renaissance England, 1570–1625* (Woodbridge: Boydell, 1997) recount her death, her funeral, and interment.

Her public images and portraits

James Phillips, *Images of a Queen: Mary Stuart in Sixteenth Century Literature* (Berkeley, CA: University of California, 1964); and Alexander Wilkinson, *Mary Queen of Scots and Public Opinion, 1542–1600* (New York: Palgrave, 2004) present contemporary views of her. See also, Pearl Brandwein, *Mary Queen of Scots in Nineteenth and Twentieth Century Drama: Poetic License with History* (New York: Lang, 1989); and Jayne Lewis, *Mary, Queen of Scots: Romance and Nation* (London: Routledge, 1998). Helen Smailes and Duncan Thomson, *The Queen's Image: A Celebration of Mary, Queen of Scots* (Edinburgh: The Trustees of the National Galleries of Scotland, 1987) reproduce exquisite copies of her portraits.

Scottish studies

Important contemporaries

Studies of Scottish individuals important to her life are useful. Frederik Schiern, *The Life of James Hepburn*, trans. D. Berry (Edinburgh: Douglas, 1880); Thomas Duncan, "The Queen's Maries," *Scottish Historical Review*, 2, 1905; A. Francis Steuart, *Seigneur Davie: A Sketch Life of David Riccio* (London: Sands, 1922); Maurice Lee, *James Stewart, Earl of Moray: A Political Study of the Reformation in Scotland* (New York: Columbia University Press, 1953); D.M. Lockie, "The Political Career of the Bishop of Ross," *University of Birmingham Historical Journal*, 4, 1953; Neville Williams, *Thomas Howard, fourth Duke of Norfolk* (New York: Dutton, 1964); I.D. McFarlane, *Buchanan* (London: Duckworth, 1981); Peter Anderson, *Robert Stewart, Earl of Orkney, Lord of Shetland, 1533–1593* (Edinburgh: Donald, 1982); David Walker, *The Scottish Jurists* (Edinburgh: Green, 1985); Margaret Sanderson, *Cardinal of Scotland: David Beaton, 1494–1546* (Edinburgh: Donald, 1986); Caroline Bingham, *Darnley: A Life of Henry Stuart, Lord Darnley, Consort of Mary Queen of Scots* (Edinburgh: Constable, 1995); Jamie Cameron, *James V: The Personal Rule* (East Linton: Tuckwell, 1998); Rosalind Marshall, *Mary of Guise: Queen of Scots* (Edinburgh: National Museums of Scotland, 2001); Pamela Ritchie, *Mary of Guise in Scotland, 1548–1560: A Political Career* (East Linton: Tuckwell, 2002); and Jane Dawson, *The Politics of Religion in the Age of Mary, Queen of Scots* (Cambridge: Cambridge University Press, 2002).

General histories, social and economic issues

For the Scottish context numerous studies are available. Only a few can be listed here. Edward Burns, *The Coinage of Scotland*, 3 vols (Edinburgh: Black, 1887); Jenny Wormald, *Court, Kirk, and Community: Scotland, 1470–1625* (Toronto: University of Toronto, 1981); Leah Leneman (ed.), *Perspectives in Scottish Social History: Essays in Honour of Rosalind Mitchison* (Aberdeen: Aberdeen University Press, 1988); Keith Brown, *Noble Society in Scotland: Wealth, Family and Culture From Reformation to Revolution* (Edinburgh: Edinburgh University Press, 2000); and Julian Goodare, *State and Society in Early Modern Scotland* (Oxford: Oxford University Press, 1999) and *The Government of Scotland, 1560–1625* (Oxford: Oxford University Press, 2004).

Religion and politics

Gordon Donaldson, *The Scottish Reformation* (Cambridge: Cambridge University Press, 1960) is the traditional survey. Michael Lynch, *Edinburgh and the Reformation* (Edinburgh: Donald, 1981) examines the queen's relationship to her capital. Essays in Norman MacDougall (ed.), *Church, Politics and Society: Scotland, 1408–1929* (Edinburgh: Donald, 1983); James Kirk, *Patterns of Reform: Continuity and Change in the Reformation Kirk* (Aberdeen: Clark, 1989); and Roger Mason (ed.), *John Knox and the British Reformations* (Burlington, VT: Ashgate, 1998) provide further revisionist nuances. See also, Michael Graham, *The Uses of Reform: "Godly Discipline" and Popular Behavior in Scotland and Beyond, 1560–1620* (Leiden: Brill, 1996). For a comparative study, see Clare Kellar, *Scotland, England and the Reformation, 1534–1561* (Oxford: Clarendon Press, 2003).

Legal and constitutional studies

The most useful are Lord Normand, intro., *An Introduction to Scottish Legal History* (Edinburgh: Stair Society, 1958); Keith Brown, *Bloodfeud in Scotland: 1573–1625: Violence, Justice and Politics in Early Modern Society* (Edinburgh: Donald, 1986); M.D. Young (ed.), *The Parliaments of Scotland*, 2 vols (Edinburgh: Scottish Academic Press, 1992–93); David Walker, *A Legal History of Scotland: Vol. 3, The Sixteenth Century* (Aberdeen: Clark, 1995); and J.H. Burns, *The True Law of Kingship: Concepts of Monarchy in Early Modern Scotland* (Oxford: Clarendon, 1996). Terry Brotherstone and David Ditchburn (eds), *Freedom and Authority: Scotland c.1050–c.1650: Historical and Historiographical Essays* (East Linton: Tuckwell, 2000); Julian Goodare, "The Scottish Political Community and the Parliament of 1563," *Albion*, 35, 2003, and "The First Parliament of Mary, Queen of Scots," *Sixteenth Century Journal*, 36, 2005. Dauvit Broun, R.J. Finlay, and Michael Lynch (eds), *Image and Identity: The Making and Re-making of Scotland through the Ages* (Edinburgh: Donald, 1998) offer interpretative essays on selected topics, including the Declaration of Arbroath. See also, Roger Mason (ed.), *Kingship and the Commonweal: Political Thought in Renaissance and Reformation Scotland* (East Linton: Tuckwell, 1998).

Architectural studies

No investigation of her life would be complete without studies of architecture, including David Breeze, *A Queen's Progress: An Introduction to the Buildings Associated with Mary, Queen of Scots, in the Care of the Secretary of State for Scotland* (Edinburgh: Historic Buildings and Monuments, Scottish Development Department, 1987); Richard Fawcett, *Scottish Architecture from the Accession of the Stewarts to the Reformation, 1371–1560* (Edinburgh: Edinburgh University Press, 1994); and Miles Glendinning, Ranald MacInnes, and Aonghas MacKechnie, *A History of Scottish Architecture from the Renaissance to the Present Day* (Edinburgh: Edinburgh University Press, 1996).

European studies

British cultural studies

Especially useful are Helena Shire, *Song, Dance and Poetry of the Court of Scotland Under James VI: Musical Illustrations of Court-Song* (ed.) Kenneth Elliott (Cambridge: Cambridge University Press, 1969); Roy Strong, *Art and Power: Renaissance Festivals, 1450–1650* (Woodbridge: Boydell,

1984); Louise Fradenburg, *City, Marriage, Tournament: Arts of Rule in Late Medieval Scotland* (Madison, WI: University of Wisconsin, 1991); A.A. MacDonald, Michael Lynch, and Ian Cowan (eds), *The Renaissance in Scotland: Studies in Literature, History and Culture Offered to John Durkan* (Leiden: Brill, 1994); Carol Edington, *Court and Culture in Renaissance Scotland: Sir David Lindsay* (Amherst, MA: University of Massachusetts Press, 1994); Janet Williams (ed.), *Stewart Style, 1513–1542: Essays on the Court of James V* (East Linton: Tuckwell, 1996); Gordon Kipling, *Enter the King, Theatre, Liturgy and Ritual in the Medieval Civic Triumph* (Oxford: Clarendon, 1998); Sally Mapstone and Juliette Wood (eds), *The Rose and the Thistle: Essays on the Culture of Late Medieval and Renaissance Scotland* (East Linton: Tuckwell, 1998); and R. Malcolm Smuts, *Culture and Power in England, 1585–1685* (New York: St Martin's Press, 1999).

Elizabethan England

Works on Elizabethan England are also too numerous for a comprehensive listing. The standard biography of the queen is Wallace MacCaffrey, *Elizabeth I* (London: Arnold, 1993), but it should be supplemented with works that examine gender issues, such as Carole Levin, *"The Heart and Stomach of a King:" Elizabeth I and the Politics of Sex and Power* (Philadelphia, PA: University of Pennsylvania, 1994); Amanda Shepherd, *Gender and Authority in Sixteenth Century England* (Keele: Keele University Press, 1994); Susan Doran, *Monarchy and Matrimony: The Courtships of Elizabeth I* (London: Routledge, 1996); A.N. McLaren, *Political Culture in the Reign of Elizabeth I: Queen and Commonwealth, 1558–1585* (Cambridge: Cambridge University Press, 1999); and Mary Hill Cole, *The Portable Queen: Elizabeth I and the Politics of Ceremony* (Amherst, MA: University of Massachusetts, 1999). Stephen Alford, *The Early Elizabethan Polity: William Cecil and the British Succession Crisis, 1558–1569* (Cambridge: Cambridge University Press, 1998) should be read in association with Jane Dawson, *The Politics of Religion in the Age of Mary, Queen of Scots: The Earl of Argyll and the Struggle for Britain and Ireland* (Cambridge: Cambridge University Press, 2002).

Conspiracies against Elizabeth

For studies of the conspiracies against Elizabeth that exonerate Mary see, for example, John H. Pollen, *Mary Queen of Scots and the Babington Plot*

(Edinburgh: Constable, 1922); and for the many condemnations of her, see A.G. Smith, *The Babington Plot* (London: Macmillan, 1936), which prints some of the documents; Conyers Read, *Mr. Secretary Walsingham and the Policy of Queen Elizabeth*, 3 vols (Oxford: Oxford University Press, 1925), *Mr Secretary Cecil and Queen Elizabeth* (New York: Knopf, 1955); and *Lord Burghley and Queen Elizabeth* (New York: Knopf, 1960). The following offer invaluable insights into the operations of spy networks: Alan Haynes, *Invisible Power: The Elizabethan Secret Services, 1570–1603* (Stroud: Sutton, 1992); John Archer, *Sovereignty and Intelligence: Spying and Court Culture in the Renaissance* (Palo Alto, CA: Stanford University Press, 1993); and John Bossy, *Giordano Bruno and the Embassy Affair* (New Haven, CT: Yale University Press, 1991) and *Under the Molehill: An Elizabethan Spy Story* (New Haven, CT: Yale University Press, 2001). See also, David Kahn, *The Codebreakers: The Story of Secret Writing* (London: Macmillan, 1967); Peter Way, *Codes and Ciphers* (London: Aldus Books, 1977); and Mark Jones (ed.) with Paul Craddock and Nicholas Barker, *Fake? The Art of Deception* (London: Trustees of the British Museum, 1990).

French histories

Only a few, relevant books on French history can be listed here: Julia Cartwright, *Christina of Denmark, Duchess of Milan and Lorraine* (New York: Dutton, 1913); Henry Evennett, *The Cardinal of Lorraine and the Council of Trent: A Study in the Counter-Reformation* (Cambridge: Cambridge University Press, 1930); N.M. Sutherland, *The French Secretaries of State in the Age of Catherine de Medici* (London: London University, 1962); De Lamar Jensen, *Diplomacy and Dogmatism: Bernardino de Mendoza and the French Catholic League* (Cambridge, MA: Harvard University Press, 1964); Frederic Baumgartner, *Henry II, King of France, 1547–1559* (Durham, NC: Duke University Press, 1988); Keith Cameron (ed.), *From Valois to Bourbon* (Exeter: Exeter University Press, 1989); Mack Holt, *The French Wars of Religion*, 1562–1629 (Cambridge: Cambridge University Press, 1995); David Potter, *A History of France, 1460–1560: The Emergence of a Nation State* (London: Macmillan, 1995); R.J. Knecht, *French Renaissance Monarchy: Francis I and Henry II* (Harlow: Longman, 1996); and Stuart Carroll, *Noble Power During the French Wars of Religion: The Guise Affinity and the Catholic Cause in Normandy* (Cambridge: Cambridge University Press, 1998).

Women's history

A knowledge of women's history is essential to an understanding of six-teenth-century culture and the writing of women's biography. See, for example, R.A. Houston, "Women in the Economy and Society of Scotland," in Houston and I.D. Whyte (eds), *Scottish Society, 1500–1800* (Cambridge: Cambridge University Press, 1989); Joy Hendry, "'Lying in the Asylum of Taciturnity:' Women's History in Scotland," in Ian Donnachie and Christopher Whatley (eds), *The Manufacture of Scottish History* (Edinburgh: Polygon, 1991); John Parsons (ed.), *Medieval Queenship* (New York: St Martin's Press, 1993); Maureen M. Meikle, "Victims, Viragoes, and Vamps: Women of the Sixteenth-Century Anglo-Scottish Frontier," in John Appleby and Paul Dalton (eds), *Government, Religion and Society in Northern England, 1000–1700* (Stroud: Sutton, 1997); Sara Mendelson and Pauline Crawford, *Women in Early Modern England, 1550–1720* (Oxford: Clarendon, 1998); Megan Matchinske, *Writing, Gender, and State in Early Modern England: Identity Formation and the Female Subject* (Cambridge: Cambridge University Press, 1998); Terry Brotherstone, Deborah Simonton, and Oonagh Walsh (eds), *Gendering Scottish History* (Glasgow: Cruithne Press, 1999); and Laurence Normand and Gareth Roberts, *Witchcraft in Early Modern Scotland: James VI's Demonology and the North Berwick Witches* (Exeter: University of Exeter Press, 2000).

Family and gender studies

Ralph Houlbrooke, *The English Family, 1450–1700* (Harlow: Longman, 1984); Mervyn James, *Society, Politics and Culture in Early Modern England* (Cambridge: Cambridge University Press, 1986); M. Lindsay Kaplan, *The Culture of Slander in Early Modern England* (Cambridge: Cambridge University Press, 1997); and Elizabeth Foyster, *Manhood in Early Modern England; Honor, Sex, and Marriage* (Harlow: Longman, 1999) explore how definitions of honor affected familial and gender relationships. For widows, see Sue Walker (ed.), *Wife and Widow in Medieval England* (Ann Arbor, MI: University of Michigan, 1993); and Sandra Covallo and Lydan Warner (eds), *Widowhood in Medieval and Early Modern Europe* (Harlow: Longman, 1999). For reproduction see, Angus McLaren, *Reproductive Rituals: The Perception of Fertility in England from the Sixteenth to the Nineteenth Century* (London: Methuen, 1984).

History of sexuality and rape

James Brundage, *Law, Sex and Christian Society in Medieval Europe* (Chicago, IL: University of Chicago Press, 1987) is required reading for insights into the history of sexuality in Europe. Rosalind Mitchison and Leah Leneman, *Sexuality and Social Control: Scotland 1680–1780* (Oxford: Blackwell, 1989); and Laura Gowring, *Domestic Dangers: Women, Words and Sex in Early Modern London* (Oxford: Clarendon, 1996) are important for an understanding of the British context. Of the numerous publications on rape and abduction, the following are useful: Sylvana Tomaselli and Roy Porter (eds), *Rape* (Oxford: Blackwell, 1986); Beverly Brown, Michele Burman and Lynn Jamieson, *Sex Crimes on Trial: The Use of Sexual Evidence in Scottish Courts* (Edinburgh: Edinburgh University Press, 1993); Jocelyn Catty, *Writing Rape, Writing Women in Early Modern England: Unbridled Speech* (London: Macmillan, 1999); Georges Vigarello, *A History of Rape: Sexual Violence from the 16th to the 20th Century*, ed. Jean Birrell (Cambridge: Polity, 2001).

Rituals and symbols in an historical setting

Victor Turner, *From Ritual to Theatre: The Human Seriousness of Play* (New York: Performing Arts Journal Publications, 1982), studies the drama of human relationships. Peter Burke, *The Historical Anthropology of Early Modern Italy: Essays on Perception and Communication* (Cambridge: Cambridge University Press, 1987); and Mary Hazard, *Elizabethan Silent Language* (Lincoln, NE: University of Nebraska Press, 2000) examine the use of body language. William Coster, *Baptism and Spiritual Kinship in Early Modern England* (Burlington, VT: Ashgate, 2000) explores godparents' roles. For questions about preparation for death and for martyrdom, see K. Jankofsy, "Public Executions in England and in the Late Middle Ages: The Indignity and Dignity of Death," *Omega: The Journal of Death and Dying*, 10, 1979; and Anne Dillon, *The Construction of Martyrdom in the English Catholic Community, 1535–1603* (Burlington, VT: Ashgate, 2002).

Governmental and legal structures of early modern Europe

Ernest Satow, *Satow's Guide to Diplomatic Practice*, 5th edn (Harlow: Longman, 1979); J.H. Elliot, "A Europe of Composite Monarchies," *Past and Present*, 137, 1992; Richard Mackenny, *Sixteenth Century*

Europe: Expansion and Conflict (London: Macmillan 1993*);* and Hendrik Spruyt, *The Sovereign State and Its Competitors: An Analysis of Systems Change* (Princeton, NJ: Princeton University Press, 1994) reveal the complexity of early modern diplomacy and monarchical structures. Jenny Kermode and Garthine Walker (eds), *Women, Crime, and the Courts in Early Modern England* (London: UCL Press, 1994); and Malcolm Gaskill, *Crime and Mentalities in Early Modern England* (Cambridge: Cambridge University Press, 2000), investigate trial procedures and cases.

Medical studies

For evidence of acute intermittent porphyria, see Norman Moore, *History of the Study of Medicine in the British Isles* (Oxford: Clarendon Press, 1908); Ida Macalpine and Richard Hunter, *George III and the Mad-Business* (London: Lane, 1969); and Sara Jayne Steen, "'How Subject to Interpretation:' Lady Arbella Stuart and the Reading of Illness," in James Daybell (ed.), *Early Modern Women's Letter Writing, 1450–1700* (New York: Palgrave, 2001). F.F. Cartwright, *A Social History of Medicine* (Harlow: Longman, 1977) offers a good survey. See also, Georges Vigarello, *Concepts of Cleanliness: Changing Attitudes in France*, trans. Jean Birrell (Cambridge: Cambridge University Press, 1988).

INDEX

Note: Aristocrats are indexed under their titles rather than their family names

Routledge History

England under the Tudors
Third Edition

G. R. Elton

'the best full-length introductory history of the period . . . written with great verve, it will delight both the scholar and the general reader' *The Spectator*

'Students of history owe Elton major debts. He has shown that political history is still worth investigation, that it offers the possibility of exciting discovery and genuine debate. He has demonstrated that scholarly work can be presented in prose that is witty, muscular, clear and above everything, readable' *Times Education*

Pb: 0-415-06533-x

Available at all good bookshops
For ordering and further information please visit:
www.routledge.com

Routledge History

A Political History of Tudor and Stuart England: A Sourcebook

Edited by Victor Stater

Covering a period characterized by conflict and division, this wide-ranging single-volume collection presents the accounts of Yorkists and Lancastrians, Protestant and Catholics, and Round-heads and Cavaliers, side by side. It provides a crucial opportunity for students to examine the institutions and events that moulded English history in the early modern era at first hand.

Hb: 0-415-2743-6
Pb: 0-415-2744-4

Available at all good bookshops
For ordering and further information please visit:
www.routledge.com